Encyclopedia of Reproductive Technologies

Encyclopedia of Reproductive Technologies

Edited by

Annette Burfoot

LONDON AND NEW YORK

First publishing 1999 by Westview Press

Published 2018 by Routledge
52 Vanderbilt Avenue, New York, NY 10017
2 Park Square, Milton Park, Abingdon, Oxon OX14 4RN

Routledge is an imprint of the Taylor & Francis Group, an informa business

Copyright © 1999 Taylor & Francis

All rights reserved. No part of this book may be reprinted or reproduced or utilised in any form or by any electronic, mechanical, or other means, now known or hereafter invented, including photocopying and recording, or in any information storage or retrieval system, without permission in writing from the publishers.

Notice:
Product or corporate names may be trademarks or registered trademarks, and are used only for identification and explanation without intent to infringe.

Library of Congress Cataloging-in-Publication Data
Encyclopedia of reproductive technologies / edited by Annette Burfoot.
   p. cm.
  Includes bibliographical references and index.
  ISBN 0-8133-6658-5
  1. Human reproductive technology—Encyclopedias. 2. Infertility—Treatment—Technological innovations—Social aspects—Encyclopedias. 3. Fertilization in vitro, Human—Encyclopedias.
  I. Burfoot, Annette J.
  RG133.5.E537 1999
  616.6'9206'03—dc21   98-53131
                                                                       CIP

ISBN 13: 978-0-367-00753-9 (hbk)

*This book is dedicated to my beloved nephew,
Patrick James Duncan Harvie (1983–1998)*

Contents

List of Tables and Figures   xi
Preface   xiii
List of Acronyms   xv

Part One
Theories of Reproduction—Ancient to Contemporary,
Annette Burfoot   1

1. Historical Perspectives of Human Reproduction, *Nancy Tuana*   5
2. Infant Feeding, *Marjorie Altergott*   15
3. Sex Preference, *Elizabeth Mathiot-Moen*   23
4. Genetic Engineering, *Patricia Spallone*   27
5. Genetic Diagnosis, *Patricia Spallone*   31
6. New Definitions of Family, *Erica Haimes*   36
7. Response of the Catholic Church to New Reproductive Technologies, *Paul Lauritzen*   42
8. Reprotech: A Feminist Critique of the Language of Reproductive Technologies, *Robyn Rowland*   46
9. New Reproductive Technologies—Women and Science, *Sue Rosser*   50
10. New Reproductive Technologies as Dystopia, *David N. James*   53

Part Two
Early Reproductive Technologies,
Annette Burfoot   59

11. Birth Technology, *S. Nan Schuurmans, James J. Boulton, Patricia A. Stephenson, and Sheryl Burt Ruzek*   63
12. Birth Technologies: Critical Perspectives, *Dorothy C. Wertz*   75

13	Breastfeeding, *Marjorie Altergott*	79
14	Infant-Feeding Technologies, *Marjorie Altergott*	83
15	Contraception Technologies, *Susan P. Phillips*	92
16	Contraception—Ethics, *Joan C. Callahan*	99
17	Diethylstilbestrol (DES), *Ellen 't Hoen*	105
18	Menstrual Disorder Technologies, *Emma Whelan*	109
19	Female Circumcision/Female Genital Mutilation, *Nahid Toubia*	114
20	Abortion Technologies, *Richard Boroditsky*	118
21	Abortion—Ethics, *Christine Overall*	122
22	Adoption and Restrictions on Abortion—Ethics, *David N. James*	125
23	Prenatal Harm, *Joan C. Callahan*	128
24	Informed Consent and Women in Labor, *Rosalind Ekman Ladd*	132
25	Reproductive Health in the Workplace, *Regina H. Kenen*	135
26	Contemporary Midwifery, *Vicki Van Wagner*	138

Part Three
Early Infertility Treatments,
Annette Burfoot — 145

27	Artificial Insemination, *Rona Achilles*	149
28	Artificial Insemination Policy, *Anne Donchin*	154
29	Psychosocial Implications of Donor Insemination, *Rona Achilles and Ken Daniels*	160
30	Lesbian Access to Donor Insemination, *Mary Anne Coffey*	166
31	Male Infertility, *Douglas T. Carrell and Ronald L. Urry*	171
32	Ovulation Induction, *Patricia A. Stephenson*	180
33	Risk Perception and Health Screening, *Claire D. F. Parsons*	188
34	Prenatal Diagnosis Technologies, *Richard T. Hull*	193
35	Prenatal Diagnosis—Critical Perspectives, *Abby Lippman and Richard T. Hull*	198

36 Sex Selection, *Helen Bequaert Holmes and Elizabeth Mathiot-Moen* ... 203

Part Four
Advanced Infertility Techniques,
Annette Burfoot ... 207

37 In Vitro Fertilization—Overview, *Robert Gore-Langton and Susan Daniel* ... 211

38 In Vitro Fertilization—Historical Development, *Robert Gore-Langton and Susan Daniel* ... 218

39 Ovarian Suppression by GnRH Agonists, *André Lemay* ... 222

40 Human Pituitary Hormones and Creutzfeldt-Jakob Disease, *Lynette Dumble* ... 229

41 In Vitro Fertilization—Culture Media, *Robert Gore-Langton and Susan Daniel* ... 236

42 In Vitro Maturation and Ova Freezing, *Kathy Munro* ... 242

43 In Vitro Fertilization and Male-Factor Infertility, *Michelle A. Mullen* ... 247

44 Gamete Intrafallopian Transfer (GIFT), *Richard T. Hull* ... 251

45 In Vitro Fertilization—Risks, *Michelle A. Mullen, Judith Lorber, and Linda S. Williams* ... 255

46 Counseling, *Ken Daniels* ... 261

47 Selection and Assessment for Treatment, *Ken Daniels* ... 265

48 Egg Donation, *Erica Haimes* ... 269

49 Surrogacy, *Laura M. Purdy and Helen Bequaert Holmes* ... 272

50 "Baby M" Surrogacy Case, *Sharyn Roach Anleu* ... 280

51 World Health Organization Report on the Place of In Vitro Fertilization in Infertility Care, *Patricia A. Stephenson with Marsden G. Wagner* ... 283

52 Advanced Infertility Technologies and Occupational Environments, *H. Patricia Hynes* ... 289

53 Informed Consent and Advanced Infertility Technologies, *Françoise Baylis* ... 293

54	Legislation—United Kingdom, *Deborah Lynn Steinberg*	298
55	Legislation—The Netherlands, *Marta Kirejczyk*	303
56	Legislation—France, *Jean Cohen*	307
57	Legislation—Australia and New Zealand, *Sharyn Roach Anleu*	310
58	Legislation—Canada, *Annette Burfoot (with advice from Health Canada)*	317
59	Legislation—The United States, *Anne Donchin*	320
60	Legislation—Germany, *Anne Waldschmidt*	324

Part Five
Reproductive and Genetic Science,
Annette Burfoot 329

61	Fetal Tissue Research and Applications, *Michelle A. Mullen*	333
62	Embryo Research, *Patricia Spallone*	337
63	Embryo Research—Legal Issues, *Sharyn Roach Anleu*	341
64	Cloning Technologies, *Robin Woods*	347
65	Cloning—Ethics, *Laura Shanner*	356
66	Preimplantation Genetic Diagnosis, *Andrea L. Bonnicksen*	361
67	Genetics—Discrimination, *Regina H. Kenen*	364
68	Genetic Counseling, *Dorothy C. Wertz*	367
69	Ectogenesis, *David N. James*	370
70	Genetic Screening and German-Based Eugenics—Old and New, *Anne Waldschmidt*	373

About the Editor and Contributors 381
Index 389

Tables and Figures

Tables

6.1	Family relationships created through third-party conceptions	39
11.1	Rates of cesarean delivery, cross-national comparisons	71
39.1	Clinical utilities of ovarian suppression by GnRH agonists	223

Figures

1.1	Internal female genitalia	7
1.2	Veins to the left and right ovaries	10
1.3	Spermatozoon with homunculus	12
39.1	GnRH analogs and the female hormonal cycle	224
64.1	The somatic cell division cycle	348
64.2	The two divisions of meiosis in males	349
64.3	The two divisions of meiosis in females	349
64.4	Fertilization and the zygote	350
64.5	Origin of clones by cell separation or embryo splitting	351
64.6	Cloning by nuclear transplantation	352

Preface

The birth of Louise Brown in 1978 signified a remarkable shift in medical and scientific intervention in human reproduction. Before this time, human reproductive technologies were limited to contraception, relatively crude assisted-conception techniques such as artificial insemination, and interventions during established pregnancies and at birth. Louise was the first "test tube" baby, the product of in vitro fertilization, or IVF, and was the first person born as a result of assisted conception outside the body of a woman. Since her birth, other conception-based and postconception technologies have emerged. One of the more controversial developments involves genetic screening and the genetic engineering of preimplanted embryos. The following encyclopedic survey provides clear descriptions of the key reproductive technologies of assisted conception from IVF to cloning. More important, it contextualizes them both historically and critically.

The text emphasizes recently developed reproductive techniques and introduces them to those unfamiliar with the technologies. Technical entries are written in an accessible manner so that those without a scientific background can understand. The text also covers the technological precedents (such as contraception and birth technologies) and the controversies and criticism surrounding recent developments. The prime purpose of this book is to provide a holistic view of the complex world of reproductive technologies and to bridge the gap between science and society. The selection of entries allows the reader to find in one place both the necessary technical explanations of an increasingly complex field and the social and historical contexts of these developments.

The text is organized into five thematic areas. It begins with a critical overview of the history of reproductive theory from classical Greece to the present with an analysis of the language of new reproductive technologies. The second part focuses on contraception and abortion, along with historical and critical perspectives and debates on these issues. The text moves from postconception interventions to conception and preconception technologies and their respective social and critical environments. The third part focuses on older, established technologies of assisted conception such as artificial insemination and donor insemination. Critical issues include lesbian and single women's access to such technologies as well as shifting psychosocial dynamics in the area of donor insemination and secrecy. The fourth part is devoted to advanced infertility technologies, such as IVF, along with associated issues from health risks to global sociolegal implications. Female infertility is addressed in most of these entries; a separate entry for male infertility is included. The last part of the text examines genetics and genetic engineering as they relate to advanced infertility technologies. Again, both clearly explained technical entries (such as preimplantation techniques and cloning) and examinations of issues arising from various perspectives are provided. Special attention is given to Germany due to its problematic history with eugenics and genetic control.

The volume as a whole allows for a quick and comprehensive assessment of the increasingly complex world of human reproduction and technical intervention. Each part is introduced. Individual entries are designed to provide information in isolation as far as possible, although in many cases the reader would benefit from using the index for cross-referencing to related entries. Following each entry is a list for further reading. Dollar figures are U.S. unless otherwise stated.

The Social Science and Humanities Research Council of Canada and the Queen's University Advisory Research Committee provided essential financial support for this project. Editorial assistance was provided by Heather Dietrich and Jill Smith. Helen Bequaert Holmes and Jeffrey Nisker assisted with the entry list, identifying contributors, and with Internet searches at the final stage of publication. Research assistants were Lore Fredestrom, Olga Kitts, and Lorie Scheibelhoffer. Secretarial support was provided by June Pilfold, Geetha Rengan, and Kimberley Sanders and Internet research by Joan Westenhaefer. Lisa Wigutoff (Westview) provided genial and constructive long-distance editorial support. Jenn Price and Marigold Rogers gave a home to the final stage. Wylie Burke provided a model for maturity under pressure, and Tyler Burke was generous in her accommodation. Oscar is a cherished and constant companion. Finally, I am indebted to Frank Burke as my respected colleague for teaching me by example how to copyedit the entire manuscript. I thank him as a loving partner for his continual encouragement and support.

Annette Burfoot
Brighton, U.K.

Acronyms

AID (or DI)	artificial insemination by donor
AIF	artificial infant feeding
AIH	artificial insemination by husband (artificial insemination homologous)
AMA	American Medical Association
APGAR	a scoring method developed by Virginia Apgar to quickly assess the well-being of the newborn
ASHG	American Society of Human Genetics
ASRM	American Society for Reproductive Medicine (formerly American Fertility Society)
BABI	blastocyst analysis before implantation
CASA	computer-aided sperm analysis
CB	Children's Bureau (United States)
CDF	Congregation for the Doctrine of the Faith (Vatican)
CECOS	French Federation of Centers for Cryopreservation of Eggs and Sperm
CJD	Creutzfeldt-Jakob disease
CMV	cytomegalovirus
D and C	dilation and curettage
D and E	dilation and evacuation
DBCP	dibromochloropropane
DES	diethylstilbestrol
DHHS	Department of Health and Human Services (United States)
DI	donor insemination
EAB	Ethics Advisory Board (United States)
EBSS	Earle's balanced salt solution
EFM	electronic fetal monitoring
ELSI	Ethical, Legal and Social Implications program (United States)
EPA	Embryonic Protection Act (Germany)
ET	embryo transfer
FASA	fetal anatomic sex assignment
FDA	Food and Drug Administration (United States)
FIVNAT	IVF National (France)

FSH	follicle-stimulating hormone
GAMS	Groupe Femmes pour l'Abolition des Mutilations Sexuelles (France)
GIFT	gamete intrafallopian transfer
GnRH	gonadotropin-releasing hormone
hCG	human chorionic gonadotropin
HEPT	hamster egg–human sperm penetration test
HFE	Human Fertilisation and Embryology Act (United Kingdom)
hGH	human pituitary growth hormone
HIV	human immunodeficiency virus
hMG	human menopausal gonadotropin
HOS	hypo-osmotic sperm-function assay
hPG	human pituitary gonadotropin
HTF	human tubal fluid
HUAM	home uterine activity monitoring
ICSI	intracytoplasmic sperm injection
IUD	intrauterine device
IVF	in vitro fertilization
LH	luteinizing hormone
LHRH	luteinizing hormone–releasing hormone
LTOT	low tubal ovum transfer
MEM	minimum essential medium
NBCC	National Bioethics Consultative Committee (Australia)
NGO	nongovernment organization
NIH	National Institutes of Health (United States)
NRT	new reproductive technology
Pap	Papanicolaou (smear)
PD	partial zona dissection
PGD	preimplantation genetic diagnosis
PHS	Public Health Service (United States)
PID	preimplantation genetic diagnosis
PMS	premenstrual syndrome
PZD	partial zona dissection
R-AFS	Revised American Fertility Society classification
RAINBO	Research, Action, and Information Network for the Bodily Integrity of Women (United States)
RU-486	the abortifacient pill
SCID	severe combined immunodeficiency disease
SCNT	somatic cell nuclear transfer
SET	surrogate embryo transfer
SI	self-insemination
SPA	sperm penetration assay

Acronyms

SRACI	Standing Review and Advisory Committee on Infertility (Australia)
STD	sexually transmitted disease
SUZI or SZI	subzonal insertion
TBA	traditional birth attendant
TOT	tubal ovum transfer
TOTS	tubal ovum transfer with sperm
UNICEF	United Nations International Children's Emergency Fund
WHO	World Health Organization
ZIFT	zygote intrafallopian transfer

Part One
Theories of Reproduction—Ancient to Contemporary

Reproduction theory has changed little over time, and its language continues to mediate people and their procreativity. The two main issues, the value of gender and the control of procreation, persist throughout a considerable history of human reproductive thought. Within some of the earliest philosophical writings from classical Greece lie the first coherent theories of human reproduction. Moreover, treatises such as Aristotle's on human reproduction form the basis of an approach to understanding regeneration in a way that values male contributions and their stated worth over those of females. These views, which include male seed theory and the notion of the homunculus (the entire human form is contained in a sperm), continued well into the sixteenth century in Western Europe. They also served as precursors to underlying philosophies of reproduction developed during the scientific revolution, which extend into contemporary debates surrounding new reproductive technologies and genetic engineering. Within new reproductive technologies women's breeding capacities are emphasized over experiences and rights of maternity. Embryos are separated from the pregnant woman and become the subject of public property disputes. Men gain reproductive options that increase their chances of genetic continuity. In addition to gender bias exist concerns with the general fragmentation and control of humanity. Also, the site and purpose of reproduction have radically shifted, and genetics has become a determinant of human relations and human value.

The first theories of human reproduction were limited to what could be observed outside the body. The visible elements of reproduction—semen, menstrual fluid, pregnant women's swollen bodies, birth, and lactation—were artfully arranged within early debates on the meaning of human reproduction. Common to most explanations right up to the scientific revolution was the superior quality assigned to semen: Although it was readily acknowledged that women were the primary site of reproduction, women's procreativity was usually given no proactive or determining power in explaining reproduction between men and women. Women were often described in terms of a vessel or carrier and the provider of the material but not the form. Men's procreativity, in contrast, was usually assigned the essential, formative role in the process. Even with the advent of tools such as the microscope and with modern scientific methods including the dissection of internal reproductive organs, these biased views remained.

Contemporary reproductive theories are similar in terms of gender bias to their precedents but are formulated in a different manner. By the early twentieth century, generalized philosophical discussions of human reproduction were replaced almost entirely by a dominant discourse of science and medicine. This discourse has become commonly accepted as truth and the way to confirm realities including the meaning and value of human reproduction, and it persists in denigrating female procreativity. Infant-feeding technologies, popularized at the onset of contemporary medical and scientific professions at the turn of the nineteenth century, provide a good example. Since pregnancy and birth were medicalized at this time, science became interested in the components of nursing. Researchers were particularly fascinated with what constituted human milk and whether it could be improved upon. This scientific attention raised doubts of the value of nursing generally and led to a worldwide industry in infant formulas with highly questionable impacts on infant health and survival, particularly in developing countries.

Perhaps one of the most extreme forms of denigration of female reproductivity occurs with sex selection within societies where a male preference dominates. Selection issues for both men and women arise with the advent of genetic engineering and screening. Other forms of fragmentation, particularly in women's procreativity, are evident in the new reproductive technologies, especially in vitro fertilization (IVF), egg donation, embryo freezing, and transfer and surrogacy arrangements. For the first time, women experience a level of reproductive uncertainty similar to that of men. In the past women were always certain how their gametes were used in reproduction and who their children were, whereas men were not. Presently, with IVF and egg and embryo donation, women's genetic contributions in reproduction are as mobile as men's, and new formations of family result.

In the late 1800s, science began exploring the genetic constituents and mechanisms in human reproduction. Finally the earlier, obviously gender-biased theories of reproduction were disputed: Women and men were found to contribute equally in terms of genetic codes to their offspring. However, these discoveries also allowed for a new, more interventionist basis for eugenic practices. Previously, controlling for inherited traits was a passive activity based on the observation of patterns in observable traits and controlled through selective breeding. With the development in genetic engineering technologies, procedures could be speeded up enormously and the traits themselves could be distilled and directly transferred without researchers having to rely on relatively long natural reproductive cycles. These interventions have created new expectations with regard to reproducing people. There is heightened public attention to genetic screening as a responsibility, especially for the mother as the predominant site of reproduction, to ensure that undesirable traits are not continued. Scientific and medical claims for remarkable prediction abilities with genetic screening also raise the specter of vulnerabilities to genetic-based illnesses forming new bases of discrimination at or even before birth. Genetic engineering of plants and animals raises questions of long-term effects of genetic tampering and the issue of ownership and control over life-forms and their reproductivity. Underlying all these concerns are the questions How are undesirable traits determined and by whom? and Are we playing God?

The Catholic Church is particularly critical of reproductive medicine and genetic science for their fragmentary effects on and unquestioned license to intervene in human reproduction. The fundamental difference in the church's approach from others rests with the object of its concern. The church is concerned with the integrity of a family unit based on a church-sanctioned union of men and women as the only legitimate site of reproduction. People and life generally are deemed part of God's domain and thus should not be constituted as the property of each other. Also, human intervention in this reproductive context should be kept to a minimum and should not necessarily extend to what is possible through medical and scientific practice.

Alternatively, feminists and others critical of recent developments are concerned with the integrity and well-being of people's procreativity regardless of church-sanctioned notions of reproduction. The new language of reproduction itself can be seen to deny and fragment women's procreativity; women's abilities to control scientific discourse remain limited. This brave new world of reproductive and genetic replication can be compared with Orwellian-like predictions of technological development generally and the implications for reproduction in particular.

one

Historical Perspectives of Human Reproduction

NANCY TUANA

Classical theories of human reproduction consistently ascribed superior powers to the male principle. Some theories were quite extreme, limiting woman's contribution to the nourishment of the male seed. Others allowed that women contributed seed but argued that their seed was inferior.

From the classical period, the biological writings of Aristotle (384–322 B.C.) influenced reproductive theory well into the sixteenth century. Aristotle believed that the male contributed seed that was responsible for determining the form and function of the organism. He depicted the female principle as supplying only the blood upon which the male imposed form. Aristotle supported this position by arguing that the female did not contribute seed to generation. He claimed that women were impotent. Aristotle equated menstrual fluids with the blood males were able to transform into semen and argued that women lacked sufficient heat to turn this blood into potent seed.

Aristotle's tenet that women produced no semen had numerous ramifications for his understanding of human creation. He supported the view that the fetus was contained within the male, who placed it in the female. The male imparted the *form* of the fetus to the female. Aristotle employed the metaphor of a carpenter carving out a bed to explain the process of conception. In conception, the woman provided the raw material, just as the tree provides the wood. But it was the man who, like the carpenter, determined the function of the object to be produced and gave it its form. The female body became the workplace, in effect, in which the male crafted a human life. Aristotle reinforced his thesis of male-dominant generation by arguing that it involved nothing material; he thus made the implicit assumption that nonmaterial substance has a higher degree of perfection than material substance. Using the analogy of the carpenter, Aristotle depicted male semen as a tool that moves upon the material within the womb and imparts form and motion but does not become a part of the fetus.

Aristotle's view of the primacy of the male principle of creation was consistent with both the metaphysical views of his time, which depicted women and female traits as inferior, and other scientific theories of generation. His embryological theory, however, was extreme in holding that only the male contributed seed. Many classical theorists, including Anaxagoras (500–428 B.C.), Empedocles (490–430 B.C.), Hippocrates (460–377 B.C.), and Parmenides (born 515 B.C.), believed that the fetus was the result of a combination of male and female semen, though all uniformly maintained that the woman's contribution was less potent.

Hippocrates claimed that generation could result in six types of individuals depending on the particular combination of seed. A mix of male and female seed would produce a man if the male seed dominated. If the father contributed the male seed and the mother the female seed, the offspring would be courageous. If the dominant male seed was from the mother and the female seed from the father, the resulting individual would be a hermaphrodite. A mix of male and female seed where the female seed dominated would result in a female. If the dominant female seed originated from the father, the daughter would be "bold yet graceful," but if it originated from the mother, she would be "brazen and mannish." If both the mother and the father contributed male seed, the offspring would become "a man who is brilliant in soul and strong in body." The sixth possible individual would result from a mixture of female seed from both parents and would be the "most female and very well-endowed" (Hippocrates 1943: 269, 271, 267, 269). Note that the characteristics resulting from dominant female seed are less perfect than those resulting from dominant male seed.

The physician Galen (A.D. 129–199), although strongly influenced by the Aristotelian worldview, agreed with Hippocrates on the issue of women's semen. However, he went beyond the Hippocratic position in offering a biological explanation of its inferiority. Galen, adopting the Aristotelian belief that women lacked men's superior heat, concluded that women's genitals were less fully formed than men's and thus less

Historical Perspectives of Human Reproduction 7

perfect. Galen depicted women's genitals as identical to those of men, although underdeveloped and internal: unable, because of a defect in heat, to mature and migrate outside her body. Since her organs of generation were not fully formed, the obvious inference was that her semen was also imperfect: scantier, colder, and wetter. The history of anatomy attests to the power of Galen's analysis of woman's genitals. For centuries, anatomical drawings of women's internal genitalia would bear an uncanny resemblance to man's external genitalia (see Figure 1.1).

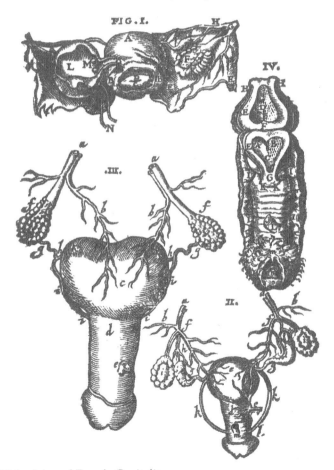

FIGURE 1.1 Internal Female Genitalia.

SOURCE: Ambroise Paré, *Oeuvres Complétes d'Ambroise Paré* (Paris: J. B. Bailliere, 1840–1841).

Galen accepted as true the popular classical view that male seed was produced in the right testis and female seed in the left. On the basis of this belief, Galen was able to construct a biological explanation of the inferiority of female seed. Using very creative anatomy, Galen argued that the blood vessels feeding the right testis and right side of the uterus first passed through the kidney, thus providing cleansed blood. However, he insisted that those feeding the left testis and left side of the uterus did not pass through the kidney and thus provided uncleaned blood. The impure blood feeding the left side contained less heat, resulting in the production of imperfect seed. Since woman was conceived out of impure blood, she was colder than man.

The Perpetuation of Male Generative Primacy

Aristotelian biology, revised by the work of Galen, remained authoritative for many centuries well into the sixteenth century. Later Christian theorists, believing that the ultimate creative principle, God, was male, had little trouble accepting Aristotle's view that the male was the primary creative force in human generation. Saint Gregory of Nyssa (335–394), adopting this theory, argued that the embryo was implanted by the male into the female. Saint Thomas Aquinas (1224–1274) compared the generation of humans to the creation of the world: Just as God alone can produce form in matter, the active force in human generation is in the semen of the male with the female providing only matter.

The views of Jewish commentators also reflect the influence of Aristotelian and Galenic biology. The school of Judaic, Midrashic thought, starting around the second century, depicted generation in an identical manner to that of Aristotle. According to Judaic texts, a man's sperm acts upon the woman's menstrual blood, causing it to come together and giving it form. A mother's womb is depicted as full of standing blood, which flows out during menstruation. But at God's will, a drop of whiteness enters and mixes with the blood to form the child. This is likened to a bowl of milk: When a drop of rennet falls into it, it congeals and becomes cheese; if not, it remains as liquid milk.

The anatomical tradition, from 1200 to 1700, perpetuated the Aristotelian and Galenic view of human reproduction. Although the predominant view was Galenic in allowing imperfect potency for female seed, a number of anatomists such as Ricardi Anglici (1180–1225) and Giles of Rome (1243–1316) supported the Aristotelian position that female semen is so imperfectly developed that it can provide only the least perfect of all the causes of generation—the material. Such theorists typically employed a molding metaphor to describe the mechanism by which man's sperm gives form to that of woman.

The Galenic explanation for the weakness of female seed, and ultimately for woman's inferior role in generation, was accepted by the majority of theorists within the anatomical tradition, including Albertus Magnus (1206–1208), Alessandro Benedetti (1450–1512), Alessandro Achillini (1463–1512), and Andres de Laguna (1499–1560), and was contained within one of the most influential medical texts of the fifteenth and sixteenth centuries, *Aristotle's Masterpiece*. The seeds of the man continued to be perceived as the active and formative agent; the woman's seed was depicted as playing a role only in providing the matter upon which male sperm imprinted form.

Dissection up until the sixteenth century was generally used to illustrate treatises of thinkers such as Galen. However, as numerous discrepancies between these traditional texts and the conditions found in cadavers were uncovered, there was a gradual realization among anatomists that the theories needed revision. The anatomist Andreas Vesalius of Brussels (1514–1564) is credited with founding modern anatomical practices. Despite his work, and despite the fact that careful attention to the actual structure of the veins and arteries of the testicles and ovaries would refute them, many anatomists persisted in the view that female seed was defective because of the impure blood that fed it. In Vesalius's depiction of the reproductive organs of women (see Figure 1.2) the vessel feeding the left ovary (a) originates in the renal artery (b) that carries uncleansed blood, while the right ovary is fed from the cleansed blood of the dorsal artery (c). This anatomical misconception was in no way the result of ignorance of human female anatomy, for Vesalius based his drawings of the female reproductive system on dissections of at least nine women's bodies. It is not surprising that even an anatomist as careful as Vesalius would perpetuate such an error, for the scientific theory he had inherited demanded this "fact." The belief that female seed arose from the "serous, salty, and acrid" blood of the left testis was the only viable explanation of the perceived physiological differences between women and men.

Niccolo Massa (1485–1569), the Italian doctor and anatomist, provides an interesting case study of the power of such a bias. Massa appears to have recognized Galen's anatomical error, for in his *Introductory Book of Anatomy*, he claimed that the vessels feeding the left ovary and testicle originate from the same source as those that feed the right. Despite this acknowledgment Massa continued to insist that female seed was weaker than male seed. Amazingly, his explanation of the imperfection of female seed is identical to that of Galen! He claimed that from the left "testicle"

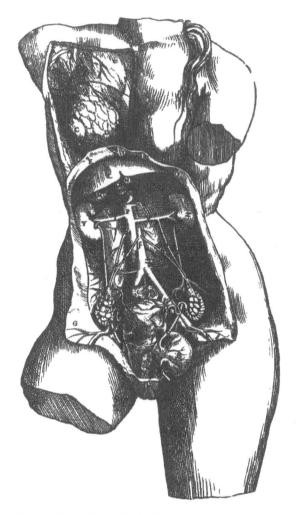

FIGURE 1.2   Veins to the Left and Right Ovaries.

SOURCE: Andreas Vesalius, *De Humani Corporis Fabrica* (Rome: Per Ant. Salamanca et Antonio Lefrerj, 1560). Courtesy of the Library of Congress.

of both the woman and the man a watery blood was emitted from which a weak sperm was created.

Despite the so-called corrections of anatomists like Massa, it would take over a century for the implications of Galen's anatomical error to be generally recognized. For example, at the end of the seventeenth century, Herman Boerhaave (1668–1738) acknowledged the mistake but proceeded to explain it with yet another piece of creative anatomy. He claimed that the veins and arteries of the left ovary and testicle were wrapped in a "capsule" or "tunic" that made their point of origin more difficult to see than that of the right ovary and testicle. Simply put, the belief in female generative inferiority was so strong that it dictated observation for centuries.

Ovism and Animalculism

In the seventeenth century, a new theory took hold that had significant effects on the science of embryology. From Aristotle to Harvey (1578–1657), embryologists believed that new life was produced through gradual development from unorganized matter, what we now call an epigenetic theory of development. Form was seen as evolving from the actions of the male semen upon the blood of the uterus or from the mixture of the semen of the two parents. But the idea of an evolution of complexity from unstructured material lost favor toward the end of the seventeenth century because of the general scientific commitment to a mechanistic worldview and the insufficiency of mechanical explanations for the gradual development of living organisms.

The epigenetic view was replaced by the belief that development was the result of the growth or unfolding of preexisting structures. This was known as preformation doctrine. This theory was formulated initially in the works of Nicholas Malebranche (1638–1715), Claude Perrault (1613–1688), and Jan Swammerdam (1637–1680), who claimed that there was never evolution of complexity in nature but only increase in size of preformed parts. Fetal development was likened to the enlargement of the little leaves in a bud: The structures of the entity were all there from the beginning. For approximately a century, beginning in the last quarter of the 1600s, preformation doctrine supplanted epigenetic theory.

An important consequence of preformation theory was the belief that the seed of subsequent generations could reside only in a single parent and that generation could no longer be the result of a mixture of semen. The only question was whether the miniature being was in the female egg (ovism) or the male sperm (animalculism). Early preformationists, influenced by studies of chicken eggs, tended to be ovists, positing the female as the source of this seed and arguing that the male parent provided only a stimulus that caused the outermost seed to begin its growth. However, the situation changed when Louis Dominicus Hamm, the assistant of Antoni van Leeuwenhoek (1632–1723), while looking at human seminal emissions under a microscope, saw "spermatic animalcules." In a series of correspondences with the Royal Society beginning in 1677, Leeuwenhoek claimed to have confirmed Hamm's discovery and concluded that these animalcules were the source of embryos. To counter the arguments of ovists, he also studied female ovaries and declared that these mammalian organs were useless ornaments. Echoing centuries of tradition, Leeuwenhoek insisted that nourishment of the male seed was the sole function of the female. To account for the generation of two sexes,

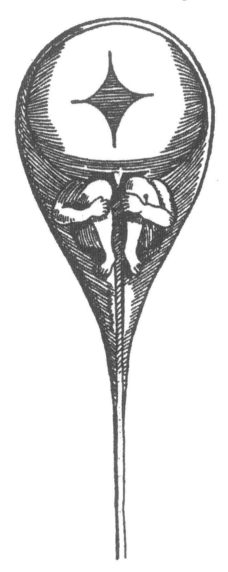

FIGURE 1.3 Spermatozoon with Homunculus.

SOURCE: Nicholaus Hartsoeker, *Essai de Diotropique* (1694). Courtesy of the Library of Congress.

Leeuwenhoek claimed to have observed two kinds of spermatozoa, one that would give rise to males, the other to females.

Nicholaus Hartsoeker (1656–1725) was the first scientist to illustrate the appearance of a fetus contained within a spermatozoon (see Figure 1.3). Hartsoeker did not pretend to have seen such a being himself but claimed that if one could see through the skin that hid it, one might see it as represented in his illustration.

Although ovists were initially without rivals, their theory quickly went out of favor once the male analogue to the egg was observed. Within two decades, animalculism was the favored view and continued to be held for almost a century. Clearly, the popularity of animalculism and its quick ascendancy were rooted in the centuries-old bias of male primacy in generation. Consistent with this, animalculist George Garden published on "modern theories of generation" in 1691 and argued that the egg, although essential to development, provided none of the form of the fetus. The ovum supplied only the nutriment necessary for the unfolding of the embryo already fully formed in the sperm. Martin Frobenius Ledermuller (1719–1769) compared the small seminal animalcule developing in the mother to the seed developing in the field. Even Erasmus Darwin (1731–1802), as late as 1794, held that the male provides the form or rudiment of the embryo, whereas the female provides only the oxygen, food, and nidus.

In short, the history of embryology from Aristotle to the preformationists illustrates the ways in which gender values shaped the process of scientific investigation. Belief in the primacy of male generative power was such a fundamental tenet of cosmogony that it permeated embryology for centuries.

FOR FURTHER READING

Aristotle. 1984. "Generation of Animals." Trans. A. Platt. In J. Barnes, ed., *The Complete Works of Aristotle*. Princeton: Princeton University Press.

Boerhaave, Herman. 1757. *Dr. Boerhaave's Academical Lectures on the Theory of Physics*. London: N.p.

Cole, F. J. 1930. *Early Theories of Sexual Generation*. London: Oxford University Press.

Feldman, David. 1974. *Marital Relations, Birth Control and Abortion in Jewish Law*. New York: Schocken.

Galen. 1968. *On the Usefulness of the Parts of the Body*. Trans. M. T. May. Ithaca: Cornell University Press.

Garden, George. 1961. "A Discourse Concerning the Modern Theory of Generation." *Philosophical Transactions of the Royal Society* 17: 474–483.

Hippocrates. 1943. *Regimen.* Trans. W.H.S. Jones. Cambridge: Harvard University Press.
Leeuwenhoek, Anthony van. 1685. "Correspondence." *Philosophical Transactions of the Royal Society* 25: 1120–1134.
Massa, Niccolo. 1975. "Introductory Book of Anatomy." Trans. L. R. Lind. In *Studies in Pre-Vesalian Anatomy.* Philadelphia: American Philosophical Association.

two

Infant Feeding

MARJORIE ALTERGOTT

Historical Context for Women's Emancipation in Relation to Infant Feeding

High-quality artificial infant feeding (AIF) is a lifesaving technology for infants unable to breastfeed. However, its acceptance for conventional use is related to the devaluation of women's biological role. Manipulation of infant feeding can be a means of social control, serving to support economic gains for an elite group of capitalists and professionals, and to support women's subordination. The AIF industry is huge with worldwide sales estimated at $2 billion annually.

Historically, women passively accepted sanctioned changes in AIF. They, like the rest of the population, were convinced by the new medical science and its tangible benefits in their lives, particularly in regard to promises of less painful and safer childbearing. Women also recognized that new contraceptive technologies could provide them with more control over their lives and were deeply involved in the struggle for legalization of birth control. But women typically did not associate AIF with either a loss or a gain of social power, and as an issue, infant feeding was absent from early-twentieth-century women's movement agendas.

In addition to birth control, women demanded the right to vote and rights to employment and education. However, women did not generally seek radical changes in their domestic role, and infant feeding, whether breast or bottle, was accepted as their responsibility. Most of their new roles were an expansion of their work at home and in charity; they became nurses, social workers, and teachers, but not scientists. They did seek to become better mothers and sought the advice of experts to teach them scientific mothering. Mothers themselves urged other mothers to seek the advice of experts rather than trust themselves or their infants' behavior. As women lost confidence in themselves and no longer shared their breastfeeding experiences, breastfeeding declined and the need for safer AIF increased. Higher-quality infant food, improved sanitation, immunizations, and antibiotics decreased infant mortality, and a midcentury attitude of indifference toward breastfeeding prevailed in industrialized nations.

Medical Sanctions on Breastfeeding

Virtually all publications from nineteenth- and early-twentieth-century general medical practice emphasize the superiority of breastfeeding. The medical profession's interest in a substitute for human milk began with a concern for the survival of infants who were increasingly not being nursed. During this time physicians acquired a substantial amount of useful, empirical information about AIF. However, they then applied this scientific method to breastfeeding, which was too intimate to study and could not be understood in the same way as AIF. Soon, as the medical profession claimed authority over infant feeding, it included breastfeeding and began to advise nursing mothers in all aspects of infant feeding.

Advice about breastfeeding from the late 1800s through the 1960s illustrates a trend. Initially, this advice reflected women's common experiences. Increasingly, professional concerns dominated women's experiences such that the advice inevitably led to unsuccessful breastfeeding. Night feedings became widely spaced and then discontinued at an early age, and strict scheduling was increasingly emphasized. Delaying the first nursing for twelve hours or more became acceptable, and daytime intervals lengthened to four hours. Breasts needed to be cleansed before and after each feeding, and sore breasts were treated with shields or chemicals such as silver nitrate. Doctors were concerned that mothers nursed their babies too often and believed this contributed to poor milk quality. Women were advised not to interrupt their sleep, and separate rooms for baby were urged. By the 1940s psychological theories of child development suggested that forced feedings due to strict scheduling could be harmful, and rules about feeding times relaxed, although training babies to be on a schedule was considered convenient.

The use of supplements increased throughout the first half of the twentieth century, and by midcentury, physicians were questioning not only the quantity but the quality of human milk. Health professionals explained that AIF could enhance breast milk's value and could be just as pleasurable for the infant as breastfeeding. Instructions from nurses reinforced physician teachings. Nursing care involved detailed, time-consuming procedures for wrapping, cleansing, and rewrapping the breasts at each nursing period.

The U.S. government, through the early Children's Bureau (CB) and the Public Health Service, also contributed to the decline of breastfeeding in the United States. The CB's primary strategy for improving child health was through the education of mothers. By 1929 its pamphlet *Infant Care* reached approximately 50 percent of American mothers, including a substantial number of poor women. Although the pamphlet extolled the value of breastfeeding, it included highly questionable, medically sanctioned advice around matters such as restrictive schedules, scrupulous cleansing of breasts, and separate sleeping rooms.

The Public Health Service (PHS) also effectively advised against breastfeeding. The PHS was concerned with the high infant mortality rate, and its primary approach was to promote sanitation. The PHS recognized that breastfeeding required no special sanitizing treatments. Instead, it focused on ensuring that the milk depots of the late nineteenth and early twentieth centuries provided clean milk for infants and children and on educating the public on milk storage and handling. Clients of these depots did have lower mortality and morbidity rates than other artificially fed babies, but this rate was not usually compared to rates among breastfed babies. Also, depots handed out free or extremely inexpensive milk, thus indirectly encouraging bottle feeding. Those that offered breastfeeding advice also provided the usual questionable, medically sanctioned information of the time.

Contemporary Issues

Over the past century of AIF development, the intensive analysis of human milk has led to dramatic improvements in infant food products. Today there are special products for infants with specific metabolic disorders, nutrient needs, and allergies. Nonetheless, a number of disasters, including microbial contamination and lack of certain micronutrients or their correct proportion, have caused serious damage and affected thousands of infants. Such incidents led several parents who were experts in health care fields or law to seek legislation for regulating infant food products. This effort resulted in the 1980 U.S. Infant Formula Act, which in its final form was a watered-down version of the originally proposed legislation. The weakening of the original version is blamed, in part, on the lack of support by U.S. medical professional organizations.

In spite of the overall increased breastfeeding rates in industrialized countries since the 1960s, the breastfeeding experience is far different now than in earlier times. More newborns are being breastfed, but the duration has decreased and only 18.2 percent of newborns were being breastfed at six months in 1991. There has also been a trend in the medicalization of breastfeeding, which is illustrated by the growth of the lactation consultant profession, certified by the International Board of Lactation Consultant Examiners. Consultants have a positive impact on women's success with breastfeeding and assume a much needed role in supporting the practice. However, consultant practices are increasingly advertising the breastfeeding paraphernalia they can provide to new mothers and are hired by the companies that produce it. Ads for nursing pads, a wide variety of manual and electric breast pumps, special clothing, breast shields, and special containers appear in both lay magazines and professional journals and are often sold with the message that they are important to the success of breastfeeding. In addition, some breastfeeding supporters are highly critical of this increased commercial interest in breastfeeding and of terms such as "breastfeeding management" because they interfere with the process and with the autonomy of nursing mothers and babies.

The monetary value of breast milk is seldom considered when assessing a national economic system. Women who do not breastfeed must purchase a milk substitute, have increased health care costs, must purchase birth control shortly after childbirth if they do not wish to become pregnant, and, if employed, often pay for child care. The monetary value of human milk has been estimated for a number of countries, including Indonesia. There it was estimated that mothers produce 1 billion liters annually and that replacing this human milk with AIF would cost $400 million plus another $120 million for increased health care costs and fertility-reduction activities. Overcoming problems of sanitation and water quality would not solve the problem of expense for employed mothers who are poor. The least expensive human milk substitutes are also the lowest quality, and even these require an excessively high proportion of a poor mother's income. The losses are not confined just to families with young children. The Philippines, like many nonindustrialized countries, imports the raw materials for its breast milk substitutes and does not reap the benefits that can be realized from industries using local resources. Also, calculations of the material value of human milk ignore the experiential value of breastfeeding.

The contraceptive effect of lactation has led to the manipulation of women's fertility through direct force or coercion both historically and contemporaneously. English seventeenth-century noblewomen were discouraged from breastfeeding to increase the number of male heirs. Slaves in the United States and the Caribbean were either encouraged to breastfeed or prevented from doing so depending on whether raising young slaves or purchasing adults was financially more advantageous to their owners. More recently, women in Korea were found to be less likely to breastfeed newborn daughters if they did not yet have a living, more valuable, male child.

Women's use of nursing as a contraceptive measure is generally given little credit. Most family planners in nonindustrialized countries, as well as those working with poor populations in industrialized countries, prefer the more scientific methods of modern contraception, particularly combined hormonal contraceptives. Because these hormonal methods interfere with milk production, they are not compatible with breastfeeding. Although these effects are known, these methods continue to be provided to breastfeeding women, who are then encouraged to bottle-feed in order not to risk infant health. Child health advocates are concerned with the decline of breastfeeding associated with implementation of family planning programs, a situation that clearly illustrates family planners' failures to work within the context of women's experience. The recently developed synthetic progestin contraceptive Norplant, which is implanted under the skin, does not appear to interfere with milk production, although caution in using it while breastfeeding is necessary because long-term effects on infants are, so far, unknown.

The decline in breastfeeding in the nonindustrialized world is the result of more than the promotion of hormonal contraceptives. Undoubtedly, the attraction and status of Western ideology are powerful. Using contraceptives and bottle feeding are ways to achieve the lifestyle of Western women and are often promoted as a means to increase women's status by making them more employable. However, a significant proportion of bottle-feeding mothers in nonindustrialized nations are not employed. And although employment of women is increasing throughout the world, being employed is not necessarily associated with increased status. Women's willingness to accept low pay and insecure employment makes them targets of the growing service industries, which view women as compliant, unorganized as a workforce, and dispensable. In fact, women have historically continued to participate in other productive work while breastfeeding, and it wasn't until industrialization that the two became apparently incompatible. How incompatible they actually are is not clear. Whereas employment undoubtedly complicates the breastfeeding experience, and employers have often discouraged mothers from initiating it or continuing with it, infant feeding methods do not consistently explain variations in employment.

The breastfeeding decline in the United States did coincide with an increase in women's employment during the early and mid-twentieth century, but the decline was significant for both employed and unemployed mothers. And it may well be the structure of the workplace, not employment itself, that is crucial to the initiation and continuation of breastfeeding. It has been noted that women's power in society is reflected in workplace structure and that breastfeeding is related to their power in social exchange. Workplaces in Western Europe often accommodate women's lactation function by providing lengthy maternity leaves, day care near or at the workplace, and nursing breaks, all of which result in high breastfeeding rates among employed women. Similar support systems existed in China in the 1970s, where 95 percent of employed mothers breastfed, sometimes through the age of two. In contrast, most employed breastfeeding mothers in the United States are expected to alter drastically the traditional practice of unrestricted breastfeeding and must supplement any breastfeeding with bottles or pump milk from their breasts for later use, an endeavor limited by inadequate storage facilities.

Theoretical Considerations of Social Support for Breastfeeding

The relationship between women's breastfeeding experience and gender relations is complex and involves the woman's role as primary caretaker of children as well as the objectification of women's bodies for men's use. Some feminist theorists cite women's sole responsibility for child care as the source of women's inferior status. Logically, shared child care is necessary to equality. Many women consciously work at creating an environment in which child care is shared by the father, other significant persons, or paid workers. Some women choose bottle feeding for this reason, and others breastfeed when with their child; other caretakers feed the baby either artificial foods or pumped breast milk when she is not.

An unexplored possibility is that the decision to bottle-feed may be made on a less conscious level and as a result of women's perception that assistance in all areas of care will be easier to obtain if she does not engage in an activity that is her exclusive responsibility. Those who theorize the effects of women's sole responsibility for child care successfully argue that women's ability to nurture children is not a biological given and that all of society would benefit from shared child care. However, they do not address the unique experiences of pregnancy, childbirth, and breastfeeding, in which biological and social roles are not completely distinguishable. Bottle feeding and shared feeding do not constitute a simple replacement of one product and experience with equal alternatives. At least a portion of a unique experience is eliminated with inseparable biological and social consequences.

Some feminist theorists call for the development of scientific technology to replace women's unique roles in biological reproduction, thereby eliminating inequality. The nature of breastfeeding does appear to be incongruent with the popular image of a liberated woman. Unrestricted breastfeeding is the sole responsibility of the mother; it requires frequent close contact and flexibility in order to meet unpredictable infant needs, and it results in spontaneous physical sensations, all of which seem to contradict the notion of control over one's body, a central theme of the women's movement. Women may resist engaging in this activity, which has great power for maintaining health and for developing deep human relationships, out of fear that it will limit them to oppressive traditional roles. However, the decision not to breastfeed for the previous reasons clearly raises questions about what women mean by control.

The AIF industry replaces a woman-made product, supports the man-made workplace structure, and benefits corporate interests. Although women's bodies are no longer being used directly when they bottle-feed, it is not clear they are free from being controlled. In fact, they avoid the control natural forces exert while breastfeeding but then fall under the control of professional protocols and technological systems. Also, choosing not to breastfeed raises questions about the value of women's biological functions and whether it is necessary to forfeit these in order to achieve equality.

A leading feminist theorist, Mary O'Brien, also addresses the sociobiological consequences of motherhood and offers an additional viewpoint for understanding how women's status is woven into the social construction of reproduction. She hypothesizes that men's consciousness of reproduction is discontinuous because their biological experience involves no physical connection to the reproductive process beyond the transfer of sperm. Women's consciousness, however, is continuous, proceeding from intercourse through pregnancy, then through birth, and finally through breastfeeding. Because of this, O'Brien hypothesizes, men develop artificial means of maintaining continuity through creations such as social institutions that ensure knowledge of paternity. She does not specifically refer to breastfeeding, but it follows that AIF and shared infant feeding may be other means of creating such an artificial continuity.

Feminists have also drawn attention to the distinction between the two functions of the female breast, sexual and maternal, as a social construction of female sexuality. In many Western countries, public breastfeeding is far less tolerated than using breasts in a sexual context to boost commercial sales. Images of naked or near-naked women are often used to sell cars, perfume, and so on; yet nursing women have been arrested for breastfeeding on a beach and are often asked to leave restaurants or other public places. The social stigma against this type of exposure of the female breast is so strong that many nursing women are so embarrassed and fearful of a negative response that they nurse their infants in public bathroom stalls.

The potential of breastfeeding as a sexual experience for mothers and their children may also be considered a social threat to a social order where such pleasure and fulfillment are sanctioned only in interactions between women and men. As the child grows older and the interaction between the nursing pair intensifies, social taboos regarding incest and lesbianism may seem at risk of being violated, and the relationship becomes even less compatible with patriarchal models of female sexuality.

FOR FURTHER READING

Beasley, A. 1991 "Breast Feeding Studies: Culture, Biomedicine and Methodology." *Journal of Human Lactation* 7(1): 7–14.

Boston Women's Health Book Collective. 1995. *The New Our Bodies, Ourselves*. New York: Simon and Schuster.

Chodorow, Nancy. 1978. *The Reproduction of Mothering*. Berkeley: University of California Press.

Gaskin, Ina May. 1987. *Babies, Breastfeeding and Bonding*. South Hadley, Mass.: Bergin and Garvey.

Hardyment, C. 1983 *Dream Babies*. New York: Harper and Row.

Newton, N. 1972. "Interrelationship Between Various Aspects of the Female Reproductive Role." *Psychosomatic Medicine in Obstetrics and Gynaecology: 3rd International Congress, 1971*: 388–390.

O'Brien, Mary. 1981. *The Politics of Reproduction*. Boston: Routledge and Kegan Paul.

Palmer, G. 1988. *The Politics of Breastfeeding*. London: Pandora.

Van Esterik, P. 1989. *Beyond the Breast-Bottle Controversy*. New Brunswick, N.J.: Rutgers University Press.

three

Sex Preference

ELIZABETH MATHIOT-MOEN

Both contemporary medicine and folklore reveal a widespread social desire to attain children of a preferred sex. Discussions of sex selection have been traced as far back as 2000 B.C. in China. Until very recently the only sure way to achieve it was through infanticide. This method was followed in the 1970s with fetal sexing and sex-selective abortion. By the 1990s it became possible to detect the sex of an embryo ex utero and, it is claimed, to sort male- and female-determining sperm. In many cases, sex selection per se is not the primary aim of contemporary reproductive technologies but instead is a necessary or accompanying factor in prenatal diagnosis and the identification of male fetuses or embryos at risk of sex-linked disorders. Worldwide, however, these technologies are increasingly being used to identify, select, and, in some cases, destroy embryos that display no other "defect" than the fact of being female.

Gender Differences in Access to Life

The elimination of unwanted females has been and remains widespread. High levels of excess female mortality among infants, children, and adults were found in Europe and European-settled countries well into the nineteenth century and are still found today in less affluent nations. The reverse—widespread killing of males because of a preference for females and general disdain for males—is virtually unknown.

In the past, excess female mortality was often the result of direct killing, whereas today deliberate neglect and overwork usually cause intentional and unintentional killing of females. Also, female infanticide, bride burning, dowry deaths, widow killing, and murders masked as suicide are not uncommon in India, China, and surrounding areas. In the United States and other more affluent nations, one might argue that the killing of females as a group is sublimated in wife battery and sexual assault. Also, a preference for boy children persists in these nations, especially as the oldest or only child. In these wealthier countries there is some stated willingness to use sex-selection technologies to meet these desires. It is believed that this trend may increase when affordable and reliable methods of sex selection that do not require abortion appear on the market.

Research on sperm separation has focused on capturing male sperm. The use of gender-neutral sex-selection techniques against females is growing internationally as these technologies are promoted and justified as an advancement in family planning that will both reduce fertility rates and enable a greater choice in family composition. In India, sex-selection technologies (especially amniocentesis and abortion) are blatantly advertised as ways to have sons or avoid paying dowry for daughters. As pre-implantation genetic diagnoses advance, a question arises: Will pre-implantation techniques be promoted as a way to select males, just as sex-selective abortion has been used to discard females?

Social, Ethical, and Political Issues

Since new reproductive technologies, especially those that do not require abortion, allow the elimination of females in ways that may be more culturally, morally, and legally palatable than the traditional means, it is important that they be taken into account in sociological theories of gender stratification and eugenics. Author Gena Corea claims that many sociologists do not see preconception or preimplantation elimination of females as victimization. Typically the moral implications of these practices are not questioned, and assurances are made without evidence that only a few will use sex-predetermination methods once they are available and that any increase in the number of males relative to females will be initial and temporary.

Sex selection also raises the issue of eugenics. If ethnocentrism, class elitism, and racism were important components of eugenics earlier in this century, might not sex-selection technology allow sexism to enter as an important component of a new eugenics? Singapore has already tried sex-based eugenics, and there is evidence that China and India might turn to these measures to bolster their fertility-control policies. Moreover, given the near universality of male dominance and related social structures, norms, customs, and laws that prevent females from moving up status hierarchies, sex selection on the grounds that males are superior to females could be justified or even required. In fact, sex selection may further advantage males to the extent that there is a correlation between being firstborn and enjoying social success.

Ethical discussions of sex selection are highly speculative and are often concerned with anticipated positive and negative effects of a predominantly male or female population. These deliberations are generally limited by essentialist beliefs that males are inherently violent, aggressive, and competitive, whereas females are inherently gentle, nurturing, and cooperative. Some think the predominantly male society that is likely to result from unobstructed sex selection will enhance the status of a precious few females; others think it will lead to further degradation. The experience of India suggests the latter. There are disagreements on other counts as well. Some ethicists label sex preference as irrational and sex selection as immoral. Others believe that sex-selective abortion is of the same class as abortion for genetic defects and that women have a right to abort a child for any serious reason.

Some feminists, noting the intensity of research and the increasing use of sex-selective technologies against females, are concerned that traditional femicide, isolated cases of killing undesired females, may evolve into gynicide, or the calculated and widespread extermination of women and women's cultures. Others, such as Joseph Fletcher, see concerns over sex-selective abortion as a topic for ridicule:

> The assumption that the male gender is better and more desirable is a barefaced piece of male chauvinism and androcentric psychology. To suppose that fetal sex choice and freedom of abortion would mean the throwing out of "worthless females" is both hilarious and foolish. If men were stupid enough to do it (they aren't) the women would soon set things straight. (1974: 184)

Evidence accruing during the subsequent decade and a half shows that sex selection—research and practice—has become a serious business and that Fletcher overestimated both the wisdom of men and the power of women.

Physicians are put in a bind by some prospective parents who strongly desire a child of a specific sex, because if sex typing is not done, the mother will have an abortion to be sure of not having a child of the undesired sex. Nevertheless, as the technology progresses, clinicians are becoming more tolerant of sex determination and sex selection, and to avoid abortion, some are supporting further development of techniques that enable sex preselection through the sorting of sperm.

Finally, on the issue of women's reproductive rights and freedoms, there is no consensus and little regulation. New sex-selection techniques are seen as a triumph for family planning by some but as a superficial technological fix for severe sociocultural problems by others. Some claim the technologies enhance individual choice and are a liberating force for women; others view them as a new means of social control and a death knell for females. There is little agreement regarding the regulation of sex-selection technologies.

FOR FURTHER READING

Corea, Gena. 1985. *The Mother Machine*. New York: Harper and Row.

Boetzkes, Elisabeth. 1999. "Equity, Autonomy, and Feminist Bioethics." In Anne Donchin and Laura M. Purdy, eds., *Embodying Bioethics: Recent Feminist Advances*. Boulder, Colo.: Rowman & Littlefield.

Fletcher, Joseph. 1974. *The Ethics of Genetic Control*. Garden City, N.Y.: Anchor.

Guttentag, Marcia, and Paul F. Secord. 1983. *Too Many Women? The Sex Ratio Question*. Beverly Hills, Calif.: Sage.

Moen, Elizabeth. 1991. "Sex Selective Abortion: Prospects for China and India." *Issues in Reproductive and Genetic Engineering* 4: 231–249.

Warren, Mary Anne. 1985. *Gendercide: The Implications of Sex Selection*. Totowa, N.J.: Rowman and Allanheld.

four

Genetic Engineering

PATRICIA SPALLONE

Gene manipulation, the linchpin of the "biotechnology revolution," affects almost every level of human existence, from the food we eat and how it is grown; to health care and how it is administered; to how we have babies; and to our perceptions of ourselves, other living things, and nature itself. The term "genetic engineering" was coined in 1965 to denote a range of micromanipulations of the reproductive or hereditary process; that is, manipulations at the level of the cell and of the DNA (genes) within the cells.

Gene Manipulation

Gene manipulation, with its techniques of gene splicing, gene rearranging, and gene cloning, allows scientists to break species boundaries as never before possible. The genes of viruses, bacteria, people, trees, insects, and other living things can be moved into foreign organisms. For instance, a firefly gene has been introduced into tobacco plants to make the mature plants glow. In terms of human genetics, gene manipulation allows scientists to isolate and study genes individually.

Cloning, the production of genetically identical organisms by asexual reproduction (without any combination of egg and sperm cells), is one example of micromanipulation of the reproductive and hereditary processes. By the late 1960s, scientists had successfully cloned a toad by replacing the nucleus of a toad's egg cell with a nucleus of a cell from a mature toad. The toad that grew from the egg was genetically identical to the mature toad whose cell nucleus was used. By 1973, hybrid DNA

(DNA formed from combining DNA from two different sources) had been created in a test tube, and DNA foreign to bacteria had been transferred into bacteria. These developments were the result of new techniques of gene manipulation that allowed scientists to introduce, delete, or otherwise change the DNA in living cells of an organism.

In 1974, concerned over the risk of causing a human disease through genetically altered bacteria, eleven molecular biologists called for a partial and temporary voluntary moratorium worldwide on gene manipulation experiments. The moratorium was short-lived, and genetic engineering became an everyday occurrence in laboratories all over the world. The change in attitude was partly due to an apparent consensus among scientists over the safety of gene manipulation and partly due to commercial interests. Eager to reinvent the commercial successes of the computer industry, venture capitalists in concert with academic researchers, as well as large transnational corporations, embraced gene manipulation as the key to a new industrial revolution.

The "Biotechnology Revolution"

One of the earliest negative international responses to genetic engineering came from rural development organizations concerned with the impact of biotechnology on the world's food resources and the need to reorient our thinking and practices to ensure ecologically sound and socially just global development. Concerned commentators argue that although biotechnology presents a new model of industrial growth based on living things, there is continuity with old models of farming and industrialization, and patterns of land exploitation of Third World resources and peoples can be repeated. Ownership and control of land and genetic resources are a central theme in North-South relations, more so now since gene manipulation technology has put a price tag on genes. Biotechnology can thus be seen as a nexus of commerce, ethics, and social relations. The 1987 report of the Federal Republic of Germany's Committee of Enquiry on Prospects and Risks of Genetic Engineering recognizes genetic engineering as a technology for the control of humankind and nature. What kind of control, how, by whom, why, and to what benefit all became important questions. However, in response to tensions around these concerns, the scientific establishment continues to lobby for its right to pursue knowledge unimpeded and to chiefly regulate itself.

Subsequently, organizations such as the Berlin-based international information and communication clearinghouse, the Gene Ethics Network, founded in 1986, emerged to facilitate a broad public dialogue about the objectives, applications, dangers, and consequences of genetic engineering and to discuss possible alternatives. Members of these organizations argue that rather than solving societies' problems of hunger and disease, biotechnology is destined to continue social inequalities and environmentally risky patterns of farming and dependence of the Third World on the First World, where the biotechnology industries flourish.

Human genetics raises specific issues concerning the uses of genetic information to discriminate against people. Genetic discrimination by insurance companies and others prompted some concerned citizens in the United States to call for protective legislation. Feminist responses, although diverse, have included all of these concerns but are notable for their recognition of the links between genetic engineering and reproductive technology.

Reproductive Engineering and Biotechnology

In vitro fertilization (IVF) offers another avenue for genetic research and genetic screening on the fertilized egg in the laboratory dish. Genetic technology includes new genetic diagnostic tests and genetic therapies that are used on IVF embryos and on fetuses in a woman's womb. In the early 1970s, some of the social consequences of genetic control of human reproduction were questioned, but only briefly during in-house scientific debates on "the new biology." Questions were raised about the experimental nature of the methods, about the unknown physical risks to babies born as a result of IVF, and about scientists "playing God."

Whereas critical questions were being raised in many quarters regarding the risks of reproductive engineering to farm animals or the social repercussions of biotechnology in areas such as agriculture, similar questions have not been raised as widely in connection with the impact of biotechnology on women and women's reproductive capacities. Feminists argue that the new technologies have developed without adequate consideration of the impact on the status of women or of people with disabilities. They claim that questions about social judgments of normality and health have not been adequately addressed. They also argue that as human reproduction changes, so too do human relationships. A critical philosophical analysis of biotechnology is offered by Indian ecofeminist Vandana Shiva, who maintains that industrial exploitation of the fertility of all living things—of the soil, of human beings, of life itself—is the foundation of the biorevolution.

FOR FURTHER READING

Council for Responsible Genetics. 1990. "Position Paper on Genetic Discrimination." *Issues in Reproductive and Genetic Engineering* 3(3): 287–290.

Edwards, Jeanette, et al. 1993. *Technologies of Procreation: Kinship in the Age of Assisted Conception.* Manchester: Manchester University Press.

Etzioni, Amitai. 1973. *Genetic Fix: The Next Technological Revolution.* New York and London: Harper and Row.

German Bundestag III. 1987. *Report of the Committee of Enquiry on Prospects and Risks of Genetic Engineering.* Bonn: N.p.

Hall, Stephen S. 1988. *Invisible Frontiers: The Race to Synthesize a Human Gene.* London: Sidgwick and Jackson.

Juma, Calestous. 1989. *The Gene Hunters: Biotechnology and the Scramble for Seeds.* London: Zed Books.

Kevles, Daniel J. 1985. *In the Name of Eugenics.* New York: Knopf.

"The Molecules of Life." 1985. *Scientific American.* Special issue 253(4).

Shiva, Vandana. 1988. *Staying Alive: Women, Ecology and Development.* London: Zed Books.

Spallone, Patricia. 1989. *Beyond Conception: The New Politics of Reproduction.* London: Macmillan; South Hadley, Mass.: Bergin and Garvey.

Spallone, Patricia, and Deborah Lynn Steinberg, eds. 1987. *Made to Order: The Myth of Reproductive and Genetic Progress.* Oxford: Pergamon.

Stanworth, Michelle, ed. 1987. *Reproductive Technologies: Gender, Motherhood and Medicine.* Cambridge, U.K.: Polity.

Wheale, Peter, and Ruth McNally. 1988. *Genetic Engineering: Catastrophe or Utopia?* Brighton, U.K.: Harvester Wheatsheaf.

five

Genetic Diagnosis

PATRICIA SPALLONE

Genetic engineering revolutionizes and expands the study of genetic disease. As a consequence, a growing number of conditions of the human body and mind are the subject of gene analysis, genetic testing, and genetic screening. Areas of application include prenatal diagnosis of embryos and fetuses during pregnancy, screening of newborn infants, and screening of children and adults. There has been an increase in the number and range of genetic diagnostic tests for inherited traits and diseases, and for predispositions to certain noninherited diseases such as some forms of cancer. The expansion of genetic testing on embryos, fetuses, children, and adults has legal, medical, employment, and reproductive implications.

Gene Analysis

Before the 1970s, there were only three ways to diagnose diseases known or thought to be inherited: (1) through the study of inheritance patterns by observing which members of a family were affected, (2) by taking blood samples to diagnose conditions with biochemical (mostly protein) tests, (3) by looking under a microscope for structural abnormalities of the cells and chromosomes. Chromosomes are the threadlike structures in the nucleus of a cell where the genes are packaged. They are large enough to be observed under a microscope.

Genetic engineering changed the scope of genetic diagnosis. Now it is possible to isolate and manipulate genes (pieces of DNA) to study relationships between genes and physical characteristics. The same technology is used to create lucrative diagnostic tests. For instance, if the presence of a particular gene is associated with a condition, it is possible to create a gene probe to search an individual's DNA to see if he or she carries the gene in question. A gene probe is a sequence of DNA that matches and recognizes a sequence among the DNA being analyzed. Diagnostic gene probes alone had an estimated market worth of at least $500 million by 1992.

Correlations between genes and medical conditions are varied. Some genetic conditions are inherited; others are due to damage or mutation of the genetic material in either an egg cell, a sperm cell, a fertilized egg (embryo), or a fetus during pregnancy. Whereas some illnesses are associated with the presence of a gene, others are associated with a lack of one. Many disorders are associated with a defective protein (gene product). Still others are called multifactorial, a result of a complex web of many genetic, environmental, and other factors. There are over 4,000 known inherited single-gene traits, including genetic disorders (such as multiple sclerosis); these are defined as caused by a single change in the structure of an individual's DNA. The number of identified multifactorial traits and disorders is growing but remains more open to question.

Intensified efforts are being directed toward the identification of genetic factors associated with conditions as diverse as asthma, cleft palate, some kinds of cancers, mental illnesses such as manic depression and schizophrenia, and allergies. These conditions are both unique and complex in their origins and effects, often involving external influences such as nutrition, infection, toxins in the environment, sex, race, and standard of living. Commentaries on actual gene discoveries reveal that they are not as straightforward as headlines and premature scientific announcements may suggest. For example, the gene marker first thought to be associated with manic depression in a closed community of Amish people of northern Pennsylvania in the United States was not found elsewhere.

Genetics and Medicine

Medical and scientific interests in the pathology of genes in the 1960s produced the theory that "abnormal genes" should be viewed as causal agents of disease, just as bacteria or viruses are considered causal agents. Some geneticists proposed that all diseases have a genetic component. Genetic-engineering technology provides methods to explore genetic components of varied origin. In this sense, the new genetics follows in the footsteps of Western scientific medicine, which seeks to find a singular primary cause of an illness, either biological or psychological. The limitations of this approach are most obvious in the field of mental health. For example, two years after the genetic basis of schizophrenia was apparently discovered, another medical study showed that the improved health of mothers is a crucial factor in the substantial fall in the number of people admitted to the hospital in the United Kingdom for schizophrenia since the 1960s. The researchers concluded that improved nutrition and maternal health, which came in with the welfare state in the mid-1940s, were key.

An alternative to fixating on one cause of an illness is offered by psychiatrist Suman Fernando, who argues that biochemical and genetic influences are in a dynamic relationship with each other and with other social influences. Thus clinicians are not forced to identify some health states and people as pathological; mental illness can be understood as disturbances of balance within individuals, families, and societies. However, it must be noted with caution that new genetic theories of human behavior are being formulated in ways that recognize such complexity but still emphasize the biological and genetic characteristics of individuals. Most researchers accept the view that complex human behaviors are the result of many factors, but there remains an increased interest in finding biological factors (genes, hormones, etc.) that predispose some individuals to behavioral tendencies. A most controversial example is the wider acceptance of a greater role for biology in understanding the causes of male violence, crime, antisocial behavior, and sexual orientation.

The Hypersusceptible Person

Researchers, especially in cancer research, suggest that automated genetic profiles should be used to identify so-called susceptible individuals. The rationale for this is that some individuals have an inherited susceptibility to certain diseases. The occupational disease asbestosis, a serious and often fatal lung condition caused by exposure to asbestos fibers, is now thought to be more prevalent in individuals with a genetic predisposition to it.

The theory of hypersusceptibility originated in the 1960s in the field of industrial toxicology (the branch of medical science dealing with the effects of poisons). The hypersusceptible worker provides a model for explaining the ill effects from exposure to hazardous workplace chemicals. The theory relies on measurements of enzyme deficiencies in the blood of some (not all) people who fell ill from exposure to hazardous chemicals in the workplace. Since enzymes are gene products, the supposition is that getting sick from exposure is ultimately a gene problem. But this evidence is criticized by other scientists who argue that it is built on unproven premises and sloppy reasoning.

Workplace screening for hypersusceptibility in the United States during the 1960s was challenged by trade unionists, civil rights groups, and women's groups. For example, women of childbearing age had often been excluded from jobs on the grounds that certain industrial environments posed risks of chromosomal damage to a fetus. Under U.S. law, women's groups argued, employers are obliged to make the workplace safe for all workers. Other arguments opposing screening were based on constitutional rights to privacy and equal opportunity, on the right to work, and on illegal discrimination against people with disabilities.

Predictive Medicine

Genetic engineering brings the basic theory of hereditary vulnerability back into the limelight. Some molecular biologists working on the human gene mapping project suggest that eventually a complete genetic profile of an individual soon after birth will reveal that person's disease state. How will genetic profiling improve health care, especially when already existing opportunities to improve people's health are so often bypassed? The answers to such questions have been vague at the least.

Critical observers warn of the discriminatory use of genetic information by employers and insurance companies, and within the community. Another ethically fraught outcome is mass population screening. What happens when several genetic factors contributing to susceptibility to a pervasive disease, such as heart disease, have been identified? To group people who are at risk, and who could (and should) take preventative measures, would require massive and complicated population screening. Gene analysis enables a profound shift in medicine. Emphasis can now be placed on the power of predictive screening as a new definition of preventative medicine, which demotes the traditional means of forestalling illness by attention to social and environmental factors (nutrition, standards of living, and so on) and good primary health care.

The European Union's original proposal for funding a European human gene mapping project was subtitled *Predictive Medicine*. Its aims were criticized strongly by several grassroots and political groups, including the (then) vibrant coalition of European Green Parties, whose Women's Bureau argued that the project individualizes health care to the detriment of the individual. Although few professionals would deny the importance of social and environmental factors in health, genetic medicine as it is being played out today concentrates heavily on the genetic factors of illness and on individual solutions while diminishing environmental and social factors, and at the expense of public health solutions. This emphasis away from such wider solutions may be the most far-reaching long-term consequence of an expanded emphasis on genetic diagnosis.

FOR FURTHER READING

Bains, William. 1989. "Disease, DNA and Diagnosis." *New Scientist* 122(1663): 48–51.

CIBA Foundation. 1996. *Genetics of Criminal and Anti-social Behaviour*. Chichester: John Wiley.

Fernando, Suman. 1990. "The Same Difference." *New Internationalist* (July): 24–25.

Gill, Michael. 1988. "Molecular Genetics and Schizophrenia." *British Medical Journal* 297: 1426.

Marx, Jean, ed. 1989. *A Revolution in Biotechnology*. Cambridge: Cambridge University Press.

Milunsky, Aubrey, and George J. Annas II, eds. 1980. *Genetics and the Law II*. New York: Plenum.

Nelkin, Dorothy, and Lawrence Tancredi. 1989. *Dangerous Diagnostics: The Social Power of Biological Information*. New York: Basic Books.

Rose, Steven, R. C. Lewontin, and Leo J. Kamin. 1984. *Not in Our Genes: Biology, Ideology and Human Nature*. Harmondsworth: Penguin.

Spallone, Pat. 1992. *Generation Games: Genetic Engineering and the Future for Our Lives*. London: Women's Press.

six

New Definitions of Family

ERICA HAIMES

Implications of assisted-conception techniques include innovations in family formations and the notion of parents and children and wider kinship ties. Even though the original motivation to use the new reproductive technologies might initially have a narrower focus (to become a mother or to become a father or to have a child), these wider consequences are as important.

The first point is that each person who has achieved parenthood through the use of assisted conception may find that the individual is considered merely one fragment in a wider mosaic of parenting relationships. For example, it is now common in medical and academic literature to find the woman's role divided into three types of motherhood: the genetic mother, the carrying mother, and the nurturing mother. This fragmentation then has the curious effect of raising questions about how best to label the woman who combines all three elements. Similarly, a man could be either a genetic father or a nurturing father or both. A distinction is now also made between genetic and gestatory surrogacy: The former applies to the situation when the "surrogate mother" provides the egg, the latter when she carries an embryo for the "commissioning parents." Whereas this terminology is important in identifying the different elements of the process to parenthood, another, more prosaic, distinction occurs in everyday usage: that between biological and social parents. The entrance of this distinction into common parlance is an indication of the impact the new reproductive technologies have had on everyday understanding of family relationships. As legislation is emerging to regulate the deployment of the new reproductive technologies, it has become increasingly necessary to provide legal definitions of "mother" and "father" of the resultant child to prevent disputes. For example, the British Human Fertilisation and Embryology Act (1990) defines the woman who carries and gives birth to the child as the legal mother whatever her genetic relationship to the child. In the case of surrogacy, the commissioning parents can apply for a court order to be legally defined as the child's parents. The same act defines the husband of any woman receiving assisted-conception treatment as the father of the resultant child provided he has consented to the treatment. If he refused consent, however, and if he can prove that he is not the child's genetic father, that child will legally be fatherless. Such distinctions reflect the particular Euro-American view of parenthood as grounded in biology, since any other type of parent-child relationship is seen as social and hence artificial.

A second major theme in discussions of parenthood achieved through assisted conception is the question of whether individuals seeking such assistance should be required to satisfy criteria not applied to those achieving parenthood without assistance. Should the provision of assistance be accompanied by various screening procedures? Debate has focused on whether treatment should be provided for unmarried heterosexual couples, single women, lesbian couples, and, albeit to a lesser extent, single men and male homosexual couples. Advisory and legislative bodies around the world have taken slightly different positions on this, but the overall picture indicates a preference in most countries for recipients of assisted conception to be stable, heterosexual (preferably, but not necessarily, married) couples with the possibility, usually to be decided at the discretion of the clinical teams, of treatment also being provided for single women (for example, in the United Kingdom and in Canada). In the United Kingdom the clinical team is required to consider the welfare of the resulting child, including that child's need of a father, before providing treatment to a woman. It can be argued that the level of concern raised about access to treatment reflects the extent to which the resultant family is perceived to be deviating from the ideological, structural, and biological profile of normal family life.

Other variations in parenting have been either introduced or expanded on by the use of assisted conception. Women receiving treatment are at greater risk of multiple births, which are in turn associated with much greater parental stress arising from lack of space, money, energy, and other resources for child care. In contrast to such sudden multiple parenting, the notion of limited parenting might be used to describe the constraints placed on gamete donors. These constraints possibly limit the number of times donors are allowed to donate to avoid the danger of later incestuous relationships. There are also the limitations placed on donors' later involvement with the resultant children. Contested parenthood occurs when a surrogate mother refuses to surrender the child she has carried or when semen donors seek paternity rights. Finally, posthumous parenting can occur for both men and women when frozen gametes and embryos are used after the death of one of the gamete contributors. Typically this last possibility occurs when a male partner stores some of his frozen semen prior to receiving other medical treatment, such as for cancer, that might render him infertile. If he then dies, his female partner can still technically be artificially inseminated, although such practice is discouraged in much of the Western world.

It is argued that the main motivation for people to use assisted conception (rather than, for example, adoption) is to have their "own" child. Increasingly people are seeking as close a biological or genetic link to their offspring as possible even if this means that only one of the parents has such a link. In assisted-conception cases where neither has that link, at least both are equally involved with the arrangements for the baby's conception and birth (as with some forms of surrogacy). What are the consequences of this motivation for the resultant child?

In fact, very little is so far known about the impact on children of being conceived through the new reproductive technologies. Since in vitro fertilization (IVF) has been available only since 1978, it is not yet possible to be clear about the long-term effects on such children. Indeed, given the low success rates of advanced infertility procedures, fewer children than might have been expected have been born from this technique. The few studies that have so far been conducted on the development of children conceived through IVF suggest that physically their progress is as good as, or better than, that of other children, but in behavioral and emotional terms, they might experience greater difficulties than other children. It may well be, however, that such problems result not directly from IVF but either from being the product of a multiple birth or from the fact that their parents might handle difficulties differently given their status as IVF parents. However, much more research needs to be done to confirm these early suggestions and (if such problems are found to be common) to identify the causal factors.

It might be expected that more would be known about children conceived through donor insemination given the much longer history, and the higher success rate, of this practice. However, that is not the case, since this method of assisted conception has been surrounded by an almost impenetrable secrecy such that most of the resultant children, and their extended families, do not know the manner of conception. Since little was known about donor insemination, this secrecy was largely unchal-

New Definitions of Family

lenged until the practice was incorporated into new reproductive technology practice (particularly in the United Kingdom, Sweden, and the United States). Once the element of secrecy was revealed in assisted conception, questions were raised about whether such secrecy was in the best interest of the child. Reference was frequently made to recent changes in adoption practice in North America, the United Kingdom, parts of northern Europe, Australia, and New Zealand, where the child's interest in his or her origins was beginning to be recognized as reasonable and legitimate. It could be argued, however, that the notion of origins in the domain of assisted conception is potentially more complex than in adoption given the range of individuals who might be involved in the child's conception, birth, and nurturing (see Table 6.1).

A variety of positions within the debate on what to tell children about their origins can be identified. First, there are those who advocate telling children nothing about the manner of conception and their genetic origins on the grounds that the social parents have a right to privacy about their fertility status and that the children might feel stigmatized and unnecessarily confused about the unusual origins. Second, there are those who argue that children should be told about how they were conceived

TABLE 6.1 Family Relationships Created Through Third-Party Conceptions

Family Created Through	Child's Relationship to Nurturing Father — Genetic	Child's Relationship to Nurturing Mother — Genetic	Child's Relationship to Nurturing Mother — Carrying	Child's Relationship to Third Parties — Genetic	Child's Relationship to Third Parties — Carrying
Donor insemination	No	Yes	Yes	Yes	No
Egg donation	Yes	No	Yes	Yes	No
Embryo donation	No	No	Yes	Yes	No
				Yes	No
Gestatory surrogacy	Yes	Yes	No	No	Yes
Genetic surrogacy	Yes	No	No	Yes	Yes
Gestatory surrogacy using donor semen	No	Yes	No	No	Yes[1]
				Yes	No[2]
Gestatory surrogacy using donor egg	Yes	No	No	No	Yes[1]
				Yes	No[3]
Gestatory surrogacy plus donor embryo	No	No	No	No	Yes[1]
				Yes	No[3]
				Yes	No[2]
Genetic surrogacy plus donor semen	No	No	No	Yes	Yes[1]
				Yes	No[2]

[1] Surrogate
[2] Semen donor
[3] Egg donor

and possibly given some idea of the type of contributor (e.g., gamete donors, surrogate mother) involved in the conception, gestation, and birth without going so far as to identify the third parties. This view is advocated on the grounds that trying to keep such matters secret would place intolerable burdens on the family and might not even be successful, but to identify the third parties, especially semen donors, would endanger the supply of donors who might fear the possibility of a long-term obligation to the child. A third position in this debate is taken by those who advocate not only telling children about the means of conception but also providing, at a later stage, full identifying information about the third party (usually taken to be, in this debate, the semen donor, though the logic of the arguments extends to egg donors and surrogate mothers). This position rests on the claim that children need access to full information about their origins, and in particular about their genetic origins, to establish a proper sense of their own identity and to provide information for medical purposes. In addition, it is argued that donors do not all necessarily wish to remain anonymous and could, therefore, in the future be selected according to their willingness to be identified to the child. Advocates of the second and third positions in the debate have also asked whose interests have most been protected by secrecy and anonymity. Though the donors' interests are most often cited, it could be argued that secrecy is in the social parents' interests too, particularly the social father in the case of donor insemination. Secrecy hides not only the fact that he is not the child's genetic father, it also hides his infertility. It might even be argued that secrecy is in the clinicians' interests too, since it makes their pivotal role in all aspects of assisted conception, but in particular in donor insemination, less open to outside scrutiny.

It can be argued that this debate could be settled by reference to international conventions of human rights that declare children's right to establish details of their identity. But in fact the international picture is quite varied, even among signatories to such conventions. In Sweden a child conceived from donated semen has the right of access, at the age of eighteen, to identifying information about the donor. In the United Kingdom, such a child can apply for information to confirm that he or she was so conceived and may be given other, nonidentifying, information about the donor. In the Netherlands it has been recommended that donors be allowed to consent to being identified in the future. In general, however, third-party anonymity has been sustained in most countries. Whether children born through assisted conception will themselves mount a campaign for access to information (which was part of the impetus behind changes in adoption practice) remains to be seen. This possibility, however, is a reminder that the children of assisted conception eventually become adults: Persistent reference to "children" serves to infantilize them and leads to a language of protection rather than of rights.

Less prominent but no less important issues that affect the children of assisted conception have already been mentioned but are given added significance when seen from the offspring's point of view. For example, it is not known what the impact of a surrogate mother handing over the newborn baby to the commissioning parents will be on her existing children; or the impact on an assisted-conception child of knowing (if the child has been told) that the child is the survivor of a selective reduction process that terminated the lives of the child's fetal siblings.

In conclusion, we can see that what has previously been regarded as a matter of fundamental biological and family ties is now open to assistance, manipulation, and negotiation. Assisted reproduction has the potential to extend ideas about family and kinship even if it is as yet being applied according to more traditional views of family life. Assisted conception also has the potential to create new areas of conflict between parents and children. Whether such potential is used to positive or negative effect, it is certainly the case that the experiences, indeed the fates, of parenthood and childhood are inextricably interwoven.

FOR FURTHER READING

Daniels, Ken, and Erica Haimes, eds. 1998. *Donor Insemination: International Social Science Perspectives.* Cambridge: Cambridge University Press.

Golombok, S., R. Cook, A. Bish, and C. Murray. 1995. "Families Created by the New Reproductive Technologies." *Child Development* 66: 285–298.

Haimes, Erica. 1990. "Recreating the Family?" In Maureen McNeil et al., eds., *The New Reproductive Technologies.* London: Macmillan.

Morgan, Derek, and Robert Lee. 1991. *Blackstone's Guide to the Human Fertilisation and Embryology Act 1990.* London: Blackstone Press.

Stacey, M., ed. 1992. *Changing Human Reproduction.* London: Sage.

United Kingdom. 1990. *Human Fertilisation and Embryology Act, 1990.*

United Nations. 1948. *1948 Universal Bill of Human Rights.* UNdocA/811. New York: UN.

seven

Response of the Catholic Church to New Reproductive Technologies

PAUL LAURITZEN

In 1987, the Vatican's Congregation for the Doctrine of the Faith (CDF) issued an instruction on reproductive technology entitled *Donum Vitae: Instruction on the Respect for Human Life in Its Origin and on the Dignity of Procreation*. Since the CDF is responsible for assisting the pope in overseeing Catholic theology, including Catholic moral theology, it is part of the magisterium, or teaching authority, of the church, and its pronouncements represent the official teaching of the church. Thus even though an instruction does not carry the same weight as other types of teaching documents, for example, encyclicals, it is an authoritative document of the church hierarchy and, in this case, defines official Catholic teaching on the new reproductive technologies.

Donum Vitae is divided into three parts plus an introduction and conclusion. The introduction sets out some of the basic presuppositions about human life and history that inform the Catholic perspective on human reproduction as well as some of the fundamental moral principles that will be applied in the remainder of the document in order to reach particular moral conclusions. Part 1 examines the use and treatment of human embryos given the technologies of in vitro fertilization (IVF), embryo flushing and transfer, and prenatal diagnosis of genetic defects. Part 2 discusses particular reproductive interventions such as IVF, artificial insemination by the husband, donor insemination, and surrogate motherhood. Part 3 takes up the relationship between the moral and civil law and calls for action on the part of political authorities to stop the spread of these technologies. The instruction is highly critical of assisted reproduction, explicitly condemning artificial insemination with either husband or donor sperm, IVF of all sorts, surrogate motherhood, and almost all manipulations of human embryos. A close reading of the instruction shows that the rejection of reproductive technology is supported by essentially three lines of argument, two of which are familiar from Catholic teaching on other controversial social issues.

The first line of argument is consistent with church teaching on abortion and the moral status of the fetus: Human life begins at conception, and embryonic life must thus be safeguarded and treated with dignity from the very first moment of its existence. On the basis of this concern to protect fetal life, the church condemns as illicit the cryopreservation and destruction of human embryos typically associated with IVF, the gestation of human embryos in nonhuman animals or in artificial uteruses, nontherapeutic experimentation on embryos, and prenatal diagnostic tests directed to aborting defective fetuses.

The second line of reasoning used to oppose interventions in the reproductive process is related to the Catholic Church's teaching on contraception, specifically to what the church sees as a special nature in the transmission of human life in marriage. According to the church, human procreation is irreconcilably different from the transmission of other forms of life; it is intentional and purposive and therefore governed by laws. These laws are given by God and written in the very being of man and woman. One such law is that intercourse, love, procreation, and marriage belong together. Quoting the 1968 encyclical on contraception, *Humanae Vitae*, the CDF reaffirms church teaching that an inseparable connection, willed by God and unable to be broken by man on his own initiative, exists between the two meanings of the conjugal act: the unitive meaning and the procreative meaning. The implications for reproductive technology are clear: Just as contraception separates what it is never permitted to separate by allowing for union without the possibility of procreation, so does reproductive technology make possible an impermissible separation by providing for procreation without union. The problem with contraception is that although intercourse and love may be held together, procreation is split away. The problem with artificial reproduction is that although procreation and love may be held together, intercourse is split away.

The third line of reasoning is connected to what the CDF sees as the legitimate nature of the human person in bodily form. The church's stated point of view is that because a person is a "unified totality" of body and soul, it is wrong to treat a person in a way that reduces him or her to either mere body or mere spirit. The final line of argument in *Donum Vitae* is thus that reproductive technology is dehumanizing because it treats human reproduction as merely material. Since it reduces human procreation to the union of gametes, reproductive medicine is unconcerned with how this union is brought about. By allowing for noncoital procreation, reproductive technology diminishes the full significance of human reproduction. It simultaneously turns our bodies into mere instruments of our wills—thereby dividing us against ourselves—and disembodies procreation in a way that sets the stage for the objectification and commodification of reproduction.

Responses to Catholic teaching on the new reproductive technologies have been varied. For example, the Ethics Committee of the American Fertility Society issued an explicit rejoinder to the instruction in which it attempted to rebut every substantive conclusion articulated by the church. By contrast, many liberal Catholics accept church teaching on forms of assisted reproduction that involve the use of donor gametes or surrogates but reject church teaching that forbids artificial insemination with the husband's sperm or IVF using a married couple's gametes. Finally, some feminists have condemned as appalling the instruction's failure to discuss the effects of the new reproductive technologies on women, particularly given the extensive discussion of their effects on fetuses.

FOR FURTHER READING

American Fertility Society Ethics Committee. 1988. "Ethical Considerations of the New Reproductive Technologies in Light of 'Instruction on the Respect for Human Life in Its Origin and on Dignity of Procreation.'" *Fertility and Sterility* 49(2): i–7S.

Congregation for the Doctrine of the Faith. 1987. *Instruction on Respect for Human Life in Its Origin and on the Dignity of Procreation: Replies to Certain Questions of the Day*. Publication no. 156-3. Washington, D.C.: United States Catholic Conference.

Coughlan, Michael J. 1990. *The Vatican, the Law and the Human Embryo*. Iowa City: University of Iowa Press.

O'Connell, Laurence J., et al. 1987. "Responses to the Vatican Document on Reproductive Technologies." *Health Progress* 68: 45–65.

Pellegrino, Edmund D., John Collins Harvey, and John P. Langan, eds. 1990. *Gift of Life: Catholic Scholars Respond to the Vatican Instruction*. Washington, D.C.: Georgetown University Press.

Raymond, Janice. 1987. "Fatalists and Feminists: They Are Not the Same." In Patricia Spallone and Deborah Lynn Steinberg, eds., *Made to Order*. Oxford: Pergamon Press.

Shannon, Thomas A., and Lisa Sowle Cahill. 1988. *Religion and Artificial Reproduction: An Inquiry into the Vatican Instruction on Respect for Human Life in Its Origin and on the Dignity of Human Reproduction*. New York: Crossroad.

Vacek, Edward V. 1988. "Notes on Moral Theology: Vatican Instruction on Reproductive Technology." *Theological Studies* 49: 114–115.

eight

Reprotech: A Feminist Critique of the Language of Reproductive Technologies

ROBYN ROWLAND

"Reprotech," the language of the new reproductive technologies, helps to construct a context for reproductive technology that both softens its reality and redefines women as fragmented body parts and children as products. Within this discourse, infertility is presented as the primary issue at stake; yet the infertile include a broad range of people, including women on in vitro fertilization (IVF) because of their male partner's infertility. Increasingly, language conflates the woman undergoing IVF with the couple. For example, so-called surrogate mothers are sought to incubate embryos for couples. Although statistics for IVF are rarely represented as failure rates even though after fourteen years between 90 and 95 percent of women exposed to IVF fail to have babies, medical scientists repeatedly give misleading success rates, often including pregnancy rates in those for live births.

Embryos

IVF for the first time allows the human embryo to be available for ex utero manipulation and research. Debates around the rights and wrongs of embryo experimentation led to interesting manipulations of language in the course of a public outcry against early IVF practice in humans during the 1980s in the United Kingdom. The embryo was retermed a "pre-embryo" and finally a "fertilized egg" by the medical profession in order to avoid the implication that the subjects of experimentation were human. Embryos can be operated upon, are effectively parentless, yet are also commonly portrayed in the media as awaiting adoption. Embryos have been involved in custody battles as if they were in vitro children, especially in the United States. Embryos in IVF procedures are typically categorized in terms such as "poor quality" or "high caliber" and may be "wayward" if they do not perform correctly, that is, if they do not implant, which is the tendency with IVF.

Women's and men's body parts become personified in different and revealing ways. IVF practitioners and researchers commonly refer to "nubile," "young," and "youthful" ova as the most desirable ones for fertilization. Sperm is allocated child status and has a father. In so-called surrogacy arrangements, the man donating the sperm and using a woman's womb is regularly described as the "father" even though his sole role up until the baby's birth, such as in the case of "Baby M," is limited to that of sperm donor. In this case the contracting father and sperm donor, Richard Stern, was given fatherhood status by Superior Court of New Jersey judge Harvey Sorkow: "At birth, the father does not purchase the child. It is his own biological genetically related child. He cannot purchase what is already his" (Superior Court of New Jersey 1987: 1157). The discriminatory validation of fatherhood over motherhood was obvious when Stern was defined as the father compared to "this alternative reproduction vehicle," as the judge described Mary Beth Whitehead, the birth mother. In discussions of donor insemination and children's attempts to trace their genetic fathers, paternity is valued over maternity where mothering is defined as relationship and fatherhood signifies the sperm as the life source.

Fetus Personification

As the embryo becomes personified, so too does the fetus. In an advertisement by Hewlett-Packard in 1988, a new "fetal trace transmission system" was featured. With this system, heartbeat traces can be communicated and recorded over standard telephone lines linking women in their homes with hospitals and doctors' offices, avoiding the necessity of practitioners speaking with, touching, or seeing the woman at all. The advertisement for this system carried a large photograph of a fetus looking very childlike within a supposed amniotic sac. The caption in large letters read: "Today, Jennifer made her first long-distance telephone call." Medical, law, and ethics journals increasingly refer to fetal "rights" and "personality." With ultrasound, the fetus is no longer screened by the woman's body but is available for real-time, "live" viewing and therefore manipulation. This visualization reveals an active creature on screen and produces a new individual patient with distinct medical problems that can be diagnosed and treated. This personification of the fetus at the same time leads to a dehumanization of women and the loss of associated rights. Within the growing and exciting field of in utero medicine the fetus becomes preeminent as the woman recedes. Conflicts between doctors and birth mothers over fetal diagnosis and therapy arise. Their resolutions are increasingly portrayed as difficult and even tragic events for physicians, as moral arguments that the woman's life is more important than that of the fetus become less convincing. Serious morbidity and handicap in the mother are no longer commonly assumed as more grave than such morbidity and handicap in the fetus.

Women Dismembered

The language of dismemberment is important in constructing women's increasing alienation from their bodies and from motherhood, signifying a loss of control over themselves as whole people. Women are natural resources "harvested" for eggs and become restricted in the scientific literature to eggs, ovaries, and wombs. IVF researchers often refer to women as "endocrinological environments." In the Baby M trial, child psychologist Lee Salk called women "surrogate uteruses," and the American Fertility Society in its ethics report discussed women as "therapeutic modalities."

Women often report being treated like animals during IVF: hamsters on a wheel, a prized cow, a chick waiting to lay eggs. The alienation of women from their bodies is also evident particularly in discussion of so-called surrogate motherhood. "Surrogate" is itself a misnomer, indicating that the woman is somehow a substitute and not the "real" mother. Thus birth mother is often characterized as a "host womb." Other terminology includes the "gestational surrogate," the "gestational mother," and the "host mother." Increasingly, however, the term "mother" is not used in the description of surrogates and the woman may be described as being involved in "prenatal adoption" or as an "agent of gestation."

Alienation of Women

In an astonishing development in new reproductive technology research in the late 1980s a "back-to-nature" trend emerged. This development was one in which a woman incubated her own embryos inside her body. This technique purportedly *allows* the woman to be a human incubator for her own embryos. Instead of the eggs and sperm being combined and stored for forty-eight hours in a petri dish and a laboratory incubator, they go into a tiny tube that is put into the woman's vagina and held in place by a diaphragm. Another example of women's alienation from their procreativity is evident in terms of fetal medicine where women are reduced to a uterine operating room and are described as the best intensive-care unit for the fetal patient. Finally, there are recent speculations within the medical profession that women who have recently died or are brain dead could serve as surrogate, gestational mothers.

Children as Products

Because of the enormous commercial investment in this area of research, the packaging and sale of reproductive technology are reflected in language. Test-tube babies have "hit the stock market" and "mail-order babies" are available through surrogacy brokers such as the U.S. company Surrogate Mothers Limited. An ironic counterpoint to the current language of reproduction is in the Latin root of "obstetrician," *obstet*, which means "to stand in the way."

FOR FURTHER READING

American Fertility Society. 1990. "Ethical Considerations of the New Reproductive Technologies." *Fertility and Sterility* 53(6), supp. 2.
Andrews, Lori B. 1989. *Between Strangers: Surrogate Mothers, Expectant Fathers and Brave New Babies*. New York: Harper and Row.
Corea, Gena. 1985. *The Mother Machine*. New York: Harper and Row.
Edwards, Robert, and Patrick Steptoe. 1980. *A Matter of Life*. London: Hutchinson.
Rowland, Robyn. 1992. *Living Laboratories: Women and Reproductive Technology*. Indiana University Press.
Superior Court of New Jersey. 1987. "In the Matter of Baby M, a Pseudonym for an Actual Person." 217 N.J. Super. 313, 525 A.2d 1128, March 31.
Wood, Carl, and Alan Trounson. 1989. *Clinical in Vitro Fertilization*. 2nd ed. London: Springer-Verlag.

nine

New Reproductive Technologies— Women and Science

SUE ROSSER

Since the late 1970s feminist historians, philosophers of science, and feminist scientists have pointed out areas of gender bias in science, particularly biology. Once the possibility for androcentric bias was discovered, feminist scholars (including scientists) set out to explore the extent to which it had distorted science. They recognized potential distortion on a variety of levels of research and theory: the choice and definition of problems to be studied, exclusion of females as experimental subjects, preconceptions in methodology used to collect and interpret data, and bias in theories and conclusions drawn from the data. They also began to realize that since the practice of modern medicine depends heavily on clinical research, any flaws and ethical problems flowing from gender bias in this research are likely to result in inequity in medical treatment that results in poorer health care in disadvantaged groups.

An aspect of medical research of particular concern for women's health is reproduction. The new reproductive technologies have been criticized because of their potential physical and psychological health risks for women and because they provide men with more control over reproduction. In addition, having a huge preponderance of male leaders sets the priorities for medical research, clearly affecting the choice and definition of problems for research. Research on conditions specific to females tends to receive low priority, funding, and prestige, although women make up half the population and receive more than half the health care. The Women's Health Initiative was launched by the American National Institutes of Health in 1991 to study the problem. The study investigated women and cardiovascular diseases, cancers, and osteoporosis in an attempt to raise the priority of women's health and to provide baseline data on previously understudied causes of death in women. Additional examples that might also be included in such a study include dysmenorrhea, incontinency in older women, and nutrition in postmenopausal women.

In contrast to a low priority on women's health, significant amounts of time and money are expended on clinical research on women's bodies, particularly in connection with reproduction. From 1900 until the 1970s in the United States considerable attention was devoted to the development of contraceptive devices for females rather than for males. Furthermore, substantial clinical research has resulted in increasing medicalization and control of pregnancy, labor, and childbirth with relatively little intervention in male reproductivity. Feminists have criticized the conversion of a normal, natural reproductive process that historically was controlled by women into a clinical, and often surgical, procedure controlled by men. More recently, they have focused on new reproductive technologies such as amniocentesis, in vitro fertilization, and artificial insemination as scientific and medical means are sought to overcome infertility.

The scientific community has often failed to include females in animal studies in basic research as well as in clinical research, unless the research centered on controlling the production of children. The reasons for exclusion (cleaner data from males due to lack of interference from estrus or menstrual cycles, fear of inducing fetal deformities in pregnant subjects, and higher incidence of some diseases in males) can be defended on the basis of financial and health-risk considerations. However, such an exclusion results in drugs that have not been adequately tested on women subjects before being marketed and in a lack of information about the etiology of some diseases in women.

Perhaps more women in decisionmaking regarding the design and funding of clinical research would result in more interdisciplinary research to study issues of women's health care. Menstruation, pregnancy, childbirth, lactation, and menopause, for example, are complex phenomena and require more than the range of methods of study provided by a single discipline. Such an interdisciplinary approach could also be applied to reproductive technologies and other complex problems to benefit all health care consumers, male and female.

Researchers outside the mainstream and those likely to lose power and good health through reproductive technologies are much more likely to be critical of such technologies. Male researchers may be less likely to see flaws or question reproductive technologies that reinforce their superior status in society. In order to eliminate bias, the community of scientists undertaking research on reproductive technologies needs to include individuals of varied and diverse backgrounds in terms of race, class, gender, sexual orientation, and nation of origin. Only then is it less likely that the perspective of one group will bias technology designs, approaches, subjects, and interpretations.

FOR FURTHER READING

Birke, Lynda. 1986. *Women, Feminism and Biology.* New York: Methuen.

Hamilton, Jean. 1985. "Avoiding Methodological Biases in Gender-related Research." *Women's Health Report of the Public Health Service Task Force on Women's Health Issues.* Washington, D.C.: U.S. Department of Health and Human Public Service.

Harding, Sandra. 1986. *The Science Question in Feminism.* Ithaca, N.Y.: Cornell University Press.

Healy, Bernadine. 1991. "Women's Health, Public Welfare." *Journal of the American Medical Association* 264(4): 566–568.

Pinn, Vivian, and Judith LaRosa. 1992. "Overview: Office of Research on Women's Health." *National Institutes of Health.* Special issue: 1–10.

ten

New Reproductive Technologies as Dystopia

DAVID N. JAMES

Beginning as early as Plato, utopian literature has concerned itself with attempts to reconstruct and control human reproduction. But to many twentieth-century writers, the negative consequences of new reproductive technology far outweigh its advantages. Two of the most important twentieth-century literary dystopias in which the dangers of new reproductive technology are addressed are Aldous Huxley's *Brave New World* and Margaret Atwood's *The Handmaid's Tale*. These novels are situated within the historical context of utopian writing that began with Plato because, as Krishan Kumar, one of the most important contemporary scholars of utopias and dystopias, has argued, the histories of utopian and dystopian thinking are closely intertwined. So I will treat two contemporary dystopias, Margaret Atwood's account of coercive surrogate motherhood and Marge Piercy's *Woman on the Edge of Time*, as responses to earlier utopias including Aldous Huxley's account of biotechnology and the eugenics-inspired works of H. G. Wells and the British biologist J.B.S. Haldane. Viewing dystopian warnings as responses to utopian hopes reveals both the continuity and the evolution of thought about the social effects of reproductive technology.

The story of utopian reproductive reordering can be traced, as can the story of utopia, beginning with Plato's *Republic*. Plato's ideal city is like a healthy body: Each part functions in harmony with the rest. There are three classes corresponding to the three functions of the ideally just city-state: wise leaders, soldiers for defense against external enemies, and workers to provide food and the other necessities of life. Education is to be the same for all until differences in natural ability reveal to which of these three functional classes each student belongs. Plato advocated a system of common marriage among the rulers or guardians in which all children were to be regarded as common offspring. To maximize the natural abilities of future citizens, Plato was the first to recommend a system of selective eugenic breeding. Drawing an analogy between the selective breeding of domesticated animals and human reproduction, Plato argued that wise and good guardians are more likely to produce wise and good offspring. Hence Plato argued that the best men must have sex with the best women as frequently as possible and that the most inferior men and women must not reproduce.

This cluster of beliefs concerning "natural" human inequality, the inheritability of qualities, and the inegalitarian political implications of these supposed facts of nature have been of great ideological significance throughout Western history—not only in the era of aristocratic rule but in political movements such as national socialism in Germany—and continue widely in the present day as well. Although few subsequent writers echoed Plato's call for the abolition of families, his calls for what has come to be known as eugenics (literally "well born," a term coined by Charles Darwin's cousin, Francis Galton, in 1883) found enthusiastic support in the early decades of the twentieth century. The growing use of intelligence testing, combined with racial stereotyping, xenophobia, and social Darwinism, produced a reinvigorated "science" of eugenics in Europe and North America. The involuntary sterilization of the "feebleminded" found wide public acceptance in the United States, and the U.S. Supreme Court ruled such practices constitutional in the 1924 *Buck v. Bell* case. Conversely, the most influential dystopian writer of that era, H. G. Wells, was thoroughly in the mainstream when, in *A Modern Utopia* of 1905, he said: "It is our business to ask what will Utopia do with its congenital invalids, its idiots and madmen, its drunkards and men of vicious mind, its cruel and furtive souls, its stupid people, too stupid to be of use to the community, its lumpish, unteachable and unimaginative people?" (136). Wells's answer was: "These people will have to be in the descendent phase, the species must be engaged in eliminating them . . . The breed of failure must not increase, lest they suffer and perish, and the race with them" (136–137).

In this climate of opinion J.B.S. Haldane produced the first utopia of modern biotechnology, *Daedalus*, in 1928. Haldane's utopia, though of little literary merit, further popularized and promoted eugenic engineering of human reproduction both to eliminate diseases (negative eugenics) and to promote desirable traits such as intelligence (positive eugenics). Haldane coined the word "ectogenesis" (extra-uterine gestation), and he imagined that it would become routine by the end of the twentieth century:

> The small proportion of men and women who are selected as ancestors for the next generation are so undoubtedly superior to the average that the advance in each generation in any single respect, from the increased output of first-class music to the decreased convictions for theft, is very startling. Had it not been for ectogenesis there can be little doubt that civilization would have collapsed within a measurable time owing to the greater fertility of the less desirable members of the population in almost all countries. (Haldane 1924: 67)

Partly as an answer to Wells and Haldane, and long before midcentury Nazi sterilizations and other inhumanities were carried out under the banner of maintaining racial purity, Aldous Huxley published in 1932 the most famous dystopian novel of the twentieth century: *Brave New World*. Huxley's frightening vision is of an alienated, dehumanized clone world where genetically identical individuals are created in vitro to serve society's needs. Huxley's brave new world of 632 A.F. (after Ford), like Plato's republic, has dispensed with families and raises its children in state nurseries. Ectogenesis and genetic engineering create infants who then are educated through subliminal repetition.

Rather than Plato's crude scheme of eugenics—which Plato admits would need to be propped up with a "noble lie" by the guardians—the ectogenesis scene that opens Huxley's novel shows in embryo the potentialities of biology on the verge today of being realized: human cloning, ectogenesis, and genetic engineering. Huxley showed how these new reproductive technologies might someday be combined with psychological conditioning to produce a society where the nature and meaning of reproduction were completely redesigned to serve social stability and control.

The citizens of *Brave New World* range in intelligence from the apelike Epsilons to the highly intelligent Alphas. Turning Haldane's optimism upside down, Huxley shows the dehumanization inherent in using biotechnology to engineer reproduction and education. Reproduction in *Brave New World* has become a production process to serve the needs of a society that, like Plato's ideal city, is based on a caste system. The biggest difference is the degree of control made possible in the design of individual citizens through modern techniques of biological and psychological manipulation.

In contrast to Plato's *Republic*, however, there is no need to control the appetite for pleasure in *Brave New World*. Quite the contrary, the promiscuous sex, the mass entertainment experienced by all of the senses (the "feelies"), and the universal, frequent resort of brave new worlders to a hangoverless, psychoactive drug ("soma") create one of literature's most memorable and damning portrayals of the shallowness of a hedonistic paradise. Unable to overcome this engineered fit between desire and the satisfaction of desire, the protests of protagonist John Savage for freedom, creativity, and individuality fall on uncomprehending ears. The suicide of this "savage" outsider to the brave new world is the pessimistic note on which Huxley's novel ends.

Haldane was not the only early-twentieth-century writer to imagine a liberating future because of new reproductive technology. One such vision, the first feminist utopia making explicit use of reproductive technology, is *Herland* (1915) by Charlotte Perkins Gilman. Herland is a peaceful, socialist society peopled entirely by women. The women of Herland reproduce themselves by way of parthenogenesis. Men have been absent for 2,000 years, and with them have gone the violence, inequality, and oppression they created.

Unlike Gilman, the contemporary novelist Marge Piercy, in her 1976 *Woman on the Edge of Time*, sees sexist institutions, not men, in need of replacement. Piercy envisions the twenty-second-century Mattapoisett, which is an ecologically enlightened, agrarian society where population is controlled and the virtues of small-scale production are practiced. In Mattapoisett, just as in the societies of the *Republic* and *Brave New World*, monogamous marriage has been abolished as an oppressive institution. Reproduction is no longer carried out in women's bodies. As a guide explains to Consuelo, a visitor from our time,

> It was part of women's long revolution. When we were breaking all the old hierarchies. Finally there was that one thing we had to give up too, the only power we ever had, in return for no more power for anyone. The original production: the power to give birth. Cause as long as we were biologically enchained, we'd never be equal. And males never would be humanized to be loving and tender. So we all became mothers. Every child has three. To break the nuclear bonding. (98)

Far from Piercy's prediction of a benign future for new reproductive technology is Margaret Atwood's chilling dystopia the Republic of Gilead, found in her *Handmaid's Tale* (1986). Inspired by feminist criticisms of commercial surrogacy and animated by the increased political power of fundamentalist Christianity, Atwood depicts a United States that has, by the end of the twentieth century, become a theocracy animated by a reactionary ideology of "women's place." Offred (of-Fred), the narrator of the novel, like all women in Gilead, is known only by her keeper's name. The lack of civil liberty, the burning of books, and the omnipresent Eyes, or secret police, echo the most famous dystopian novel of totalitarianism, George Orwell's *1984*. But the fate of women in Gilead is Atwood's particular focus.

Their fate is to endure the backlash of all backlashes: Women are compelled to work as housekeeping Marthas, as prostitute Jezebels, or, like Offred, as handmaids to the men in power—as reproductive surrogates in an increasingly less fertile world. Forced to wear red clothing and utterly lacking privacy and political rights, women are reduced to a form of reproductive slavery. The handmaid must submit to coitus with a high-ranking official while lying between the legs of the official's wife—an infertile woman who will rear any offspring produced by this passionless impregnation. The rulers of Gilead justify their coercive surrogacy as analogous to the Old Testament story of how Abraham "took to himself a handmaid" after failing to impregnate Sarah.

Gilead is, at least on the surface, a puritanical society with women veiled, nonreproductive sex banned, and pornography burned. Abortion and divorce are illegal, and only heterosexual marriage is permitted. In *Brave New World*, "mother" is a dirty word; in Mattapoisett, it is a word signifying nurture without biological connection; in Gilead, according to a strict patriarchal scripture, it is a holy word. Along with such contemporary feminists as Rosemary Tong and Mary O'Brien, Atwood is less concerned with the dehumanizing possibilities of biotechnology than with how control over human reproduction, be it high-tech or low-tech, connects with control over women. By losing control over their reproductive lives, the women of Gilead have lost all other freedoms. At the same time, the loss of these other freedoms has led inexorably to the loss of control over reproduction. Of central importance for Atwood, as for many contemporary feminists, is who is to develop and use new reproductive technology, not the nature of that technology in itself.

Fears of losing control—of reproduction and of reproductive technology—have helped fuel twentieth-century dystopias. The utopian hopes for such technologies, often echoing eugenic dreams as old as Plato, have continued to be influential. In response to such utopian optimism, dystopian writers have revealed the darker potentialities of new reproductive technology. Utopian and dystopian perspectives have constantly interacted, and together they have helped to shape the actual development and critiques of new reproductive technologies.

FOR FURTHER READING

Atwood, Margaret. 1986. *The Handmaid's Tale*. Boston: Houghton Mifflin.
Gilman, Charlotte Perkins. 1915. *Herland*. Reprint 1979. New York: Pantheon Books.

Haldane, John B.S. 1924. *Daedalus*. New York: Dutton.
Huxley, Aldous. 1932. *Brave New World*. New York: Harper and Row.
Kumar, Krishan. 1987. *Utopia and Anti-Utopia in Modern Times*. Oxford: Basil Blackwell.
O'Brien, Mary. 1981. *The Politics of Reproduction*. London: Routledge and Kegan Paul.
Piercy, Marge. 1976. *Woman on the Edge of Time*. New York: Fawcett Crest Books.
Plato. 1992. *The Republic*. Trans. George. A. Grub. Revised by C.D.C. Reeve. Indianapolis, Ind.: Hackett.
Tong, Rosemarie. 1989. *Feminist Thought: A Comprehensive Introduction*. Boulder: Westview Press.
Wells, H. G. 1905. *A Modern Utopia*. Reprint 1967. Lincoln: University of Nebraska Press.

Part Two

Early Reproductive Technologies

In the current climate of technological advancement in reproductive technologies and genetic engineering, a considerable number of previous and "low-tech" interventions in human reproduction tend to be lost or taken for granted. The history of birth technologies, for example, extends back to prehistory in the form of crude contraceptive devices, aids to birth and nursing, and alternatives to breastfeeding newborns. Also, there is now considerable routine technological intervention in common aspects of human reproduction: In most developed countries pregnancy and childbirth are the most common reasons for hospitalization, and obstetrical interventions (medical and surgical) are the predominant procedures performed in hospitals. It is important to examine the history of reproductive technology as well as contemporary assumptions about technological requirements for reproduction to appreciate fully reproductive technologies as products of social and political pressures. Without appropriate scrutiny, one is inclined to view technological applications as self-determining and an automatic response to social progress rather than the work of dominant interests.

Because women's bodies are the most obvious site of reproduction, it is not surprising to find the considerable history of reproductive interventions focused on women. As a profound and highly involved event culturally and physically, birth was one of the first and most persistent foci of interest to every society. Yet there is little evidence of the complex treatment of this central social activity before the advent of the European scientific revolution. Midwives were certainly the chief attendants at and around birth up to and, in most places, at least sporadically, beyond this time. There is also evidence that their knowledge of human reproduction and its complications was extensive and effective. However, beginning in the mid-1800s, there was a radical transition from a midwife-controlled environment of reproduction to one dominated by a growing profession of physicians. By the beginning of the twentieth century the transition was almost complete, as midwifery practice was either unauthorized or highly limited in most Western and developed countries.

Alongside this history of medical professional development and the movement of birth into the medical sphere runs a history of increased technological intervention in birth. As training midwives and other traditional birth attendants was likely carried out through apprenticeship and based on oral traditions, records of technological interventions preceding the advent of contemporary medical science are virtually nonexistent. Some traditional herbal drugs and remedies have been appropriated by medical practice, such as using ergot for stimulating labor, a part of common medical practice today. Predominantly, however, medically sanctioned technologies of reproduction were developed over the past three centuries. One technology in particular, the forceps, was instrumental in shifting the control of birth away from midwives and women to the predominantly male medical profession. The argument used increasingly by physicians that reproduction is a fundamentally dangerous enterprise worthy of considerable medical attention was another way in which midwives were removed from the birthing scene as unskilled and ineffective attendants. As surgery improved (largely due to an understanding of infection and sterile techniques), cesarean sections became another common yet controversial birth technology, and in many developed nations today they are used in up to 25 percent of births. Monitoring laboring women with sophisticated electronic devices has also become standard procedure and provides another apparent justification for the professionalization of attention and for hospital births.

About the same time most Western births were being moved into hospitals (the turn of the nineteenth century), public health initiatives and scientific curiosity created the alternative infant-feeding movement. Just as women giving birth was reconstituted as an event requiring sophisticated medical intervention, breastfeeding as the best way of nourishing a newborn child was replaced. An entire industry, which continues to flourish today, was built on the notion that mother's breast milk was inadequate, should be supplemented or replaced relatively soon in the infant's life, and could be improved upon with scientific baby formulas.

With twentieth-century advances in drug production, women's reproductivity was exposed, largely on an experimental basis, to a variety of chemical interventions. DES, a synthetic estrogen, was routinely used in women to prevent miscarriages between the 1940s and 1970s despite reports that indicated it did not prevent spontaneous abortion. In 1971 a link between the drug and a rare form of cancer in the female offspring of women using it was established and prescriptions for DES halted. The estrogen-based oral contraceptive pill has a similar history in terms of experimentation on women with very high initial doses. Currently, oral contraceptives used by women are the most common form of contraception and contain relatively small hormonal doses. Although contraceptives can provide women with a much-desired control of reproductivity, their experimental development and the predominance of contraceptive methods for women rather than for men mean that women's health is more at risk than men's. This is particularly the case for women in developing and underdeveloped nations, where international concerns for population growth assert themselves through aggressive population-control programs. Also, drugs and contraceptive methods outlawed in developed countries because of health risks are often distributed through some of these programs to boost the profits of large pharmaceutical and medical supply companies.

Recent developments in hormone therapy in menstruating and menopausal women have also contributed to the notion of women's reproductivity as both problematic and deficient. Menstrual disorders provide a good case in point. Despite little knowledge of what causes painful periods generally and endometriosis specifically, surgery and high-level hormonal interventions are now used to treat the symptoms. At first, the symptoms were construed by the medical profession as largely psychological. Now the treatment program provides women with some pain relief, but it is accompanied by significant risk. Also, the social construction of treatment tends to reduce and skew women's complex experience of menstruation. Similar reasoning, though with more extreme effect, accompanies female genital mutilation. Mostly practiced in Africa, it tends to be distinguished by northwestern nations as barbaric and "other" even though it is based on the same Western notions of female reproductivity and sexuality as requiring technological intervention to improve and control them.

One of the best examples of socially determined reproductive technologies is abortion. Despite medical advances in abortion techniques, which finally make them safe and relatively easy to employ, public debates over the morality of terminating pregnancy prohibit many women from accessing abortion. Intense arguments as to when life begins have prevented women's safe and ready access to abortion and have impeded physicians' adoption of abortion as medical practice. More recently, opposition to abortion has led to violent attacks on abortion clinics and their staff. Women seeking to terminate their pregnancies also face a common misperception that the pregnancy is their fault and that they are viewing abortion casually and callously as birth control. It is also argued that given the large amount of adoption demands, abortion should be restricted or even forbidden. In contrast, feminists argue that safe and accessible abortion is a key aspect of women's reproductive autonomy.

"Prenatal harm" is a relatively new term that continues the debate over the status of the fetus and poses a threat to women's reproductive autonomy. Besides abortion, the term also refers to pregnant women's behavior, especially the abuse of drugs and alcohol. The term and attendant public concern tend to focus on the woman and blame her for becoming a noxious or insufficient fetal environment through neglect or substance abuse. Most Western courts in dealing with claims based on these assumptions have been reluctant to rule against the pregnant woman, as such rulings would usher in the highly problematic precedent of fetal personhood and the kind of litigation it would allow. Nonetheless, there are tendencies to recognize the fetus as a patient within medical practice even though all medical attention to the fetus must go through the body of a woman and even though, legally, the fetus is not a separate patient.

In another direction, a recent trend in reproductive health broadens the scope of attention to include the environment. Contrary to the typical focus on the woman's body as the primary site of reproduction, there is increasing concern for environmental effects on reproduction. Because women have long been banned from work and especially certain types of work due to their reproductive capacities, employment equity poses interesting issues in terms of reproductive health in the workplace.

Despite an increase generally in attention to informed patient consent (resulting chiefly from increased medical litigation), women in labor remain largely without the power to challenge physician-led interventions. In response to this situation and to the increased medicalization of women's reproductivity, women, chiefly in developed countries, have led a movement to return women to positions of control over their reproductivity. Typically this movement counters the medical claim that birth is normally a dangerous event with the assertion that when the mother is in good health, pregnancy and birth do not require the interventions standardized by the 1960s in medical practice. This movement also seeks to reestablish the normal birthing site outside hospitals and in specially designed, women-centered birthing centers and the home. Partly as a result of this movement and partly due to governments' interests in lowering health care costs, midwives are returning as legitimate practitioners but within a newly negotiated role that acknowledges the medical model and defers to physicians in high-risk cases.

eleven

Birth Technology

S. NAN SCHUURMANS, JAMES J. BOULTON,
PATRICIA A. STEPHENSON, AND
SHERYL BURT RUZEK

The history of birth technology is shaped by three major factors: advances in medicine, methods, and instruments that date back to before the Middle Ages; sociopolitical change; and feminist issues around female midwives and male physicians and around the autonomy and control of the childbearing woman.

From earliest recorded times until the Middle Ages, midwifery was performed by women for all women, peasants and queens alike. From the fifteenth to seventeenth centuries, midwives were highly respected in Europe, and childbirth occurred at home. The earliest and most influential book on midwifery dates back to 1513 and was written by the German physician Eucharius Rosslin. First published in German, the book was translated into Latin as *De Partu Hominis* and later into English as *The Byrth of Mankynde*. An excerpt from the English translation reads,

> The midwife herself shall sit before the laboring woman and shall diligently observe and waite, how much, and after what meanes the child stirreth itself. ... [The midwife is encouraged to] instruct and comfort the party, giving her good meate and drinke, [all the while] giving her hope of a good speedie deliverance, encouraging and enstomacking her to patience and tolerance. [The midwife is] not to let the woman labour before the birth come forward and show itself. [She must not let the mother push until the head is visible, or she] will labour in vain, her strength will be spent and that is a perillous case.

Many of the directions, such as individual labor support and delayed pushing in the second stage of labor, are still proving effective and are advocated today for positive obstetrical outcomes.

By the end of the seventeenth century, the industrial revolution had changed most aspects of life. Medicine and related disciplines took on a mechanistic view of the world with their drive toward standardization, specialization, and centralization. The rise of universities brought the development of medicine and midwifery as regulated specialties. (Since the former was restricted to those who knew Latin, it excluded most women practitioners who were not formally educated.) The Industrial Revolution also increased the use of forceps and cesarean sections and increased knowledge about the medical care of women in childbirth.

The movement of people to the cities and the formation of a class of working poor led to the formation of hospitals, some with lying-in wards. Early hospitals were small institutions formed for the impoverished, aged, or ill and for single mothers without resources. But as the need grew, hospitals grew larger, like the Hôtel Dieu in Paris, which served a population of 400–500 patients, including some for obstetrics. Women may also have received antenatal care at separate hostels. The physician Adolphe Pinard and a Madame Becquet, for example, opened a hostel for unsupported pregnant women in Paris in 1892. Admitted first to the hostel, these women subsequently delivered in Pinard's hospital. In North America, Marguerite de Youville and her Grey Nuns established various hospitals for the care of poor, single, pregnant women in Montreal and across Canada.

A lack of knowledge of the spread of infection and overcrowding resulted in death from puerperal sepsis for thousands of women in eighteenth- and nineteenth-century maternity hospitals. This high rate of maternal morbidity diminished considerably with the development of chlorine disinfection starting in the mid-1900s (Robert Collins), hand washing between treating patients with "chlorina liquide" (Ignaz Semmelweis), antiseptic techniques using carbolic spray (Joseph Lister), and improved ventilation (Florence Nightingale). At the Queen Charlotte Hospital in England, maternal mortality was recorded as 84.4 per 1,000 deaths in 1868, dropping to 45.7 per 1,000 in 1876 as a result of the improvement of ventilation and antiseptic techniques. Other factors affecting mortality, such as forceps delivery and cesarean section, were not well established at this time, and many women continued to die of obstructed labor, eclampsia, malposition, and hemorrhage. It is noteworthy that the incidence of maternal mortality at this time was much lower for home deliveries than for deliveries in institutions.

In the early twentieth century, the control of infection in hospitals and the introduction of anesthesia and operative obstetrics resulted in continued improvement in outcomes. The effectiveness of many scientific discoveries, such as the development of antibiotics and uterotonic drugs, standardized the education of obstetrical caregivers. Antenatal care was also enhanced by improved living standards. Furthermore, governmental health ministries began to take an active interest in maternal and perinatal mortality.

A major reduction in death from sepsis occurred with the introduction of sulphonamides in the 1930s and penicillin in 1941. The discovery and production of agents that act on the muscle wall of the uterus, such as ergot and syntocinon, led to decreased losses from postpartum hemorrhage and also aided in the management of prolonged labor. The recognition that early diagnosis of conditions such as preeclampsia with routine blood-pressure measurement during pregnancy, and the advent of drugs to treat high blood pressure and convulsions, led to a dramatic decline in mortality from this disease. The result of these and other innovations was a diminishment in maternal mortality from a rate of 5–7 per 1,000 live births in the early 1900s to 1 in 20,000 in the late 1990s in the developed world. Similarly, the perinatal mortality rate was 156 per 1,000 live births at the turn of the century in the United Kingdom compared to 6–7 per 1,000 in the late 1990s.

Common Birth Technologies

Obstetrical Forceps

Until the eighteenth century, obstetrical operations were often destructive procedures performed in attempts to save the life of the mother. These procedures included such extreme actions as dismembering and extracting the fetus with fillets (blades), hooks, snares, and bands in cases of severe cephalopelvic disproportion (narrowing of the pelvis). Although there are references to the possible delivery of living infants via operations and other technical interventions in ancient writing, the development of one of the most significant birth technologies, forceps, is usually ascribed to one of several members of the Chamberlen family. Four generations of this family practiced in England from 1600 onward, and it is not certain which of them actually invented the forceps. The success of the implement is historically credited to the invention of the two branches, each having a curved blade to fit the fetal head. Because the instrument could have been easily copied, the Chamberlens kept their invention secret by transporting it in a large box. They also performed all deliveries under cover of a large sheet with no observers present. But eventually, one Chamberlen divulged the secret to a colleague, Roger Roonhuysen, in Amsterdam around 1693. Roonhuysen formed a group, the Medical

Pharmaceutical College of Amsterdam, which maintained a monopoly on this technology by licensing practitioners, who had to pay a fee for the secret of forceps.

Meanwhile, comparable instruments were independently developed elsewhere in England and on the European continent with several important improvements. Two of these, a lock to articulate and stabilize the forceps branches and a second curve to fit the natural curve of the maternal pelvis, were devised in France and England during the eighteenth century. Another essential development in the evolution of obstetrical forceps was the enunciation of the principle of axis traction. Mathias Saxtorph, who practiced in Copenhagen from 1771 to 1800, recognized that the force of traction on the forceps should follow the natural curve of the maternal pelvis. He described a bimanual technique that was later popularized by Charles Pajot, a practitioner in Paris from 1842 to 1886. From 1860 onward, a great sequence of forceps modifications was introduced to facilitate the technique.

The forceps in current use are not, by and large, the result of recent developments. Their design has required few substantial improvements in the past sixty years. Correctly used, forceps are aligned symmetrically with the fetal head, following the bony landmarks, and traction is applied when the blades are closely aligned with the maternal pelvic curve. Determination of whether the pelvis is adequate for a forceps delivery requires expert judgment: Failure to progress in labor may be the result of a small degree of cephalopelvic disproportion, which may be an indication for forceps delivery. A significant degree of disproportion, however, becomes a contraindication to vaginal delivery by any means. In the past, many problems in obstetrics probably existed because of poor nutrition and the frequency of such conditions as rickets, which can affect the size and shape of the maternal pelvis.

Since 1980, two types of forceps delivery have properly been abandoned. High-forceps operations, where the fetal head has not entered the pelvis, have been replaced by cesarean section because of the risk of maternal or fetal injury and the increased safety of abdominal delivery. Elective low-forceps extractions, formerly performed on the premise that spontaneous delivery would not occur, have also been abandoned. Today, every attempt is made to avoid difficult forceps deliveries. Should it not be possible to obtain the correct forceps application or should the effort required for rotation or extraction of the fetus be unusual, the procedure is abandoned and cesarean section is carried out.

It is a challenge in modern obstetrical training to teach the prudent use of mid-forceps procedures in order to effectively reduce the incidence of unnecessary abdominal delivery and to strike the proper balance among appropriate interventions and thus avoid very difficult or traumatic deliveries. Modern obstetrics requires that operative vaginal deliveries have clearly documented indications such as definite evidence of fetal compromise, failure to progress, or some emergency that precludes waiting any longer for spontaneous delivery. The concept of "fetal distress" is being revisited as methods of fetal evaluation are being reviewed.

Fetal Monitoring

In-Hospital Monitoring. The stethoscope was invented in 1819 by René Laënnec, and two years later Jacques Alexandre le Jumeau, vicomte de Kergaradec, reported hearing the fetal heart when applying the stethoscope to the mother's abdomen. The original fetal stethoscope was developed by Adolphe Pinard in France. By the mid-1800s, listening for the fetal heartbeat (auscultation) became established practice in maternity hospitals. *Observations on Obstetric Auscultation* was published in 1833 to give guidelines for use in obstetrical units. It was first used routinely by the Rotunda Hospital in Dublin. It seems likely that the ability to determine whether a baby was alive was an important medical advance allowing appropriate intervention.

Electronic fetal monitoring (EFM) paralleled technological advances after World War II. Fetal heart tracings were recorded in the 1950s, and clinical application increased after Edward Hon developed the spiral scalp electrode in 1972. Hon, Roberto Caldeyro-Barcia, and Klaus Hammacher developed monitors that record fetal heart rate on paper strips and described the significance of fetal heart patterns. Because worrisome fetal heart-rate tracings had an association with abnormal fetal acid-base status and fetal asphyxia, it was hoped that routine use of EFM would lead to a reduction in the incidence of cerebral palsy. Unfortunately, most studies have failed to show any advantage of EFM over intermittent auscultation as judged by mortality, neonatal morbidity, or cerebral palsy. In addition, the use of EFM, combined with an increased concern of medical legal risk, has led in part to an unnecessary increase in the cesarean-section rate.

Home Uterine Activity Monitoring and the Treatment of Preterm Labor. Home uterine activity monitoring (HUAM) is designed to detect uterine activity that may lead to preterm labor. The objective is to detect preterm labor early so that therapy can be started early, when it is most effective. Well-designed, randomized, controlled trials have failed to demonstrate a reduction in preterm birth attributable to home uterine monitoring, per se. However, when combined with daily or weekly nurse contact, women who were prescribed home uterine monitoring as a preventive measure had a significant decrease in the incidence of preterm birth when compared to controls. The HUAM monitor is a censoring device that women apply to the abdomen for an hour twice a day to record uterine contractions. The information is transferred by telephone to a perinatal monitoring center or a physician's office. Typically the woman has daily contact with a high-risk pregnancy obstetrical nurse. If the level of uterine activity exceeds a specific threshold, the woman may be given tocolytic therapy (oral and intravenous medications) to stop contractions and to prolong the pregnancy and give the fetus more time to develop in utero.

Scientific studies have shown neither home uterine activity monitoring nor tocolytic therapy to be effective in preventing prematurity. In four randomized studies comparing daily home uterine activity monitoring to frequent nurse telephone contact alone, no statistically significant differences in outcome have been shown. In 1991 the U.S. Food and Drug Administration (FDA) approved use of the device only for early detection of preterm labor in women who had a previous preterm birth. The FDA did not approve the system for preventing prematurity per se. The distinction is important because there is scant evidence that this costly technology benefits patients.

The efficacy of the device is particularly controversial because of growing questions about the safety and efficacy of tocolytic therapy. In a 1992 Canadian study of ritodrine, the only drug approved by the FDA for preventing preterm labor, there was no significant benefit in terms of perinatal mortality or morbidity over that of the placebo. In addition, women who used ritodrine had more complications, such as chest pain and cardiac arrhythmias. In the United States, terbutaline, a similar drug, is often used to treat preterm labor, although it is not approved by the FDA for this use. The lack of efficacy of tocolytic therapy calls into question the entire home uterine monitoring procedure because early detection is not beneficial unless there is effective treatment.

Home monitoring of high-risk pregnancies is targeted for growth by home health care companies, although controversies over efficacy have slowed reimbursement. In the United States, FDA approval has been given to only one company's monitor, and use is approved only for women past their twenty-fourth week of pregnancy who have histories of previous preterm births. Any claim for or promotion of the device that goes beyond the approved indication is illegal and could lead to regulatory action by the FDA. Although the FDA does not consider cost or cost effectiveness in the approval process, cost clearly is an issue in assessing actual benefit. Home uterine activity monitoring costs over $100 a day. The American College of Obstetricians and Gynecologists estimates that it averages $5,616 per patient followed. If 30 percent of pregnant patients were monitored, the cost would be over $6 billion per year in the United States alone. Blue Cross and Blue Shield insurers regard home uterine activity monitoring as investigational but estimate that 40–50 percent of its member plans reimburse for it under specified conditions. Aggressive marketing of the technology has led women to believe that there is established benefit. Some insurers have been sued for failing to reimburse for the device despite the lack of evidence of efficacy and growing concerns over maternal risks from tocolytic drugs.

Episiotomy

The use of episiotomy, or surgical enlargement of the vaginal orifice during delivery, seems to have paralleled the shift of birth management from midwives to physicians. Episiotomy was first discussed by Fielding Ould in 1742 and was advocated during the eighteenth and nineteenth centuries only for extremely difficult births. It was not until the early 1900s that prominent physicians began to advocate increased use of episiotomy.

At the turn of the century, episiotomy was rarely performed, and less than 5 percent of women delivered in hospitals. By the 1950s, 80 percent of all North American births occurred in hospitals, and episiotomy was considered routine for 50–90 percent of cases. Perceived benefits of episiotomy include prevention of tears into the rectum, prevention of trauma to the infant, and prevention of long-term dysfunction of the pelvic muscles. However, studies in the 1980s did not demonstrate any of the above for normal deliveries, and by the early 1990s, the routine application of the procedure had been challenged.

Cesarean Section

Historical Development. Cesarean section involves the abdominal delivery of the baby by incising the abdominal and uterine walls. "Section" is an early word for abdominal entry, now replaced by the term "laparotomy." The term "cesarean section" is one of historical curiosity, and no direct association with the Roman emperors has been found. The word may have been first used in a treatise on abdominal delivery published in 1581. Postmortem abdominal delivery was practiced in antiquity and was at one time decreed in Roman law. Through the Middle Ages, it was likely reserved for the salvage of the infants of important persons, and numbers of notable survivors have been recorded in the literature. Ancient literature and medical papers from the eighteenth and nineteenth centuries tell of women being delivered abdominally by laypersons, or indeed by themselves, with instances of survival.

The first successful abdominal deliveries on living patients may have been performed in the early fifteenth century by the German midwife Guetgin. By the late sixteenth century the procedure was recommended, but it was to be undertaken only under the most desperate circumstances of prolonged, obstructed labor. In these situations, the mother and baby were already seriously compromised, and death was generally accepted as the probable outcome for both. Prior to the availability of practical anesthesia in the nineteenth century, the procedure must have been horrifically painful.

The usual causes of death were hemorrhage, either operative or secondary to uterine atony (failure), infection, ileus (intestinal obstruction), and thromboembolism (blocked blood vessels). The high rate of death associated with cesarean section led surgeons to explore variations of the procedure in the hope of improving the chances of maternal survival. The uterine incision was generally left open or barely closed. Closure of the abdominal incision was almost inevitably lethal, since blood, serum, and contaminants then had free access to the abdominal cavity without the possibility of egress. Several solutions were postulated over a period of decades. These included variations on removing the uterus as a source of bleeding and infection, exteriorizing the uterine incision, and seeking to approach without entering the abdominal cavity. In 1876, Eduardo Porro performed the first subtotal hysterectomy following abdominal delivery, and its success prompted several surgeons to experiment with modifications. However, even though more experience was gained, the maternal mortality remained high.

The first true extraperitoneal cesarean section was performed by Ferdinand Ritgen in Germany in 1821. In the meantime, meticulous closure of the uterine incision was explored but was not entirely satisfactory because of the nature of the available suture material. In 1881, Ferdinand Kehrer performed the first low-segment transverse incision with closure. Several American and European obstetricians urged practitioners to recognize the indications for cesarean section before the operation became hopeless, in an attempt to reduce maternal mortality. In 1908, Bernhard Krönig performed the first cesarean section under the bladder (retrovesical), utilizing a vertical incision. In 1921, John Martin Munro Kerr of Glasgow, together with Eardley Holland, introduced the retrovesical transverse incision, which is now the preferred procedure.

Until the mid-nineteenth century, hospitals were dangerous places because of accumulated bacterial contaminants. After Joseph Lister revolutionized surgery (circa 1867) by advocating antisepsis, the literature and scientific meetings began to include discussions regarding postoperative care, and extensive treatises were published on the subject. By the late nineteenth century, more attention was also being paid to postoperative fluid balance. Absorbable sutures improved wound healing. The discovery of uterotonic agents in the first decade of the twentieth century permitted control of blood loss from the uterus. Improvements in antisepsis and postoperative care, along with development of absorbable suture material, antibiotics, and uterotonic agents, made cesarean section less risky. The discovery of blood groups by Karl Landsteiner in 1901 set the stage for blood transfusion, although its use in civilian populations was limited until after World War II.

Modern Trends. With the new surgical technique, transverse lower-segment incision, and improvements in sterile technique and methods of anesthesia administration, maternal and perinatal mortality associated with cesarean section has decreased dramatically. Even so, until recently, obstetrical providers were conservative in their management of difficult labor and delivery with cesarean section. In industrialized countries up until 1970, only about 5 percent of births were by cesarean section, but thereafter, the rates began to climb (see Table 11.1). By the early 1980s in some countries (most notably the United States, Canada, and Australia), the cesarean rate had exceeded levels that could be justified on the basis of medical need.

Researchers began to look for nonmedical explanations for the increasing rates. Variation in cesarean-section rates was found to be associated with geographical region, expected method of payment and type of medical insurance coverage (private insurance is associated with higher rates), provider convenience, malpractice worries, type of birth attendant (midwife, general practitioner, obstetrician), and type of hospital. For the latter, differentiating factors included size, affiliation (or lack of) with a university, presence of high-risk neonatal care, and type of ownership (public, private, religious).

Lower-segment cesarean section is used almost exclusively. Classical cesarean section is unusual, but it could be indicated when large fibroids occupy the lower segment or when the size of the fetus precludes delivery through the lower segment. For lower-segment cesarean section, a transverse incision is made in the lower segment of the uterine wall. Possible skin incisions are vertical or transverse. One clinical trial compared the two categories of skin incision and was unable to demonstrate statistically

TABLE 11.1 Rates of Cesarean Delivery, Cross-National Comparisons

Country	1979/1980	1987/1988
Czechoslovakia	4.0	7.7
Denmark	10.7	12.1
Finland	11.9	14.4
France (part)	9.6	12.0
Netherlands	4.7	7.2
Scotland	10.7	14.4
USA	16.5	24.1

SOURCES: Lomas and Enkin 1991; Stephenson 1992; Grandjean et al. 1990.

significant differences in terms of the need for blood transfusion, postoperative anemia, average operating time, or febrile morbidity. The transverse incision is preferable for cosmetic reasons. The type of skin incision and mode of delivery depend on the presentation of the fetus, the position of the placenta, and whether the pregnancy is single or multiple.

Four methods of anesthesia are commonly used for cesarean section: general, epidural, spinal, and local infiltration. Selection method depends on whether the operation is emergency or elective, the experience of the person administering the anesthesia, the equipment available, whether the woman is experiencing complications, and the preference of the woman. Proper positioning of the woman for the operation is essential. Randomized clinical trials indicated that a left lateral tilt relieves the pressure of the uterus on the vena cava and thus helps prevent neonatal depression.

Cesarean section must be viewed as a lifesaving operation. Still, it is not without risks, and potentially avoidable deaths still occur. The maternal mortality ratio associated with cesarean sections (40.9 per 100,000 births) is four times that associated with vaginal delivery (9.8 per 100,000 births). Maternal mortality from cesarean section per se is difficult to estimate, since some of the deaths are caused, at least in part, by the condition that led to the cesarean. Nevertheless, the maternal death rate associated with elective repeat cesarean sections (17.9 per 100,000) is twice that for all vaginal deliveries and four times that for uncomplicated vaginal deliveries (4.9 per 100,000). The main causes of maternal death associated with cesarean section are hemorrhage, sepsis, pulmonary embolism, and anesthesia accidents.

Most forms of maternal morbidity are higher after cesarean than after vaginal birth. There are risks of infection, of operative injury (damage to the bladder, accidental extension of the uterine incision, damage to the uterine vessels), and of negative effects on fertility. The adverse effects of anesthesia and/or cesarean section on the fetus (depressed APGAR score, higher rates of respiratory distress, and increased perinatal mortality in subsequent pregnancies) are well known.

Current Trends

Through the late 1980s and the 1990s, there has been growing concern over excessive cesarean-section rates, and the use of this procedure is now being carefully monitored. The incidence of true cephalopelvic disproportion has diminished. There has been a gradual but definite and favorable change in pelvic architecture since the 1960s to the extent that the evaluation of pelvic bony anatomy is no longer central to obstetrical teaching. Also, women who have had a low-segment cesarean section are no longer routinely booked for sections for consequent births. Forceps deliveries and vaginal breech deliveries are also being revisited as alternatives to cesarean sections with an emphasis on careful diagnosis. Irregular fetal heart patterns on continuous monitoring may have led to the overuse of cesarean section, and modern trends in medical practice call for caution in the assessment of fetal distress.

Birth technology continues to evolve. Along with better standards of living, birth technology has resulted in marked improvement in both maternal and perinatal outcomes, but not without some costly experiments. In addition, because of relatively poor standards of living, advances in birth technology have not reached most areas of the developing world. Maternal and perinatal mortality rates there still reach alarming proportions. Today, obstetric caregivers also grapple with the effects of overreliance on mechanistic technology. There is a renewed interest in applying practices that aid the mother to summon her own resources. More emphasis is being placed on the autonomy of the mother, involvement of the family, and infant bonding. The modern goal is to use birth technology where it has proven benefit and otherwise to allow the birth process to occur spontaneously.

FOR FURTHER READING

Canadian Pre-term Labor Investigators Group. 1992. "Treatment of Pre-term Labor with the Beta Adrenergic Agonist Ritodrine." *New England Journal of Medicine* (July 30): 308–312.

Cartwright, F. F. 1968. *The Development of Modern Surgery from 1830*. New York: T. Y. Crowell.

Das, K. 1929. *Obstetrical Forceps, Its History and Evolution*. St. Louis, Mo.: C. V. Mosby.

Grandjean, H., et al. 1990. *Enquête sur les Naissances Vivante et les Décès Avant 28 Jours dans Cinq Régions et Quatre Départements Français: Rapport de Fin d'Etude.* Toulouse: Laboratoire de Recherche Clinique et Biologique en Reproduction, INSERM.

"Home Monitors for High-risk Pregnancies Get Critical Look." 1992. *Health Technology Trends* (September): 3–5.

Labarge, Margaret Wade. 1986. *A Small Sound of the Trumpet—Women in Medieval Life*. London: Penguin.

Lomas, J., and M. Enkin. 1991. "Variations in Operative Delivery Rates." In I. Chalmers, M. Enkin, and M.J.N.C. Keirse, eds., *Effective Care in Pregnancy and Childbirth*. Vol. 2. London: Oxford University Press.

McCraw, Ronald K. 1989. "Recent Innovations in Childbirth—Dangerous Proposals, Harmless Fads or Wave of the Future?" *Journal of Nurse Midwifery* 34(4): 206–210.

McKay, W. J. 1905. *The Preparation and After-Treatment of Section Cases*. London: Bailliere, Tindall and Cox.

O'Dowd, M. J., and E. E. Philip. 1994. *History of Obstetrics and Gynaecology*. New York: Parthenon.

Paul, R. H. 1994. "Electronic Fetal Monitoring and Later Outcome: A Thirty Year Overview." *Journal of Perinatology* 14(5): 393–395.

Pearson, J., and G. Rees. 1991. "Technique of Cesarean Section." In I. Chalmers, M. Enkin, and M.J.N.C. Keirse, eds., *Effective Care in Pregnancy and Childbirth*. Vol. 2. London: Oxford University Press.

Petitti, D. B., et al. 1991. "In-Hospital Maternal Mortality in the United States: Time Trends and Relation to Method of Delivery." *Obstetrics and Gynecology* 59(1): 6–12.

Radcliffe, W. 1989. *Milestones in Midwifery and the Secret Instrument*. San Francisco: Norman.

Sachs, B. P., S. Hellerstein, R. Freeman, F. Frigoletto, and J. C. Hauth. 1991. "Home Monitoring of Uterine Activity. Does It Prevent Prematurity?" *New England Journal of Medicine* 325(19): 1374–1377.

Stephenson, P. A. 1992. *International Differences in the Use of Obstetrical Interventions*. Copenhagen: World Health Organization Regional Office for Europe.

Trolle, D. 1982. *The History of Caesarean Section*. Acta Historica Scientiarum Naturalium et Medicinalium series. Copenhagen: C. A. Reitzel.

Wertz, Richard W., and Dorothy C. Wertz. 1989. *Lying-In: A History of Childbirth in America*. Exp. ed. New Haven and London: Yale University Press.

twelve

Birth Technologies: Critical Perspectives

DOROTHY C. WERTZ

Until the mid-nineteenth century, birth was a women's event attended by midwives. Ninety-five percent of the time, both mother and child survived. Some colonial midwives delivered 3,000 to 4,000 babies in the United States without a fatality, but when something went wrong, midwives had few technologies. They could reposition a breech birth and deliver the child feet first (a maneuver called podalic version). By the eighteenth century, if their techniques failed, midwives called a male barber-surgeon (a tradesman without formal education) to dismember the fetus to save the mother's life. Typically, the few men who witnessed birth saw it as a flawed, disastrous process needing improvement.

The forceps, the first instrument that could deliver a live baby, probably evolved from midwives' attempts to deliver impacted babies by placing spoons on either side of the head. When men began to take an interest in birth, in the early seventeenth century, the English barber-surgeon Peter Chamberlen developed a lock to hold the spoons together. Like many medical entrepreneurs, the Chamberlen family kept the new instrument a family secret for over a century and became accouchers (male midwives) to the royal family. Forceps may have taken more lives than they saved before Pasteur's bacteriological discoveries of the 1860s. Early models had no curves to fit the birth canal or the baby's head, often tore the mother's soft tissue, and were not disinfected or even washed. Sources of infection were unknown and infections were usually blamed on patients.

A mother and infant might survive a forceps birth only to die of puerperal fever several days later. No one would credit her death to the instruments used during birth.

Forceps were among the few recognized medical procedures before 1880. They helped male doctors gain control over birth, preparing the way to lucrative family practice in an increasingly competitive atmosphere. English laws forbade midwives from using them; educated midwives wrote and campaigned against them as harmful and unnecessary. In America, no laws restricted use, but midwives could not afford instruments and generally believed them to be unnecessary. To demonstrate professional superiority and to justify higher fees, male doctors constantly used them.

In the first half of the nineteenth century, U.S. medicine turned in a heroic fashion to medical procedures and pills of all kinds in order to manage birth. Bloodletting and mercury were favorite, and dangerous, treatments for laboring women. Originally a German midwife's discovery, ergot, a fungus that grows on rye, was appropriated by the medical profession and used by physicians starting in the 1830s to strengthen labor contractions. Although still used to induce labor, ergot derivatives can be dangerous.

The only labor analgesia available to midwives for centuries was wine. In 1847, James Simpson of Edinburgh introduced chloroform, and in 1848, Walter Channing of Boston introduced ether. Queen Victoria's choice of chloroform in 1853 helped to silence religious objections that women should suffer in childbirth as the curse of Eve. Both anesthetics were probably used only at the last moment, after the worst pain had passed. Thus women demanded something that would obliterate the entire experience of pain during labor and delivery. In 1914, at the outbreak of World War I, German doctors developed a method called "twilight sleep," which combined morphine (a powerful painkiller) with scopolamine, an amnesiac that took away memory. American women campaigned for this method, and twilight sleep (without morphine) became the analgesic of doctors' choice until the 1960s. Local anesthetics such as spinals and epidurals were developed between the 1940s and 1960s.

Before the bacteriological discoveries of the 1860s to 1880s, medicine placed little value on cleanliness. Fortunately, the United States escaped the puerperal fever epidemics that killed half or more of women delivering in European maternity hospitals in the mid-nineteenth century, largely because it had few maternity ("lying-in") hospitals. Pasteur's discovery of the cause of puerperal fever (1880) and the use of antisepsis made hospital birth safer. By the 1920s, hospitals, formerly the refuge of poor women, were advertising to attract middle-class women. By the 1930s, most urban births in the United States occurred in hospitals. This trend followed in most of Europe after World War II.

Antisepsis and the move from home to hospital made proliferation of new technologies possible. The cesarean section, once routinely fatal for the mother and therefore performed only after she was dead, became a viable operation once infection could be prevented. By the 1890s, doctors were performing cesarean sections on living mothers, only half of whom survived. Like other technologies, the operation was overused. In 1930, a commission investigating maternal deaths in New York City decried the high cesarean rate of 5 percent. Development of safe blood transfusions and sulfa drugs (the first antimicrobials) in the mid-1930s, followed by penicillin in the 1940s, helped decrease the risks and increase the use of the operation. Cesarean sections are now performed in 25 percent of U.S. births. This rate has been criticized as too high and as a reflection of physicians' concerns over being sued for complications arising from birth rather than of genuine medical indications.

North American society has consistently sought technological improvements to birth. In the 1920s birth was described as akin to the mother's falling on a pitchfork and the baby having its head slammed in a barn door. It was deemed by the medical profession to be far better to make a surgical cut (episiotomy) in the mother's tissues and to lift the baby out with forceps so as to protect its brain from the mother's birth canal. Outlet (or lower) forceps and episiotomies became routine in U.S. births for over fifty years until the 1980s. Other developed nations eventually followed the U.S. lead and have also instituted more technology in birth. Since at least 1900, women and doctors have cooperated in the search for perfect babies, regarding sophisticated technology as the best insurance. However, many of these technologies were adopted without clinical trials. Fetal heart monitors for asphyxiation appeared in the 1970s and have become routine. Starting in the early 1970s, prenatal diagnosis through ultrasound, amniocentesis, and eventually chorionic villus sampling provided a window on the womb to diagnose fetal abnormalities. Movements for natural childbirth have not succeeded in reducing the amount of technology.

There is no evidence that widespread use of sophisticated technology in itself increases survival rates or improves health, especially if there are social inequities in care. In fact, nations that provide basic prenatal care to all and that use less technology at birth have lower maternal and infant mortality rates than the United States, which uses a good deal of birth technology.

FOR FURTHER READING

Cianfrani, Theodore. 1960. *A Short History of Obstetrics*. Springfield, Ill.: Thomas.
Cutter, Irving S., and Henry R. Viets. 1964. *A Short History of Midwifery*. Philadelphia: Saunders.

Davis-Floyd, Robbie E. 1992. *Birth as an American Rite of Passage.* Berkeley: University of California Press.
Findlay, Palmer. 1939. *Priests of Lucina: The Story of Obstetrics.* Boston: Little, Brown.
Graham, Harvey. 1951. *Eternal Eve: A History of Gynaecology and Obstetrics.* Garden City, N.Y.: Doubleday.
Leavitt, Judith Walzer. 1986. *Brought to Bed: Childbearing in America, 1750–1950.* New York: Oxford University Press.
Oakley, Ann. 1984. *The Captured Womb: A History of the Medical Care of Pregnant Women.* Oxford: Basil Blackwell.
Speert, Harold. 1958. *Obstetric and Gynaecologic Milestones.* New York: Macmillan.
Thoms, Herbert. 1933. *Chapters in American Obstetrics.* Springfield, Ill.: Thomas.
Wertz, Richard W., and Dorothy C. Wertz. 1989. *Lying-In: A History of Childbirth in America.* Exp. ed. New Haven and London: Yale University Press.

thirteen

Breastfeeding

MARJORIE ALTERGOTT

Infants who are exclusively breastfed need no additional food or water. Contemporary medical professionals suggest adding other foods beginning between the fourth and sixth months of life, although supplemental foods in some cultures are offered much later during the first year. Unrestricted breastfeeding is an intimate experience involving extensive skin-to-skin contact during which each participant sees, touches, smells, hears, and senses the movements of the other. Because of the frequent interaction, mothers and babies can develop an acute awareness of each other, sensing each other's moods and anticipating movements. For women, the complex hormonal, neurological, and emotional interactions associated with breastfeeding contribute to changes in blood flow and temperature, contractions of the uterus and other muscles, nipple erection, a sense of pleasure and well-being, and perhaps other responses not currently documented. Although it is seldom recognized, infants also respond physiologically and sensually. Human milk is quite diluted, and babies must nurse often to obtain adequate nourishment. Although it has been postulated that the dilution is an adaptation to ensure constant monitoring and stimulation to enhance the infant's cognitive development and a close mother-infant bond, dilution and frequency of contact are more likely the result of an evolving process combining physiological and behavioral factors.

The length and frequency of nursing episodes vary from minutes to hours. They also vary with babies and mothers, infant age, and within any twenty-four-hour period. Because of this, and because nursing can be so integrated into daily activities, some mothers find it difficult to count the number of discreet nursing episodes within a specific time period. Night feedings are important to the maintenance of milk supply, and nursing with both breasts for most feedings, although not absolutely necessary, helps ensure milk production in both breasts and can help prevent breast infections. Women in traditional societies seldom nursed less than two years, and continuing through the third, fourth, and even fifth years of the child's life was not uncommon. Thus the amount of time spent in nursing can exceed that required for pregnancy or birth and may be comparable to the time women devote in a lifetime to the intimate portions of adult sexual relationships. The success and duration of breastfeeding are negatively affected by mother-infant separation, delayed first feedings, scheduled feedings, and interruptions in breastfeeding with formula and other foods. Artificial foods take longer to digest, increase intervals between feedings, and can lead to inadequate breast stimulation. Also, the processes of extracting liquids from bottles and from the human breast are different, and newborns often have difficulty nursing after using substitutes.

Human milk production and flow are responses to hormones and neurological events and are influenced by other physiological and psychological factors and the mother's overall health status, although even poorly nourished mothers can provide highly nutritious milk for their infants for an extended period. Milk production adapts to individual infant needs during the first weeks of life by responding to the frequency and length of suckling. Production is inhibited when the breasts are not completely emptied or when the nipples receive insufficient stimulation, and flow can be inhibited when mothers are under stress. Chemicals and rough treatment of nipples increase the likelihood of soreness because these destroy the protective outer cells and remove beneficial oils. Nipple shields used for sore nipples interfere with the natural suckling process and with success in establishing lactation and, along with restricted schedules, can delay healing.

Substantial documentation exists of the biological value of breastfeeding for infants. Human milk is a unique substance, sometimes used for its healing properties by ancient societies. Among its many significant physiological benefits are its antiinfective and antiallergenic properties. Breast milk not only passively confers protection on the infant but also actively stimulates the infant's immune system. In addition, human milk promotes growth and development, including that of the central nervous system. Breastfeeding has been associated with the prevention of sudden infant death syndrome and with positive cognitive development. Cultural practices have varied widely, and data on the needs of infants are primarily based on artificially fed babies, helping create uncertainty as to the physiological needs of breastfed infants.

Even less attention is given to physiological benefits of breastfeeding for women. The decreased risk for postpartum hemorrhage is well established, and there is an association between breastfeeding and the temporary remission of diabetes mellitus to various degrees. There is also evidence of a protective effect for breast cancer and osteoporosis. There is a dearth of information concerning the effect of breastfeeding on human behavior and interrelationships. Scholars believe that bonding is enhanced by mother-infant interaction during the first hours after birth. This is thought to be an especially sensitive period, and there is evidence that separation at this time may have long-term negative effects on the mother-infant relationship, making a deep bond more difficult to achieve. Most likely, infants' and children's interactions with their mothers, as well as with other socially significant people, are highly relevant to the development of personality and social relationships. Researchers are currently investigating the effect of attachment security on stress and social competence. The role of breastfeeding in attachment security has not been addressed, but the recent research may suggest avenues for studying and understanding the relationship further.

An often overlooked effect of lactation is the suppression of conception. The physiological milieu of unrestricted and unsupplemented lactation inhibits ovulation, menstruation, and conception. Estimates of pregnancy occurrence during lactational amenorrhea vary from 1 to 11 percent. This wide range exists primarily because definitions of breastfeeding vary, and research often fails to differentiate between supplemented and exclusive breastfeeding. Keeping this in mind, an international multidisciplinary group of experts found breastfeeding to account for more contraceptive effect than all reversible contraceptives provided by family planning programs. This expert panel concluded that exclusive breastfeeding for the first six months after birth results in less than a 2 percent chance of pregnancy. The ability of lactation to prevent pregnancy has been known since ancient times, and it has undoubtedly been used by women to limit fertility, a practice that has served to stabilize population size.

The majority of women and babies have the physiological capacity for breastfeeding. However, many different customs have been associated with it. Beliefs about colostrum (the substance secreted from the breast during late pregnancy and for up to several days after birth) and about the introduction of other foods and weaning, as well as rituals to enhance milk quality and quantity, vary widely among cultures. Information on ancient chants and potions to support breastfeeding has been accumulated by anthropologists. These interventions were used to protect milk, remedy problems with milk or its supply, or treat infected breasts. Also, herbal remedies have been passed down through generations, and although no longer widely used in industrialized societies, they are described in contemporary historical and natural health literature. In spite of immense cultural variation in beliefs and customs, women in most traditional societies—which have changed relatively little over many centuries—and most likely the majority of women in many contemporary societies breastfeed without restriction.

FOR FURTHER READING

Jelliffe, D., and E. Jelliffe, eds. 1981. *Advances in International Maternal and Child Health*. New York: Oxford University Press.

Kennedy, K., R. Rivera, and A. McNeilly. 1989. "Consensus Statement on the Use of Breastfeeding as a Family Planning Method." *Contraception* 39(5): 477–491.

Klaus, M., and J. Kennel. 1982. *Parent-Infant Bonding*. St. Louis, Mo.: C. V. Mosby.

Lawrence, R. 1989. *Breastfeeding: A Guide for the Medical Profession*. St. Louis, Mo.: C. V. Mosby.

Minchin, M. 1989. *Breastfeeding Matters*. Alfredton, Victoria: ALMA.

Riordan, J., ed. 1980. "Pleasure and Purpose: The Sensuousness of Breastfeeding." *Journal of Obstetrical, Gynaecological and Neonatal Nursing* 9(2): 109–112.

Stuart-Macadam, P., and K. Dettwyler, eds. 1995. *Breastfeeding: Biocultural Perspectives*. Hawthorne, N.Y.: Aldine de Gruyer.

World Health Organization. 1981. *Contemporary Patterns of Breastfeeding: Report on the WHO Collaborative Study on Breastfeeding*. Geneva: WHO.

fourteen

Infant-Feeding Technologies

MARJORIE ALTERGOTT

Artificial infant feeding (AIF) is one of the most successful and widely used reproductive technologies to date. It can completely replace the lactation function of women's breasts that was once essential for the continuation of human life. Breastfeeding rates in industrialized countries most likely began a slow decline in the eighteenth century, but significant changes occurred in the first half of the twentieth century, coinciding with improvements in AIF. After World War II, breastfeeding rates declined dramatically. Estimates of breastfeeding rates by 1970 in the United States range from 18 percent to 25 percent at birth, decreasing to about 5 percent at six months of age. A renewed interest both within the scientific community and among many women who desired to experience the full range of their reproductive abilities led to an increase, peaking in the early 1980s, when 59.7 percent of new mothers breastfed at birth. A slow but persistent decline then occurred, reaching a low in 1990, when 51.5 percent of newborns were breastfeeding. Since then, breastfeeding has slowly increased. However, breastfeeding with supplemental foods rather than exclusive breastfeeding accounts for much of this increase. Also, the duration appears to be declining, and surveys suggest that much of the discontinuation actually occurs early in the postpartum period.

There are large discrepancies in breastfeeding rates of women from different social categories. In industrialized countries, women from the less privileged minority groups and economic levels have significantly lower breastfeeding rates, a situation reversed in many nonindustrialized countries. Other industrialized nations generally followed the U.S. pattern over the twentieth century, although at a somewhat slower pace and seldom reaching figures as low. Nonindustrialized countries exhibited a slower trend of decreasing breastfeeding rates, but AIF is being rapidly incorporated into the lives of women there as well.

Infant-feeding technology affects not only the vast majority of childbearing women and their infants but, because of its economic and health consequences, all people living in the world. Its significance is compounded when we recognize that breastfeeding traditionally continued for years, not weeks or months, as is currently practiced. Artificially fed infants in nonindustrialized countries are significantly more likely to die than breastfed babies. Contaminated water and utensils and improper administration partly explain the difference. The loss of protection afforded by breastfeeding in an impoverished environment, where an increased likelihood of disease and malnutrition comes from a variety of sources, is also significant. Presently in industrialized countries, due to a relatively higher quality of health care and generally low infant mortality rates, the links between AIF and infant mortality are difficult to detect. Where research has concentrated on First World infant morbidity, the superior health, in the short and long term, of breastfed infants has been substantiated, as has a positive effect on cognitive development.

Early History

Artifacts believed to be infant-feeding vessels used between 1000 and 3000 B.C. include animal horns and Egyptian pottery shaped in the form of a woman. Greek vessels, vase-shaped with a handle and sometimes a spout, date back to 1000 B.C. Similar Roman artifacts from the first few centuries A.D. also exist. Images of humans suckling from other animals appear in Greek and Roman mythology. Ancient Indian texts reveal that cow's or goat's milk was acceptable should human milk not be available, but it is not clear whether this milk was provided through the direct suckling of animals or with the aid of a vessel. Feeding or sucking horns are mentioned in European writings from the ninth through the fifteenth centuries A.D. These and boat-shaped vessels appear in Medieval artwork, and clear records of direct suckling of other animals during this era also exist.

Anthropological evidence suggests glass was used for AIF as early as the first few centuries A.D., wood and leather appear in the fifteenth and sixteenth centuries, metal vessels were used at least by the sixteenth century, and porcelain was used from the eighteenth century onward. Artificial nipples were first mentioned in early Greek writings (A.D. 1 to 500). Upright bottles with teats appear in artwork from the sixteenth century, and bottles with screw tops appeared between A.D. 1600 and 1700. Nipples were constructed from leather, parchment, linen, or animal skin, and sometimes from an animal teat.

Honey was commonly recommended as the first additional food in ancient Greek and Roman writings. In the Middle East, animal milk and eggs were suggested, and a first food in ancient India was boiled rice. Numerous recipes for infant foods appear in Medieval literature, most using milk or broth and a locally grown grain. Sometimes sugars and flavorings were added, and the use of wine or other spirits was not unusual. The extent to which these vessels and artificial feedings were used for newborns and young infants is not clear. However, it is clear that at least some young infants were given such foods, sometimes as a substitute for breast milk. This was particularly true when a wet nurse could not be found or when wet-nursing was frowned upon, as was the case in parts of seventeenth- and eighteenth-century Europe.

Wet-Nursing

In spite of the lengthy historical record of artificial infant feeding, anything other than human milk for newborns was often fatal until this century, and wet-nursing was a more viable alternative. Wet-nursing suggests women have long been willing to share their reproductive abilities with other women, although we know little about the practice from women's point of view. Evidence that wet-nursing was practiced in ancient times exists, and it probably occurred long before recorded history. Wet nurses appeared to be highly valued, and the special relationship that developed between nurses and nurslings was often maintained throughout the life span. Most likely, the early practice of wet-nursing was confined to women caring for infants whose mothers died or were incapacitated. Some were temporarily assisting other mothers at difficult times, a practice occasionally engaged in today.

There is more recent historical evidence that some women experienced wet-nursing as a form of oppression, as illustrated in the common practice of American slaves who nursed the infant of an owner. Other women used wet-nursing as a means of self-support in a number of societies in which wet nurses were paid. The extent of wet-nursing varies with the particular era and culture; however, most historical records indicate that lower-class wet nurses primarily served the upper classes.

Nineteenth-Century Developments: Baby Formula

Successful artificial infant feeding became possible as the result of scientific developments in the 1800s. These developments included affordable sterilizable containers and the refining of rubber to make it more pliable and adaptable to the container as well as to the infant's sucking reflex. The discovery of the basic components of food permitted the modification of animal milk, and early-twentieth-century discoveries of some essential micronutrients decreased the hazards associated with AIF. The developing fields of bacteriology and sanitation were essential to safe AIF and provided information needed to control infectious and often fatal diseases spread through contaminated foods and containers.

Scientists utilized their knowledge to develop infant-feeding formulas. At first, in the mid-1800s, these were simply diluted cow's milk with added cream and milk sugar to make something more closely resembling human milk. In the latter decades of the 1800s, formulas were often cooked with wheat flour or malt. The German chemist Justus von Liebig provided the world with the first commercial infant food in the 1860s. By the 1870s, Henri Nestlé from Switzerland had distributed his product throughout Europe, Australia, and the United States. Mellin's baby food was developed and popularized in England at the end of the nineteenth century. But the United States, where Wagner's Infant Food, Eskay's Albuminized Food, and Horlick's Malted Milk became well-known household products, led the way in the mass production of commercial infant foods.

The new infant-food companies advertised in women's magazines, primarily circulated among the upper classes, and offered free booklets on child care. They used illustrations of chubby smiling babies and testimonials of new mothers, often asserting that their food was as good as mother's milk and even superior. Some promised to ease the responsibility of motherhood and claimed they could prevent colic. Poor women, who could not afford these products, were instructed to use less expensive condensed or evaporated milk even though their adequacy was controversial.

The young infant-food companies recognized the value of physician support and were soon advertising in medical journals, providing doctors with free samples, and presenting their products at professional meetings. They spoke to doctors in technical terms to assure them that their products were developed on scientific principles. Meanwhile, physicians were increasing in status and developing a strong professional organization. The new sciences allowed them to visibly affect the lives of their patients. Their technical knowledge was beyond the grasp of most people, who seldom questioned their advice. Some physicians concentrated on child health, and particularly on the problem of infant mortality. It was clear that infant feeding was an important factor for survival, and it became a cornerstone of the developing field of pediatrics. These early pediatricians did not at first accept commercial foods but developed their own formulas.

The U.S. method, also known as the Boston or the percentage method, was developed by Thomas Rotch, a faculty member of Harvard Medical School. Complicated calculations were used to determine exact formulas for individual infants, which were to be based initially on an analysis of the mother's milk. Strict attention was paid to the exact percentages of fat, protein, and carbohydrate, and formulations ideally required a milk laboratory. The Chicago, or caloric, method, which actually originated in Germany, was especially concerned with overall caloric value. The two schools of thought disagreed about the desirable amount of protein and fat and the degree to which each of these was the root of digestive problems.

Although the percentage method dominated throughout the turn of the century, its time-consuming calculations and laboratory work were eventually rejected in favor of simply prescribing commercially prepared formulas that had been improved as new information became available. However, the development of these methods and the professional dialogue they created had far-reaching effects on physician-mother relationships. They firmly placed infant feeding on scientific ground, created an area of expertise that helped legitimize pediatrics as a specialty, and instilled in the minds of physicians (and eventually mothers) that women were incapable of grasping the complexities of infant feeding.

While physicians were increasingly prescribing commercially prepared foods for their patients, they became aware that infant-food companies that provided feeding instructions to mothers were a threat to their own authority. The American Medical Association (AMA) assigned its Committee on Foods the responsibility of determining which products were suitable for advertising in its journal. The committee accepted advertisements from companies that advertised only to the medical profession or that instructed mothers to follow physicians' advice, but not from those that refused to remove instructions from their packaging. Other medical journals followed AMA decisions in their advertising policies, placing pressure on companies to conform.

Recent Technological Developments

Milk banking, more available in Europe than North America, is an alternative to AIF for infants whose mothers cannot nurse. Since its establishment in the early 1900s, a number of methods for preserving and storing human milk have been tried. Early measures included the addition of H_2O_2 and drying. Freezing appears to be the superior method and is now virtually the universal technique. Raw frozen human milk retains almost the original nutrient status and maintains a low bacterial count if collected under sanitary conditions. The fear of transmitting AIDS decreased the number of milk banks in the 1980s, and the potential to spread this as well as other serious diseases has led the Human Milk Banking Association of North America to recommend strict screening of donors and heat treatment of donor milk. Currently, most human milk is dispensed through physician prescription and goes to those babies whose survival may depend on it, such as those with certain immune diseases, gastrointestinal malformations, and extreme prematurity. Because mothers of premature babies produce milk with unique qualities most suitable for the developmental stage of their infants, they are often urged to extract their milk so it can be frozen and then fed to their infants even before they are medically judged to be capable of suckling.

"Lacto-engineering" human milk, which involves new methods for extracting and recombining specific components of milk from various donors to produce human milk formulations for infants with special needs, is being explored. Human milk is considered a food, not a medication, and therefore is not covered by most health insurance providers and is usually not regulated by drug-approval agencies. How much regulation over banked human milk should exist is currently being discussed by legal experts. Women in North America are not paid for their donation, but in Europe mothers may be paid a nominal fee. The U.S. cost of banked milk to consumers varies from approximately $1 to $2.75 per ounce.

Exporting Artificial Infant Feeding to Nonindustrialized Countries

AIF was introduced to nonindustrialized countries chiefly after World War II, when scientists became concerned with world population growth and widespread hunger in poor nations. Surplus dried cow's milk was shipped to these countries and distributed with the aid of the World Health Organization (WHO) and the United Nations International Children's Emergency Fund (UNICEF). The milk was often used to attract mothers to the clinics, where they were also offered the same questionable advice and instructions about breastfeeding that were offered in industrialized countries. Typically these women were urged to wean early to protect their health and that of their infants. It eventually became obvious that contaminated water, lack of sanitary facilities, lack of knowledge about proper handling of the substitute milk, and the nutritional inadequacy of skimmed cow's milk were contributing to an increased rate of infant mortality. Numerous statistics indicating higher survival rates for breastfed infants have since been compiled. As a result, international development organizations such as WHO and UNICEF became active proponents of breastfeeding in nonindustrialized nations. However, proprietary food companies took advantage of the criticism of cow's milk as a human milk substitute and claimed their products as superior to both.

A number of companies, Nestlé being the most notorious because of its large share of the nonindustrialized world market and its aggressive marketing practices, produced energetic campaigns to sell its formulas to poor women of these nations. They used billboards and flyers of chubby healthy babies, and sometimes "milk nurses" not necessarily educated in nursing, to promote their products. The resulting decrease in breastfeeding contributed significantly to the high infant mortality rates because of problems with sanitation, inadequate communication, poverty, and lower health status in general as the result of environmental conditions.

In the 1970s, consumer groups became active in publicizing the results of bottle feeding. Films such as *Bottle Babies* (Krieg 1975) and a British charity's pamphlet *The Baby Killer* (Muller 1974) stimulated public sympathy and action. The Infant Formula Action Coalition, a U.S.-based ethical marketing advocacy group, organized a Nestlé boycott beginning in 1975, which received worldwide support. Consumer action motivated the U.S. Congress to support international cooperation to address the decline in breastfeeding. The International Pediatric Association filed a resolution to support breastfeeding. However, the American Pediatric Association was reluctant to support any action perceived as negative by the formula industry. The lack of action by this and other U.S. professional organizations has been criticized by breastfeeding advocates, who link it to the financial benefits physicians receive through industry support of research and conferences.

The concern about infant feeding culminated in the 1979 WHO Meeting on Infant and Young Child Feeding, where the various consumer advocacy groups formed a coalition called the International Baby Food Action Network to represent their concerns. The meeting resolved that a code for marketing breast milk substitutes be developed. The International Code of Marketing Breast Milk Substitutes was passed at the 1981 World Health Assembly with three nations abstaining and a single no vote by the United States on the grounds of constitutional incompatibility. The code is a recommendation to be implemented by each country in the way it desires, and WHO has no enforcement authority. It asks AIF companies not to advertise or idealize their products; not to provide gifts to mothers or health workers; and to consider the climate, water supply, and storage capabilities in the areas in which they sell their products. Many parts of the world reacted to the U.S. no vote with outrage, and the vote did increase public awareness.

A recent review indicates that the code has stimulated government and professional action to support breastfeeding in many countries around the world. This support has occurred in spite of AIF supporters in the United States who successfully projected breastfeeding activists as political extremists, causing some groups to refrain from supporting the international struggle. In other parts of the world, breastfeeding advocates continue to lack political and financial power to enforce the code. In 1984 Nestlé finally agreed to comply with the WHO code, and the boycott ended. Only four years later, in 1988, the U.S.-based Action for Corporate Responsibility reinstated a boycott against Nestlé and American Home Products (Wyeth Laboratories) because of their failure to comply with the code. Even in industrialized countries where public support for the code is high, pamphlets that violate the code continue to be provided to new mothers, and free samples are commonly given to maternity patients. The current boycott has now spread to seventeen nations. However, the International Lactation Consultant Association's decision not to endorse the boycott may indicate declining support for this type of action.

There is an ironic twist to this chain of events, resulting from the intertwining of changes in professional knowledge and practice with the emergence of a code to inhibit unethical marketing of breast milk substitutes. Since the middle of the twentieth century, when breastfeeding declined rapidly, the duration of nursing has declined. It was common for physicians to recommend cow's milk after weaning from the breast even at the age of three months, and after several months of formula feeding for babies who were not breastfed. Since the 1970s, such cow's milk feeding has been questioned, and many pediatricians in the industrialized world are now recommending either breast milk or formula as the only milk product for the first year of life. This recommendation has expanded the market for formula considerably, offering infant-food companies an opportunity to give cursory support to breastfeeding and then to promote their product as "follow-up milk." The term "follow-up milk" is important because it illustrates a loophole in the text of the code, which refers only to breast milk substitutes. Formulas are now being purchased by an increasing number of mothers who breastfeed for less than a year, many of whom will purchase formulas for more months than the mothers who did not breastfeed at all during the middle decades of this century.

Nongovernment organizations (NGOs) have continued to play an important role in breastfeeding promotion during the 1990s. The Innocenti Declaration of 1990, resulting from a global initiative, stresses the empowerment of women as well as the need to end manipulative media, social constraints, and obstacles within health systems. The World Alliance for Breast-feeding Action, an umbrella organization of NGOs that advocate breastfeeding, has actively worked toward implementation of the Innocenti Declaration. It has organized activities such as the Annual Worldwide Breast-Feeding Week and the Baby-Friendly Hospital Initiative (which approves hospitals that satisfy ten criteria as baby friendly). The alliance also campaigns for mother-friendly workplaces.

FOR FURTHER READING

Apple, R. 1987. *Mothers and Medicine: A Social History of Infant Feeding*. Madison: University of Wisconsin Press.
Arnold, L. 1992a. "Human Milk Storage and Preservation in the Early 1900s." *Journal of Human Lactation* 8(2): 91–92.
Arnold, L. 1992b. "North American Milk Banks." *Journal of Human Lactation* 8(4): 225–226.
Chetley, A. 1986. *The Politics of Baby Foods*. London: Francis Pinter.
Jelliffe, D., and E. Jelliffe, eds. 1981. *Advances in International Maternal and Child Health*. New York: Oxford University Press.
Krieg, Peter. 1975. *Bottle Babies*. Manchester, U.K.: Workers Film Association.
Lester, G. 1992. *The International Code of Marketing of Breast Milk Substitutes: Survey of National Legislation and Other Measures Adopted (1981–1991)*. Geneva: World Health Organization.
Mantell, J. 1992. "ACTION and the Boycott." *Lactation* 8(1): 5.
Muller, M. 1974. *The Baby Killer*. London: War on Want.
Palmer, G. 1988. *The Politics of Breastfeeding*. London: Pandora.
Stuart-Macadam, P., and K. Dettwyler, eds. 1995. *Breastfeeding: Biocultural Perspectives*. Hawthorne, N.Y.: Aldine de Gruyter.
Winikoff, B., and V. Laukaran. 1989. "Breast Feeding and Bottle Feeding in the Developing World: Evidence from a Study in Four Countries." *Social Science and Medicine* 29(7): 859–868.

fifteen

Contraception Technologies

SUSAN P. PHILLIPS

Contraception is the prevention of conception or impregnation in a woman. Interference with any aspect of fertilization or implantation of a fertilized egg can prevent pregnancy. Mechanical or chemical barriers may be used to block the production of egg or sperm, alter their function, obstruct fertilization (the meeting of egg and sperm to form an embryo), or alter the uterine environment to prevent implantation. Abortion, described elsewhere, can also be considered a contraceptive method. Information about the way a contraceptive works, its failure rate, risks, noncontraceptive benefits, costs, and availability are required to make an informed choice. There is no best method because risks and benefits vary from person to person.

The Menstrual Cycle and Fertilization

The average menstrual cycle is twenty-eight days. By convention, day one refers to the first day of bleeding or menses. During the follicular phase (day one until ovulation), the shedding of the lining of the uterus (menses) is followed by increasing pituitary production of the follicle-stimulating hormone (FSH) and the luteinizing hormone (LH). FSH stimulates the development of several follicles in the ovary, one of which assumes dominance by days five to seven. The follicles in turn produce an increasing amount of estrogen, which initiates regrowth of the lining of the uterus and signals the pituitary to decrease FSH production and dramatically increase LH production. Ovulation occurs about ten to twelve hours after the peak of this LH surge. The developing follicle releases an egg that travels through the fallopian tube toward the uterus. The subsequent luteal phase is uniformly thirteen to fifteen days long. The remains of the follicle, now called the corpus luteum, produces progesterone, which further develops the uterine lining. If pregnancy does not occur, various feedback systems trigger a decline in production of estrogen, progesterone, FSH, and LH. The uterine lining is shed, and the cycle begins again. A woman is most likely to conceive if fresh sperm are already present in the reproductive tract when ovulation occurs. Sperm remain viable for two to three days; the egg survives for about twenty-four hours.

Hormonal Methods

The Birth Control Pill

Since the early 1960s oral contraceptives have been used by more than 100 million women worldwide. Although dosages of the estrogens and progesterones that are combined in the most common oral contraceptive, the Pill, have decreased over the years, failure rates for proper use have remained less than 1 percent per year of use. The separation of pill taking from the act of intercourse makes this method a particularly appealing form of contraception, as does its easy reversibility.

The Pill works primarily, but not solely, by blocking ovulation. Estrogen also speeds up the passage of the egg through the reproductive tract, inhibits implantation by altering the uterine environment, and augments destruction of the corpus luteum. Progesterone thickens cervical mucus, which inhibits the transport of sperm, slows the passage of the egg, and interferes with both implantation and the sperm's ability to penetrate the egg.

In most industrialized countries the Pill is prescribed by a health care worker who determines whether it is safe for the woman involved, checks her blood pressure, and completes a pelvic exam with pap smear and infection screen. Combined oral contraceptives are taken daily for twenty-one days starting by day seven of the menstrual cycle. They are then stopped for seven days, during which time the woman should have a light or normal period. Some manufacturers provide seven placebos or sugar pills to be taken during this week so that pills are taken continuously. To decrease some side effects, oral contraceptives should be taken at about the same time each day. Because the woman may ovulate after missing one pill, an alternate method of birth control should be used for the remainder of the cycle.

There are many side effects associated with the Pill. Although not harmful, spotting or breakthrough bleeding can be irritating. Periods may become lighter or disappear altogether. Headaches, weight changes, nausea, loss of libido, and depression have all been associated with use. More serious although less common risks include hypertension, stroke, increased blood clotting (or deep venous thrombophlebitis that can cause pulmonary embolus), heart attack, and some cancers including breast cancer. Some of these side effects are improved by switching brands of pills to alter the balance or type of estrogen or progesterone. Others are the result of any oral contraceptive use. The Pill has both contraceptive and noncontraceptive benefits. It is relatively safe, effective, and easy to use. It decreases the heaviness and pain of menstruation as well as the risk of developing cancers of the ovary and uterus.

There are some absolute contraindications to oral contraceptive use. Women who have had breast cancer, clotting disorders, strokes, heart disease, or liver disorders should not add to their risk by taking oral contraceptives. Relative contraindications include migraine headaches, hypertension, and smoking (for women over age thirty-five). Because many medications can decrease the effectiveness of the Pill, and the Pill can alter the action of some medicines, women should discuss potential interactions with their health care provider.

Progesterone-Only Contraceptives

Progesterone alone can prevent pregnancy by inhibiting ovulation, changing cervical mucus to block sperm penetration, preventing implantation, and destroying the corpus luteum. Oral-contraception risks associated with estrogen in the Pill, such as clotting disorders and heart disease, are avoided. Progesterone can be taken orally, injected, implanted, or inserted vaginally. The progesterone-only pill, or minipill, actually contains less progesterone than combined hormone pills. Failure rates may be slightly higher: about 2 per 100 women per year. Unlike combined pills, the progesterone-only pill does not decrease milk supply in lactating women. Pills are taken once daily, at the same time. After the pack is finished, the next pack is begun on the following day. A gap of more than about twenty-seven hours between pills increases the risk of contraceptive failure. Pills are prescribed by a health care provider, who should monitor care. The minipill often causes irregular periods, spotting, and prolonged cycles. Ovarian cysts are seen somewhat more frequently in women on these progesterone-only pills, as are ectopic pregnancies.

Injections of medroxyprogesterone (Depo Provera) given at three-month intervals have been available for decades in many countries. The ease of use (four injections per year) and effectiveness (less than 1 failure per 100 woman years—"woman year" denotes one woman using a particular method for one year) have made this method particularly popular in developing countries. Injections usually cause amenorrhea (no menstrual periods). As a result, despite some controversy, medroxyprogesterone has been used with institutionalized, developmentally challenged patients who have difficulty with menstrual hygiene. Risks include delayed fertility after stopping injections, a mild though measurable decrease in bone density due to lack of estrogen production, and a possibly increased susceptibility to breast cancer. Animal studies showed a significant increase in breast cancers; however, human studies have not confirmed this. Some women experience excessive uterine bleeding, loss of libido, weight gain, headaches, depression, or dizziness. As with oral progesterone-only contraceptives, injectable progesterone does not increase blood pressure or thromboembolic problems.

Since the late 1980s, Norplant implants have been available. Six strawlike capsules of long-acting progesterone are surgically inserted under a woman's skin. They provide five years of highly effective contraception (failure less than 1 per 100 woman years), after which they must be surgically removed. Removal at any time carries a risk of infection, and menses may become irregular. Advantages parallel those described for other progesterone methods.

Morning-After Pill

Following unprotected intercourse at midcycle, use of the morning-after pill reduces the likelihood of pregnancy from approximately 20.0 percent to 1.5 percent. A large combined dose of estrogen and progesterone is taken within seventy-two hours of intercourse and then again twelve hours later. The birth control pill Ovral is often used by giving two pills initially, then two more after twelve hours. Menstrual bleeding should occur within twenty-one days. Because the dose of hormone is large, nausea sometimes accompanies its use.

Barrier Methods

Condoms

For thousands of years, penile coverings have been used to prevent pregnancy. Most male condoms are now made of rubber. They are of varying shapes and colors. Some have spermicide or lubricant coatings. The noncontraceptive benefits of condoms have added to their acceptability and availability since the 1970s. Because condoms with spermicide limit transmission of sexually transmitted diseases (STDs) such as HIV, herpes, and hepatitis B, their use has been promoted as a public health rather than a contraceptive measure. They are readily available and relatively inexpensive.

Condom effectiveness is dependent on proper use. The condom should be unrolled over an erect penis, leaving a space at the tip to collect ejaculate. Even with proper use condoms will break approximately once in every 150 times they are used. Leakage can occur after intercourse as the penis returns to nonerect size. Overall failure rates range upward from about 2 percent. Risks of condom use, other than pregnancy, are minimal. Some people develop allergies to either rubber or spermicides. Petroleum jelly products can break down the condom and should not be used as lubricants. Recently, a female condom has been marketed in North America. It is more costly than the male condom but offers women more control over pregnancy and STD prevention. The condom is inserted into the vagina. Risks and benefits are otherwise similar to those with the male condom.

Spermicides

Spermicide is a chemical barrier, applied vaginally, that prevents sperm from entering the uterus. Most commonly known as nonoxynol-9, it can be incorporated into gels, foam, creams, or suppositories. These can be used alone or in combination with a mechanical barrier that holds the spermicide in place next to the cervix. They are generally most effective if inserted into the vagina between fifteen and sixty minutes before intercourse. Although skin irritation or allergies may result from use, spermicides are otherwise quite safe. Foam and foam in suppository form are the only spermicides that can be used alone. Their high failure rate (up to twenty-five pregnancies per woman year of use) is greatly reduced by use with condoms, diaphragms, or cervical caps.

Diaphragms, Caps, and Sponges

The diaphragm is a dome of rubber with a flexible rim. When the diaphragm is properly fitted it tucks behind the pubic bone at the front of the vagina and covers the cervix. By holding spermicidal jelly against the opening to the uterus, it acts as both a chemical and mechanical barrier. Since the effectiveness of the spermicide declines after application, intercourse should occur within thirty to sixty minutes of insertion. The diaphragm is left in place for six hours afterward, then removed and washed with soap and water. It can be reused for several years. Failure rates range from about two to twenty pregnancies per woman year of use.

The cervical cap, which fits directly over the cervix, is somewhat similar to the diaphragm in action and effectiveness. It is smaller than a diaphragm, made of rubber, and should be partially filled with spermicide. Although more difficult to insert than the diaphragm, it can remain in place for several days. Petroleum jelly products can break down the diaphragm or cap and should not be used as a lubricant.

The Today Vaginal Sponge is a single-use sponge that contains spermicide. It does not require fitting by a health care provider and is relatively easy to insert into the vagina, covering the cervix. Contraceptive effect lasts for twenty-four hours.

Intrauterine Devices (IUDs)

For at least the past century, objects of some kind have been inserted into the uterus to prevent pregnancy. Although their mechanism of action is not known, IUDs most likely immobilize sperm, inhibit fertilization, and alter the uterine environment to prevent implantation. Currently, IUDs are either made of plastic wound with copper wire or filled with progesterone. The IUD is inserted directly into the uterus by a health care provider. This quick but painful procedure is easier if the woman has had a baby. Because the presence of the IUD in the uterus can spread infection (particularly gonorrhea or chlamydia), screening for these diseases should precede insertion, and the IUD should be removed if infection subsequently occurs. The IUD can remain in place for years and is, as a result, a very inexpensive form of contraception.

In the 1970s an increased risk of pelvic infection in women with IUDs (particularly the Dalkon Shield) was identified. Fearing lawsuits, many U.S. IUD manufacturers ceased production and marketing within the United States, although remaining supplies were sold to developing countries.

Rhythm Method and Coitus Interruptus

For religious or personal reasons there are some people who rely on natural family planning for contraception. By checking either basal body temperature or cervical mucus, one may be able to identify ovulation. A finding that ovulation regularly occurs around day fifteen, for example, signals that abstaining from intercourse from days eleven to eighteen should prevent pregnancy. Body temperature often drops slightly just prior to ovulation, then rises by about half a degree Celsius with ovulation, remaining elevated until menses begins. A few days before ovulation, cervical mucus becomes clear, wet, slippery, and stretchy. This mucus disappears with ovulation. Since abstention must begin four days before ovulation, these signs are useful only if they indicate that the timing of ovulation does not vary. The fertile time of a subsequent cycle can then be anticipated.

Coitus interruptus, or withdrawal of the penis from the vagina prior to ejaculation, must be mentioned as a method, since it is widely used in parts of the world despite its high failure rate (about 20 percent).

Recent Developments

Despite press reports of imminent breakthroughs, the range of contraceptives available has not really expanded since the late 1970s. Attempts are ongoing to deliver progesterone via a ring that can be inserted into the vagina to provide three months of protection. Variations on the potency and implantation methods for long-term progesterone contraceptives are being researched. Oral-contraceptive manufacturers frequently develop new combinations of estrogen and progesterone that are not necessarily safer or more effective but instead are attempts at increasing market share. The contraceptive market is a huge and lucrative one, but those who now profit from it have little incentive to search for new, safer, less expensive alternatives.

Research is under way on male antifertility agents including gossypol, androgens, estrogens, progestins, progestin-androgen combinations, GnRH (gonadotropin-releasing hormone) antagonists and agonists, inhibin (a derivative of glycerine), antiandrogens, enzyme inhibitors, hormone antibodies, and antisperm antibodies. Thermal methods inhibiting production of fertile sperm and mechanical damage to sperm by application of ultrasound are also under investigation. None of these male contraceptives is near mass production or distribution.

FOR FURTHER READING

Canada. Health Canada, Health Protection Branch, Drugs Directorate, Special Advisory Committee on Reproductive Physiology. 1994. *Oral Contraception.* Ottawa: Canadian Communications Group.

Canadian Consensus Conference on Contraception. 1998. *Journal of the Society of Obstetricians and Gynaecologists of Canada* 20(5): 483–489.

Hatcher R., et al. 1990 (updated every few years). *Contraceptive Technology.* New York: Irvington.

Journal of the American Medical Association. Contraceptive Information Center: http://www.ama-assn.org/special/contra.htm.

sixteen

Contraception—Ethics

JOAN C. CALLAHAN

The most significant ethical issues that surround contemporary contraception are those involving abortion, the continued medicalization of reproduction, dangers to women, availability to minors, informed consent, and the imposition of contraceptive technologies as punishment.

Definitions and the Problem of Abortion

True contraceptive technologies do just what their name implies, namely, preclude conception. The most effective true contraceptive intervention is male or female sterilization. Most other technologies for women popularly known as contraceptives have prevention of conception as their primary action but include secondary actions that have effects after conception should fertilization occur. For example, so-called oral contraceptives have prevention of ovulation as their primary action. But should breakthrough ovulation and fertilization occur, oral contraceptives have "backup" mechanisms that interfere with implantation or support of an embryo. Similarly, intrauterine devices (IUDs) may act as true contraceptives or they may act by interfering with the implantation of an embryo. An IUD is a foreign object in the uterus, and a woman's body responds by attempting to neutralize it. This is done by increasing the number of phagocytic leucocytes (destructive white blood cells) in the uterus, making it an inhospitable environment for either sperm or an embryo. Thus when an IUD is in place, it is particularly difficult for sperm to traverse a woman's uterus. However, some sperm may well get through (particularly in long-term IUD users), and fertilization can occur. When this happens, successful birth control is effected by a woman's inflamed uterus's inability to support an embryo. So-called contraceptive technologies that have these secondary birth control actions are sometimes called "interceptives," since they intercept the conceptus after fertilization but (generally) before implantation. This interceptive feature of contemporary birth control technologies, however, raises the issue of abortion. That is, since most who are opposed to abortion hold the view that a person exists from the time of human fertilization onward, simply calling a technology an "interceptive" rather than an "abortifacient" does not bypass the abortion issue raised by the use of any birth control technologies with so-called interceptive actions. Interestingly, the interceptive actions of ordinary oral contraceptives seem not to be widely known (or they are widely known and are just ignored in the abortion debate). There has been no movement toward banning them, as there has been in the case of RU-486, which has been roundly condemned by those who have opposed elective abortion. The controversy over RU-486, however, is not limited to its frankly abortifacient properties.

RU-486 and the Medicalization of Reproduction

Feminists have long worried about the medical profession's control over both limiting and assisting human reproduction. RU-486 has been hailed by some feminists as finally placing postcoital contraception in the hands of women. That claim, however, has been seriously challenged by other feminists who have pointed out that deployment of RU-486 still requires examination by a physician, prescription of the drug, reexamination after the induced menstruation, and suction abortion if the contents of a woman's uterus have not been entirely emptied. (For a description of RU-486 see Chapter 20.) The feminists who emphasize these features of the drug's deployment have urged women to temper their enthusiasm for utilizing RU-486, which they argue can involve even more interaction with the medical profession than a simple suction abortion.

Proponents of RU-486, however, have further argued that there is reason to believe that the drug might prove to be a valuable treatment for breast cancer, since as many as one-third of breast cancers involve tumors with an abundance of progesterone receptors, and the tumors are dependent on progesterone for survival. RU-486 may be able to block progesterone receptors in these cancer cells just as it is able to block progesterone receptors in a woman's endometrium, which is how the drug induces menstruation. There is also hope that RU-486 might serve as a treatment for Cushing's syndrome, for endometriosis, and as an aid in cervical dilation to allow vaginal deliveries in cases where cesarean section might otherwise seem necessary.

These hopes for RU-486, however, raise a set of additional worries, also voiced by feminists who have been urging women to proceed with caution in endorsing the drug—namely, concerns about the safety of women.

Dangers to Women

Ever since the early trials on and quick dissemination of oral contraceptives, there has been a continuing concern about the safety of women in both the testing and application of contraceptive technologies. High doses of estrogen in the early versions of the very popular oral contraceptive the Pill placed women at extremely serious risk of cardiovascular disease and certain cancers. Decreasing estrogen doses and the introduction of estrogen-progestogen combination pills lowered these risks, and the so-called minipill, which contains a low daily dose of progestogen only, eliminates the risks associated with taking estrogen. However, despite the decrease in exogenous estrogen in current formulations, combination oral contraceptives can still present grave cardiovascular (and other) risks to certain women (particularly women who smoke), and forms of progesterone have been associated with breast cancer. Individual family medical histories are critical considerations for every woman in deciding whether to take oral contraceptives.

Intrauterine devices have also raised serious questions regarding women's safety. As mentioned previously, IUDs function by disrupting a woman's uterus, keeping it in a state of immune response, much as if there were infection. In addition, IUDs have not infrequently been associated with pelvic inflammatory disease, which has caused the death of a number of women and has resulted in infertility for many others. IUDs are also associated with ectopic pregnancies (implantation outside the uterus, usually in the oviduct) and septic abortions, which can be extremely dangerous for women. Women with certain characteristics (for example, those who have not had children, those with multiple sex partners) are at greater risk than others for some of these problems. But for women for whom oral contraceptives and sterilization are out of the question, an IUD might be the birth control method of reasonable choice.

Newer systemic technologies (such as RU-486, injectables, and implants) and local drug-delivery systems (such as sponges impregnated with spermicide) all raise worries about women's safety. Until these technologies have been tested for a number of years, their long-term consequences will not be known. At the same time, pregnancy is not an innocuous condition, and it can be life threatening for some women. A significant moral question is whether contraceptive technologies that are known to be risky or whose long-term effects remain uncertain should still be available in order to afford women who wish to avoid pregnancy a maximum number of options.

Availability to Minors

The ready availability of contraceptive devices and drugs to minors has been opposed on two main grounds. First, it is argued that such availability will encourage sexual activity. Second, it has been argued that because female contraceptives other than simple barrier methods can be dangerous, these should not be prescribed for or applied to young women without parental consent. The presumed empirical link between use of contraceptives and sexual activity has not been demonstrated. Even more important, it has been argued that condoms should be made readily available to minors (through schools) as protection against sexually transmitted diseases, including AIDS.

The question of the safety of minors is more complex. Since, as we have seen, steroidal contraceptives and IUDs can be seriously dangerous, especially to some very young women, the questions here revolve not only around parental rights but also around the special duties of parents to protect their children. One objection is that a minor acting alone may not have knowledge of facts about either her own or her family's history that might contraindicate the application of a given contraceptive method. One response to this objection is that preventing the harm that can result (including an unwanted pregnancy) justifies a physician's prescribing contraceptives for minors. There are also concerns about a minor's ability to give a genuinely informed consent to a possibly dangerous medical intervention.

Informed Consent

The issue of informed consent arises in several ways in regard to contraception. There are, for example, questions connected to the facts just discussed. Do women know and accept that these technologies might prevent birth by acting after fertilization? Are they clear on the risks involved with the technologies they accept? Are minors able to give genuinely informed and voluntary consent to potentially dangerous contraceptive interventions? Further, there are worries about informed consent when contraceptive technologies are applied in nations or among groups where those in power are concerned to limit population growth. It is known, for example, that without their knowledge or consent, women have had IUDs implanted or sterilizations done after giving birth. In other cases, women have been injected with contraceptive preparations without their knowledge or consent. Even where there are attempts to get informed consent, the quality of consent may leave much to be desired. For example, the implementation of China's one-child policy brought with it enormous pressures on women to undergo abortion or to accept IUDs or sterilization after having a child. In other cases, particularly in developing nations, women have "consented to" insertion of IUDs without having any clear idea of the risks they were undertaking. These devices have included unacceptably dangerous ones, such as the infamous Dalkon Shield. And in still other cases, individuals have been offered incentives to accept contraception that raise extremely serious questions about coercion. In addition to raising pressing questions about the wisdom and morality of attempting to address population problems with contraceptive technologies rather than with changes in the social and economic conditions that lead to "overproduction" of children, such problems with informed consent and coercion are closely related philosophically to another issue—namely, contraception as punishment.

Court-Ordered Contraception

In the 1990s, especially in the United States, there has been an increase in cases of court-ordered contraception. More precisely, there have been an increasing number of instances where judges in child-abuse and neglect cases and cases involving failure to provide child support have given those convicted a "choice" of contraception or incarceration. Some long-acting contraceptives seem particularly prone to be involved in this kind of situation. For example, less than a month after approval of Norplant in the United States, a judge offered a woman convicted of child abuse Norplant as a condition of probation. In another case in the United States, which led to considerable public outrage, a woman who was convicted of molesting her sons agreed to be sterilized in order to avoid an extended prison term. The case involved the woman's husband, who was also convicted of molestation. Part of the outrage was based on the judge's ruling that he would give both the woman and her husband probation if she (but not he) would consent to sterilization. As of 1998, no U.S. sentence or condition of probation involving restriction of the capacity to bear children had been upheld on appeal. But not all of these cases have been appealed. In particular, there have been cases in which men who have fathered numerous children or failed to pay child support have elected sterilization to avoid incarceration. The moral issues here have to do not only with acceptably informed and acceptably voluntary consents but also with questions of justice (including questions regarding justice across genders, races, and classes), as well as with the question of the purported "right" to reproduce.

FOR FURTHER READING

Associated Press. 1993. "Woman Who Molested Sons Agrees to Sterilization." *New York Times* (January 31): 13.

Baulieu, E. 1989. "Contagestion and Other Clinical Applications of Ru 486: An Antiprogesterone at the Receptor." *Science* 245: 1351.

Callahan, Joan C. 1996. "Contraception or Incarceration: What's Wrong with This Picture?" *Stanford Law and Policy Review* 7(1): 67–82.

Hartmann, Betsy. 1995. *Reproductive Rights and Wrongs: The Global Politics of Population Control and Contraceptive Choice.* Rev. ed. Boston: South End Press.

Key, T.J.A., and M. C. Pike. 1988. "The Role of Oestrogens and Progestogens in the Epidemiology and Prevention of Breast Cancer." *European Journal of Clinical Oncology* 24: 29.

Knight, James W., and Joan C. Callahan. 1989. *Preventing Birth: Contemporary Methods and Related Moral Controversies.* Salt Lake City: University of Utah Press.

Lewin, T. 1991. "Implanted Birth Control Device Renews Debate over Forced Contraception." *New York Times* (January 10): A20.

Pike, M. C., B. E. Henderson, M. D. Krailo, A. Duke, and S. Roy. 1993. "Breast Cancer in Young Women and Use of Oral Contraceptives: Possible Modifying Effect of Formulation and Age at Use." *Lancet* 11: 926.

Raymond, Janice G. 1995. "RU-486: Progress or Peril?" In Joan C. Callahan, ed., *Reproduction, Ethics, and the Law: Feminist Perspectives.* Bloomington: Indiana University Press.

Russo, J., and I. H. Russo. 1987. "Biological and Molecular Bases of Mammary Carcinogenesis." *Laboratory Investigation* 57: 112.

Warwick, Donald. 1982. *Bitter Pills: Population Policies and Their Implications in Eight Developing Countries.* Cambridge: Cambridge University Press.

seventeen

Diethylstilbestrol (DES)

ELLEN 'T HOEN

Diethylstilbestrol (DES), a synthetic estrogen, was first fabricated in 1938 by the British biochemist E. C. Dodds. Since the 1940s, DES has been prescribed to millions of pregnant women worldwide to prevent miscarriages. This practice was based on the unverified hypothesis that spontaneous abortion was caused by a lack of progesterone and that DES was able to stimulate the production of progesterone by the body. Since the 1970s many adverse effects for the users of DES and their children have become known. In 1953 a U.S. study by W. E. Dieckmann showed that DES was not effective in the treatment of habitual spontaneous abortion. Nevertheless, the use of DES to treat complications during pregnancy continued as a common practice. The package insert of the Dutch manufacturer Dagra lists fourteen different indications for DES prescription, including morning sickness.

In 1971 the American gynecologist A. L. Herbst established a connection between DES and a rare type of vaginal cancer, clear cell adenocarcinoma, which occurred among daughters of women who had taken DES during pregnancy. That same year the American Food and Drug Administration contraindicated DES for use during pregnancy. By then an estimated 3 million women in the United States alone had used the product. Prescription of DES during pregnancy continued in Europe later than 1971. In the Netherlands and the United Kingdom, DES was used until 1975, in France until 1977, and in Spain until 1981.

DES is still being produced and is available under a variety of brand names. According to the World Health Organization, DES remains available in many countries but only for the treatment of certain hormone-dependent carcinomas. However, a survey of prescribing guides in nine developing countries in Asia, Latin America, and Africa shows a variety of indications for use of DES in women, including suppression of lactation after childbirth, primary amenorrhea, menstrual or fertility problems, menopause, and acne.

Risks of the Use of DES During Pregnancy

After the discovery of the link between vaginal cancer and DES exposure, more effects of the drug have become known. Women prescribed DES during pregnancy have an increased risk of developing breast cancer. Exposure to DES also causes benign changes in the genital tract in both daughters and sons that can lead to fertility and pregnancy problems. Many DES daughters have benign vaginal epithelial changes such as adenosis. They have an increased risk for ectopic pregnancy, miscarriage, and premature labor. They are also at risk for cervical and vaginal dysplasia and carcinoma in situ. DES daughters need special gynecological examinations annually. These examinations need to be performed by a gynecologist who is experienced and familiar with DES-related problems.

Fortunately, clear cell adenocarcinoma is rare, occurring in 1 per 1,000 to 1 in 10,000 DES daughters. But it affects mainly women in their early twenties, and the treatment involves extensive and disfiguring surgery or radiation. Women who are unaware of their exposure often receive unnecessary treatment or are confronted with misdiagnosis. Knowing you are a DES daughter may also have implications for choices concerning contraceptives, treatment with fertility drugs, and pregnancy. Because of the many uncertainties of the effect of DES on the health of DES daughters, some doctors advise caution in the use of fertility-related medicines and hormonal contraceptives.

DES Action Groups

Out of frustration with the medical profession's initial lack of interest in the DES problem and the reluctance of governments to develop policies to deal with it, DES-exposed women have formed action groups all over the world. These groups have joined together in DES Action International to call for a worldwide ban on DES. The main aims of DES Action groups are to trace as many DES-exposed people as possible, to provide information to both the public and the medical profession about DES, to provide support and counseling for DES-exposed people, and to cooperate with relevant organizations to encourage the development of policies with regard to the DES issue. DES Action sees the DES case as an example of a medical failure that could be repeated if appropriate lessons are not learned. DES Action has also questioned the rapid spread of new reproductive technologies such as in vitro fertilization (IVF) and pointed to the similarities between the DES history and the present developments around IVF.

The DES Cancer network was formed from DES Action groups. This is a support and information network by and for the women who suffer from cancer of the vagina or cervix. The cancer network and DES Action are the driving forces behind legal action taken by DES daughters against the manufacturers of DES. The first lawsuit against a pharmaceutical company was won in the United States when, in 1981, a DES daughter was granted $500,000 in damages. This case was followed in the United States by other successful legal challenges.

Many obstacles remain in addressing legal liability. In the Netherlands a group of DES daughters spent six years in court proceedings only to establish the right to hold a group of manufacturers liable. The main problem is that many DES daughters cannot identify the individual manufacturer of the product that was given to their mother. In a recent decision of the Dutch Supreme Court, the way was paved for assigning liability to groups of manufacturers. International support in cases like this has proven to be extremely important. There is a constant flow of information, suggestions, and support among the DES Action organizations and the lawyers who represent DES daughters.

FOR FURTHER READING

DES Action: http://www.desaction.org.

Dieckmann, W. E., M. E. David, et al. 1953. "Does the Administration of Diethylstilbestrol During Pregnancy Have Therapeutic Value? *American Journal of Obstetrics and Gynaecology* 66: 1062.

Greenberg, E. R., A. B. Barnes, L. Resseguie, et al. 1984. "Breast Cancer in Mothers Given Diethylstilbestrol in Pregnancy." *New England Journal of Medicine* 311: 1393–1398.

Kleiverda, Gunilla. 1990. "How Can We Provide Appropriate Medical Care for DES-Exposed Women?" In Barbara Mintzes, ed., *DES: A Drug with Consequences for Current Health Policy*. Utecht, the Netherlands: DES Action.

Netherlands Supreme Court. 1992. *Ruling of 9 October*. The Netherlands First Division no. 14.669. (Official English translation of the judgment available.)

Robboy, S. J., K. L. Noller, P. O'Brien, et al. 1984. "Increased Incidence of Cervical and Vaginal Dysplasia in 3980 Diethylstilbestrol-Exposed Young Women." *Journal of the American Medical Association* 252: 2979–2983.

Smith, O. W. 1948. "Diethylstilbestrol in the Prevention and Treatment of Complications of Pregnancy." *American Journal of Obstetrics and Gynaecology* 56: 821–834.

Stillman, R. J. 1982. "In Utero Exposure to Diethylstilbestrol: Adverse Effects on the Reproductive Tract and Reproductive Performance in Male and Female Offspring." *American Journal of Obstetrics and Gynaecology* 142: 905.

't Hoen, Ellen. 1990. "Diethylstilbestrol: The Effects on the Health of Users and Their Children." *Women and Pharmaceutical Bulletin.* Amsterdam: Wemos/HAI International Group on Women and Pharmaceuticals.

eighteen

Menstrual Disorder Technologies

EMMA WHELAN

Menstrual disorder technologies are surgical, conceptual, and pharmaceutical techniques and tools used to diagnose and treat menstrual disorders. Common disorders include amenorrhea (an absence of menstruation); dysmenorrhea (painful menstruation); premenstrual syndrome (PMS); and abnormal, dysfunctional, or excessive uterine bleeding. Also included are those technologies used to treat gynecological diseases associated with menstrual disorders, such as endometriosis, which is often accompanied by dysmenorrhea and excessive uterine bleeding. There are many menstrual disorder technologies. The ones discussed here are most often used in the treatment and diagnosis of dysmenorrhea and endometriosis.

Surgical Technology: The Laparoscope

A surgical procedure called a laparoscopy must be performed to diagnose definitively the cause of many menstrual disorders. The patient is given a general anesthetic, and a small incision is made, usually just below the patient's navel. A needle is inserted through the incision, and carbon dioxide gas is pumped through the needle into the patient's abdomen to distend it. The needle is removed and replaced with a laparoscope, a thin tube with a light source at one end and a telescopic eyepiece at the other. The surgeon is now able to view the patient's pelvic organs through the laparoscope. Other instruments may be inserted through incisions in the lower abdomen and/or through the cervical os. These may be used to move the uterus and thereby facilitate visualization of the entire pelvis, to perform biopsies, or to assist in the removal of diseased tissue (often done with a laser that is attached to the laparoscope).

Many of the procedures now performed via laparoscopy were once performed using the older technique of laparotomy, which involved a larger "bikini cut" incision. Some gynecologists have questioned whether results obtained via laparoscopy are comparable to those obtained via laparotomy. However, because laparoscopic surgery does not require large incisions, it has certain advantages over laparotomy: decreased patient recovery time, shorter hospital stays, decreased operating time, decreased cost, and higher patient acceptance.

As with many medical specialties, the surgeon's observation of pathology is often considered a more reliable measure of the patient's "real" bodily state than the patient's own reports. Surgical visualization supplants the patient's embodied experience as the arbiter of truth. Thus the woman who suffers from dysmenorrhea may be constructed as an unreliable symptom reporter if the cause of her pain cannot be surgically visualized.

Conceptual Technology: The R-AFS Classification

Laparoscopy facilitates the use of another technology, a conceptual one used specifically in the diagnosis and treatment of endometriosis: the Revised American Fertility Society (R-AFS) classification. Through the completion of a standardized form, the surgeon records the location, extent, and severity of endometriosis lesions and adhesions and categorizes the patient according to one of four stages of severity. Surgical visualization (typically via laparoscopy) is a precondition for the use of this taxonomy.

The R-AFS classification was developed as a way for physicians to compare the results of various therapies on fertility outcomes, but not on pain relief. Therefore, the highest scores are allocated to endometriosis in areas where it is most likely to affect fertility. Only the degree of visible anatomic disease is taken into account. However, many gynecologists argue that pain symptoms are related to disease activity and that small endometriosis lesions are often more active and therefore may cause more pain than large ones. Therefore, the stage to which a patient is assigned says little, if anything, about the degree of pain or other symptoms she may experience. Nevertheless, the R-AFS classification is routinely used to classify patients who are being treated for endometriosis-related dysmenorrhea.

The objectivity of the R-AFS taxonomy has been questioned by many prominent endometriosis specialists; for example, its staging system has been criticized as arbitrary, based more upon anecdotal clinical evidence than good comparative research, and coding across surgeons has been found to be unreliable in some studies. Also, although pain is a more commonly reported symptom of endometriosis than infertility, this classification of endometriosis focuses on infertility and not pain. It prioritizes women's fertility over their desire for pain management, thereby emphasizing a traditional conception of women's social role.

Pharmaceutical Technology: Hormonal Manipulation

A wide array of pharmaceutical therapies is used to treat menstrual disorders. Some therapies, such as nonsteroidal antiinflammatory drugs, target particular symptoms; most therapies used to treat these disorders modify or interrupt the menstrual cycle through hormonal manipulation. These include birth control pills, progesterone, danazol, and GnRH agonists.

Many of the therapies currently used to treat menstrual problems were not developed for that purpose. For example, medroxyprogesterone acetate, a progestogen marketed under the brand names Depo Provera for the injectable form and Provera for the tablet form, was originally developed in the 1950s in Brazil as a preventive treatment for premature labor and miscarriages. It was found ineffective for that purpose. In the 1960s, it was approved as a treatment for cancer. In 1992, after years of lobbying on the part of Upjohn (the manufacturers of the drug), Depo Provera was approved as a contraceptive. Currently in some Western countries, it is an approved treatment for endometriosis and an unapproved but common treatment for PMS, dysmenorrhea, and other functional menstrual disorders.

Using progesterone for PMS is a highly controversial treatment. Studies regarding its efficacy in the treatment of PMS have been few and flawed. In five placebo-controlled studies, rectovaginally administered progesterone was found to be no more effective in relieving PMS symptoms than a placebo. However, a U.S.-based consumer organization called PMS Action argues that progesterone is an effective treatment for PMS, based on its members' experiences and the anecdotal evidence of Katharina Dalton, a British PMS medical specialist. In support of this argument, Virginia Cassara, the founder of PMS Action, criticizes studies that assert only a placebo effect for progesterone because (1) progesterone appears to have a cumulative effect, and most studies do not allow sufficient time for the drug to take effect before measuring its efficacy against placebo; and (2) by the time a woman is prescribed progesterone for PMS, she has usually tried a great many other therapies unsuccessfully and would be unlikely to give undue credit to progesterone. If anything, she would expect it, like all the other therapies, to be ineffective. Whatever the true palliative value of progesterone in the treatment of PMS, it certainly seems to be true that in the treatment of menstrual disorders, we are witnessing a progression to more complex therapies, and simpler, local-acting hormonal treatments (like progesterone and the birth control pill) are increasingly out of vogue among clinicians.

In North America, GnRH agonists are marketed under the brand names Lupron (leuprolide acetate), Synarel (nafarelin acetate), Zoladex (goserelin acetate), and Suprefact (buserelin acetate). They were originally developed as a treatment for prostate cancer. When they were found to induce a state of pseudomenopause in women, they began to be used in the treatment of menstrual disorders. They have been approved as a treatment for endometriosis in several countries including Canada and the United States and are being clinically evaluated as a treatment for premenstrual syndrome, dysmenorrhea, dysfunctional uterine bleeding, and many other nonmenstrual women's health problems.

The action of the GnRH agonists (at the level of the pituitary and hypothalamus) may have far-reaching effects on the rest of the body, as suggested by the long list of side effects for each. GnRH agonists, for example, are known to cause bone-density loss. Addback therapy, or the administration of small amounts of estrogen to offset this effect of GnRH agonists, is being evaluated. This addition of estrogen obviously intensifies technological intervention. It also increases the cost of treatment, and GnRH agonists are already the most expensive medical treatment for endometriosis. Few published, randomized-control studies of treatments for menstruation-related pain exist; thus there is little evidence that the more expensive therapies (danazol and GnRH agonists) are any more effective in relieving endometriosis pain than cheaper therapies such as the birth control pill, whose side effects have been more thoroughly investigated.

FOR FURTHER READING

American Fertility Society. 1985. "Revised American Fertility Society Classification of Endometriosis." *Fertility and Sterility* 43(3): 351–352.

Audebert, A.J.M. 1990. "Current Classifications of Endometriosis: Practical Concerns." In D. R. Chadha and V. C. Buttram Jr., eds., *Current Concepts in Endometriosis.* New York: Alan R. Liss.

Cassara, V. 1988. "A Consumer Organization's Perspective." In L. H. Gise, ed., *The Premenstrual Syndromes.* New York: Churchill Livingstone.

Friedman, A. J. 1990. "Laparoscopy, Hysteroscopy, and Laser Surgery." In K. J. Ryan, R. Berkowitz, and R. L. Barbieri, eds., *Kistner's Gynaecology: Principles and Practice.* Chicago: Year Book Medical.

Gomibuchi, H., et al. 1993. "Is Personality Involved in the Expression of Dysmenorrhea in Patients with Endometriosis?" *American Journal of Obstetrics and Gynecology* 169(3): 723–724.

Groff, T. R. 1989. "Classifications." In R. S. Schenken, ed., *Endometriosis: Contemporary Concepts in Clinical Management*. Philadelphia: J. B. Lippincott.

Gruhn, J. G., and R. R. Kazer. 1989. *Hormonal Regulation of the Menstrual Cycle*. New York: Plenum Medical Book Company.

Lorber, Judith. 1997. "If a Situation Is Defined as Real . . . : Premenstrual Syndrome and Menopause." In *Gender and the Social Construction of Illness*. Thousand Oaks, Calif.: Sage.

Miller, R. M., and R. A. Frank. 1992. "Zoladex (Goserelin) in the Treatment of Benign Gynaecological Disorders: An Overview of Safety and Efficacy." *British Journal of Obstetrics and Gynaecology* 99, supp. 7: 37–39.

Roseff, S. J., and A. A. Murphy. 1990. "Laparoscopy in the Diagnosis and Therapy of Chronic Pelvic Pain." *Clinical Obstetrics and Gynecology* 33(1): 137–144.

Shohat, Ella. 1992. "'Laser for Ladies': Endo Discourse and the Inscriptions of Science." *Camera Obscura* 29: 57–89.

Waller, K., and R. W. Shaw. 1995. "Endometriosis, Pelvic Pain, and Psychological Functioning." *Fertility and Sterility* 63(4): 796–800.

nineteen

Female Circumcision/ Female Genital Mutilation

NAHID TOUBIA

Female circumcision is a ritualistic cutting of parts of the genitals of girls as a rite of passage into womanhood. It is performed in preparation for socially defined female sexual and reproductive roles. This custom has also been termed female genital mutilation because it causes substantial anatomical and functional damage. An estimated 130 million girls and women in the world have undergone some form of female circumcision, and 2 million are at risk every year. This amounts to 600 females per day, or five per minute, suffering mutilation.

In modern times female circumcision/genital mutilation is practiced primarily in Africa and among small minorities in Asia. The possibility of the continuation of the practice on the part of African and Asian immigrants to new countries causes anxiety and debate in these countries. The state's obligation to protect children and observe universal standards of human rights is juxtaposed against the call for cultural tolerance and acceptance of social diversity. The twenty-seven African countries where female circumcision/genital mutilation is practiced are Benin, Burkina Faso, Cameroon, Central African Republic, Chad, Côte d'Ivoire, Djibouti, Egypt, Ethiopia, Eritrea, Gambia, Ghana, Guinea, Guinea-Bissau, Kenya, Liberia, Mali, Mauritania, Niger, Senegal, Sierra Leone, Somalia, Sudan, Tanzania, Togo, Uganda, and Zaire. In Asia these practices are known among a very small ethnic group, the Bohra Daodi Muslims, in India. The practice is not currently reported in Indonesia or Malaysia, although the noncutting clitoral cleaning or pricking rituals of the past are still practiced by some. Some reports from Yemen and Oman document the selective tribal practice of female circumcision/genital mutilation, but prevalence and the type performed in these two countries are not known. Meanwhile, in Europe and North America some physicians still perform a malelike circumcision on women who fail to reach orgasm. The practice is questionable. Other genital cosmetic surgery operations are performed in Europe and North America on adult women who believe that their genitals are abnormal or ugly.

Female circumcision/genital mutilation is a cultural, not religious, requirement in Africa. It is practiced equally by Muslims and Christians (Catholics, Evangelists, and Orthodox), by one Jewish group, and by followers of indigenous African religions. Many followers of these religions and sects do not even know about the practice. A common misconception is that the practice is linked to Islam; but Islam does not require it, and the vast majority of the world's Muslims do not know about it. The exact history and origin of female circumcision/genital mutilation are not known. Currently it is prevalent along a broad belt across central Africa and along the Nile valley with a probable focal point of origin around southern Egypt or northern Sudan. Some suggest that the practice was started by the Pharaohs, but no conclusive evidence has been found to substantiate this hypothesis.

Girls undergo circumcision usually between the ages of four and twelve years; but in countries like Uganda, girls fifteen to eighteen and eligible for marriage display their courage by being circumcised in public. More modern families occasionally circumcise their girls in infancy, but this is very rare. A girl may be circumcised alone or with a group of her relatives or tribal peers. With urbanization, most of the rituals surrounding the actual cutting have faded, but circumcision has persisted as a stand-alone event unaccompanied by ceremonial celebrations. Female genital mutilation can take many forms; the most common are

1. Clitoridectomy: partial or total removal of the clitoris.
2. Excision: removal of clitoris and labia minora.
3. Infibulation: removal of the clitoris and labia minora and incision of the labia majora, which are then stitched into a "skin hood" that covers the vagina.

Other rare forms of mutilation involve different forms of incision or stitching around the vagina and are reported in Africa and among some indigenous people on other continents. Because of the sensitive nature of the area of the genitals and its rich blood supply, female genital mutilation causes many physical complications. Shock, bleeding, infections, cysts, ulcers, fistulae, and infertility are among the more common. Psychosexual problems also occur, many of which are long lasting.

African physicians have exposed and criticized female circumcision/genital mutilation since the 1950s. Today the growing African women's movement is raising its voice against the practice. The Inter-African Committee on Traditional Practices Affecting the Health of Women and Children was started by African women following a conference in Dakar, Senegal, in 1984. It currently has affiliates in most countries where the practice occurs. Organizations have also been started by immigrant women. They include FORWARD and the London Black Women Health Action Project in the United Kingdom, GAMS (Groupe Femmes pour l'Abolition des Mutilations Sexuelles) in France, Women's Health in Women's Hands in Canada, and RAINBO in the United States. Many other African women's organizations dealing with women's health and rights are becoming active in fighting against female circumcision/genital mutilation as a reproductive and sexual rights violation and a health hazard.

Because of the severe nature of this practice to control women's sexuality and reproduction and because it occurs primarily in Africa, it has generated many controversies. At the center of the controversy is the way in which Western media and some feminist groups represent the practice as a barbaric ritual of inferior societies rather than one form of patriarchal society's control of women. The absence in the Western press of exposure of efforts by African women (and men) to combat this practice leaves the common representation of the issue at best patronizing and in some cases titillating in a bizarre way. In the past few years, the increased collaboration and networking between women's organizations in Africa and the women's health and human rights movement all over the world have helped overcome this rift between the women's movements in the South and the North. The view of progressive African women working on this issue is that the practice of female circumcision/genital mutilation is a health hazard and a human rights violation and must be stopped. Their statements welcome the support and collaboration of all the people of the world if given in the spirit of equality and justice. The work toward stopping the practice promises to become an important test for the international women's movement on how to develop its ethics of collaboration across race, culture, and national boundaries.

Following major world conferences on human rights, population, and women, UN organizations—namely the World Health Organization, the UN International Children's Emergency Fund (UNICEF), and the UN Fund for Population Activities—have been giving significant attention to female circumcision/genital mutilation. Policy statements have been published, and programs of actions are being charted. Other international health and development assistance organizations, both governmental and nongovernmental, are becoming active in the efforts to stop this practice. Research efforts are under way to identify the true extent of the practice and the underlying causes for its continuation. Behavioral and psychological research is also being designed to understand the reasons for women's compliance in and perpetuation of the practice. The social and gender constructs that keep women bound to damaging social norms, and the psychological mechanisms they develop to live with violence and degrading treatment, must be identified in order to establish means of reversing the acceptance of this practice.

FOR FURTHER READING

Baasher, T. 1979. "Psychological Aspects of Female Circumcision." In *Traditional Practices Affecting the Health of Women and Children*. WHO/EMRO technical publication no. 2. Geneva: World Health Organization.

Dirie, M. A., and G. Lindmark. 1991. "A Hospital Study of the Complications of Female Circumcision." *Tropical Doctor* 21(4): 146–148.

El Dareer, A. 1983. "Attitudes of Sudanese People to the Practice of Female Circumcision." *International Journal of Epidemiology* 112(2): 138–144.

Gordon, D. 1991. "Female Circumcision and Genital Operations in Egypt and Sudan: A Dilemma for Medical Anthropology." *Medical Anthropology Quarterly* 5: 3–14.

Toubia, Nahid. 1995. *Female Genital Mutilation: A Call for Global Action*. New York: Women Ink.

Toubia, Nahid, and Susan Izett. 1998. *Female Genital Mutilation: An Overview*. Geneva: WHO.

Van Der Kwaak, A. 1992. "Female Circumcision and Gender Identity: A Questionable Alliance." *Social Science and Medicine* 135: 777–787.

World Health Organization Technical Workshop Group. 1995. *Female Genital Mutilation*. WHO/FRH/WHD/96.10 (July 17–19). Geneva: WHO.

twenty

Abortion Technologies

RICHARD BORODITSKY

Induced, or therapeutic, abortion is the voluntary and deliberate termination of pregnancy. Ideally, every woman seeking abortion should have a complete medical history and physical examination and should have appropriate clinical and laboratory investigations to confirm the pregnancy and its gestation and to rule out concomitant disease. Such women should receive supportive and sympathetic counseling responsive to their circumstances. To provide appropriate information and support, health practitioners caring for these women must be comfortable with all the options available.

The gestational age and the experience and preference of the surgeon determine the method selected to induce abortion. Major complications (relating to anesthesia, hemorrhage, uterine perforation, infection, etc.) arise as gestational age increases. The death rate with first- and early-second-trimester abortion is much less than that with term- or third-trimester pregnancy.

Surgical Abortion

First-Trimester Procedures: Vacuum Aspiration or Suction Dilation and Curettage (D and C)

Usually vacuum aspiration can be performed easily and safely under local anesthesia. Premedication with analgesics and/or sedation can be used if necessary. In the case of extremely tense patients, general anesthesia can be used. Natural or synthetic osmotic dilators, which are hygroscopic (expanding when wet), can be preinserted in order to bring about gradual and safe dilatation of the cervix, reducing the risk of cervical laceration and uterine perforation.

The surgical procedure entails blocking the areas involved (paracervical or uterosacral) with local anesthesia followed by gradual, gentle dilation of the cervix with tapered dilators if necessary. The uterine contents are then evacuated with a vacuum aspirator or suction curette. Further exploration of the uterine cavity with a sharp curette may be performed to ensure a complete emptying of the uterus.

Second-Trimester Procedures

Dilation and Evacuation (D and E). There is a considerable amount of controversy regarding which method of pregnancy termination in the second trimester is safest, which produces the least stress for the patient and provider, and which is the most cost effective. However, dilation and evacuation is safer than instillation abortion procedures, and both are safer than hysterotomy and hysterectomy. Until sixteen weeks of gestation, the D and E procedure is definitely safer than instillation procedures; and in experienced hands, modern D and E methods used after sixteen weeks greatly reduce morbidity and mortality.

Overnight placement of several osmotic dilators is usually sufficient preparation prior to eighteen weeks, but beyond this time, the use of serial sets of osmotic dilators over two days is preferable. The D and E procedure can be performed under local anesthesia with intravenous analgesia and/or sedation. If multiple or serial osmotic dilators are used, it is usually unnecessary to further dilate the cervix. The uterus can usually be evacuated up until sixteen weeks of gestation with a large suction curettage or with the use of extraction forceps. After sixteen weeks, a combination of suction curettage followed by extraction of the fetal parts and placenta with extraction forceps ensures evacuation of the uterine cavity. In order to decrease bleeding during the procedure, one can employ various oxytocic (to produce uterine contractions) or vas-pressor (to decrease blood flow) medications either intravenously or directly injected into the uterus.

Very few centers perform D and E procedures in the very late second trimester. For those that do, additional modifications to the procedure have been developed using multistage osmotic dilator treatments and urea injection into the amniotic sac, followed by extraction after labor begins and after fetal maceration has occurred.

Hysterotomy and Hysterectomy. Hysterotomy is essentially an early classical cesarean section. With today's technology, there is rarely an indication for this procedure as a primary method for abortion. The morbidity and mortality associated with this procedure are far greater than for any other technique. If pregnancy coexists with a separate condition for hysterectomy, such as a precancerous condition of the cervix or ovarian cancer, this condition may be an indication for a gravid hysterectomy, which has an even greater associated morbidity and mortality.

Medical Induction of Abortion

First Trimester

The antiprogestational compound mifepristone (RU-486) is being used in several industrialized countries (including France, where it was developed) to induce abortion at very early gestations. This compound interferes with the woman's hormonal cycle in the early stages of pregnancy and induces a spontaneous abortion much like a miscarriage. Its effectiveness is increased to approximately 95 percent by the addition of a low-dose prostaglandin analog to empty the uterus. It also appears that mifepristone may have a very useful role in producing cervical softening and ripening prior to pregnancy termination in both the first and second trimesters. Its use to induce abortion is being investigated intensively. However, to date, it has not been approved for use in most countries.

Second Trimester

Various medications and methods of drug administration have been used to induce uterine contractions and termination of pregnancy in the mid- to-late second trimester. Intra-amniotic injections of substances such as prostaglandin F2-alpha, urea, or hypertonic saline (20 percent) have been effective and usually stimulate uterine emptying within twenty-four hours. Concentrated intravenous infusion of oxytocin has also been effective. At present, the most commonly used compound is prostaglandin F2-alpha given by intra-amniotic injection; however, the prostaglandins are also effective when given intramuscularly, inserted into the extra-amniotic space, or administered orally or intravaginally. Preinsertion of multiple or serial osmotic dilators for all cases of medical induction of abortion shortens the induction time and decreases the risk of cervical laceration and uterine rupture.

FOR FURTHER READING

Aurech, O. M. 1991. "Mifepristone (RU486) Alone or in Combination with a Prostaglandin Analogue for Termination of Early Pregnancy: A Review." *Fertility and Sterility* 56(3): 385–393.

Hern, Warren M. 1984. *Abortion Practice.* Philadelphia: Lippincott.

Winkler, C. L. 1991. "Mid-second Trimester Labor Induction: Concentrated Oxytocin Compared with Prostaglandin E2 Vaginal Suppositories." *Obstetrics and Gynaecology* 77(2): 297–300.

twenty-one

Abortion—Ethics

CHRISTINE OVERALL

There are two general ethical questions about abortion: For what reasons, if any, is abortion morally justified? and Under what circumstances, if any, should abortion be legally available? The first is a question about individual decisionmaking; the second, about social policy. Much of the philosophical debate about the justification of abortion has focused on two crucial issues: whether the human fetus is a person or human being in the moral sense, and what importance should be attributed to women's right to reproductive autonomy. Three of the main ethical positions on abortion—conservative, liberal, and moderate—are distinguished primarily by the ways in which they assess these two issues. The fourth position, developed by feminists, differs from the first three because it offers a contextual and political analysis of abortion.

According to the conservative position, human entities are persons from conception; hence the fetus is a person with a right to life. Since abortion involves the killing of the fetus, it is almost always intrinsically wrong and should be illegal. Conservatives regard themselves as coming to the protection of vulnerable human beings who are unable to help themselves. Prohibitive or restrictive laws on abortion are not merely the enforcement of religious morality but are an extension of the laws against homicide. Conservatives may grant that making abortion difficult to obtain can cause hardship for some women and that women will resort to illegal abortions in some cases. Nevertheless, these facts cannot override the overwhelming moral wrongness of ending the life of a human person.

For conservatives, the rights of the fetus are morally paramount: The well-being of one person, the pregnant woman, is not sufficient to justify the killing of another, the fetus. The fact that some pregnancies may occur as a result of rape or incest is unfortunate, but the origin of the pregnancy in no way increases the pregnant woman's entitlement to an abortion because the fetus is still an "innocent" person and, for that reason, entitled to live. The only case in which abortion is not morally wrong is when the woman's own life is threatened by the continuation of the pregnancy; under such circumstances, abortion is a matter of self-defense.

According to the liberal position, human beings do not become persons with a right to life until birth. Hence, abortion is a matter private to the woman because no other person is affected. The rights of women are morally paramount: Women are entitled to be self-determining, to control their bodies, and to decide whether they will reproduce. Laws that prohibit or restrict abortion are an unjustified imposition of conservative morality and result in an unwarranted tampering with individual liberties. The only policy goal should be that abortions are available and safely performed; no other legal regulation of the procedure is necessary.

Liberals defend their position on abortion policy primarily in consequentialist terms, that is, by reference to its likely outcomes. Liberals argue that the consequences of making abortion widely and freely available are positive: Fewer unwanted children are born, and children who are born are wanted and appreciated; women are able to end pregnancies that result from acts of rape or incest and pregnancies in which the fetus is known to have disabilities; and women do not have to compromise their health by resorting to illegal and unsafe abortions.

Clearly a major source of disagreement between conservatives and liberals is the moral status of the fetus. However, in an influential paper, "A Defense of Abortion," Judith Jarvis Thomson (1984) argues that even if the conservative claim that the fetus is a person with a right to life is accepted, abortion can nonetheless be morally justified. She suggests that abortion is permissible because the fetus has no moral right to use of the pregnant woman's body even if it needs it to live.

The moderate position on abortion claims that both liberals and conservatives err in their assumption that the fetus has the same moral status throughout its entire nine-month development. Instead, moderates argue for a gradualist approach, according to which the fetus acquires moral status and significance during gestation and becomes a human person as its central nervous system develops. Thus abortion is morally permissible early in pregnancy, and social policy should make abortions easily available during that time. As the pregnancy progresses, abortion becomes progressively more difficult to justify in that reasons for abortion have to be more and more serious to make it morally right. Toward the end of the pregnancy, only very serious concerns about threats to the life of the pregnant woman would justify abortion.

Feminist views on the ethics of abortion share with the liberal position its emphasis on women's right to reproductive autonomy, but they differ from it in several important respects. First, feminists reject the assumption made by all three of the other positions that the fetus has an absolute moral status—whether person, nonperson, or potential person—that is independent of the woman gestating it and her life circumstances. Instead, they argue that fetuses have a relational moral status; their moral significance is a function of the value ascribed to them by the pregnant women in whose bodies they grow. Second, feminists offer political analyses of the conditions of sexual domination and oppression under which women become pregnant and raise children. They argue that the ethics of abortion should not be detached from an appraisal of the patriarchal conditions that make sexual and reproductive self-determination for women difficult or even impossible. Third, feminists include within the scope of abortion ethics questions about access to abortion and the medical treatment both of women who continue their pregnancies and of those who seek abortions. Typically, feminists wish to promote all aspects of reproductive freedom, usually defined as the conditions under which women are able to make truly voluntary choices about their reproductive lives.

FOR FURTHER READING

Jaggar, Alison. 1976. "Abortion and a Woman's Right to Decide." In Carol C. Gould and Marx W. Wartofsky, eds., *Women and Philosophy: Toward a Theory of Liberation*. New York: Putnam.

Lake, Randall A. 1986. "The Metaethical Framework of the Anti-Abortion Debate." *Signs: Journal of Women in Culture and Society* 11: 478–499.

Noonan, John T., Jr. 1984. "An Almost Absolute Value in History." In Joel Feinberg, ed., *The Problem of Abortion*. Belmont, Calif.: Wadsworth.

Petchesky, Rosalind Pollack. 1984. *Abortion and Woman's Choice: The State, Sexuality, and Reproductive Freedom*. Boston: Northeastern University Press.

Ramsey, Paul. 1975. "The Morality of Abortion." In James Rachels, ed., *Moral Problems: A Collection of Philosophical Essays*. 2nd ed. New York: Harper and Row.

Rothman, Barbara Katz. 1989. *Recreating Motherhood: Ideology and Technology in a Patriarchal Society*. New York: W. W. Norton.

Sherwin, Susan. 1992. *No Longer Patient: Feminist Ethics and Health Care*. Philadelphia: Temple University Press.

Sumner, L. W. 1981. *Abortion and Moral Theory*. Princeton: Princeton University Press.

Thomson, Judith Jarvis. 1984. "A Defense of Abortion." In Joel Feinberg, ed., *The Problem of Abortion*. Belmont, Calif.: Wadsworth.

Warren, Mary Anne. 1984. "On the Moral and Legal Status of Abortion." In Joel Feinberg, ed., *The Problem of Abortion*. Belmont, Calif.: Wadsworth.

twenty-two

Adoption and Restrictions on Abortion—Ethics

DAVID N. JAMES

Many have been struck by an apparent paradox: Abortion is freely available in most industrialized nations, but at the same time millions of infertile couples are seeking to adopt newborns. Some respond that coercive antiabortion laws should be enacted so that more infants become available for adoption. Such a proposal, however, falls short of satisfying norms of justice, utility, and liberty. George Schedler, a philosopher and lawyer, has argued that even if we set aside all appeals to their personhood or intrinsic value, fetuses still have instrumental value as precious "natural resources." Apart from their present value for embryo research, fetuses will eventually develop into infants who would be valued by infertile couples seeking to adopt. Society is justified in imposing coercive restraints on individual freedom to protect endangered species, forests, and other natural resources, so why not in this case also?

Schedler begins with a point made by Mary Anne Warren, a philosopher who wrote a classic defense of abortion in the 1970s. In a later postscript to this article, Warren (1988) investigated why late abortion is morally permissible, whereas infanticide is impermissible. According to Warren, the moral difference between killing late-term fetuses and killing newborns is that killing the latter, when there are couples eager to adopt, is like squandering a precious natural resource. But, Schedler says, Warren overlooks the fact that there is also a demand that fetuses be brought to term. Furthermore, society could compensate women for any lost opportunities they might forgo to complete a pregnancy. The happiness and opportunities of loggers are adversely affected by forest conservation measures, so "why could fetuses not be regarded as having as much value as forests we protect from destruction?"

The small number of young, healthy babies up for adoption is an unfortunate fact. Intrusive home studies, bureaucratic red tape, painful uncertainties, and years of waiting are some of the unfortunate consequences of the small supply of adoptive babies relative to demand. But would it be just for society to coerce pregnant women to continue unwanted pregnancies to provide childless couples with adoptive children? The coercion, Schedler suggests, could be minimized by focusing on late abortions, which are rare: Ninety-eight percent of abortions in the West take place before twenty weeks, and abortions performed after twenty-four weeks are very unusual.

What sort of women seek late abortions? Who would be those whose liberty would be restricted in this scenario? The most common groups would be women too poor to seek medical attention earlier; women unaware of the signs of pregnancy or of the significance of these signs, including mentally retarded women; and women paralyzed from acting earlier by fear, ambivalence, denial, or guilt. Norms of justice exist to protect the vulnerable from exploitation, and what is most impressive about this list is the extreme vulnerability of these women. A serious injustice would be involved in imposing coercive burdens on those already distressed and damaged to provide benefits to those seeking to adopt, who as a rule are both older and more affluent.

From a purely utilitarian point of view, the argument for coercive pregnancy to benefit the childless is also unconvincing. Schedler argues that the harms of abortion are less than the harms of compulsory childlessness. But this view mistakenly minimizes the burdens of compulsory pregnancy, childbirth, and adoption and mistakenly maximizes the burdens of childlessness. Though involuntary infertility, of course, differs from voluntary childlessness, it is important that the voluntary choices of some single people and some couples to remain childless can be explained only by recognizing that childlessness is not always an unfortunate case. Choices to forgo children may make possible other worthwhile uses of time and energy. Some may choose a child-free life. Others may and often do find ways to nurture children who are not their own. Despite the feeling of loss that may persist for the involuntarily infertile, childlessness is still not like disabilities, such as paralysis and blindness, that nobody freely chooses in order to pursue alternative lifestyles.

Nor should we assume that the burdens of coercive pregnancy, childbirth, and adoption would end as soon as the pregnancy is over, since the burdens may only begin at this point. Curiosity about how the child is turning out, sad memories of the birthday, and guilt about having been unable to provide for her own "flesh and blood" are sometimes lifelong burdens for women who relinquish infants for adoption.

Philosophers have long recognized how difficult it is to actually carry out a utilitarian calculation of total harms and benefits for any policy. In the end these utilitarian issues are not the decisive ones. Given the central place of autonomy in modern ethics, it is crucial not to devalue women's liberty to make reproductive choices. Without the freedom to make medical decisions and reproductive choices, women would be systematically deprived of the liberty to live independent lives. However sympathetic we must be to the real burdens of infertility, hard-won reproductive freedoms should not be surrendered. Norms of justice, utility, and liberty all support the conclusion that the case for coercive laws restricting access to abortion is unsound.

FOR FURTHER READING

Glendon, Mary Ann. 1987. *Abortion and Divorce in Western Law: American Failures, European Challenges.* Cambridge: Harvard University Press.

James, David N. 1990. "Abortion, Coercive Pregnancy, and Adoption." *Philosophy in Context* 20: 53–64.

Schedler, George. 1989. "Viewing Fetuses as Scarce Natural Resources." *Philosophy in Context* 19: 21–31.

Warren, Mary Anne. 1988. "On the Moral and Legal Status of Abortion" and "Postscript on Infanticide." In Joel Feinberg, ed., *The Problem of Abortion.* Belmont, Calif.: Wadsworth.

"Who Gets Abortions?" 1990. *Society* 27: 3.

twenty-three

Prenatal Harm

JOAN C. CALLAHAN

The debate over prenatal harm centers on the moral and legal status of the fetus. Despite a long tradition of the law not recognizing fetuses as persons, in the late 1990s there have been a number of attempts to control or punish pregnant women in instances of actual or presumed prenatal harm. These attempts have included the incarceration of pregnant women, the imposition of medical and surgical treatments (such as cesarean sections), and legal action against women after the birth of their children. Commentators in medical, legal, philosophical, and popular literature have divided on the question of the moral legitimacy of interfering with or punishing women in order to prevent prenatal harm. Among those who argue in favor, some assert that a human being is a person with the full rights of persons from fertilization onward, and others claim that advances in medicine and technology have made fetuses patients with the attendant rights of all human patients; still others point to the future rights and interests of the persons fetuses will eventually become. Opposing arguments either reply directly to those advanced for interfering with or punishing women or contend that legal action against pregnant women ignores the social condition that can give rise to prenatal harm.

Arguments for Prenatal Personhood

Arguments in favor of intervening in a woman's pregnancy to prevent prenatal harm or punishing women for causing prenatal harm are based on the notion that personhood begins at fertilization and so are interwoven with the debate on abortion. Although there is no sound philosophical argument for the position that personhood must be recognized from fertilization onward, and although prenatal human beings have not been treated as persons by the law, some recent court cases in the United States, unrelated to the issue of prenatal harm, have taken the view that in the disposition of frozen embryos a human conceptus is an "unborn child." Further, recent legislative attempts to regulate abortion in a number of U.S. jurisdictions (including Arkansas, Idaho, Illinois, Kentucky, Louisiana, Missouri, Montana, Nebraska, North Dakota, Pennsylvania, South Dakota, and Utah) have asserted that "life begins at conception."

There have been several attempts to add a so-called human life amendment to the U.S. Constitution that would assign the full range of constitutional rights to human beings from fertilization onward. If these rights were to be applied to prenatal human beings, those who deliberately abort for reasons less than self-defense and those who assist them would be subject to the sanctions attached to the deliberate killing of innocent persons. Birth control technologies with potential abortifacient effects would be available only to those for whom pregnancy would be life threatening. And women who are seen to harm or otherwise impose noxious experiences on their fetuses would be liable for charges of assault and battery even if their actions caused no discernible harm to their fetuses.

It is likely that the implications of prenatal personhood have kept the legislators and judges who agree with its rationale from legislating it. The penalties for illegal abortions in jurisdictions with restrictive abortion laws remain far less than the penalties for murder in the same jurisdictions. There has never been an attempt in the United States to prohibit or limit the use of intrauterine devices or steroidal oral or implanted contraceptives even though these can prevent birth through abortion. Nor has any U.S. jurisdiction questioned the judgment that a woman's life should be saved at the expense of her fetus. The position that full persons are present from fertilization onward, then, is actually held by very few even though the rhetoric of prenatal personhood is often deployed to justify state attempts to control pregnant women.

Arguments for the Fetus as Patient

Some have argued that advances in medicine and technology have made fetuses patients with the rights accruing to all patients. It is now possible to assess the health status of the fetus from a very early stage, arguably since conception with prenatal genetic diagnosis. Also some medical screening of the fetus has been routinized in most industrialized countries. There are now medical specialties in fetal pharmaceuticals, surgery, and general medical care, and expectations for pregnant women to submit to the medical profession's fetal care are rising. Women who are socially vulnerable, such as pregnant substance abusers, are increasingly forced into fetal treatment of various kinds. However, a being's capacity to be effectively treated medically or surgically does not dictate its moral status. We do not, for example, afford human rights to nonhuman animals even though we medically and surgically treat them.

Arguments for the Interests of Future Persons

Arguments for forcing pregnant women to submit to medical or surgical interventions for the sake of the fetus can also be based in the interests of the persons prenatal human beings will eventually become. In their most plausible form, these arguments distinguish potential persons and future persons and hold that even if abortion is morally permissible and permitted by law, pregnant women should not make decisions or act in ways that might seriously impede the interests of future persons. It is difficult to see how anyone could, in principle, disagree with the moral appropriateness of this position. Disagreements do arise, however, on the question of whether this position should allow serious intrusions in women's lives and the punishment of women.

A common legal argument for the justification of this position contends that when a woman becomes pregnant and elects to bring that pregnancy to term, she has voluntarily relinquished her rights in favor of a future person. But the concept here is not one of waiver but forfeiture. The argument rests on comparing prenatal cases to pediatric cases. It is generally agreed that the state is entitled to interfere with parents' rights in order to provide medical care or other basic needs for children whose parents will not or cannot so provide. But prenatal cases are not the same as pediatric cases, since anything that is done to or for a fetus must be done through the body of a woman. Further, even if the analogy could be made, it would imply that parents could be subject to all sorts of bodily impositions for the sake of their children (enforced organ transplants, for example). Such impositions have not been allowed.

Feminist Responses

In addition to the objections that have been previously mentioned against interfering with and punishing women to prevent prenatal harm, some feminists have argued that acting on prenatal harm will result in more damage than good. The fear of potential legal sanctions will discourage those women who are "at risk" of causing prenatal harm from seeking appropriate prenatal care. Blaming or punishing such women for not doing the best for their future children in societies that have continued to cut funds for prenatal education, care, and nutrition is highly contradictory, unfair, and an abuse of public welfare principles. Policies based on prenatal harm allow societies to proclaim an interest in the well-being of future children while letting many children languish below the poverty level, failing to provide drug treatment centers for pregnant women, and ignoring toxins in workplaces and the natural environment that can cause preconceptive and prenatal harm through men as well as women. Most feminists' approach to the issue of prenatal harm is that we must cease interfering with and punishing individual women and attend to the social problems that continue to compromise the well-being of women and children: poverty; the general oppression of women; violence against women; lack of appropriate sex education; rampant drug use; pregnancy in the very young; limited access to prenatal education and prenatal care; and limited access to treatment for drug abuse, particularly for pregnant women.

FOR FURTHER READING

Annas, George J. 1986. "Pregnant Women as Fetal Containers." *Hastings Center Report* 16(6): 13–14.

Callahan, Joan C., and James W. Knight. 1992. "Prenatal Harm as Child Abuse?" *Women and Criminal Justice* 3(2): 5–33.

Gallagher, Janet. 1987. "Prenatal Invasions and Interventions: What's Wrong with 'Fetal Rights.'" *Harvard Women's Law Journal* 10: 9–58.

Gallagher, Janet. 1989. "Fetus as Patient." In Sherrill Cohen and Nadine Taub, eds., *Reproductive Laws for the 1990s*. Clifton, N.J.: Humana Press.

Gallagher, Janet. 1995. "Collective Bad Faith: 'Protecting' the Fetus." In Joan C. Callahan, ed., *Reproduction, Ethics, and the Law: Feminist Perspectives*. Bloomington: Indiana University Press.

Johnsen, Dawn. 1987. "A New Threat to Pregnant Women's Autonomy." *Hastings Center Report* 17(4): 33–40.

Kolder, V.E.B., J. Gallagher, and M. T. Parsons. 1987. "Special Article: Court-Ordered Obstetrical Interventions." *New England Journal of Medicine* 316: 1192–1196.

Lenow, Jeffrey. 1983. "The Fetus as Patient: Emerging Legal Rights as a Person?" *American Journal of Law and Medicine* 9: 1–29.

Mathieu, Deborah. 1985. "Respecting Liberty and Preventing Harm." *Harvard Journal of Law and Public Policy* 8: 19–55.

Parness, Jeffrey A. 1985. "Crimes Against the Unborn: Protecting and Respecting the Potentiality of Human Life." *Harvard Journal on Legislation* 22: 97–172.

Robertson, John A., and Joseph D. Schulman. 1987. "Pregnancy and Prenatal Harm to Offspring: The Case of Mothers with PKU." *Hastings Center Report* 17(4): 23–33.

Rodgers, Sanda. 1989. "Pregnancy as a Justification for Loss of Judicial Autonomy." In Christine Overall, ed., *The Future of Human Reproduction*. Toronto: Woman's Press.

twenty-four

Informed Consent and Women in Labor

ROSALIND EKMAN LADD

Recent changes in attitudes and practices concerning childbirth—from a hospital-based, physician-directed model to a woman-centered, less medicalized model—have been inspired in large part by the recent move of Western women to take control of this and many other aspects of their lives. They also reflect the more general trend in medicine away from a form of paternalism where physicians make decisions for their patients and toward informed consent in virtually every aspect of the doctor-patient relationship.

Although women are given many choices about the use of various reproductive technologies and are required to give legal consent through often elaborate contractual arrangements and disclaimers (e.g., in the instance of in vitro fertilization), one of the last holdouts of the power of the physician to make unilateral decisions for others is in relation to the woman in labor. Typically, women entering hospitals for childbirth are asked to sign blanket consent forms providing the physician with the power to perform any procedures he or she deems necessary. This consent effectively removes any obligation on the part of the physician to obtain further specific agreement for such procedures as induction of labor, fetal monitoring, or cesarean section. This circumvention of informed consent reflects a number of assumptions about women in labor and childbirth that are usually false and often involve unwarranted generalizations about women, as well as a misunderstanding of the nature of medical decisionmaking in general.

In the United States, the formal requirement for informed consent for medical research was initially a recommendation of the Belmont Report (1978) and later became a legal requirement applying to all medical treatment. It is based in part on a judicial opinion of Justice Cardoza (1914) that every adult of sound mind has a right to determine what shall be done with his or her body. Although initially greeted with skepticism by physicians who argued that nonprofessionals cannot understand enough to give truly informed consent, it is widely accepted today and widely appreciated as a protection for the physician as well as the patient.

In order to achieve valid informed consent, certain conditions must be met. The patient must be (1) informed (given truthful, adequate information in a form that is understandable), (2) competent (rational and capable of making reasonable decisions), and (3) noncoerced (able to make a voluntary choice). Typically for women in labor, each of these required conditions for informed consent is challenged. Because they are laypersons (and because they are women, some allege), it is assumed that they cannot understand the medical complexities surrounding birth and thus cannot be adequately informed. Because they are feeling pain and anxiety or, conversely, because they have been given medications for pain control, they are often assumed to be irrational and incompetent as decisionmakers. Because they do not have the option of refusing treatment and walking out, their decisions cannot be voluntary. A woman's ability to provide informed consent is also undermined when there is a perceived conflict of interest between the woman and her fetus in situations where the well-being of one can be achieved only at some cost to the other.

There is an overriding belief that all decisions about childbirth are medical decisions and thus are best made by medical professionals. It is a misconception, however, to think that making a medical decision is the same as knowing scientific facts. Medical science may tell us the best means to a given end, but values and preferences are always involved in choosing that end. For example, the use and timing of anesthesia during labor depend on a woman weighing her desire for pain relief against concerns for the well-being of her fetus. Physicians are experts in terms of scientific knowledge, but values and preferences are the prerogative of each individual in a pluralistic society. A medical decision is the combination of scientific and value-based considerations and thus should involve practitioners and patients equally.

If the role of values and preferences in decisions about childbirth is acknowledged and if women are well informed so that by the time they are in labor they are relatively free of anxiety, the assumption of incompetence of women in labor will be eliminated and the right to informed consent and shared decisionmaking will be realized.

FOR FURTHER READING

Applebaum, Paul S., Charles W. Lidz, and Alan Meisel. 1987. *Informed Consent: Legal Theory and Clinical Practise*. New York: Oxford University Press.

Faden, Ruth R., and Tom L. Beauchamp with Nancy M.P. King. 1986. *A History and Theory of Informed Consent*. New York: Oxford University Press.

Grice, S. C., J. D. Eisenach, D. M. Dewan, and M. L. Robinson. 1988. "Evaluation of Informed Consent for Anesthesia for Labor and Delivery." *Anesthesiology* 69(3A): A664.

Knapp, Robert M. 1990. "Legal View of Informed Consent for Anesthesia During Labor." *Anesthesiology* 72(1): 211.

Ladd, Rosalind Ekman. 1989. "Women in Labor: Some Issues About Informed Consent." *Hypatia* 4(3): 37–45. Reprinted 1992, in Laura Purdy and Helen Bequaert Holmes, eds., *Feminist Medical Ethics: New Perspectives*. Bloomington: Indiana University Press.

Overall, Christine. 1987. *Ethics and Human Reproduction: A Feminist Analysis*. Boston: Allen and Unwin.

twenty-five

Reproductive Health in the Workplace

REGINA H. KENEN

Reproductive health issues for women in the workplace are basically the same worldwide. What is vastly different is the degree to which women are exposed to workplace hazards and stress, the adequacy of their pregnancy and maternity benefits, and the quantity and quality of available child care facilities, if any. Also, too little attention has been given to male reproductive hazards in the workplace even though it is known that toxic substances can affect both men's and women's ability to conceive or bear healthy children and can affect the health of future children. Exposure to some pesticides, cancer drugs, lead, viruses, and X rays, as well as stress, increasing violence against women, and excessive lifting of heavy weights, are just a few workplace conditions that can have adverse reproductive effects.

The International Labor Office projects that by the year 2000, 830 million women will be in the labor force worldwide. In many Western, industrialized nations, they make up more than 50 percent of the workforce. The Inter-American Development Bank estimates that in Latin America and the Caribbean, 27 percent of the labor force is women. This figure represents a fourfold increase in the number of women wage earners since 1950. The majority of these women will be part of the labor force during one or more of their pregnancies.

Women tend to be segregated into specific jobs. In Latin America, North America, and Europe most women work in the service sector; in Asia and Africa, they are employed in agriculture, where exposure to toxic pesticides remains a major problem. Women's disadvantaged social and economic status, as well as biological differences, needs to be addressed before true equality in the workplace is achieved.

Until recently, women's work received little attention from health researchers. The kinds of jobs that women typically hold are characterized by long hours of monotonous and repetitive work that puts great pressure on eyesight, joints, and tendons (particularly bad for pregnant workers) and results in additional stress-related disorders. So far scientists have not been able to determine any direct causal connection between video display use and reproductive harm. However, women who use video displays intensively for the entire workday are considered to be at greatest risk. The effect of intensive video-display-terminal work on reproductive health remains inconclusive, and the potential risks for men of this type of work have barely been studied. Given the uncertainty about adverse reproductive effects in many types of work settings, a policy that allows for both men and women trying to conceive to transfer temporarily to other types of jobs without penalty seems to be the most prudent approach.

Internationally, legislative reforms, legal suits, workers' action programs, workplace health and safety initiatives, and union action are geared toward the protection and promotion of reproductive health in the workplace for women and in some cases for men as well. In Mexico, some forty families in which the pregnant worker had miscarriages or stillbirths are suing an electronics plant for failing to warn employees about toxic chemicals and for its failure to provide protective equipment. In Costa Rica, approximately 150 banana plantation workers who became sterile are suing the company for exposing them to the pesticide DBCP (dibromochloropropane), which has been banned in the United States.

Most industrial countries have some type of regulation controlling substances hazardous to health, equal opportunity and maternity rights, and benefits laws. Maternity leave and access to medical care have been stipulated in international rights conventions such as the U.N. Convention on the Elimination of All Forms of Discrimination Against Women. However, in many (especially developing) nations, these rights have not been implemented. Except for a few European countries, the lack of adequate child care facilities for working mothers continues to be a major problem.

Reproductive health in the workplace remains a major health and social policy issue throughout the world. The European Community has issued work-related directives that indirectly and directly affect reproductive health in the workplace. These directives set out general goals and duties and general principles for employers to follow in protecting the health and safety of workers. The five directives that particularly affect reproductive health in the workplace focus on (1) the use of personal protective equipment, (2) the manual handling of loads, (3) the use of display-screen equipment (video display units), (4) exposure to carcinogens and biological agents, and (5) pregnant workers. The Pregnant Workers Directive (Collins 1994) is the most important piece of European Union legislation affecting pregnant workers because it covers not only health and safety but also maternity leave and pay. In the United States, a highly advanced industrial nation, the National Institute of Occupational Safety and Health still includes reproductive disorders among the ten leading workplace-related diseases. Conditions are worse in most of the developing countries.

FOR FURTHER READING

Blank, R. 1993. *Fetal Protection in the Workplace: Women's Rights, Business Interests, and the Unborn.* New York: Columbia University Press.

Boston Women's Health Collective. 1998. "Environmental and Occupational Health." In *Our Bodies Ourselves for the New Century.* New York: Simon and Schuster.

Collins, H. 1994. *The EU Pregnancy Directive: A Guide for Human Resource Managers.* Oxford: Blackwell Business.

Graebner, W. 1984. "Doing the World's Unhealthy Work." *Hastings Center Report* 14: 4.

Kenen, R. 1993. *Reproductive Hazards in the Workplace: Mending Jobs, Managing Pregnancies.* New York: Haworth Press.

Kenen, R. 1998. *Pregnancy at Work: Health and Safety for the Working Woman.* London: Pluto.

LaDou, J., ed. 1986. "The Microelectronics Industry." *Occupational Medicine: State of the Art Reviews.* Special issue 1.

Latin American and Caribbean Women's Health Network, ISIS International. 1991. "Labor Pains: Women's Health on the Job." *Women's Health Journal* (Fall): 29–52.

Nelson, L., R. Kenen, and S. Klitzman. 1990. *Turning Things Around: A Women's Occupational and Environmental Health Resource Guide.* Washington, D.C.: National Women's Health Network.

Schrag, S. D., and R. Dixon. 1985. "Occupational Exposures Associated with Male Reproductive Dysfunction." *Annual Review of Pharmacology and Toxicology* 25: 567–592.

Shepard, T. 1995. *Catalogue of Teratogenic Agents.* 8th ed. Baltimore: Johns Hopkins University Press.

Thomas, J. A., and B. Ballantyne. 1990. "Occupational Reproductive Risks: Sources, Surveillance, and Testing." *Journal of Occupational Medicine* 32: 547–554.

U.S. Congress, Office of Technology Assessment. 1985. *Reproductive Health Hazards in the Workplace.* OTA-BA-266. Washington, D.C.: U.S. Government Printing Office.

twenty-six

Contemporary Midwifery

VICKI VAN WAGNER

The World Health Organization's Definition of a Midwife: She must be able to give the necessary supervision, care, and advice to women during pregnancy, labour and the postpartum period, to conduct deliveries on her own responsibility, and to care for the newborn and the infant. This care includes preventative measures, the detection of abnormal conditions in mother and child, the procurement of medical assistance, and the execution of emergency measures in the absence of medical help.

She has an important task in counselling and education—not only for patients, but also within the family and community. The work should involve antenatal education and preparation for parenthood and extends to certain areas of gynaecology, family planning and child care.

She may practice in hospitals, clinics, health units, domiciliary conditions or any other service.

—**Kitzinger 1988**

Midwifery is now the art and science of caring for women during pregnancy and childbirth and caring for the new mother and baby during the first weeks of the newborn's life. Midwifery is also an ancient practice common to most cultures around the world. Most of the world's babies are born with a midwife assisting the mother throughout labor and birth, but the status of midwifery varies widely around the world. In Scandinavian countries, where midwives are highly respected professionals, all pregnant women see midwives for maternity care. In some parts of North America and the Third World, midwifery is not legally recognized and may be illegal. In most countries, midwives were an integral part of the health care system but have lost status over the past fifty years as medical dominance and the use of technology in childbirth have increased. An international movement of midwives and women supporting them has both criticized this trend and sought to reverse it.

Physiologically, if the mother is healthy, birth is usually a normal, healthy event. Both feminist and consumer critics point out that obstetric care is focused on pathology, and as a result, women can be subjected to unnecessary surgery and other medical procedures. In this view, some women and their families complain that the medical model ignores the profound social and emotional implications of the birth process, turning a potentially joyous event into a clinical routine. A growing body of medical research indicates that many of the procedures that have been considered a routine part of obstetric care, for example, episiotomy, are not based on scientific evidence and have no proven benefit for mother or baby. The effectiveness of contemporary midwifery in providing safe care with low rates of intervention is well documented internationally.

Decoding the language used to name the midwife and to describe her role in helping the mother to give birth reveals some of the politics of childbirth. The term "deliver the baby" is common in everyday speech but is avoided by those midwives and childbirth activists who advocate women's control over the process of childbirth. The term implies that the care provider rather than the mother is in the active role. Many prefer "assists the mother to give birth" because this phrase more accurately reflects the midwifery philosophy of support and respect for the woman's strength and ability. Others, in the same spirit, suggest that the midwife be described as the one who "catches" the baby. In French the verb *recevoir* is used; the midwife "receives" the baby. However, these terms also present problems. Midwives who advocate an approach that makes women the central figures in the birth process have been stereotyped by opponents as being handholders rather than skilled professionals. The words "assist" and "catch" do not convey the degree of responsibility the midwife takes for the health and well-being of mother and baby. Internationally, many midwives refer back to the root meaning of the words for midwife. The French *sage-femme* and the Dutch *verloskundige*, both of which mean "wise woman," convey respect for the midwife's skills and knowledge. The meaning of the old English word *midwyfe*, "with woman," is often cited as more helpful in conveying the centrality of the laboring woman to the midwife's role. Also, like the Danish and Norwegian *jordemoder*, these terms reveal the long history of the profession.

It is only in the past century that medicine has dominated childbirth. Feminist historians have thoroughly documented the rise of medical obstetrics in the late 1800s, the attempts of medicine to discredit midwifery, and the move of birth from home to hospital. At the turn of the century, European and North American medical propaganda painted the midwife as unskilled, uneducated, and unsanitary. In some places midwives survived this campaign by organizing for the formal education and licensing of midwives. In most European countries this strategy worked, and midwifery continued to be a vital community-based service in many countries until the mid-twentieth century. However, in many countries midwifery has been gradually eroded and has increasingly played the role of assistant to physicians, as obstetrics has become more technological and medicalized. In most developed countries, policies of routine institutionalization of childbirth mean that very few women give birth outside the hospital, although the available scientific research does not provide evidence of benefits to either mother or baby in low-risk situations. Moving the usual site of birth to the hospital undermined the autonomy of both women and midwives.

Holland is a notable exception and is often held up as the model midwifery system. In Holland, midwives and physicians work as colleagues, respecting each other's expertise and distinct roles in the health care system. There, 50 percent of women choose to give birth at home assisted by midwives, a choice that is supported by the health insurance system, the government, and the medical profession. In contrast, in twentieth-century North America, midwifery was nearly eradicated when governments complied with the powerful medical lobby and passed legislation making midwifery illegal. This resulted in a medical monopoly over childbirth that modern midwives and childbirth activists have had to struggle to change. In other places, the medicalization of childbirth has resulted in midwifery being viewed as second-class care, functioning as an adjunct to medical care or as a part of nursing rather than as an autonomous and separate profession. In some cases, midwives are supported by governments and other health workers only when and where physicians are not available.

Traditional midwives (often referred to as traditional birth attendants, or TBAs) provide an important health service in many Third World countries. They have usually learned their skills from older women in the community rather than through formal training. In countries where poverty means that many women are not in optimal health, pregnancy and childbirth are critical periods in the lives of women and children, and midwives are seen as vital primary health care workers. Traditional midwives can be utilized by the formal health care system as an indigenous resource and have been a central part of the WHO's "Safe Motherhood" initiative. Many Third World midwives working in poor or war-torn countries are without access to medical backup and have very limited supplies of drugs and equipment even though, by necessity, their scope of practice involves dealing with many complications and emergencies.

Since the late 1980s, community development workers have pointed out that the health and well-being of women are central to the health of the community as a whole. In Third World countries, maternal mortality, or death associated with pregnancy or childbirth, is still the major cause of death for women and occurs at a far greater rate than in industrialized countries: 1 in 16 in Africa versus 1 in 3,700 in North America. The International Confederation of Midwives has worked jointly on the Safe Motherhood Project with the World Health Organization to address these problems.

International Trends in Midwifery

In the latter half of the twentieth century technological intervention in childbirth has increased exponentially. Medical bodies have acknowledged that the rate of cesarean section has risen to an inappropriately high level in many industrialized countries. In North America the rate currently ranges from 19 to 24 percent. In contrast, in Holland, where midwifery and home birth are an accepted part of the health care system, the rate is 6 percent with equal or superior outcomes in terms of perinatal mortality.

In many parts of the developed world, midwives have become a focal point for those who wish to reclaim childbirth from medicalization and institutionalization. As the use of birth technologies has increased, so has the demand for midwives to play a role as the advocates of women's choices in childbirth and the guardians of the normal physiologic process. An international consumer movement to lower rates of intervention and redefine birth as a normal life event has challenged midwives who have become part of the medical system in many countries to rethink their role in providing maternity care. Movements in both Britain and Denmark called "Know Your Midwife" have pressured midwives to return to caseload systems rather than shift work in order to provide continuity of care. In many parts of North America where midwifery practice had virtually disappeared, an underground of lay practitioners evolved to meet the need for alternatives to institutionalized childbirth. This underground has developed into a popular social movement seeking the recognition of autonomous, community-based midwifery practice. In places such as the state of Washington (the United States) and in several Canadian provinces, midwives and their supporters gained status and established midwifery education programs. In Ontario, British Columbia, and Alberta (Canada), midwives have won the same right to govern themselves as held by the medical and nursing professions. In New Zealand an active movement of both women and midwives has transformed midwifery from a devalued and subservient position to a strong and autonomous one. In Britain, a parliamentary report called *Changing Childbirth* (1993) recommends widespread changes to increase the autonomy of midwives, expand women's choices to include home birth, and increase continuity of care.

In order to support women's choices, midwives have asserted that they must be autonomous practitioners accountable to the women they care for and to the standards of practice set by midwives rather than to a supervising physician or an institutional employer. Midwives from all around the world have begun to resist the loss of status as primary caregivers that leaves them to work as obstetrical nurses or physicians' assistants. This movement for autonomy and accountability to women rather than to institutions and the medical model seeks to reverse the gradual erosion of the midwife's legitimacy and scope of practice and to reestablish pregnant women as the central decisionmakers in childbirth.

In a new model of care, midwifery focuses on normal childbirth as a part of the continuum of the life of a woman and her family. Midwives' trust in the normal birth process allows room for the social, cultural, and emotional aspects of birth. The essence of the new model is that the midwife follows the woman throughout pregnancy, labor, and postpartum rather than care being fragmented among staff in antenatal clinics, labor and delivery wards, and postpartum workers in the hospital and the community. Called continuity of care, this approach allows a meaningful relationship to develop between a woman and her midwife. In order to provide continuity of care, the midwife works in a small group practice that takes responsibility for sharing the care of the woman and baby.

The midwife also follows the woman's choices, supporting and monitoring rather than directing the process of normal childbirth. The midwife informs, educates, and supports the woman and family in their decisionmaking process. The midwife accepts full professional responsibility for the woman's care but in a model based on a nonauthoritarian partnership. The midwife's view of birth as a healthy process, her relationship with each individual woman and family, and her commitment to the woman as primary decisionmaker allow the midwife to support the woman to choose not only how but also where to give birth. Home birth has become symbolic of returning power over birth to women and their families.

The midwife's expertise is in facilitating the normal process, in supporting the woman to use the many nonmedical techniques that can also prevent problems from arising. For example, there is evidence that simple methods such as walking, squatting, and being cared for by a constant companion help to avoid unnecessary intervention, reduce pain, and help prevent prolonged labors. Also, the midwife is highly skilled at monitoring the well-being of mother and baby and detecting abnormalities. In cases where complications occur and the midwife refers to a specialist, the former becomes the advocate for the woman in the appropriate use of birth technology. The midwife's role in facilitating informed choice is of particular importance when technological intervention becomes necessary.

As the international midwifery community works toward reclaiming autonomy for both women and midwives, it faces many challenges. The proliferation of birth technology and the struggle over resources in the health care system mean that little money is available for women-centered approaches to improving maternity care. Successful efforts in this direction have often been the result of active consumer organizations and midwives' associations working closely together. The future of midwifery, like its history, is closely linked to much wider social issues about women's autonomy and control of reproduction. Midwives have the potential to create a model of reproductive health care that shifts the system away from dependence on technology, experts, or institutions and places women at the center.

FOR FURTHER READING

Chalmers, Iain, Muray Enkin, and Marc J.N.C. Keirse. 1995. *Effective Care in Pregnancy and Childbirth*. London: Oxford University Press.

Donnison, Jean. 1977. *Midwives and Medical Men*. London: Heinemann.

Kirkham, Mavis. 1986. "Feminist Perspectives in Midwifery." In C. Webb, ed., *Feminist Practice in Women's Health Care*. London: John Wiley.

Kirkham, Mavis J., and Elizabeth R. Perkins. 1997. *Reflections on Midwifery*. London: Balliere Tindall.

Kitzinger, Sheila. 1988. *The Midwife Challenge*. London: Pandora.

Kleiverda, G. 1990. *The Transition to Parenthood: Women's Experiences of Labour*. Amsterdam: Department of Obstetrics and Gynecology, Academisch Medisch Centrum.

Kroll, Debra, ed. 1996. *Midwifery Care for the Future: Meeting the Challenge*. London: Balliere Tindall.

Litoff, Judy, ed. 1986. *The America Midwife Debate*. Westport, Conn.: Greenwood Press.

Martin, Emily. 1987. *The Woman in the Body: A Cultural Analysis of Reproduction*. Boston: Beacon Press.

Phaff, J. M., ed. 1986. *Perinatal Health Services in Europe: Searching for Better Childbirth*. London: Croom Helm.

Rothman, Barbara Katz. 1982. *In Labour.* New York: W. W. Norton.
Sullivan, Deborah A., and Rose Weitz. 1988. *Labour Pains: Modern Midwives and Home Birth.* New Haven: Yale University Press.
United Kingdom Department of Health. 1993. *Changing Childbirth: Report of the Expert Maternity Group (The Cumberledge Report).* London: HMSO.
Wertz, Dorothy C. 1983. "What Birth Has Done for Doctors: A Historical View." *Women and Health* 1, supp.: 7–24.
Wertz, Richard W., and Dorothy C. Wertz. 1989. *Lying-In: A History of Childbirth in America.* Exp. ed. New Haven and London: Yale University Press.
World Health Organization. 1987. *Safe-Motherhood: Helping Women off the Road to Death.* Geneva: WHO.

Part Three
Early Infertility Treatments

Infertility treatment has entered the scene relatively late in terms of reproductive practices. Initial practice was based on the assumption of fertility. The focus was on women once pregnancy was established and on avoiding pregnancy and birth with contraception and abortion. The treatment of infertility began as highly experimental and was explored by doctors and scientists in the mid-nineteenth century but did not become routine within medical practice until the mid-twentieth century. Preceding the substantial developments in assisted conception of the 1980s, commonly referred to as the new reproductive technologies, there were three basic approaches to infertility: artificial insemination, biochemical interventions within women's reproductive cycles, and pregnancy screening. The field of artificial insemination has recently given more attention to male infertility. Pregnancy screening represents a shift in the conceptualization of infertility, especially since the 1960s, to include the notion of improved fertility.

Artificial insemination is one of the earliest reproductive technologies in contemporary medical practice. The procedure was first tried by scientists and doctors interested in increasing the body of scientific knowledge around reproduction and pushing the medical ability to control reproductivity. Addressing the plight of infertile heterosexual couples was not the motivation for these early explorations. Eventually, however, artificial insemination, especially donor insemination, or DI, was adopted as routine practice in the treatment of infertility by the growing subprofession of obstetricians and gynecologists. This development is important from two different perspectives. First, insemination with sperm that is not from the partner in a heterosexual relationship has raised concerns with paternal rights and responsibilities. These concerns have restricted the medical and state-sanctioned insemination practice in differing ways worldwide. Second, the procedure, which is relatively simple to perform, can be done without medical supervision and offers women reproductive choice. This aspect of the issue has also influenced recent international insemination policy.

The insemination of a woman with a donor's sperm is a complex social process. It has long been practiced secretly for several reasons. A man with fertility problems was considered a source of embarrassment. In addition, a nongenetically related child poses a serious threat to genuine fatherhood and masculinity. And finally, donors do not want to be held responsible (particularly financially) for their genetic offspring. As male infertility has become gradually recognized both in reproductive medicine and more broadly in the social sphere, the need for secrecy has diminished. Also, the DI child's interests are now addressed, and often these children are told of their genetic lineage. Nonetheless, the donor's identity usually remains unknown, and recent legislation tends to shield donors from liability and responsibility for their genetic offspring.

Initially the technique of artificial insemination, whether using sperm from "the husband" (AIH) or from a donor (DI) was restricted to placing the sperm in the uterus of a fertile woman at the time of her ovulation. The procedure has become more complicated with the development of medical protocols that include hyperovulation and microimplantation of the sperm into the egg to increase the success rate of fertilization. Also there are concerns about passing on sexually transmitted diseases that have led to complicated sperm-screening procedures and thorough sperm-donor screening prior to insemination. These developments have helped establish DI as a potentially dangerous and complicated procedure that requires medical supervision. Also, as DI has become more commonly practiced, more attention has been paid to the registration and tracking of donors to avoid unwanted interrelations and oversaturation of one donor's genetic contributions in a given population. The medical profession has often been used to provide this recording service. Women, especially those not in heterosexual relationships, have used DI to procreate outside the traditional bonds of marriage. The medicalization of the procedure along with moral stands that procreation should occur only within marriage or marriagelike arrangements has led to a recent trend in some places to restrict DI. However, this restriction remains virtually impossible to police, and self-insemination continues to operate to some degree outside state control and without medical authorization.

Meanwhile, male infertility begins to be more seriously and more thoroughly examined by the medical and scientific professions than ever before. The level of inquiry has moved beyond simple sperm-level counts to more detailed and complex semen analysis. Also, a greater understanding of the function of sperm production and fertilizing action is being pursued. Male reproductive hormones are also under investigation, as are ways of removing sperm in cases where the ejaculate is insufficient for reproduction. Partly due to this reorientation of infertility research to the male, pressure for women to undergo DI is relieved. However, pressures grow for more invasive assisted-conception techniques on women, particularly in vitro fertilization and microinjection of sperm into the egg. As with female infertility, currently there is little available in the way of cures for male infertility, and treatments of its symptoms continue to implicate women in terms of medical interventions.

Artificial insemination has helped fuel a more intense level of medical intervention in the female reproductive cycle, particularly in the form of hormonal replacement and control. One of the earliest uses of hormones to treat women's infertility was the infamous drug DES, used in the attempted prevention of spontaneous abortion or miscarriage. This early intervention proved dangerous and was also ineffective. So-called fertility drugs to induce hyperovulation proved to markedly increase women's chances of becoming pregnant in a variety of situations, including when the infertility was of unknown cause—the most common type of infertility. Hyperovulation is now routinely used in medically supervised artificial insemination as well as in virtually all advanced assisted-conception techniques. Hyperovulation, in turn, has assisted the development of an even higher level of hormonal intervention in the form of GnRH analogs, which suspend all female reproductive hormonal activity. These conceptive artificial hormones are not applied without considerable risk to women, however, both in the short and long term, and their use has begun to be critically examined.

There has been a trend since the 1960s to include the notion of improved fertility within infertility treatment. The increased ability to view and assess the fetus in pregnant women, now called prenatal screening, has opened up a host of medical interventions designed to treat the pregnancy and genetically test the fetus. Medical-risk perception generally has expanded dramatically, and if we keep in mind that the predominant focus of medical attention in most developed countries is pregnancy and childbirth, we can easily understand how women's reproductivity is the most affected by this trend. As the first physicians in the contemporary practice of medicine relied on a pathologizing of birth to bring this aspect of female procreativity under their authority, so does prenatal screening construct pregnancy from a very early stage as risky and worth medical surveillance. Arguments continue between medical authorities and those resisting the medicalization of pregnancy and birth as to the relative benefits of routinely checking every woman's pregnancy visually and for genetic abnormalities.

With the development since the 1970s of serum-screening technologies in pregnant women, especially amniocentesis, came the by-product of sex selection. Although prenatal sex selection, particularly for choosing male children, has long been of social interest in a variety of cultural settings, screening technologies made it possible for the first time. Capitalization on the social desire to choose the sex of children has followed, especially in the United States and developing countries, where pressures to have male children are great. Screening for both genetic abnormalities and sex selection raises the serious prospect of a new eugenics, a prospect intensified within advanced assisted-conception practices and genetic engineering.

twenty-seven

Artificial Insemination

RONA ACHILLES

In its most rudimentary form, artificial insemination is simply an alternative to sexual intercourse. Sperm acquired through masturbation is placed manually in the woman's cervical canal at the time of ovulation. When practiced in medical settings, artificial insemination involves two major categories. These are commonly defined by the relationship of the inseminated woman to the man who is the source of the sperm: artificial insemination by donor (AID), increasingly referred to as donor insemination (DI, to avoid confusion with the disease AIDS), and artificial insemination by husband (AIH). Technically, the latter acronym refers to artificial insemination homologous. When used outside of medical settings and without the assistance of physicians, DI is referred to as self-insemination or alternative insemination.

History

There are two histories of artificial insemination: the history of a medical practice and the history of alternative insemination by laypeople as a method of achieving pregnancy without sexual intercourse. Information about both is scarce as a result of the typical secrecy involved. Documented records of artificial insemination in humans go back well over 100 years in the United States and over 200 years in the United Kingdom. Artificial insemination with animals dates even earlier with stories, for example, about fourteenth-century Arabs who impregnated the mares of their enemies with the semen of inferior stallions. The biologist Lazzaro Spallanzani is accredited with using artificial insemination in dogs in

1784. In humans, the first reported instance of artificial insemination by husband was in London in 1793, when John Hunter collected sperm from a man suffering from hypospadias (inability to ejaculate sperm) and inseminated the man's wife with reported success. In the United States, AIH was performed by J. M. Sims in 1866 on six women. His very low success rate has been attributed to his confusing menstruation with ovulation. Although the freezing of sperm was recorded as early as 1776, the first recorded use of frozen sperm in humans was in the 1940s and 1950s in the United States. In 1909, an article in a medical journal recounted an incident involving donor insemination twenty-five years earlier, dating the first known instance of DI as 1874. A woman was inseminated with the sperm of "the best looking member" of the physician's medical class while she was anesthetized. When the woman became pregnant, the doctor, William Pancoast, told her husband, who requested his wife not be told. The author of this 1909 article is the sperm donor. This incident is particularly significant, since it holds within it all the elements of the clandestine practice of DI.

The nonmedical history of artificial insemination is largely unknown. A second-century Talmudic story about conception achieved in bathwater contaminated with semen and a thirteenth-century story about a rabbi warning women to be careful of bed linens on which a man other than her husband has slept indicate a lengthy history of alternative insemination. As one author argues, this nonmedical history suggests that DI existed in the public consciousness longer than the history of medical practice. Networks of women have developed in several countries (for example, Canada, the United States, and the United Kingdom) since the 1970s to assist women in finding sperm donors, to negotiate their relationship with them, and to provide support for the insemination.

Techniques

AIH is used when a woman's male partner has a fertility problem such as too few sperm (oligozoospermia) or some abnormal sperm. The sperm is treated by concentrating it in smaller volumes, separating out the viable sperm, or increasing sperm motility through the use of drugs. Other occasions for use include cervical-factor infertility (when a woman's cervical mucus rejects her partner's sperm), idiopathic infertility with an unknown cause, impotence, and vaginismus. In addition, men undergoing treatments that might damage their sperm, such as chemotherapy, may choose to freeze their sperm for later use by their partner. Generally speaking, the method of insemination used in AIH is intrauterine, which means that the semen is placed inside the woman's uterus with a catheter.

Unlike AIH, where sperm is treated to increase its fertilizing capacity, DI is not, strictly speaking, a treatment for male infertility. DI is used when a woman's male partner has untreatable infertility or untreatable semen abnormalities or has had a vasectomy. DI is also used to avoid the transmission of a genetic disease and historically, when a couple's blood type was incompatible. Women who are single or in a lesbian relationship may also use artificial insemination by donor to get pregnant. In these cases, DI is more accurately described as a social arrangement rather than a treatment. The physician's role in this arrangement is that of sperm broker, matching a fertile man with a fertile woman in order to conceive a child.

In DI medical practice, donors are selected and screened by medical personnel, and physicians may also screen recipients. The sperm donor and the recipients are generally unknown to each other, and this anonymity is regarded as essential to the success of the procedure. In the past, medical guidelines have recommended that the child conceived through DI not be told of his or her origins and that no one be told about the method of conception. Current medical guidelines are less certain about the benefits of secrecy. Since the late 1980s, the medical practice of DI has changed dramatically as a result of two factors. One is the advent of AIDS, which requires that sperm donors be tested for HIV antibodies. Current practice requires that a donor be tested and his sperm frozen for six months. Then the donor must be retested on an ongoing basis. The second factor is the development of other assisted-reproduction technologies such as in vitro fertilization and embryo transfer (IVF and ET), which have accelerated advancements in the field of infertility treatments. These advances have meant that sperm is now tested thoroughly for sexually transmitted diseases and screened for genetic problems, resulting in up to 95 percent of donors being rejected by some sperm banks. Women undergoing insemination may be subject to a variety of fertility evaluations, as well as the use of fertility drugs, despite the absence of a proven fertility problem. Methods of insemination have also become more invasive with the increasing use of intrauterine insemination as well as the introduction of direct intraperitoneal insemination (injection of sperm into the perineum) and intratubal or fallopian insemination, which may require anesthesia to inject sperm directly into the fallopian tubes.

More recently, intracytoplasmic sperm injection (ICSI) has had an impact on donor insemination. With ICSI, an egg is injected with a single sperm to facilitate fertilization. This technique is generally used with IVF for couples with male-factor infertility who do not want to use DI (the male partner's sperm is usually used to fertilize the egg). Since IVF with ICSI has higher fertilization rates than IVF without ICSI (but lower than donor insemination), many couples may want to try IVF with ICSI before attempting donor insemination. Ultimately, this procedure costs more and is more complex technologically. When IVF with ICSI is successful, DI is not required. However, IVF with ICSI can also be used with donor sperm, so it is unclear at this point what the full impact of ISCI on DI will be. Women who use self-insemination may do so in order to avoid unnecessary medical interventions to become pregnant, to negotiate a different arrangement with their donor, or because they are single and lesbian and thus denied access to medicalized DI. Self-insemination requires only a fertile and willing sperm donor and knowledge of the timing of ovulation.

Risks

The medical risks posed by artificial insemination in its simplest form are identical to the risks accompanying sexual intercourse. They include the transmission through semen of sexually transmitted diseases such as chlamydia, gonorrhea, cytomegalovirus, hepatitis B and C viruses, and HIV. Risks with medicalized procedures vary according to the attendant therapies and methods of insemination. Intrauterine insemination, for example, includes risks of bleeding, cramping, infection, and uterine contamination. Drugs to induce ovulation also increase the risks of the procedure and include luteal phase defect (inadequate production of progesterone), hydatidiform mole (a mass of cysts), premature aging of the ovary, ovarian cancer, ectopic pregnancy, and multiple pregnancies. Diagnostic procedures such as hysterosalpingography (an X ray of fallopian tube function) include risks such as intense pain during the procedure, radiation damage, adhesions, and pelvic inflammatory disease. With donor insemination, intermarriage between half-siblings is a risk that increases with the number of children conceived with the same donor, especially within smaller geographical regions. There is no evidence of other physical risks to the children conceived, but long-term studies have yet to be undertaken to evaluate outcomes of various methods of insemination where more invasive therapies and drug treatments have been employed to assist with conception.

FOR FURTHER READING

Achilles, Rona. 1992. *Donor Insemination. An Overview*. A report for the Canadian Royal Commission on New Reproductive Technologies. Ottawa: Canadian Communications Group.

Allen, N. C., et al. 1985. "Intrauterine Insemination: A Critical Review." *Fertility and Sterility* 44(5): 569–580.

American Fertility Society. 1980. *Report of the Ad Hoc Committee on Artificial Insemination.* Birmingham, Ala.: American Fertility Society.

American Fertility Society. 1990. "Ethical Considerations of the New Reproductive Technologies." *Fertility and Sterility* 53(6), supp. 2.

Bunge, R. G., and J. K. Sherman. 1953. "Fertilizing Capacity of Frozen Human Spermatozoa." *Nature* 172: 767–768.

Finegold, W. J. 1964. *Artificial Insemination.* Springfield, Ill.: Charles C. Thomas.

Francoer, R. T. 1977. *Utopian Motherhood. New Trends in Human Reproduction.* 3rd ed. South Brunswick, N.J.: A. S. Barnes.

Freedman, B., et al. 1987. "Non-Medical Selection Criteria for Artificial Insemination and Adoption." *Clinical Reproduction and Fertility* 5(1–2): 55–66.

Gregoire, A. T., and R. C. Mayer. 1965. "The Impregnators." *Fertility and Sterility* 16(1): 130–134.

Holmes, H. B. 1988. "Risks of Infertility Diagnosis and Treatment." *Infertility: Medical and Social Choices.* Contractor documents, vol. 4. Washington, D.C.: Office of Technology Assessment.

Liljestrand, Petra. 1988. "Patriarchy Undated: Artificial Insemination by Donor." Unpublished thesis. University of California at Berkeley.

Small, E. C., and R. N. Turksoy. 1985. "A View of Artificial Insemination." *Advances in Psychosomatic Medicine* 12: 105–123.

twenty-eight

Artificial Insemination Policy

ANNE DONCHIN

Though artificial insemination has been practiced for over a century and has been readily obtainable through medical channels since the 1930s, its use did not become a social policy issue until after World War II. Few oppose the technique itself, except religious groups that object to masturbation or noncoital reproduction, but these opponents sometimes permit the practice if a permeable condom is used to collect semen. Artificial insemination by husband (AIH) is seldom regarded as a social policy issue. Public controversy has centered predominantly on donor insemination (DI). Even though DI is often used in combination with other conceptive technologies, such as in vitro fertilization (IVF) and intracytoplasmic sperm injection (ICSI), a few countries (e.g., Brazil, Egypt, and Libya) prohibit DI but allow and may even encourage IVF. Many countries permitting DI impose restrictions on medical practitioners, donors, and recipients.

The practice gives rise to a tangle of legal problems about adultery, bloodlines, legitimacy, and the assignment of rights and duties to donors, recipients, and progeny. The position of the medical practitioner as intermediary raises additional policy issues: the permissible scope of physician discretion in selecting and screening donors and recipients and the use of eugenic criteria in pairing them. A third set of issues that has recently come under increased public scrutiny pertains to the widespread practice of withholding from children knowledge of their biological origins. Though varying cultural traditions may influence the ranking of these issues, all bear on public policy.

Separation of the Roles of Biological and Social Father

The assignment of paternal obligations varies with cultural traditions. For example, the French language distinguishes explicitly between biological father (géniteur) and social father (père). In English "to father a child" links paternity to the act of conceiving. Accordingly, French law incorporates the presumption that a mother's husband is the father of her child, whereas the English legal tradition places greater emphasis on the concept of illegitimacy. Hence the need for specific legislation to address the legal status of DI children is more pressing in some countries (Australia, Canada, and the United Kingdom) than others (France or Spain). Those with legal codes that did not already stipulate that the husband of a birth mother is the legal father have instituted legal reforms to that effect. A few include an exception if the husband or partner does not grant explicit consent to DI. Where other legal criteria are still used to establish paternity (e.g., the mother's marital status at the time of conception), the use of sperm donors may give rise to conflicting claims to paternal rights or concurrent disavowals of parental duties. Where physicians are required by law to maintain records identifying donors (see further on), donors are generally released from any future paternal obligations. Some countries have also made provisions for single women to have sole parental responsibility. A few explicitly prohibit access to DI by single women.

Intervention of Medical Practitioners

Costs to recipients vary considerably depending upon the screening procedures employed, the presence of underlying fertility problems, and variations in the practice of individual physicians. Some combine DI with procedures to determine the precise time of ovulation and others administer hyperovulatory drugs. National health programs cover all costs in a few countries. In the United States, insurance covers only about half the cost for half the recipients. Most countries permit payment of sperm donors, though some compensate only for transportation and lost working hours. French policy explicitly excludes payment in order to encourage altruistic donation.

Access to DI is often limited not only by medical factors but by such nonmedical considerations as marital status, sexual preference, age, and psychological characteristics. The Netherlands is the only country that specifically prohibits the exclusion of recipients on the basis of nonmedical criteria. Some countries explicitly exclude unmarried women (Sweden, Ireland). Others allow those in long-standing heterosexual relationships (France, Norway, the United Kingdom), and a few (Spain, Netherlands) also grant access to single women who meet certain criteria. The United Kingdom's Human Fertilisation and Embryology Act (1990) requires clinics administering the technique to take into account "the welfare of the child." The authority that implements the act was initially reluctant to stipulate factors clinics should consider. However, in the wake of news that a convicted sex offender was being treated for infertility, the authority did include a list of limiting factors in the fourth edition of its code of practice (U.K. Human Fertilisation and Embryology Authority 1998). Single women are not specifically excluded, but many practitioners withhold DI from all who are not in a stable heterosexual relationship. In countries that do not regulate medical practice, physicians customarily impose their own nonmedical criteria. A recent survey of clinics offering the service in the United States indicated that 80 percent of those who requested treatment were accepted and that over half of those rejected for nonmedical reasons were unmarried. By contrast, men who request semen storage for future AIH use are rarely, if ever, rejected for the reasons applied to women. In the United States recipients are twice as likely to be screened as donors.

Standards and Records

Standards of practice have changed considerably in recent years, increasing the need for a medical intermediary to administer what is basically a very simple procedure. The use of frozen sperm has become the norm to minimize risk of transmitting the HIV virus and other diseases, to identify transmissible genetic and chromosomal abnormalities, and to minimize frequent use of the same donor within small geographical areas. In 1985 the American Association of Tissue Banks published standards (widely used in many other countries) directing member sperm banks to use only frozen semen with a two-month quarantine period (since extended to six months) and periodic donor rescreening to test for the presence of disease. Similar standards were adopted by the American Fertility Society in 1986 (subsequently revised in 1988 and 1990). Yet in 1987 the U.S. Office of Technology Assessment found that 22 percent of those doing DI used only fresh sperm. Countries that regulate the practice directly are able to impose greater conformity with professional standards of quality control and technical proficiency. There is far less unanimity about the desirability of genetic screening, its extent, and the use of the physician administering the procedure as the screening agent. Many physicians are not adequately trained in genetics to screen donors, and clinics that practice the technique seldom have personnel qualified to provide well-informed genetic counseling. To minimize the risk of consanguineous (interrelated) marriage a number of countries limit the number of times the sperm of a single donor can be used. The specific number is usually relative to the size of the affected population. However, enforcement of such regulations requires meticulous record keeping and follow-up, particularly if frequency is to be correlated with birth rather than insemination.

Record keeping varies from informal records closeted in the offices of individual physicians to centralized repositories explicitly designated for the purpose. Past practice, which shrouded the DI transaction in secrecy, still influences record-keeping practices in many localities. In the United States only about half of the physicians who offer DI services keep records adequate to identify the donor. Physicians often value donor anonymity more highly than social and individual concerns about disease transmission, consanguineous marriage, or children's interests in obtaining information about their own origins. A number of countries have recently passed regulations mandating uniform record-keeping standards, both to facilitate enforcement of limitations on the permissible number of inseminations from a single donor and to balance the interests of donors, recipients, and potential children.

The French donor-insemination system, established in the early 1970s by Georges David, a physician with experience in hematology and blood banking who later specialized in the biology of sperm, has attracted widespread international attention. The French Federation of Centers for Cryopreservation of Eggs and Sperm (CECOS) now consists of twenty autonomous nonprofit organizations that regulate the acquisition, storage, and distribution of 90 percent of the frozen sperm used in France. Federation policy seeks to transform sperm donation into a socially acceptable solution to infertility by giving it altruistic meaning and eliminating the social stigma and ethical objections attached to it.

Several advisory commissions work to harmonize practice to correspond with policy and adapt it to changing medical and social conditions. They establish common technical and ethical standards and coordinate joint research projects. Donors must be married men who have at least one healthy child and have secured their wife's consent. Recipients must be heterosexual women who are either married or established in long-term relationships. The male partners of recipients must either be infertile or carriers of a serious disease transmitted by sperm. The relationship between the genetic parents is depersonalized by the maintenance of strict anonymity. The number of times a donor can contribute is carefully controlled.

Individual CECOS banks bring problem cases before the appropriate CECOS advisory commissions. Some involve genetic-screening practices that aim to match donor and recipient to minimize transmitting genetic anomalies. Embryo donation was not formerly offered by the CECOS banks (the National Ethics Commission having recommended against it), but new legislation (Loi de bioéthique, 1994) now allows for the practice. The federation has been faulted for its moralistic stance and inefficiency, since clinics often cannot secure enough sperm to meet recipient demand.

Children's interests have increasingly become a policy issue. Until recently, secrecy was favored both in medical literature and procedural guidelines. But increasing recognition of DI as a socially acceptable option undermines the rationale for deception. Also, because many countries now open adoption records to mature children, the practice of concealing comparable information from DI children is more difficult to justify. At issue is whether to provide to children (1) medical information about their biological parents and (2) specific information identifying the donor. A number of countries including Australia, Sweden, the United Kingdom, and Canada have recommended or established guidelines allowing the first. In 1985 Sweden became the first country to mandate the second; however, sperm can be provided only to married women whose husbands have given their irrevocable written consent to becoming a father, and paternity is strictly defined to preclude paternity lawsuits against the donor. The Swedish experience is being carefully observed as other countries continue to review their policies.

FOR FURTHER READING

Achilles, Rona. 1992. *Donor Insemination: An Overview.* A report for the Canadian Royal Commission on New Reproductive Technologies. Ottawa: Canadian Communications Group.

David, G., and J. Lansac. 1980. "The Organization of Centers for the Study and Preservation of Semen in France." In G. David and W. S. Price, eds., *Human Artificial Insemination and Semen Preservation.* New York: Plenum Press.

Glover, Jonathan, et al. 1989. *Fertility and the Family: The Glover Report on Reproductive Technologies to the European Commission.* London: Fourth Estate.

Jalbert, P., et al. 1989. "Genetic Aspects of Artificial Insemination with Donor Semen: The French CECOS Federation Guidelines." *American Journal of Medical Genetics* 33: 269–275.

Morgan, Derek, and Robert Lee, eds. 1991. *Blackstone's Guide to the Human Fertilisation and Embryology Act, 1990.* London: Blackstone Press.

Novaes, S. 1986. "Semen Banking and Artificial Insemination by Donor in France: Social and Medical Discourse." *International Journal of Technology Assessment in Health Care* 2: 219–229.

Novaes, S. 1989. "Giving, Receiving, Repaying: Gamete Donors and Donor Policies in Reproductive Medicine." *International Journal of Technology Assessment in Health Care* 5: 639–657.

Smart, Carol. 1987. "Law and the Problem of Paternity." In Michelle Stanworth, ed., *Reproductive Technologies: Gender, Motherhood and Medicine*. Minneapolis: University of Minnesota Press.

U.K. Human Fertilisation and Embryology Authority. 1998. *Code of Practice*. 4th ed. London: Human Fertilisation and Embryology Authority.

U.S. Congress, Office of Technology Assessment. 1988a. *Artificial Insemination: Practice in the United States*. Washington, D.C.: U.S. Government Printing Office.

U.S. Congress, Office of Technology Assessment. 1988b. *Infertility: Medical and Social Choices*. Washington, D.C.: U.S. Government Printing Office.

twenty-nine

Psychosocial Implications of Donor Insemination

RONA ACHILLES AND KEN DANIELS

General Psychosocial Implications

Similar to other reproductive technologies that separate sexual intercourse from reproduction, donor insemination (DI) can alter the usual parameters of time and space in reproductive behavior. Reproductive partners need no longer be in the same location at the same time. Indeed, they no longer need to meet or know each other in any way. Freezing of sperm allows for different time frames including the possibility that a man's sperm may be used to conceive a child after his death. In addition, sperm may be manipulated before insemination, as it is in sex predetermination techniques. As well, the medicalization of conception that occurs with DI moves conception from the private to the public realm and grants the medical profession control over who becomes a parent. This process also has eugenic consequences in the screening of both donors and recipients.

With artificial insemination by husband (AIH), the psychosocial implications are minimal, since aside from the stress associated with all infertility treatments, the practice of AIH replicates reproduction by two partners through sexual intercourse. In DI, the traditional interpersonal dynamics of reproduction are substantially altered. DI mothers conceive their children with men who are unknown to them. In many cases, they have no information about the biological father of their child. In some instances, depending on the discretion of the physician or sperm-bank policy, they may have nonidentifying information about the sperm donor. A DI father consents to his female partner conceiving and bearing the child of a man who is unknown to him and will rear a child whose biological father is perhaps unknowable. Children conceived through DI may or may not be told about their genetic origins. If they are told, it is not likely (unless they live in Sweden, Austria, or Victoria in Australia) that they will be able to find out any information about their biological fathers. In some practices, records are not kept linking participants, and even if they are kept, no access to them is possible. Sperm donors may be the biological fathers of many children about whom they know nothing.

These interpersonal dynamics of DI raise questions about what constitutes a family, the meaning of biological ties, and the consequences of anonymity and secrecy in the current practice of donor insemination. Women using self-insemination can negotiate different arrangements with their donors. Donors may be unknown or have a variety of different relationships with the recipient and resulting child. In other words, sperm donors may play roles as different as distant uncle or equal coparent. The implications of these arrangements are profound for both family structure and function. These arranged conceptions, much like arranged marriages, eliminate the romantic and sexual components integral to traditional parental relationships. Until new laws are created, however, the donor may pose a custody threat to women, such as lesbian DI mothers, who may be perceived as unfit by the courts.

The issue of secrecy or openness in relation to DI has much to do with societal factors. In its early history DI was vilified as adultery, an abomination against nature, and a threat to the institutions of marriage and the family, for example, by the archbishop of Canterbury in 1948. Even today, the practice is not covered in the media in the way that, for example, IVF is. The difficulty in recruiting donors from the public at large probably reflects general lack of awareness about DI rather than disapproval. Because of the uncertainty of public reaction, many doctors advise couples and donors to keep their participation a private matter. Under these circumstances, it would be easy to understand if donors felt they were taking part in something illicit and underhanded. There is a need for greater understanding of parenting relations resulting from DI. The separation of genitor from parenting functions has long been accepted in relation to adoption, yet community acceptance of this separation in relation to DI is still at an early stage. Problems with DI acceptance are connected with perceptions of legitimate fatherhood.

Psychosocial Issues for Men

One in six couples requires specialist help for infertility. It is thought that approximately 25 percent of infertility can be traced to a male factor, but infertility services are offered within the gynecological specialty of medicine, which has women as its focus. Very little attention has been devoted to male infertility except via donor insemination (DI), where the male partner may become a bystander as the doctors and his female partner work toward solving the problem for which he is seen to be responsible.

Two sets of men are involved in DI: the consumers (infertile men, men who risk passing on hereditary diseases, or men with irreversible vasectomies) and the providers (semen donors). The recipient male and the donor male are inextricably linked not at the physical or biological level but rather at the psychosocial level. The linkage and its meanings for both sets of men have not been explored in detail, partly because the donor is usually portrayed as donating to the couple. However, it is also important to acknowledge that the donor fulfills a function for the recipient male.

The Recipient Male

Typically the recipient male experiences as loss the inability to father a child biologically. As with all loss, there is grief and mourning. Many men are influenced by prevailing social and cultural attitudes, which prescribe that they should father children and which link procreation with the continuance of the human race. Each man responds to these societal attitudes according to the way he views himself, in particular to the value he accords himself.

Although behaviors are personal in that they emerge from the individual, they all manifest at the interpersonal and often social levels. A loss of libido or even potency, for example—albeit temporary with most men—is felt by the partner. She too may experience a loss of libido. Both are likely to question whether there is any point in having intercourse. The female partner may also be the focus of aggressive behavior. Many men, on discovering their infertility, withdraw and offer their partners a divorce or separation on the basis that they are not able to fulfill their social role and that the female should have a "second opportunity." It is important that before DI is entered into, the male and his partner have the opportunity to work through the grief and deal with the issues of self-esteem and relationship as well as the implications of donor insemination.

Another facet of interpersonal relationships is the social father's connection to his nongenetically related child or children. One of the concerns expressed by women prior to starting DI is whether their partners will relate well and normally to the child. However, there is evidence that these fathers develop, in the main, very strong bonds with children conceived via DI and participate in their upbringing more than many biological fathers do.

The infertile male has to adjust to being different from other males. His "normal" role cannot be fulfilled, and this circumstance affects his social relationships, particularly given the confusion in most societies concerning the link between sexuality and procreation. Infertile men report that other men link the inability to father children with sexual inadequacy. Fearing possible rejection and misunderstanding, many do not discuss their infertility with others. DI has been used as a way of protecting the male from stigmatization by giving the appearance that he and his partner have had children. Doctors used to encourage this subterfuge; now greater openness is encouraged.

Semen Donors

DI also has psychosocial implications for donors. They are drawn from many different sources: medical students attached to hospitals where infertility services are provided, fathers about to undergo vasectomies or whose wives are currently undergoing IVF treatment, members of the general public, and members of the doctors' own personal networks. Male volunteers may be drawn from a wide range of occupations and may be married or unmarried, heterosexual or homosexual. It appears that the characteristics of donors depend largely on the method of recruitment.

Many people question the motives of semen donors. In 1960, the Feversham Committee in the United Kingdom suggested that donors were abnormal and unbalanced. Today, many assume that donors participate for money only (as vendors rather than donors), but studies produce varied results. In the United States, several studies showed that about two-thirds of semen donors would be unwilling to donate if payment were withdrawn. In Australian and New Zealand studies, although money was mentioned by donors as a benefit, altruism was the main motivation. Other studies from elsewhere support this view, and in many countries either no payment at all or only compensation for expenses is provided. Among the many reasons hypothesized for donation are to help make up for a personal tragedy in the donor's life, to boost self-esteem, to satisfy curiosity about scientific procedures, and to have many progeny.

Semen donors wish, in the main, to be anonymous. This issue is especially important to the recipients of donor insemination. However, it is not uncommon for donors to express a desire to know whether offspring have resulted or to have information about the recipients. Studies have found that about half of donors think the child has a right to know of his or her genetic origins; almost the same number indicated that they would still donate if the child or children could contact them at the age of eighteen. Many other donors remain distanced from their actions, not wanting to know about the recipients or whether children resulted. The situation varies from country to country and study to study.

Traditionally, donors have been discouraged by practitioners from asking questions about the other parties in the DI transaction, but this approach fails to address the personal implications for the donor of his biological link with the offspring and his psychosocial link with the DI couple. In fact, the act of donating is broadly social as well as personal. The relationships the donor has with clinic staff, partner, and friends provide feedback that helps with the decisionmaking process. It is often the recognition by the donor's network of the act, rather than the act itself, that helps the donor feel good about his decision. This validation may help explain why most donors tell partners and friends—who also experience psychosocial effects. The donor's wife, for example, may have a variety of reactions to the idea of her husband's semen being used by another woman. She may even feel robbed or invaded by being asked to share her husband's procreative ability.

The recipients, the DI child, and the general community generally provide very little or no feedback to the donor. Commonly, donors have been discouraged from even thinking about the recipient couple and the resulting children. Although little work has been done in this area, it seems wrong to assume that the donor will have no thoughts or feelings about the couple he has assisted.

FOR FURTHER READING

Allen, N. C., et al. 1985. "Intrauterine Insemination: A Critical Review." *Fertility and Sterility* 44(5): 569–580.

American Fertility Society. 1990. "Ethical Considerations of the New Reproductive Technologies." *Fertility and Sterility* 53(6), supp. 2.

Archbishop of Canterbury, Report of a Commission Appointed by His Grace. 1948. *Artificial Human Insemination.* London: Society for the Propagation of Christian Knowledge.

Boyarsky, R., and J. Boyarsky. 1983. "Psychogenic Factors in Male Fertility: A Review." *Medical Aspects of Human Sexuality* 17: 86h–86t.

Czyba, J. C., and M. Chevret. 1979. "Psychological Reactions of Couples to Artificial Insemination with Donor Sperm." *International Journal of Fertility* 24: 240–245.

Daniels, K. R. 1986. "Psychosocial Issues Associated with Being a Semen Donor." *Clinical Reproduction and Fertility* 4: 341–351.

———. 1989. "Semen Donors: Their Motivations and Attitudes to Their Offspring." *Journal of Infant and Reproductive Psychology* 7: 121–127.

_____. 1991. "Relationships Between Semen Donors and Their Networks." *Australian Social Work* 44: 29–35.

Daniels, Ken, and Erica Haimes. 1998. *Donor Insemination: International Social Science Perspectives.* Cambridge: Cambridge University Press.

Holmes, H. B. 1988. "Risks of Infertility Diagnosis and Treatment." *Infertility: Medical and Social Choices.* Contractor documents, vol. 4. Washington, D.C.: Office of Technology Assessment.

Purdie, A., et al. 1992. "Identifiable Semen Donors: Attitudes of Donors and Recipient Couples." *New Zealand Medical Journal* 105: 27–28.

Robinson, J. N., R. G. Forman, A. M. Clark, D. M. Egan, M. G. Chapman, and D. H. Barlow. 1991. "Attitudes of Donors and Recipients to Gamete Donation." *Human Reproduction* 6: 307–309.

Rowland, R. 1983. "Attitudes and Opinions of Donors on an Artificial Insemination by Donor (AID) Programme." *Clinical Reproduction and Fertility* 2: 249–259.

Schover, L. R., R. L. Collins, and S. Richards. 1992. "Psychological Aspects of Donor Insemination: Evaluation and Follow-up of Recipient Couples." *Fertility and Sterility* 57: 583–590.

Snowden, R., and G. D. Mitchell. 1981. *The Artificial Family: A Consideration of Artificial Insemination by Donor.* London: George Allen and Unwin.

Snowden, R., G. D. Mitchell, and E. M. Snowden. 1983. *Artificial Reproduction: A Social Investigation.* London: George Allen and Unwin.

United Kingdom. Feversham Committee. 1960. *Report of the Departmental Committee on Human Artificial Insemination.* Cmnd 1105. London: Her Majesty's Stationery Office.

thirty

Lesbian Access to Donor Insemination

MARY ANNE COFFEY

Although donor insemination is essentially a simple procedure that has been medicalized, little is known about DI outside medical settings, and even less has been documented. The aura of secrecy that surrounds the medical practice of insemination has served to hide the evidence of male infertility in heterosexual couples and to limit public discussion of its important social and political ramifications. The tendency toward secrecy, and the widespread cultural preference for heterosexual couples as the ideal parental configuration for assisted reproduction, have meant that for lesbians (and single heterosexual women), access to DI through Westernized medical channels is extremely limited or nonexistent. For the same reasons, self-insemination has been a virtually invisible method of conception but one practiced increasingly by single women of heterosexual and lesbian persuasion (at least those living in Western liberal democracies).

The initial association of DI with medical practice and the married state continues and has influenced the formulation of criteria for the evaluation of recipients. As might be expected, these criteria tend to reduce or eliminate the chances of insemination for women who are not linked through a marital or common-law union to an infertile male partner. In the literature on single motherhood by choice (including DI as one reproductive option), the term "single women" includes a number of disparate groups, making meaningful comparison of research findings difficult. "Single" is commonly used to denote unmarried, never-married, separated, divorced, or widowed women, as well as those in common-law relationships similar to marriage. In addition, because the term indicates the lack of a legally recognized marital relationship to a male partner, it includes every lesbian woman whether or not she has a partner. A legal and social status (perhaps, more precisely, a lack of status) therefore becomes a criterion for offering or withholding a medical procedure.

The reasons given for limiting access by single women have included concern about the ability of single women to provide socially and economically for a child; the possible negative effects of an absent father on later sex-role behavior; fear that, if the mother is lesbian, the child may become homosexual or be stigmatized and that the mother's homosexual relationship may be unstable; and the possible illegality of inseminating single women. Although research fails to indicate any cause for alarm and despite the literature expressing at least guarded approval for accepting single and lesbian applicants, most DI practitioners continue to reject women without a male partner and consider lesbians to be unsuitable candidates for insemination.

Virtually every government that has considered access to DI (now commonly included with new reproductive technologies) by lesbians has advocated a restrictive approach. In the United Kingdom, for example, legislation restricts access to couples in a "loving, stable, heterosexual relationship." It is posited that it is generally better for children to be born into a two-parent family, with both father and mother, even though there is no substantiation of this hypothesis. (In the Warnock Report, which led to British legislation regarding reproductive technology, the authors acknowledge the fundamental weakness of the position: "We recognize that it is impossible to predict with any certainty how lasting such a relationship will be.") As Robert Blank points out, the question of allowing single or lesbian women access to DI has rarely been approached explicitly, and when it is, access is usually denied. More positive views include Spanish proposals for legislation to allow DI for single women and assisted reproduction for homosexuals and the 1993 report of the Canadian Royal Commission on New Reproductive Technologies, which recommends that lesbians have equal access to all assisted-reproduction services.

Although restricted access is almost universally advocated, few jurisdictions have actually attempted to impose legal sanctions on self-insemination, recognizing that enforcement would be impossible. Brazil, Egypt, and Libya prohibit DI entirely; twenty-one U.S. states require that DI be performed by a physician, with Georgia treating noncompliance as a felony. Some U.S. legal commentators have argued that restrictions on access to assisted reproduction by single women violate a constitutionally protected right to procreate. They advocate an expanded definition of family that recognizes in law the reality of lesbian and other nontraditional family configurations. In Canada, some federal and provincial government advisory bodies have clearly preferred that access to assisted reproduction be limited to married or common-law couples but have hesitated to recommend that restrictions on access by single women be legislated, fearing that such a restriction would violate provincial human rights codes. Currently, in both the United States and Canada, medical discretion is relied on to achieve heterosexually restricted access.

In many jurisdictions, limiting access to DI and attempting to police self-insemination (SI) is considered a restriction on reproductive choice and a violation of the basic human right to procreate. Due to the simplicity of the SI procedure, criminalization is virtually impossible to implement. Even though they are impractical to enforce, legislated limitations on access could reinforce an atmosphere of secrecy and make SI use covert. Making SI an underground process is not likely to be in the long-term best interests of children conceived in this manner. Ironically, attempts to discourage single women and lesbians from using DI may encourage and increase SI. There is already an increasing demand for DI by lesbians and single heterosexual women, and underground networks of women have developed since the early 1970s in the United Kingdom, the United States, and Canada to facilitate SI. Although very little research has been done anywhere on the use of nonclinical SI by single heterosexual and lesbian women, it is apparent that SI is expanding.

Technically, SI is a very simple procedure for most women; the most complex aspect of SI is finding a donor. Women who do not wish to be sexually involved with a man must find their own donor for SI. The spread of AIDS in the gay male population has reduced lesbians' insemination options, since gay men often acted as donors in the past. Gay or straight men who test negative for HIV infection over a six-month period and who use safe-sex practices in the interim are considered to be suitable donors. Safety concerns point to the need for increased access to anonymous HIV testing and to sperm banks. An unknown donor is the preference for lesbians who do not wish to risk a custody battle, and for single heterosexual women who prefer solo parenting. Since access to frozen sperm from anonymous donors is expensive and not generally available to lesbians, fresh sperm is often used. To ensure anonymity, an intermediary or sperm runner may be asked to transport the sample from donor to recipient. Despite custody concerns, lesbians who choose a known donor often choose a friend or relative of their partner. The biological father may actively parent the child or play a more distant role.

No exact figures on the number of births resulting from SI in any jurisdiction are available, although there is general agreement that it is a common practice and likely increasing. Estimates are that between 1,000 and 3,000 children in the United States and Europe have been conceived recently by lesbians using donor insemination. In 1985 it was reported that at least 1,500 unmarried women a year in the United States are artificially inseminated despite the difficulty of gaining access to DI services. Therefore it is likely that SI is used by a numerically small but significant minority of women. The SI movement has grown in both numbers and sophistication. Because of concern by single women and lesbians over possible custody disputes with a known sperm donor, contracts have been drafted; these remain untested in the courts. Recent debates have focused on the possible harmful effect on children of having an unknown and unknowable donor father, since knowledge of one's biological parents is considered to be socially and medically important in Western societies.

Since the simplicity of the SI procedure makes attempts at regulation futile, a sensible public policy approach would ensure, minimally, that anonymous HIV testing be widely available. In terms of nondiscrimination, access to sperm banks, DI programs, and all other reproductive and fertility services should be accessible to all women without regard to marital status or sexual orientation. Lesbians (together with gay men, poor people, individuals with physical challenges other than infertility, and people of color) know that the usual criteria for entry into assisted-reproduction programs privilege heterosexual marital relationships and those with the ability to pay for lengthy and expensive medical procedures. It is therefore likely that lesbians simply do not attempt admission to new reproductive technology clinics even if they have a fertility impairment. This does not mean that lesbians who do seek access to new reproductive technologies (NRTs) and DI do so without question or that they are disinterested bystanders. In countries where lesbian and feminist political movements emerged as NRTs were proliferating rapidly and receiving widespread media coverage, gay and lesbian activists have challenged the possible negative health and social effects of NRTs on women and children, the inflated success rates of NRTs, and the discriminatory policies of NRTs and DI.

FOR FURTHER READING

Arnup, Katherine, ed. 1995. *Lesbian Parenting: Living with Pride and Prejudice.* Charlottetown, P.E.I.: Gynergy Books.

Blank, Robert H. 1990. *Regulating Reproduction.* New York: Columbia University Press.

Harvard Law Review. 1990. "Sexual Orientation and the Law." Cambridge: Harvard University Press.

Hornstein, Francine, and Cheri Pies. 1988. "Baby M and the Gay Family." *Outlook* 1: 78–85.

Kritchevsky, Barbara. 1981. "The Unmarried Woman's Right to Artificial Insemination: A Call for an Expanded Definition of Family." *Harvard Women's Law Journal* 4: 1–42.
United Kingdom. 1990. *Human Fertilisation and Embryology Act, 1990.*
Warnock Committee. 1984. *Report of the Committee of Enquiry into Human Fertilisation and Embryology.* London: Her Majesty's Stationery Office.

thirty-one

Male Infertility

DOUGLAS T. CARRELL AND
RONALD L. URRY

It was traditionally assumed by many scientists and clinicians that the female was nearly always responsible for problems with reproduction. This attitude undoubtedly slowed advances in male reproductive physiology; fortunately, this situation is gradually changing. First, males are beginning to understand their role and responsibility in fertility and infertility. Second, sensitive and informed practitioners and health care personnel are becoming more available to work with men undergoing testing and treatment, helping to reduce the humiliation and embarrassment previously common to male infertility patients. Last, recent advances in testing for and treating sperm defects have dramatically changed the prognosis for many patients. Because of these changes in society, medical training, and scientific knowledge, evaluation and treatment of male infertility have become both common and highly successful.

Diagnosis of Male Fertility Potential

Semen Analysis

Semen analysis is the first test used to determine a male's fertility potential; in some areas it may be the only test available. It is often poorly performed by technicians with little or no training, in which case the minimal information obtained does not greatly aid in the diagnosis of a potential male fertility problem. In addition, semen quality can be extremely variable in any given male and thus a minimum of two to three separate analyses is necessary to determine a male's fertility potential. When performed accurately and completely, the semen analysis can provide valuable information in diagnosing and treating male fertility difficulties.

Males are usually asked to abstain from ejaculation for two to five days prior to a semen test. If the abstinence period is less than two days and the semen count or seminal fluid volume is diminished, it is difficult to know if the condition is a persistent one or due to the short sexual abstinence period. Longer abstinence periods (over seven to ten days) can result in decreased sperm motility and function.

To minimize environmental variables, the male should provide the sample in the laboratory. If an appropriate room is not available or the male can collect the sample only at another location, he is instructed to do so in a sterile, wide-mouthed container; put the lid on tightly; wrap the container in a dry towel; put the towel in a paper bag; and bring the sample into the laboratory within thirty to sixty minutes. The sample should be kept at body temperature during transport. If a male can collect a sample only by intercourse, special nonspermatocidal condoms can be provided by the laboratory. The condom is then dropped into the sterile container, and the sample is transported as described.

Once the sample has been collected, it is allowed to liquefy for twenty to thirty minutes before the analysis begins. The sample is looked at carefully, and the color is recorded. The following measurements are obtained:

1. Semen Volume. A normal volume of ejaculate is between two and five milliliters. A minimum volume of greater than one and a half milliliters ensures adequate fluid for the sperm to make good contact with the female cervical mucus after the sperm have been deposited into the vagina. Low volumes can indicate partial duct obstruction, infections, or other problems that could contribute to fertility difficulties.

2. Semen Viscosity. The thickness of the fluid is assessed on a semiquantitative scale. Samples that are highly viscous and do not liquefy within thirty minutes to one hour after collection often possess low sperm motility, reflecting possible fertility difficulties.

3. Sperm Motility. A drop of well-mixed seminal fluid is placed on a warm microscope slide and observed at both low and high power underneath a microscope. Numerous areas of the slide are observed before making a final motility determination. The percentage of sperm in each of five categories is estimated: sperm not moving (level 0), sperm with an "in place" or "shaking" motion (level 1), sperm with a random direction and sluggish speed (level 2), and sperm moving in a linear fashion with moderate speed (level 3) or good speed (level 4). Ideally at least 40 percent of the sperm should move with progressive motility (linear with

moderate to good speed, or levels 3 and 4). Low motility in an ejaculate could indicate several potential problems and result in a lower probability that sufficient sperm will get to the site of fertilization, which is normally high in the woman's fallopian tube. Therefore, quantitative sperm motility does correlate to male fertility potential.

Computer-aided sperm analysis (CASA) has recently been introduced and defines sperm-motility parameters such as curvilinear velocity, straight-line velocity, and lateral head displacement. Recent studies have indicated a correlation between sperm velocity and fertilizing ability. CASA technology offers new possibilities for the evaluation of sperm motility, and problems with consistency and accuracy are being resolved by improved quality-control measures and improved sperm-tracking capabilities.

4. Viability. Sperm are stained, most commonly with a simple eosin and nigrosin staining technique, to determine the structural integrity of the membrane. Live and dead sperm are counted with at least 50 percent live sperm considered normal. Decreased sperm viability may be associated with abnormal spermatogenesis and the presence of antisperm antibodies.

5. Hypo-Osmolarity Sensitivity. Fertilization is preceded by several changes in the sperm membrane function: capacitation, the acrosome reaction, binding to the zona pellucida, and fusion with the plasma membrane. The hypo-osmotic sperm-function assay (also referred to with the acronym HOS) evaluates sperm membrane function. Sperm are placed in a hypo-osmotic fluid, and if the membrane function is normal the sperm tails coil. Currently at least 60 percent of sperm with a normal membrane function is considered normal overall; an HOS score of less than 60 percent may be associated with decreased fertilization ability.

6. Sperm Morphology. Sperm-head shape defects can be an important predictor of male fertility problems. Certain kinds of head-shape defects (tapered sperm) can be caused by anatomical defects such as a varicocele (described further on). Two methods are most commonly employed for the critical analysis of sperm morphology. In the modified World Health Organization (WHO) technique, sperm are stained with hematoxylin and eosin and several hundred cells are counted. The counted sperm cells are divided into seven head-shape groups and then recounted and divided into seven tail-shape groups.

The Krueger, or "strict criteria," analysis employs a technique of measuring the length and width of the sperm and classifying sperm as normal only if they are within the prescribed ranges of normality. This technique results in a lower percentage of sperm classified as normal and hence is termed the "strict" evaluation. Also, it loses the advantage of classifications that include abnormal categories of sperm. Both the WHO and strict-criteria techniques have been shown to have some correlation with actual fertilizing ability.

7. Sperm Concentration. Historically, sperm concentration was the major parameter of the semen analysis. It is currently considered one of the least important correlates to male fertility potential, and a minimum count of 30 million progressively motile sperm per ejaculate is considered acceptable. Some couples achieve an unassisted pregnancy with borderline sperm counts; others remain infertile with much higher sperm counts. The latter situation is undoubtedly due to the fact that a high sperm count in no way implies normal sperm fertilizing ability. It is important to remember that fertilization and implantation are dependent on normal sperm, egg, and uterine function, and therefore it is difficult to predict fertility solely on the basis of the number of sperm unless the count is extremely diminished.

Sperm concentration can fall to a point where it is unlikely that a sufficient number of sperm will be able to reach the egg and result in fertilization. Patients with diminished sperm counts that cannot be improved with medical or surgical treatments (see further on) are candidates for sperm concentration and artificial insemination. If the count is extremely decreased, intracytoplasmic sperm injection (ICSI) is a recently developed therapy that can be employed.

8. Sperm Agglutination. Sperm are observed carefully to determine if they are "sticking" together. Sperm that tend to stick together may indicate a seminal infection or the presence of sperm antibodies. Sperm antibodies bind to specific regions of the sperm, resulting in characteristic patterns of sperm agglutination.

9. White Blood Cells. If the semen sample has increased numbers of round or amorphous cells, it is carefully stained to make sure that these are not white blood cells. Large numbers of white blood cells might indicate a reproductive tract infection in the male.

A carefully conducted series of semen analyses gives information as to whether the sperm may be able to reach the site of fertilization. Some information is also obtained as to whether the sperm can fertilize the egg. None of the parameters of the semen analysis, either alone or in combination, perfectly predict a given male's fertility potential. However, the semen analysis can provide direction for further testing and treatment.

Sperm Antibodies

As mentioned, some men have antibodies in their serum and seminal fluid that are directed against their own sperm. Upon ejaculation, these antibodies mix with the sperm and cause them to stop moving, exhibit a shaking motion, agglutinate in characteristic patterns, or, possibly, alter membrane function. Antibodies can interfere with both sperm motility and fertilizing ability. Although any male may have antibodies, the likelihood of having them is greatly increased if the patient has previously had a vasectomy and subsequent vasectomy reversal, reproductive tract surgery, a history of undescended testicles, or trauma to the testicles.

The presence of antibodies can be evaluated in the seminal fluid or serum by a number of assays. The most commonly used is the immunobead, in which antibodies can be detected either directly (bound to the patient's own sperm) or indirectly (in the patient's serum or seminal fluid). In the direct immunobead assay, washed sperm are incubated with microscopic beads coated with one of several types of antibodies. The beads bind to sperm coated with antisperm antibodies, and the percentage of motile sperm with attached beads is calculated. In the indirect assay, the patient's serum or seminal fluid is incubated with donor sperm, then assayed. Additional antisperm antibody assays include the Kibrick macroagglutination assay and the Isojima sperm-immobilizing assay. These assays together give an accurate evaluation of the type and degree of antisperm antibody activity.

Sperm-Function Assays

Within the female reproductive tract, sperm undergo a series of biochemical changes, termed "capacitation," that include an influx of calcium and an increased fluidity of the membranes. Sperm capacitation is requisite for the acrosome reaction and fertilization to occur. Inability to capacitate will prevent sperm from binding to the egg, the acrosome reaction, and fertilization.

Recently assays have been developed that evaluate the ability of in vitro–capacitated sperm to undergo the acrosome reaction following stimulation by calcium ionophore, human follicular fluid, or other chemical simulators of the acrosome reaction. The percentage of sperm undergoing the simulated acrosome reaction is usually evaluated by staining the sperm with a fluorescent probe specific for the acrosome, along with a viability stain. Only viable sperm are analyzed, since nonviable sperm may undergo a degenerative loss of the acrosome. This assay may provide valuable data to aid in an assessment of the fertilizing ability of sperm.

The most accurate test to determine sperm fertilization capability is the hamster egg–human sperm penetration test (HEPT), also known as the sperm penetration assay (SPA). This assay, when performed under a refined and strict assay protocol, has a high correlation to subsequent male fertility potential. In this process, hamster eggs with chemically removed zona pellucidae are incubated with sperm prepared in a manner similar to in vitro fertilization techniques. The assay determines if the sperm can capacitate and subsequently penetrate the zona-free hamster eggs. If the sperm can penetrate more than 15–20 percent of the zona-free hamster eggs, the probability is high that the sperm can fertilize human eggs. Decreased penetration ability is associated with a reduced ability to fertilize both in vitro and in vivo. Recent techniques aimed at improving capacitation and penetration ability via chemical stimulation, as measured by the SPA, have shown promise clinically.

The hemizona assay utilizes one-half of a human egg's outer membrane and determines if sperm can bind to this membrane. This test has been reported to correlate with fertilizing ability in vitro. The unavailability of human zonae and the technical nature of this test have limited its availability and practicality.

Physical Exam, Endocrine, and Other Evaluations

Other tests may be important in diagnosing male fertility potential. A carefully conducted physical examination determines testicular size and consistency. Since the size of the testicles is in large part due to the cells that produce sperm, smaller and firmer testicles generally indicate fewer sperm-producing cells. Physical examination is also useful to evaluate if a varicocele is present. A varicocele is a group of swollen testicular veins that usually occurs above the left testicle but can occur above either or both. One theory for the deleterious effect of varicoceles is that the swollen vessels carry increased blood to the region. Blood carries heat, and studies have shown that heat has an adverse effect on spermatogenesis. Varicoceles are often associated with altered sperm-head shapes, increased percentages of tapered sperm, decreased sperm motility, increased variability among samples, decreased sperm concentration, and other variations in sperm function. About 7–11 percent of men in the general population have a varicocele. In couples with fertility difficulties, as many as 40 percent of men have a varicocele. It is generally assumed that if a male has a varicocele of moderate size and if the varicocele appears to be having a detrimental effect on parameters of the semen analysis, the male should have the varicocele surgically removed. Removal of a large varicocele gives the male a 50–70 percent chance of having a measurable improvement in sperm quality and gives the couple a 20–50 percent chance of pregnancy.

In men who have an extremely low sperm concentration, it may be important to evaluate the reproductive hormones such as testosterone, follicle-stimulating hormone, luteinizing hormone, and prolactin. The measurement of these hormones enables the physician to determine if there is an endocrine cause for the infertility and determine if the testicles ought to be producing sperm. When the testicles lose the ability to produce sperm, follicle-stimulating-hormone levels generally rise in the male's blood due to the lack of negative feedback. By evaluating the level of this hormone in the blood, one can learn a reasonable amount about testicular function.

In patients with a decreased ejaculate volume, rectal ultrasound may be used to determine if there is an obstruction of the vas deferens and small tubes that carry the sperm from the testes. Likewise, a vasogram—a procedure where dye is put through the vas deferens (the major tubes that carry sperm)—might be ordered. These tests aid in identifying blockages that prevent sperm from being released. A male with virtually no sperm might be asked to have a testicular biopsy; a small piece of tissue is taken to determine what kinds of cells are present in the testicle and why the testicle is not producing more sperm.

Treatments for Male Reproductive Problems

Surgical Treatment

1. Varicocele Removal. As previously discussed, if a male has a varicocele, his partner is without fertility problems, and his sperm quality indicates varicocele-like alterations, surgical removal of the varicocele is warranted. Since this procedure is expensive and often results in no visible improvement of semen quality, laboratory improvement of semen quality and artificial insemination are often attempted for a reasonable period of time prior to surgery.

2. Epididymal Sperm Aspiration. Some men are born with an absence of the vas deferens, which carries sperm out of the testes. In other cases these tubules can become blocked due to scarring, obstruction, or prior vasectomy. In these cases sperm can be obtained directly from the small segment of tubes connected to the testicle (epididymis) and used to attempt pregnancy. Usually insufficient numbers of sperm are recovered to allow intrauterine insemination; however, success rates using intracytoplasmic sperm injection are good.

3. Vasectomy Reversal. Some men who have had a vasectomy eventually decide that they would like to have it reversed. Reversal involves cleaning out any residual scar tissue and reconnecting the tubes. Approximately 40–55 percent of men who have a vasectomy reversal are able to contribute to a pregnancy. The prognosis is dependent on the length of time since the vasectomy.

Medical Treatment

Unfortunately, there are no reasonable medical treatments that predictably increase the capacity of the testicle to produce sperm or increase the quality of the sperm produced. Several endocrine therapies, including medications such as clomiphene, human chorionic gonadotropin, and tamoxifen, have been used in an attempt to improve the numbers and quality of sperm. Males who have particular hormonal imbalances may be successfully treated with these medications. However, the vast majority of subfertile men are not benefited by endocrine therapy.

Laboratory-Assisted Treatment

A major advance in male fertility was developed in the early 1990s. Practitioners take a semen sample, manipulate it to concentrate the sperm, and attempt to improve sperm quality. The manipulated sperm can then be used for inseminations or advanced reproductive techniques. Some couples can benefit by simply collecting the sperm on the woman's day of ovulation and, following sperm washing (to enhance fertilizing capacity), placing the sperm directly into the uterus. Other patients benefit from more advanced laboratory techniques that improve sperm motility or fertilizing ability or that remove white blood cells or debris from the sample. For that reason, five or six cycles of intrauterine insemination are often tried before other more costly and advanced techniques. In addition, the female may be placed on drugs to cause more than one egg to mature. This "hyperovulation" provides more targets for the sperm to reach and potentially fertilize. Hyperovulation is generally tried for two to four cycles and is an intermediate step between regular inseminations and more advanced reproductive techniques in the female.

Advanced Reproductive Techniques

In the 1980s and 1990s a number of advanced reproductive techniques have been developed to treat problems that prevent the sperm from reaching the egg or limit the ability of the sperm to fertilize the egg. These techniques include in vitro fertilization (IVF), where the clinician takes sperm of poor quality and manipulates them in vitro to improve their ability to fertilize the eggs. This ability to obtain fertilization in even the most severe cases of male infertility has revolutionized its treatment. Two key developments have resulted in the ability, for almost any male with some spermatozoa, to fertilize eggs in vitro. First, chemical treatments including sperm refrigeration in a high-albumin solution, heparin treatment, or calcium ionophore treatment have been shown to stimulate capacitation and improve fertilizing ability in men with fertilization defects.

The second, dramatic development is a refinement in sperm micromanipulation techniques to the point where samples with very few sperm, and in some cases from patients who have previously been told that they have a complete lack of spermatozoa, can be used and the eggs injected directly with sperm. Intracytoplasmic sperm injection (ICSI) is now routinely used in a wide range of instances including severely decreased sperm counts, fertilization defects, and motility defects. Sperm obtained by epididymal aspiration or testicular biopsy are routinely used for ICSI. A recent study has shown that as many as 40 percent of patients previously diagnosed as azoospermic by testicular biopsy may have limited regions of active spermatogenesis from which sperm can be obtained by biopsy and used for ICSI. Pregnancy rates are nearly equal for ICSI and standard in vitro fertilization. A slight increase in sex-chromosome anomalies has been observed in children conceived by ICSI. No overall increase in birth defects has been reported at this early stage.

FOR FURTHER READING

Hillier, S. G., H. C. Kitchener, and J. P. Neilson, eds. 1996. *Scientific Essentials of Reproductive Medicine*. London: W. B. Saunders.

Keel, B. A., and B. W. Webster, eds. 1990. *Handbook of the Laboratory Diagnosis and Treatment of Infertility*. Boca Raton, Fla.: CRC Press.

Nieschlag, E., and H. M. Behre. 1997. *Andrology: Male Reproductive Health and Dysfunction*. Berlin: Springer-Verlag.

Rowe, P. J., et al., eds. 1993. *World Health Organization Manual for the Standardized Investigation and Diagnosis of the Infertile Couple*. Cambridge: Cambridge University Press.

Schumann, G. B., ed. 1985. "Laboratory Diagnosis of Male Infertility." *Clinics in Laboratory Medicine*. Philadelphia: W. B. Saunders.

Smith, J. A., ed. 1992. "Advances in Diagnosing and Treating Sperm Problems and Advanced Reproductive Techniques." In *High Tech Urology*. Philadelphia: W. B. Saunders.

Spark, R. F. 1988. *The Infertile Male—The Clinician's Guide to Diagnosis and Treatment*. New York: Plenum.

Yu, H. S. 1994. *Human Reproductive Biology*. Boca Raton, Fla.: CRC Press.

thirty-two

Ovulation Induction

PATRICIA A. STEPHENSON

Ovulation induction (hyperstimulation) involves stimulating the ovaries with chemical preparations commonly known as "fertility drugs" in order to encourage the maturation of multiple ovarian follicles. Ovulation induction may be used as a medical treatment for infertility or as a preparatory step for artificial insemination or more recently developed assisted-conception techniques. Fertility drugs have been used clinically or experimentally since the 1960s. The most commonly used drugs to induce ovulation are clomiphene citrate and human menopausal gonadotropin. More recently, ovarian stimulation for assisted-conception techniques has been preceded by the use of a gonadotropin-releasing hormone agonist. This review, however, focuses on the earlier drugs.

Pharmacology of Clomiphene Citrate

Mechanism of Action

Clomiphene citrate (or clomiphene) is a synthetic, nonsteroidal, triphenylethylene compound. The triphenylethylenes include several structurally related compounds with the ability to bind estrogen receptors in the hypothalamus: diethylstilbestrol (DES), chlorotrianisene, tamoxifen, and nafoxidine. The precise mechanism of action has not been determined, but triphenylethylenes are believed to displace locally produced estrogens from the hypothalamus in the brain, thereby augmenting the release of follicle-stimulating hormone and luteinizing hormone. This action results in the development and maturation of ovarian follicles and ova (eggs).

Dosage and Metabolic Rate

Clomiphene is given orally and is absorbed by the gastrointestinal tract. Its exact metabolism has not been established, but it appears to be metabolized in the liver and excreted in the feces. The half-life is five days, and it takes six weeks to excrete completely. It may be stored in body fat and released very slowly and accumulates at significant levels in women receiving multiple courses of therapy. The usual recommended dose is 50 milligrams per day for five days. The dosage should be increased only in those women who do not respond to a first course of therapy and should never exceed 100 milligrams per day for five days. However, standard, empirically derived, clinical protocols for ovulation induction using clomiphene involve administration of doses with upper limits of 250 milligrams daily for five days.

Uses

Clomiphene was originally intended for use in women with demonstrated ovulatory dysfunction not due to primary pituitary failure, thyroid disease, or adrenal disease. In early clinical work it was also used experimentally to treat menstrual irregularity in women not trying to conceive, endometriosis, anaplasia, or nonsystemic cancer and as a means of regulating the menstrual cycle to improve the efficacy of the rhythm method of contraception. It has also been used to treat oligospermia (low sperm count) in men.

Clomiphene is still used as a medical treatment for infertility. It is used to treat anovulatory and ovulatory women prior to artificial insemination in order to increase their chances of conception. It is used alone or in combination with chorionic gonadotropin or menotropins to stimulate the development of multiple follicles and ova in ovulatory and anovulatory women undergoing medically assisted conception. Occasionally, it is used to improve fertility in men with oligospermia.

Pharmacology of Human Menopausal Gonadotropin

Human menopausal gonadotropin (hMG), or menotropins, is a purified extract of human female urine containing follicle-stimulating hormone (FSH) and luteinizing hormone (LH). In women it stimulates the growth and maturation of ovarian follicles. The exact metabolism of hMG has not been determined. About 8 percent is excreted in urine unchanged. The half-lives of FSH and LH are biphasic and are reported to be four hours and twenty minutes, respectively, in the initial phase and seventy and four hours, respectively, in the terminal phase. hMG is administered by injections of 75 international units each of FSH and LH daily for nine to twelve days and should not be administered any longer. Dosages may be increased but should not exceed 150 international units of either hormone per day.

hMG followed by human chorionic gonadotropin (hCG) is used to induce ovulation and pregnancy in anovulatory infertile women in whom the cause of anovulation is pituitary (hormone production) insufficiency and not the result of ovarian failure. hMG may be used to induce ovulation in women with more severe ovulatory dysfunction who fail to respond to clomiphene. hMG may be used in conjunction with artificial insemination and in vitro fertilization (IVF). Less frequently, hMG is used with hCG to stimulate sperm production in men with primary or secondary hypogonadotropic hypogonadism.

Known Adverse Effects of Ovulation Induction

Minor Side Effects

The frequency and severity of side effects from clomiphene and hMG are dose related. Minor side effects (i.e., those that are not life threatening but may cause considerable discomfort or distress) are common and include ovarian enlargement, ovarian cysts, abdominal distention and bloating, nausea and vomiting, diarrhea, dermatitis, rapid weight gain, and shortness of breath. Women treated with clomiphene have also reported midcycle ovarian pain, hot flashes, heavier menses, increased appetite, increased urinary frequency, nervous tension, depression, mood swings, breast discomfort, headache, restlessness, insomnia, dizziness, lightheadedness, fatigue, reversible hair loss, and visual disturbances (blurry vision, afterimages, double vision, phosphenes, photophobia).

Multiple Pregnancy

Perhaps the most common serious side effect of ovulation induction is multiple pregnancy. Even with improved ovulation-induction protocols and intensive monitoring, it has never been possible to control precisely the number of ovarian follicles and ova that develop. When ovulation induction is used in conjunction with assisted-conception techniques (i.e., in vitro fertilization), the likelihood of pregnancy is dependent on the number of embryos transferred. This fact has encouraged the practice of transferring three or more embryos per treatment attempt. The probability of a multiple pregnancy increases with the number of embryos transferred.

Reported multiple-pregnancy rates after ovulation induction range from 8 to 13 percent when clomiphene is used and 9 to 43 percent when hMG is used. Population-based series in several countries report multiple-pregnancy rates of approximately 25 percent for assisted-conception births. The expected incidence of multiple pregnancy is less than 2 percent.

Perinatal Mortality

Perinatal mortality is high among babies born after infertility treatment. This is in large part due to the increased frequency of multiple pregnancy and to the fact that multiple births tend to be premature. Those who survive are at increased risk for major neurological handicaps: cerebral palsy, mental retardation, and sensory impairments. Perinatal mortality rates after ovulation induction only, calculated from data reported in case series, range from 0 to 262 per 1,000. When the data from the various studies are combined, the perinatal mortality rate is 45.2 per 1,000. This rate is two or three times higher than the population perinatal mortality rates for the same Western industrialized countries during similar time periods.

Perinatal mortality is no less a problem for assisted-conception pregnancies. Population-based series of the births resulting from assisted-conception techniques report perinatal mortality rates of 27.2 and 44.2 per 1,000. These rates are three and four times higher than the population rates for the respective countries.

Ovarian Hyperstimulation Syndrome

The ovarian hyperstimulation syndrome in women exposed to clomiphene and hMG is another important iatrogenic consequence of infertility treatment. The syndrome is characterized by a marked increase in vascular permeability and the rapid accumulation of fluid in the peritoneal, pleural, and pericardial cavities. These conditions, in turn, may lead to hypovolemia, hemoconcentration, electrolyte imbalance, ascites, hemoperitoneum, pleural effusion, hydrothorax, acute pulmonary distress, thromboembolism, thrombophlebitis, pulmonary embolism, stroke, arterial occlusion necessitating limb amputation, atelectasis, or death. Although there are several case reports of severe ovarian hyperstimulation syndrome with clomiphene, the affliction is more common, severe, and protracted with hMG or hCG combined with other drugs. In case series, the modal incidence of the severe form is about 1 to 2 percent. Ovarian hyperstimulation syndrome is extremely rare following natural conception.

Suspected Adverse Effects of Ovulation Induction

Extrauterine Pregnancy

Extrauterine pregnancy (ectopic pregnancy or heterotopic pregnancy) may be another serious side effect of infertility treatment, and there are several explanations for its increased incidence. Tubal adhesions, a cause of infertility, increase the risk of ectopic pregnancy. It has also been suggested that the probability of ectopic pregnancy increases according to the number of ovulations. Additionally, the high estrogen levels that result from treatment with fertility drugs may cause "tubal locking" wherein the ovum becomes isolated in a particular segment of the fallopian tube as a consequence of dysfunctional tubal contractions. Finally, the techniques used for embryo transfer in assisted-conception procedures may be associated with ectopic pregnancy.

There have been at least forty-nine reported cases of heterotopic pregnancy associated with ovulation induction alone or as part of assisted-conception techniques. Abdominal, cervical, and bilateral tubal pregnancies have been reported as well. The incidence of heterotopic pregnancy in induced pregnancies is estimated at 1 in 100, whereas in the general population, it is estimated to occur in 1 in 300 to 1 in 8,000 pregnancies.

Several case series reports do not mention ectopic pregnancy as an outcome of ovulation induction; others report its incidence after treatment to be approximately 1–5 percent. One population-based, case-control study found that the risk for ectopic pregnancy was elevated tenfold among women who had used clomiphene during the pregnancy. The majority of the exposed women, at the time of surgery, were found to have pelvic adhesions. Therefore, the elevated risk associated with clomiphene can be explained if the pelvic adhesions were related to clomiphene therapy. The reported incidence of ectopic pregnancy following assisted conception is more consistent, ranging from 5 to 7 percent. The incidence in the general population is about 1 percent.

Congenital Anomalies

More controversial is the hypothesis that ovulation induction may be a risk factor for congenital anomalies. Clomiphene has been of particular concern because it is structurally similar to DES. Clomiphene is contraindicated during pregnancy, but fetal exposure can still occur (see further on). Clomiphene has been shown in rats and rabbits to cause a variety of congenital abnormalities including cataracts, stunted limbs, cleft palate, and hydrocephalus. Limb malformations in mice following hMG exposure have been reported, but the finding has not been replicated.

Several studies have demonstrated increased chromosomal aberrations in mouse and rabbit embryos exposed to ovulation-induction agents in utero. Other studies in animal models support the hypothesis that clomiphene may produce defects similar to those that result from in utero exposure to DES. In rats and mice, clomiphene produces cellular changes in vaginal, uterine, and fallopian tube structures similar to those seen after DES exposure. The same malformations have been observed in human vaginal tissue grafted to host mice and exposed to low doses of clomiphene.

In humans, clomiphene and hMG increase significantly the incidence of chromosomal abnormalities in the embryo. One study of 1,500 first-trimester spontaneous abortions found that the rates of genetic abnormalities in fetuses exposed to ovulation-induction drugs during fertilization or in the cycle prior to fertilization were similar and higher than normal at 83 and 86 percent, respectively. Only 60 percent of abortuses from women who had not taken drugs and 61 percent of abortuses from women who had taken drugs two or more cycles prior to fertilization had genetic abnormalities. Clinical evidence varies. Numerous case reports have appeared in the literature linking clomiphene and hMG exposure of embryos to a number of abnormalities including neural tube defects, major cardiac anomalies, congenital absence of kidneys, Down syndrome, congenital retinopathy, fetal ovarian cysts and dysplasia, clubfoot, blocked tear duct, cleft lip or palate, and polydactyly (more than the usual number of fingers and toes). Yet in case series, the overall incidence of congenital anomalies in infants exposed as embryos to clomiphene or hMG is no higher than the incidence in the general population.

In population-based series of assisted-conception births, the overall incidence of congenital anomalies was nearly the same as the normal population incidence. However, the incidence of central nervous system malformations among assisted-conception babies was twice that expected. Similarly, data from birth-defects registries have shown an elevated incidence of neural tube defects among babies exposed as embryos to ovulation-induction drugs. Case-control studies examining the suspected association between ovulation-induction drugs and neural tube defects have produced mixed results.

Cancer

Ovulation induction may be a risk factor for certain types of cancers, particularly ovarian cancer. There are two main hypotheses. First, "incessant" ovulation may lead to malignant transformation. Ovulation involves repeated disruption and minor mechanical trauma to the ovarian surface. With hyperovulation, the surface may become entrapped to form an inclusion cyst. Estrogen or estrogen precursors and gonadotropins may then be involved in the differentiation, proliferation, and eventual malignant transformation of the entrapped surface. Second, persistent stimulation of the ovary by gonadotropins may have a direct carcinogenic effect or may act in conjunction with elevated concentrations of estrogens. Excessive estrogen secretion has been implicated in ovarian, endometrial, and breast cancer, and gonadotropin secretion has been implicated in ovarian cancer. These hypotheses are supported by evidence, albeit indirect, of a protective effect from factors that afford ovarian physiological rest periods (i.e., many pregnancies, lactation, late menarche, early menopause, and oral contraceptive use). Data to support concerns about a possible association between ovarian cancer and exposure to ovulation-induction drugs are accruing. There are several reported cases of ovarian and breast cancer following treatment with clomiphene or hMG.

Few investigations evaluate directly the risks for cancer associated with ovulation induction. One study of cancer in a cohort of infertile women found no increase in cancer incidence associated with exposure to fertility drugs but a moderately increased risk of breast cancer in women having hormonal infertility; women with other causes of infertility had an excess risk of cancer of the ovary and thyroid. In this study it was concluded that infertile women treated with drugs to induce ovulation did not have a higher risk of cancer than nontreated infertile women, but rather hormonal infertility preceding treatment increased the risk of developing hormone-associated cancers. A recent collaborative analysis of twelve case-control studies refuted this conclusion, finding that among women who had never been pregnant, the risk of ovarian cancer was twenty-seven times higher if fertility drugs had been taken. At most, only a small fraction of excess risk was due to infertility per se.

Hydatidiform Mole

Hydatidiform mole is a form of gestational disease in the very early embryo (a neoplasm of the trophoblast) that also includes invasive mole and choriocarcinoma. Several investigators suggest that clomiphene and hMG may be associated with the development of hydatidiform mole, although direct, causal relationships have not been established. Investigations have uncovered both genetic and environmental risk factors for the disease. Older women are at risk, which suggests that hydatidiform mole could be a consequence of aging eggs and pathologic cell division of the fertilized egg. Abnormal cell division may also result from exposure to ovulation-induction drugs. There are at least sixteen reports of complete or partial hydatidiform mole following ovulation induction. However, the disease is rare, and most case series include too few observations to detect an increase in incidence over the normal incidence for the population in question.

Conclusion

In summary, research has demonstrated that ovulation induction is associated with serious, sometimes life-threatening, events. Severe ovarian hyperstimulation syndrome still occurs in about 1 in 50 to 1 in 100 women in spite of careful monitoring. Multiple pregnancy frequently complicates ovulation-induced and assisted-conception pregnancies. Perinatal mortality is excessive. Recent data suggest that ovulation induction may also be a risk factor for extrauterine pregnancy, neural tube defects, defects in reproductive organogenesis, malignant neoplasms, and hydatidiform mole.

FOR FURTHER READING

McEvoy, G. K., ed. 1990. *American Hospital Formulary Services*. Bethesda, Md.: American Society of Hospital Pharmacists.

Ron, E., B. Lunenfeld, J. Menczer, et al. 1987. "Cancer Incidence in a Cohort of Infertile Women." *American Journal of Epidemiology* 125(5): 780–790.

Stephenson, P. 1993. "Ovulation Induction During Treatment for Infertility: An Assessment of the Risks." In P. Stephenson and M. G. Wagner, eds., *Tough Choices: In Vitro Fertilization and the Reproductive Technologies*. Philadelphia: Temple University Press.

U.S. Pharmacopeial Convention. 1990. *Drug Information for the Health Care Professional*. Rockville, Md.: USPC.

Whittemore, A. S., et al. 1992. "Characteristics Relating to Ovarian Cancer Risk: Collaborative Analysis of 12 U.S. Case-control Studies." *American Journal of Epidemiology* 15: 1184–1203.

thirty-three

Risk Perception and Health Screening

CLAIRE D. F. PARSONS

Since World War II the notion of risk has come to pervade many of the sciences and social sciences, as well as lay parlance. In health care, risk is given significance through health-screening procedures used as a means to detect actual, and predict potential, disease among currently healthy individuals and populations. The concept of screening is used in three main ways in the health services. First, screening may refer to a series of tests undertaken on a symptomatic individual in order to determine a diagnosis. This type of screening is part of clinical practice rather than a public health (epidemiological) investigation or a community health-promotion campaign. Second, screening is conducted for research purposes as a surveillance measure to estimate the prevalence of disease in the community. Third, screening may aim to identify people at risk of a particular disease. This type may include the identification of those who are considered to constitute high-risk groups even though they do not yet have the disease. Health-promotion campaigns may then be developed, such as campaigns to encourage women to undergo screening for breast or cervical cancer. Hence mass screening or population screening has sometimes been promoted as beneficial to the community.

The term "risk" has its own meanings among health providers, such as with epidemiologists, for whom risk refers to the probability that an event will occur, for example, that an individual will die or become ill within a determined period. Notions of risk factors and relative risk arise as assessments are made about the probability of getting a disease when exposed to a particular factor. For example, smokers have a different risk of developing lung cancer than nonsmokers. Health risk is calculated according to a mathematical model from a large database collected from the community. The physician attempts to apply such population statistics to an individual patient in the clinical setting, but the layperson has no such mathematical model in mind when he or she has to interpret information about personal risk.

The ultimate aim of identifying a health risk is to reduce morbidity and premature mortality while reducing the economic and social burden of disease in society. Health campaigns that focus on risk are often undertaken amid community debate (usually among the middle and upper classes) as to the benefits or otherwise of health screening. People often find it difficult to discern which of many risk factors they should give priority to reducing in their lives or whether they should participate in screening programs at all.

The Social Impact of Identifying Health Risk Through Screening

Although screening technologies have undoubtedly saved lives through the early detection of disease, a number of researchers have argued that the notion of "at risk" individuals or groups is problematic when it diverts attention away from social responsibility to the poor, who persistently carry the greater burden of disease. Screening has even been reported as harmful, resulting in a higher incidence of stress, worker absenteeism, introspection, and reduced exercise. Screening services such as mammography and cervical screening are also misused by health professionals. Debates on screening and risk are inflamed by reports in internationally respected journals such as the *Lancet* that contain research results implying that despite mass campaigns to lower cholesterol as a significant risk factor in coronary heart disease, there is still no evidence that reducing cholesterol saves lives. Indeed, researchers propose that doing so may even be harmful.

Screening has affected public health by reducing morbidity and premature death, but it is also seen to construe populations as preclinical rather than healthy. Thus it has been argued that today, people can be regarded as either sick or potentially sick. This approach has the greatest impact on women, who are the family and community health managers. It is they who most often must make the decisions for or against screening of family members, including themselves.

The uncertainty about the benefits of screening continues, a somewhat perplexing development for those responsible for health promotion. The community at large has its own ways of determining and prioritizing risk-taking behavior. Many women, for example, do perceive risks to their well-being, especially as they approach midlife, and are becoming well informed about the benefits, limitations, and hazards of screening. Some avail themselves of services to identify the medical risks that precipitate such conditions as cervical and breast cancer, osteoporosis, coronary heart disease, and even the early onset of menopause. But despite the supermarket of options including everything from supposed risk reduction of the diseases of aging to elixirs of youth, women do not always use them. Their reluctance may be due to lack of access to support facilities (transport, child care) and to socioeconomic factors (including education, occupation, income) that influence screening behavior. A small but significant number are now refusing to take part in any further screening as a result of negative experiences with health professionals undertaking the screening or the technology itself.

Lay Perceptions of Health Screening and Risk

Today, the screening of healthy populations predominantly targets women's health. However, those who use the screening services most are still those who need them least, namely, the upper-middle classes. Those who use the services and are told they are at risk, even though they do not have a disease, experience negative side effects from the screening process. For example, a study of women and breast lumps showed that women who had been told they were at risk of breast disease no longer felt healthy. They existed in a limbo of uncertainty. This labeling of an individual as being at risk is sometimes experienced as a death sentence. The woman carries the label for life, awaiting the impending doom of cancer (or another disease) striking her down.

In many countries, screening is often indiscriminately advocated for all women and can be seen as a mechanism for the control of women's lifestyles, including women's reproduction. Screening is advocated throughout pregnancy, as can be seen by the literature written for women on the multiple technologies for the pregnant woman, including chorionic villus sampling, ultrasound monitoring, and amniocentesis. Each carries its own risks for the woman and her baby. Screening is widely advocated for women facing or in the midlife transition period. A woman's cholesterol, bone calcium, breasts, cervix, uterus, hormones, and other body parts are all potential areas for the application of screening technologies. These technologies have margins of error, giving false negative and false positive results, which means women are either falsely reassured or falsely alarmed in up to 30 percent of instances (the error margin for mammography).

Reproductive and Midlife Risks

There are many studies showing that women in their reproductive years and approaching midlife have a number of their experiences defined medically and publicly as an illness. There is now substantial public discussion of the risks associated with reproduction and midlife, and health-promotion campaigns emphasize individual responsibility for minimizing risk and reducing social burdens. Australia's La Trobe University study of the social construction of menopause has shown that some women have benefited greatly from screening, whereas others show anxiety concerning the image of femaleness, desirability, and usefulness as they approach midlife and hope that undergoing screening will gain them access to medical technology fixes to the aging process. Parsons and Richards have found that perceptions of the need to undergo high-technology screening are not unrelated to a woman's perception of her own self and her body image. Health-screening campaigns have capitalized on female insecurities about notions of the perfect body and other requirements of femaleness. Also, as in other Western industrialized societies, Australian women register a high rate of morbidity in midlife, and their risk is seen as an accumulative phenomenon. For example, family problems, financial problems, the burdens associated with having children, and a health problem may individually be seen as normal; but combined, they increase the chance of being perceived as a health risk.

Screening is not a homogeneous phenomenon; for example, cholesterol screening is easy (when a reflotron machine is used) and appointments take minimal time (around ten minutes) and do not involve personal embarrassment. Along with cholesterol testing, the Papanicolaou (pap) smear may become routine, but the screening involves more emotional investment and embarrassment. Mammography is less embarrassing than a pap smear but takes longer and is not a routine test for all women. Bone-density scanning to detect osteoporosis is usually a onetime screening but is costly and time consuming.

Hormone replacement therapy is becoming a unique reproductive technology. Some studies are showing that women not only seek the therapy for reasons other than the medically acknowledged negative signs and symptoms of menopause but are also increasingly expressing guilt about being on or not being on the drugs associated with the therapy. In reality, it is not simply a matter of being on or off the drugs but is an ongoing procedure of adjustments to dosages and experimentation with brands and categories of synthetic hormones. Few women have been put on these drugs and remained on them without these adjustments, and few have not had physical, psychological, or social side effects (for example, hormone-induced headaches). Hormone replacement therapy is not a technology used to assist a woman through an illness but a lifetime commitment to replacing what has been described as "a deficiency" in aging women. This is one technology that is irrevocably changing the meaning of midlife and menopause throughout the Western world.

Conclusion

The health professions, as well as the media, promote the idea that it is wise and responsible—"an educated choice"—for women to undergo screening for a range of possible conditions. However, all health technologies, whether they require invasive procedures or not (e.g., blood or tissue samples), have an impact on the screened. Those who have a high family incidence of a particular disease may be well advised to undergo screening procedures, but there is sufficient research to show that the indiscriminate use of screening technologies is ill advised and may cause both physical and emotional harm.

FOR FURTHER READING

Backett E., A. Davies, and A. Petros-Barvazian. 1984. *The Risk Approach in Health Care*. Public Health Papers no. 76. Geneva: World Health Organization.

Christie, D., I. Gordon, and R. Heller. 1987. *Epidemiology: An Introductory Text for Medical and Other Health Science Students*. Sydney: New South Wales University Press.

Coney, S. 1988. *The Unfortunate Experiment*. Sydney, NSW: Penguin.

Gifford, S. 1989. "The Meaning of Lumps: A Case Study of the Ambiguities of Risk." In C. Janes, R. Stall, and S. Gifford, eds., *Anthropology and Epidemiology*. Boston: D. Reidel.

Greer, G. 1991. *The Change: Women, Ageing and the Menopause*. London: Hamish Hamilton.

Parsons C., and L. Richards. 1994. *Women's Perceptions of Risk in Midlife: Grounded Theory and Computer-Assisted Analysis*. Paper presented at the Qualitative Health Research Conference, Philadelphia, Pennsylvania, June.

Ratcliffe, J., and L. Wallack. 1984. "Perspectives on Prevention: Health Promotion Versus Health Protection." In J. de Kervasdoue, J. Kimberley, and W. Rodwin, eds., *The End of an Illusion: The Future of Health Policy in Future Industrialised Nations*. Berkeley: University of California Press.

Richards, L., and J. Daly. 1991. *Women's Experience of Menopause: A Qualitative Approach*. Denver: National Council on Family Relations.

Rose, G. 1985. "Sick Individuals and Sick Populations." *International Journal of Epidemiology* 14(1): 32–38.

thirty-four

Prenatal Diagnosis Technologies

RICHARD T. HULL

Examination of the fetus in utero probably first occurred almost 100 years ago when an X-ray picture was taken of a dead fetus. However, prenatal screening and diagnosis as we think of them now have been available routinely to certain groups of women and selectively to others since the late 1970s. Amniocentesis and the other technologies of prenatal screening and diagnosis currently in use provide access to fetal cells and amniotic fluid and enable the visualization of the developing fetus. These technologies allow detection before birth of all recognizable chromosomal variations, many selected developmental malformations, over 150 biochemical disorders, and fetal sex; the list continues to expand, and the techniques are being applied earlier and earlier in pregnancy.

Amniocentesis

Examination of amniotic fluid obtained by needle aspiration was first attempted in the late 1920s. Initially amniocentesis was employed as part of the effort to manage RH disease, in which blood type incompatibility between fetus and mother results in a deadly condition called erythroblastosis fetalis. Management consisted in total transfusion at birth in the so-called blue baby, so amniocentesis was performed in the last trimester of pregnancy. Advances in the 1960s and beyond in somatic cell genetics have permitted diagnosis of genetic diseases and diseases resulting from abnormal chromosomes through examination of fetal cells obtained from amniotic fluid. Depending on the quantity of cell material needed for the assay, either directly examining fetal cells or culturing them permits identification of chromosomal abnormalities (e.g., extra, partial, or missing chromosomes), of biochemical or DNA markers of various genetic disorders, or of missing gene products. The time needed for some of these diagnostic techniques, as well as temporal pressures when abortion is contemplated, necessitated amniocentesis much earlier in pregnancy (early to mid-second trimester) than previously employed. The Human Genome Project (the mapping of an entire human genome) promises a much larger range of possible diagnoses emerging from amniocentesis.

Under sterile conditions, a needle is inserted through the abdominal wall, the uterine wall, and the amniotic sac. Amniotic fluid, in which detached fetal cells float, is aspirated in a quantity sufficient to obtain several cells. Then, various tests are performed on the uncultured cells, cultured cells, and the cell-free amniotic fluid. With the development of sonography, a technique for using low-frequency sound waves reflected and transformed into visual images (similar to underwater sonar), fetuses and placentas can be visualized, making for accurate placement of the needle and thus greatly decreasing the incidence of bloody taps and consequent misleading information. The risk of fetal death from this procedure is less than 0.5 percent. Sonography has also permitted identification of twins, so that in cases where family history indicates a risk of disease, confirmation of the status of each twin is possible.

Parents generally seek prenatal diagnosis of genetic and chromosomal abnormalities when they believe their offspring are at risk for serious abnormality due to family history, age of the mother, or exposure of the fetus to environmental risks (such as rubella, cytomegalovirus, irradiation, drugs, toxoplasmosis). The most difficult dilemmas occur when amniocentesis discloses only probabilities. It is imperative that a woman seeking prenatal tests be fully informed of the inherent uncertainties and risks of any diagnostic procedures or actions that may be taken and that informed choice be ensured.

Chorionic Villus Sampling

Chorionic villus sampling (also chorion villus sampling, or chorion villous sampling) is a technique for removing tissue from the chorion—the outermost of the embryonic membranes in mammals—which is generated by the embryo and attaches with a multitude of fingerlike villi to the wall of the uterus, eventually forming the placenta. Sampling of tissue from this structure may occur as early as the seventh week of pregnancy.

A biopsy needle is introduced either through the cervix or the abdominal wall under local anesthesia and guided through the wall of the uterus to the site of implantation. A biopsy of tissue is taken from the site, and the cells of that tissue may be subjected to various genetic and chromosomal tests to detect abnormalities.

This sampling is possible in the seventh to eighth weeks, some eight to ten weeks before enough amniotic fluid has been produced to permit amniocentesis. The technique is therefore attractive to women concerned about the possibility of abnormalities in their offspring in that it potentially gives diagnoses substantially earlier than many of the mileposts of fetal development widely regarded as signaling the onset of changes in the fetus's moral standing.

Early abortions involve technically simpler abortion techniques; they may not be "simpler" for the woman. Later abortive techniques (i.e., after twelve weeks) involve methods that some may find more difficult to approve and undergo. But the significance of an early diagnosis is not limited to early abortion decisions. Early diagnosis of some conditions opens the door for those who wish to develop genetic-manipulation technologies. It allows discussion of the possibility of fetal surgery with time for the parents to weigh possible consequences. And it permits the planning for immediate medical treatment of the newborn, including delivery at a site with experienced personnel. Many of these procedures and treatments are still highly experimental, and women subjected to chorionic villus sampling may not realize that for a wide range of detectable abnormalities, the possibility of reliable corrective treatment is remote.

Chorionic villus sampling generally results in feto-maternal transfusion, or introduction of fetal blood cells into the mother's circulation. This may create an RH factor and complicate future pregnancies. Fetal-loss rates associated with this type of screening are generally 1 to 3 percent, substantially higher than for amniocentesis (ranging between 0.2 and 1.3 percent). There is also a failure rate that may run as high as 6 percent, necessitating retesting. A number of congenital abnormalities, particularly limb defects, have been associated with chorionic villus sampling. It has also been associated with a significantly higher incidence of neonatal respiratory distress (as high as 8 percent). Finally, an increased spontaneous abortion rate has been correlated with early sampling done in women over age thirty-five, rising from just below 2 percent to nearly 11 percent for women forty years and older. These observations are controversial, and not all are universally regarded as risks imposed by the procedure. Nonetheless, persons considering chorionic villus sampling should carefully weigh the possibility of risk to a healthy fetus against the diagnostic information to be gained.

Ultrasound Examinations

During these exams, high-frequency sound waves are projected into the uterus, and the sound waves that are reflected back are resolved visually to allow one to see the fetus on a television-like screen. As a tool for prenatal diagnosis, ultrasound can be used to identify certain malformations in fetuses known to be at risk. It can also be used to identify fetal sex. Most subtle malformations will not be identified when ultrasound is applied routinely on a nondiagnostic basis for pregnancy dating, although more obvious changes in the body shape and size of the fetus should be detectable.

Maternal Serum Alpha-fetoprotein Analysis

Maternal serum alpha-fetoprotein analysis is another technique on its way to becoming a universal technology for prenatal screening. It entails the withdrawal from a pregnant woman of a sample of blood that is analyzed for the presence of alpha-fetoprotein and, in some jurisdictions, a limited number of other serum constituents that tend to be found in increased or decreased levels when the fetus has a malformation of the neural tube or Down syndrome.

Screening Technologies Under Development

An increasing number of investigators have begun to report their ability to obtain and make diagnoses from fetal cells in the mother's circulation. Using increasingly sophisticated technologies, these cells, which have crossed the placental barrier and entered a woman's bloodstream, can be separated from the woman's blood cells, grown in the laboratory, subjected to procedures that amplify their genetic material, and stained with specific (fluorescent) dyes to locate the presence or absence of DNA sequences. If this approach does provide accurate results, it will, in principle, replace procedures such as amniocentesis or chorionic villus sampling with the much less invasive procedure of drawing blood.

Another approach that may become more widespread in the future is embryo or preimplantation diagnosis. In this approach, which is already used in programs of advanced infertility techniques, a very early embryo is removed from a pregnant woman (or created in the laboratory following in vitro fertilization), tested, and, if it is found acceptable, (re)placed in the uterus to continue its development. This technology has so far been used only as a research tool for the diagnosis of certain specific genetic disorders in embryos, but should it appear not to harm the child-to-be, its further application has been endorsed by many researchers (it is now being used in the state of Virginia). Its advocates have assisted public acceptance of this problematic technique by affixing it with the acronym BABI (blastocyst analysis before implantation). Preimplantation diagnosis is also presented as a particularly welcome approach; it will circumvent the abortion of genetically defective embryos because only unaffected embryos will be (re)implanted. Also, if it is technicians who judge embryos acceptable for (re)implantation, parents who in fact are at risk for transmitting genetic abnormalities don't have to know that they are carriers. Given these arguments, a broader application is not an unrealistic expectation.

FOR FURTHER READING

Bernhardt, B. A., et al. 1998. "Prenatal Genetic Testing: Content of Discussions Between Obstetric Providers and Pregnant Women." *Obstetrics & Gynecology* 91: 648–655.

Brambati, B. 1995. "Chorionic Villus Sampling." *Current Opinions in Obstetrics & Gynecology* 7: 190–116.

Canadian Early and Mid-trimester Amniocentesis Trial Group. 1998. "Randomised Trial to Assess Safety and Fetal Outcome of Early and Midtrimester Amniocentesis." *Lancet* 351: 242–247.

Centers for Disease Control and Prevention. 1995. "Chorionic Villus Sampling and Amniocentesis: Recommendations for Prenatal Counseling." *Morbidity & Mortality Weekly Report* 44: 1–12.

Greenough, A., et al. 1997a. "First-Trimester Invasive Procedures: Effects on Symptom Status and Lung Volume in Very Young Children." *Pediatric Pulmonology* 24: 415–422.

Greenough, A., et al. 1997b. "First-Trimester Invasive Procedures and Congenital Abnormalities." *Acta Paediatrica* 86: 1220–1223.

Halliday, J. L., et al. 1995. "New Estimates of Down Syndrome Risks at Chorionic Villus Sampling, Amniocentesis, and Live Birth in Women of Advanced Maternal Age. . . ." *Prenatal Diagnosis* 15: 455–465.

Nagel, H. T., et al. 1998. "Amniocentesis Before 14 Completed Weeks as an Alternative to Transabdominal Chorionic Villus Sampling: A Controlled Trial with Infant Follow-up." *Prenatal Diagnosis* 18: 465–475.

Salonen, R., et al. 1997. "Maternal Serum Screening for Down's Syndrome on Population Basis." *Acta Obstetrics & Gynecology Scandinavia* 76: 817–821.

Ville, Y., et al. 1997. "Diagnostic Embryoscopy and Fetoscopy in the First Trimester of Pregnancy." *Prenatal Diagnosis* 17: 1237–1246.

thirty-five

Prenatal Diagnosis—
Critical Perspectives

ABBY LIPPMAN AND RICHARD T. HULL

Researchers claim that prenatal diagnosis was first used for conditions generally regarded by physicians as serious and having no effective treatments. It is now available for conditions with little or uncertain impact on postnatal health and functioning; for conditions that will appear, if at all, only in adulthood; and for conditions for which treatment exists. The speed with which these new technologies have been adopted into clinical practice and the growing number of women to whom they are applied are staggering, and unfortunately there has been insufficient consideration of the many important issues implicit in, and raised by, their availability and use.

In North America, amniocentesis and chorionic villus sampling have been generally restricted for use by women whose age (usually thirty-five years and older, an arbitrary criterion) is said to put them at increased risk for Down syndrome and by women known to be at risk for having a child with some specific condition that can be diagnosed via fetal cells or amniotic fluid. Neither of the tests is done routinely among other groups of women. By contrast, almost all women experience another form of prenatal testing (even if it is not so labeled) when they receive what has become a seemingly ordinary part of prenatal care: ultrasound examination.

Maternal serum alpha-fetoprotein analysis, which is offered routinely in some U.S. states and Canadian provinces, is a screening, not a diagnostic, test. It is used only to identify women who may be at higher-than-average risk of having a child with Down syndrome or a neural tube defect. However, this screening has rather poor predictive value. Most women whose initial screening results are considered to be abnormal do not have fetuses with the conditions sought, but this is confirmed only after the completion of further tests (ultrasound and amniocentesis). The increase in applications of genetic testing and screening raises serious social and ethical concerns.

Pregnancy and Maternity

The availability and use of prenatal screening and testing in themselves change the way women experience pregnancy and maternity, the way they conceptualize children and childbearing, and the way they seek solutions to health and social problems. Although some of the changes appear to cut across racial, income, social status, and ethnic and ability groups, issues reverberate dissimilarly and in specific problematic ways according to a woman's membership in one or more of these groups.

Prenatal testing artificially separates the unique experience of pregnancy into social and biological parts, replaces how a woman feels and what she feels about being pregnant with what a biomedical procedure tells her she should feel, and requires her to adhere to test schedules rather than to her own biological and social clocks. More troubling, perhaps, is that prenatal testing in many ways removes rather than adds to a woman's control over her childbearing. In a society where warning labels and public advertisements constantly remind women that what they do can harm the fetus, offers of prenatal screening and testing are hardly neutral and even, perhaps, impossible to refuse (except for a very determined few). It cannot surprise us if a woman offered testing by an expert who implies that she is responsible for having a healthy baby perceives a need to be tested and a need to do all that is recommended. Nor can it be a surprise if a woman chooses to discontinue her pregnancy after the fetus is diagnosed as having Down syndrome when society does not really accept children with disabilities, does not provide assistance for their nurture, and still views the pregnant woman as the means to a successful reproductive outcome, defined today as a perfect baby.

Prenatal screening and testing may be presented by professionals as ways to enhance women's choices and control over pregnancy by providing information about the physical status of the fetus, but the lived experiences reported by women suggest that these choices and control warrant close questioning. Who really benefits from them? Is there real choice and control? And if so, for whom? These technologies have not yet been subjected to the women-centered social evaluations urgently needed to determine whether their alterations of pregnancy and maternity are for or against women.

Conceptualizing Children and Childbearing

Prenatal screening and testing programs are necessarily oriented to detecting certain specific conditions in the fetus or embryo. Consequently, they make value statements about the quality or acceptability of fetuses based solely on their genetic, physical, or chromosomal appearance, and these evaluations can determine which children will and will not be born. When a condition associated with what will be a disability is detected, to abort the fetus is to make a choice about the kinds of children we will have. When the condition is one of gender, to abort the fetus to facilitate what obstetricians are calling "family completion" (for them, one child of each sex) is to practice the ultimate in sexism as well as to express a rather limited view of the modern family. Whatever else it may be, then, prenatal testing followed by abortion necessarily involves the systematic selection of fetuses and some inherent degree of quality control. And it is geneticists and obstetricians who decide which qualities will be controlled via the tests they choose to offer and the women to whom they offer them. These choices, it must be emphasized, are not (strictly) medical. They are time- and place-dependent and express professional norms. Thus although abortion may be chosen by an individual pregnant woman, her decision is circumscribed by the condition's specialists (and society), who first categorize the pregnancy as worthy or not of continuation. This categorization demonstrates the eugenic aspects implicit in prenatal testing.

Solving Social and Health Problems

Prenatal screening and testing are evolving within a societal process that favors a genetic approach to health and disease, an approach that is fundamentally expensive, individualized, and eugenic. Geneticization gives priority to searching for variations in DNA sequences that differentiate people and attributes some hereditary basis to most disorders, behaviors, and physiological variations.

Geneticization as a backdrop for prenatal testing is especially worrisome because viewing health and disease through a genetic prism ignores the many factors other than heredity—social and physical environments, economic conditions, gender, race, personal behaviors, and available health services—that play critical roles. By focusing on genetics and relying on prenatal genetic testing, supposedly to protect the health of the children we bear, we displace our attention from society's role in creating illness. The social roots of handicaps are hidden, and societal responsibilities to accommodate and embrace those with disabilities are converted into individual women's obligations not only to prevent disability but to keep it from appearing among us when prevention has not been made an option. The social, political, and economic neglect of women that seriously interferes with the physical and mental development of their children is ignored even though variations in the distribution of wealth and power have far greater impact on the distribution of health than do variations in genes. Advocating and promoting prenatal screening and testing may shift the distribution of genetic variations, but serious inequities will remain at least untouched, more likely exacerbated, as economic goals of private companies and preventive (eugenic) objectives of public health departments direct their application.

When amniocentesis was introduced about a generation ago, abortion subsequent to the diagnosis of a fetal abnormality was presented as a temporary necessity until treatment for the detected condition could be devised. Over time, and contrary to stated expectations, the gap between diagnosis and treatment of disease has widened, and selection of fetuses and embryos has become ever more part of how we conceptualize childbearing. Yet we still do not know the full impact of prenatal testing on women's total health, power, and social standing.

Feminist concerns about prenatal testing are not driven by nostalgia for the past or by desires to limit women's choices. To the contrary, these concerns are solidly grounded in the recognition that how, when, why, to whom, and by whom these technologies are applied are conditioned by prevailing gendered attitudes about women, their bodies, and their social roles. Feminist critiques recognize that these technologies cannot be neutral in societies such as ours where women are disadvantaged, generally powerless, vulnerable to offers of services because of their diminished status, challenged by prejudicial norms surrounding motherhood, and delegated responsibility for family health.

Physicians have defined themselves as guardians of the fetus in their process of medicalizing reproduction, and they are reinforcing this guardianship in their geneticization of childbearing. Biomedical guardianship reduces women's autonomy and promotes the myth of the perfect child rather than the desired reality of a healthy child. If prenatal testing is to meet its stated objectives of reassuring women and reducing suffering, we must first determine if, and then how, it can be applied in a socially responsible way that respects both the variations with which women's values and needs occur in society and the variations in our health status and abilities. We must ensure that prenatal testing is liberating, not oppressive, for individuals and the societies in which we live together.

FOR FURTHER READING

Andrews, Lori B. 1966. "Prenatal Screening and the Culture of Motherhood." *Hastings Law Journal* 47: 967.

Katz, Barbara. 1998. *Genetic Maps and Human Imaginations.* New York: Norton.

Kevles, Daniel J., and Leroy Hood, eds. 1992. *The Code of Codes: Scientific and Social Issues in the Human Genome Project.* Cambridge: Harvard University Press.

Lippman, Abby. 1992. "Mother Matters: A Fresh Look at Prenatal Genetic Screening." *Issues in Reproductive and Genetic Engineering* 5: 141–154.

Malinowski, Michael. 1994. "Coming into Being: Law, Ethics, and the Practice of Prenatal Genetic Screening." *Hastings Law Journal* 45: 1435–1526.

Press, Nancy, and Carol Browner. 1993. "Collective Fictions: Similarities in the Reasons for Accepting MSAFP Screening Among Women of Diverse Ethnic and Social Class Backgrounds." *Fetal Diagnosis and Therapy* 8: 97–106.

Rothenberg, Karen H., and Elizabeth J. Thompson, eds. 1994. *Women and Prenatal Testing: Facing the Challenges of Genetic Technology.* Columbus: Ohio State University Press.

thirty-six

Sex Selection

HELEN BEQUAERT HOLMES AND
ELIZABETH MATHIOT-MOEN

Methods

Methods of ensuring fetal sex before conception, most of which are unreliable, involve the separation and the elimination or enhancement of female- and male-determining sperm. Techniques include the timing of intercourse, special douches, electrophoresis, position during intercourse, and diet. Franchised clinics and sperm firms have been opened throughout the world, featuring a method of separating sperm (the Ericsson method) that is claimed to be about 85 percent successful. In the 1990s, preimplantation diagnosis has been a focal point of research, as has been a search for a sex-determining gene. However, although researchers seek methods of sexing preimplantation embryos that will not harm the embryo, much less concern is shown for the women involved. Preimplantation sexing requires in vitro fertilization and highly invasive and potentially risky procedures. Currently the sex of a four-to-eight-cell human pre-embryo (about one day old) can be ascertained by detecting whether it has a Y chromosome.

If sex selection is to occur later in the reproductive cycle, it requires abortion. In the first trimester, methods are under development to sex fetal cells in maternal blood. There are drawbacks to this method, however. First, in the case of female fetuses, markers are required to prove that the cells are of the fetus and not of the mother. If the fetus is male, the mother must never have had a previous pregnancy (successful or not) with a male fetus because some cells from that fetus may still be circulating in her blood. Another method of sex selection after impregnation is to sex the placental cells sloughed into the cervix or obtained through chorionic villus sampling. Over a 90 percent success rate is claimed with this method. A very accurate method is the testing of second-trimester fetal cells obtained by withdrawing amniotic fluid from the uterus (amniocentesis). Just as accurate and much less invasive is sex detection by imaging fetuses through ultrasound, also in the second trimester.

Commercialization

In 1968, New York sociologist Amitai Etzioni predicted that if a simple and safe method of sex selection for males became available, investors would promote it because of its mass-market potential. Some twenty-five years later with simple, safe, but often ineffective methods in place, his prediction has come true. The sex-selection industry in North America is fostered by a social desire to control for a sex-balanced family.

Colorado entrepreneur Robert Marsik, claiming personal success with an intercourse timing method that produced a daughter to balance his family of one son, founded Pro-Care Industries, Ltd. to capitalize on his method. In 1986 Pro-Care marketed Gender Choice, pink and blue sex-selection kits, for $49.95. They contained instructions, a douche powder, and several disposable thermometers to detect ovulation. Later that year, however, the American Food and Drug Administration told Pro-Care to halt distributing Gender Choice until its efficacy was documented. Arguing that the kit was not a medical device, Pro-Care modified the instructions to say that not all scientists agreed with the theory. They also removed the douche powder and offered a money-back guarantee. Although their 1986 sales stood at $1.1 million, these dropped in 1987 after the FDA called the product a "gross deception of the consumer." When product returns in 1987 and 1988 surpassed sales, Pro-Care filed for bankruptcy.

In the 1970s Ronald Ericsson of Montana commercialized an albumin swim-up method of enriching semen with Y sperm to select for male children. His company, Gametrics Limited, sells the method to clinics, which charge customers about $500 per insemination attempt. Since manipulation of semen lowers sperm count and since artificial insemination usually has a poor success rate, the method takes many inseminations and thus can become costly. Although in 1987 Ericsson reported a success rate of 86 percent boys, some researchers in gynecology have tested sperm samples "enriched" via Ericsson's method and have reported finding no more than 50 percent Y sperm. Nevertheless, Ericsson continues to franchise new clinics, including the London Gender Clinic in England in 1992.

Physician John Stephens's commercial method of sex selection, in contrast, is effective, although it requires selective abortion. In 1984 Stephens incorporated Koala Labs in California to use ultrasound to identify fetal sex. He invented the FASA (fetal anatomic sex assignment) and promised accurate sex assignment of females at fourteen weeks and males at twelve weeks. He advertised widely in San Francisco, especially in periodicals aimed at South Asians, whose cultural norms strongly favor males over females. In 1988, after critics objected to this obvious sex selection and because routine, high-quality ultrasound was then available under California health insurance, his business began to fail. In 1990 Stephens set up a second Koala Labs in northern Washington; in 1991 he was granted a U.S. patent on FASA. He then advertised his $500-per-sex-selection service across the border in Canada via direct-mail flyers in the Punjabi language and via the *Link*, a Vancouver Indo-Canadian newspaper. Indo-Canadian feminists subsequently mounted resistance to the Koala Labs ads.

In the 1990s some doctors in in vitro fertilization (IVF) clinical practice adopted certain techniques purported to select sex. Influenced by timing theories, Ericsson's technique, and data showing slightly higher percentages of girl babies after using the fertility drug Clomid, a few well-known clinics may combine two or three approaches. Sharon Jaffe at Columbia in New York City and Mark Geier in Bethesda, Maryland, use timing in the menstrual cycle, Clomid to produce girls, and sperm separation. The Columbia team accepts requests for either sex and uses the Ericsson albumin separation; for female selection, they inject Clomid and utilize a different sperm fraction. For male selection, their results are the same as normal chance; for girls, they report 78.6 percent success. Geier's team uses a different sperm-separation technique and tries only for females; it reports 80 percent success. Other gynecologists have criticized the methods used in computing these success rates. The commercialization of sex selection demonstrates that entrepreneurs in a market economy typically will try to turn a profit whatever the technology and associated ethical questions.

FOR FURTHER READING

Canadian Royal Commission on New Reproductive Technologies. 1993b. "Sex Selection for Non-Medical Reasons." *Proceed with Care: Final Report of the Royal Commission on New Reproductive Technologies*. Ottawa: Canadian Communications Group.

Handyside, A. H., et al. 1990. "Pregnancies from Biopsied Human Preimplantation Embryos Sexed by Y-Specific DNA Amplification." *Nature* 344: 769–770.

Hicks, L. Wayne. 1990. "Gender Choice Saga Ends with Liquidation of Assets." *Denver Business Journal* (March 26): 1, 23.

Holmes, Helen Bequaert. 1995. "Choosing Children's Sex: Challenges to Feminist Ethics." In Joan C. Callahan, ed., *Reproduction, Ethics and the Law: Feminist Perspectives*. Bloomington: Indiana University Press.

Jaffe, Sharon B., et al. 1991. "A Controlled Study for Gender Selection." *Fertility and Sterility* 56(2): 254–258.

Thobani, Sunera. 1991. "More Than Sexist . . ." *Healthsharing* (Spring): 10, 13.

Vines, Gail. 1993. "Old Wives' Tales 'as Good as Sperm Sorting.'" *New Scientist* (January 30): 4.

Zarutskie, Paul W., et al. 1989. "The Clinical Relevance of Sex Selection Techniques." *Fertility and Sterility* 52(6): 891–905.

Part Four
Advanced Infertility Techniques

Advanced infertility techniques, also known as the new reproductive technologies, assisted conception, and reproductive medicine, are commonly perceived to originate with the birth in 1978 of Louise Joy Brown, the first IVF, or test-tube, baby. In vitro fertilization (IVF) heralds a new age in reproduction, as it is the first time that medical and scientific interventions have succeeded in externalizing the moment of human conception from women's bodies. Prior to this, all successful and routine reproductive interventions focused on moments preceding conception (contraception, hyperovulation, and sperm freezing) or at later stages of pregnancy and at birth. Some of these earlier developments contributed to advanced infertility techniques, most notably sperm freezing and storing; hyperovulation (developed from oral contraceptive research); and surgical techniques including laparoscopy, ultrasound-guided retrieval, and micromanipulation. There is evidence of sporadic scientific explorations of human conception dating as far back as the mid-eighteenth century. However, the development of a successful and routine medical practice around the latest stage in human reproduction began during the 1980s.

IVF forms the central component in an array of advanced infertility techniques. From early trials with natural menstrual cycles and single-egg collection, IVF routines now include suspension of all female reproductive hormonal production, complicated hyperovulation protocols, and constant and careful screening of a woman's hormonal levels and egg development. Ultrasound-guided retrieval has evolved as the norm for collecting eggs. Culture media and storing techniques have been refined in attempts to improve relatively low success rates (about 25 percent being the best rate in terms of bringing home a baby). Embryo freezing, along with the advances in screening, retrieving, and storing techniques, makes the procedure more efficient and allows for more embryo implants. Egg and embryo donation are also enabled as a result and now take a place alongside the well-established practice of artificial insemination. Attention to issues of male infertility is increasing; the most recent major technique to be adopted in advanced infertility practice is the microimplantation (intracytoplasmic sperm injection, ICSI) of single sperm into eggs collected through IVF. Highly experimental techniques include the maturation and freezing of eggs. Also, doctors and scientists continue to explore methods of improving the success rate of embryo implantation. Genetic screening of preimplanted embryos, embryo research, and ectogenesis are also implicated here but will be covered separately in Part 5.

The issues associated with reproduction prior to the development of advanced infertility techniques persist. There are concerns that the increased and increasingly sophisticated reproductive technologies threaten women's reproductive autonomy. The practice of GIFT (gamete intrafallopian transfer, an early IVF-like procedure) raises a typical set of concerns: women's bodies as the preferred site of infertility experimentation whatever the cause and misleading information used to artificially bolster success rates and legitimate unnecessary medical interventions in reproduction. IVF and related methods also carry a potential for largely unaddressed and unquantified health risks for the women exposed to these procedures. Concern tends to focus on the use of hyperovulatory hormones and those that are used to suspend all of women's reproductive hormones (GnRH analogs) during the procedures. Creutzfeldt-Jakob disease (commonly known in bovines as mad cow disease) is one recently acknowledged deadly side effect of early IVF practices with hyperovulatory drugs. Although some of these concerns are disputed, especially by those who use such procedures in medical practice, there is agreement that the use of these drugs intervenes to a greater degree and more systemically than do previous applications of reproductive or sex hormones. Partly due to the relatively recent standardization of advanced infertility techniques, long-term risk studies are not available. Another concern is that women are exposed unnecessarily to these high-level interventions and risk. Indications for the use of IVF and related techniques have altered significantly since the late 1970s and have broadened to include unexplained infertility and male infertility.

Also at issue are the legal and social implications for maternity and paternity in the face of newly possible familial arrangements. So-called surrogate motherhood is a social consequence of new reproductive technologies. Although surrogacy does not require advanced infertility techniques, it is enabled by them, particularly by the ability to transfer female gametes prior to or soon after conception. Unlike a similar transfer of male gametes in sperm donation and artificial insemination, surrogacy entails a more involved role for the woman, who gestates the gametes and must surrender the child at birth. One of the effects of contentious surrogacy cases is judicial determinations of the meaning and relative worth of women's procreativity. There are few laws globally that directly address surrogacy and related issues; thus the task of determining fair outcomes is problematic and the outcomes are highly varied. More important, in those cases where courts have attempted to resolve these matters, there is a tendency to denigrate and commercialize female experiences of pregnancy and birth in the face of newly contested paternity rights, as in the well-known Baby M case. In previous cases of gamete transfer (limited to sperm donation), concerns for paternity were restricted to legally recognizing the social father and ensuring anonymity for the donor, as well as his release from responsibility for his genetic offspring. With advanced infertility technologies (the externalization of conception, the transfer of female gametes, and genetic screening) paternal genetic lineage is made more certain than ever and is being defended intensely in both medical practice and the courts.

Selection and assessment for access to advanced infertility techniques are also problematic. Initially, the selection of only near-fertile women in the reporting of clinical success with IVF skewed the rates. Also, many assisted-conception clinics today will not accept women near menopause or with hormonal irregularities, as their chances of success are far below those of women with regular reproductive hormonal patterns. One wonders whether this restriction is out of concern for the women applying for the services or out of protectionism for success rates in a competitive private medical service industry. In almost every country, even in those whose citizens have universal access to regular health care, advanced infertility techniques are available only privately. The costs vary from place to place and according to amount and type of intervention. A typical cost in the late 1990s for a single cycle of IVF using GnRH analogs, hyperovulation, and ICSI (the usual protocol) is $10,000. A surrogacy arrangement, where financial arrangements are permitted, typically costs $25,000. Other reasons for restricted access are sexual orientation and marital status. Many assisted-conception clinics operate without state regulation and control access themselves. As a result many clinics prohibit single women and lesbians from accessing the service, relying on a commonly held perception that only heterosexual, nuclear families deserve to reproduce. The World Health Organization has examined advanced infertility technologies from a global perspective and reorients the issue of access according to international disparities. Its report highlights the need to address causes of infertility in place of using advanced infertility technologies that do not cure infertility and are beyond the means of most of the world's people. Although most resources in developed countries are used to treat the symptoms of infertility and not its causes, there is some recent interest in linking infertility with environmental factors. Meanwhile, clinics in societies that can sustain the cost of these services have adopted counseling as a way to address uninformed consent and misleading information about success rates.

Following the expansion of new reproductive technologies into routine medical practice, many countries have rushed to establish some form of legislation. The first and one of the most influential comprehensive new reproductive technology laws is that of the United Kingdom. The British Human Fertilisation and Embryology Act (1990) brought under a single piece of legislation a number of reproductive technologies, including donor insemination. The law stands out in that it explicitly restricts all human fertilization services to "stable, heterosexual couples." Most other European countries soon after adopted legislation without such a restriction. Australia and New Zealand followed with a variety of laws governing new reproductive technologies and embryology. Canada is about to adopt legislation expressly providing single and lesbian women with access to fertilization services and including provisions for embryo research. The United States remains without any comprehensive legislation and holds a voluntary moratorium on embryo research. Germany, because of its history in World War II with eugenics, has strident legal restrictions on all embryo research. However, as with most medical practices and scientific research, these restrictions are proving virtually impossible to enforce.

Scientific and medical interest in advanced infertility techniques is not limited to fertility. Assisted conception allows for the analysis and manipulation of human genetic material in a complete, live form (the embryo), which was not possible before IVF. The potential for scientific research and for various applications is widely perceived as enormous. Although a public fear of Frankenstein-like work on live embryonic humans has been soft-pedaled by reassuring explanations from the scientific and medical professions, it was chiefly this fear that generated legislation. Many scientists and doctors welcome legislative control as insurance of their access to embryonic material for research.

thirty-seven

In Vitro Fertilization—Overview

ROBERT GORE-LANGTON AND SUSAN DANIEL

In vitro fertilization (IVF) is a female reproductive technology and involves several steps. First, women normally undergo controlled hyperovulation, which produces more than the usual single mature egg per menstrual cycle. Up to twenty eggs per ovary can result from this procedure. The ova (eggs) are then retrieved and inseminated with sperm. Within forty-eight hours fertilization and cell division, or cleavage, occur, generating a number of embryos ranging from zero to twenty. After the quality of the embryos has been checked, several of the most acceptable are implanted in the woman's womb or are frozen for future implantations and for embryo research.

IVF was developed to treat infertility due to blocked fallopian tubes, but it is now also used to overcome male-factor and idiopathic (undetermined) infertility as well as infertility related to endometriosis. Attention to patient selection is important to ensure that treatment is offered to those who will benefit from the technology and that the appropriate technology is used.

Patient Selection

Patients with tubal or idiopathic infertility have the best prognosis after IVF. Some studies indicate that women with endometriosis have a poorer prognosis than women with other causes of infertility. Also, the prognosis is dependent upon the stage of endometriosis; the more advanced the disease, the poorer the prognosis. Others find that outcomes are similar for women with or without endometriosis. For couples with male-factor infertility, success rate after IVF is the poorest. If fertilization occurs, however, implantation and pregnancy rates are similar to those of couples without a male factor.

Women who are over forty or near-menopausal with elevated levels of follicle-stimulating hormone (FSH)—two states that are often associated—have a severely compromised chance of achieving pregnancy after IVF. Decreased fecundity with advancing age is due to failing ovarian function, poor ova quality, and increased incidence of ova chromosomal abnormalities along with a decline in uterine function. Subtle increases in base FSH levels signal imminent ovarian failure regardless of age and despite regular and ovulatory menstrual cycles. Measurements of base FSH are a better indicator of ovarian function than age, although both should be taken into consideration before undertaking IVF.

Hyperovulation

Initially natural ovulatory cycles were used for IVF. However, the advantages of hyperovulation soon became apparent. With increased follicular development, more ova are collected and fertilized, and more embryos are transferred. A better pregnancy rate results. Clomiphene citrate was the first drug used to stimulate multiple follicular development in women. Hyperovulation improved when clomiphene treatment was combined with menotropin therapy. However, when clomiphene and/or menotropins are used, a spontaneous luteinizing hormone (LH) surge often occurs. For successful IVF, it is essential that the beginning of the surge be accurately determined. Incorrect timing results in either ovulation and loss of ova or retrieval of immature ova, which are less likely to fertilize and cleave. Many programs cancel treatment when unexpected LH surges occur because of poor results.

A recent development in hyperovulation has been the introduction of gonadotropin-releasing hormone (GnRH) agonists and antagonists. These compounds suspend all reproductive hormonal activity in the woman. By suppressing pituitary release of gonadotropins (reproductive hormones), they virtually eliminate spontaneous LH surges. These surges are a normal stage in ovulation, but they interfere with the successful gathering of maturing eggs for IVF. The most widely used hyperovulation protocol involves pituitary desensitization (complete suspension of reproductive hormone release) by GnRH agonists started in the luteal phase (postovulation) of the previous menstrual cycle, followed by treatment with menotropins once ovarian inactivity has been achieved. Such protocols are often referred to as long protocols. There are also short (or flare) protocols, in which GnRH agonist treatment is started in the early follicular phase (preovulation) in the current menstrual cycle. Menotropin treatment starts shortly after all reproductive hormone production is suspended with administration of the GnRH agonist. Before suspension occurs, the GnRH agonist stimulates the pituitary to secrete a burst (or flare) of FSH, which promotes follicular development (ripening of the eggs) in the ovary. Ultrasound and testing of concentrations of the hormone estradiol in the blood are used to monitor hyperovulation. When follicles are mature, the hormone human chorionic gonadotropin (hCG) is administered and egg retrieval occurs thirty-four to thirty-six hours later. Increasingly, synthetic (recombinant) gonadotropins (FSH and LH) are replacing menotropins in hyperovulation. When used with a GnRH agonist, recombinant FSH effectively stimulates follicular development. Pregnancy rates after IVF are reported to be comparable to those reported with menotropin.

Ova Retrieval, Insemination, and Embryo Development

Ova retrieval was initially achieved by laparoscopy or laparotomy. Today, fluid is aspirated from ovarian follicles guided by ultrasound (transvaginal or transvesicular) and using a needle connected by tubing to a suction apparatus. The fluid aspirated is then examined for the presence of ovulatory ova (ripe eggs). With appropriate hyperovulation and monitoring, the majority of ova collected are at the ideal stage of development (metaphase II), where the first polar body (a by-product of cell division) is present. The remainder are immature (metaphase I), with or without a germinal vesicle (nucleus), and having not yet extruded a polar body. Generally, there is a period of incubation before ova are inseminated, the duration of which depends on the maturity of ova. Incubation periods of thirty minutes to thirty hours have been reported.

In conventional IVF, only motile sperm are used to fertilize eggs. There are a number of technical procedures used to separate motile from immotile sperm, white blood cells, immature sperm, debris, and seminal plasma. They include the swim-up technique, sedimentation, gradient densities, and adherence methods. Ova are routinely inseminated at a concentration of 50,000 to 100,000 sperm per milliliter of culture medium. Sperm density is often increased, however, if there is a male infertility factor involved. The overall fertilization rate of mature ova is approximately 70 percent and is indicated by the presence of two pronuclei in the egg sixteen to eighteen hours after insemination. Presence of three or more pronuclei generally indicates polyspermic fertilization (fertilization by more than one sperm). These ova do not survive and are not implanted.

On average, 85 percent of fertilized ova can be expected to cleave by forty-eight hours after the ova retrieval. Morphology and cleavage rate are used to select embryos for transfer. More advanced embryos of regular and uniform size yield better pregnancy rates than those with irregular morphology or those that contain acellular fragments. However, not all good-quality embryos implant, and poor-quality embryos are capable of implanting and producing normal pregnancies. Pregnancy rate improves as the number of embryos transferred is increased. However, the rate of multiple pregnancies also increases. Better pregnancy rates must be balanced with the risk of higher-order multiple gestations. In most IVF clinics, embryos are transferred at the early cleavage stages (two to four cells) approximately forty-eight hours after ova retrieval. However, transfer also occurs at the pronucleate stage (one day after ova retrieval), the six-to-eight-cell stage (three days after ova retrieval), and the blastocyst stage (five to six days after ova retrieval).

Luteal Phase Support and Pregnancy Diagnosis

Luteal phase support (assistance with the eggs' development after ovulation) was initially thought necessary to overcome luteal insufficiency due to removal of follicular cells during aspiration for ova retrieval. In cycles in which GnRH agonists are not used, the value of luteal support with progesterone and/or hCG is questionable; most studies reveal no, or small, improvements in pregnancy rates. In addition, it is unlikely that follicular aspiration causes luteal insufficiency. When GnRH agonists are used for hyperovulation, luteal phase defects are more common, and luteal support is of benefit.

Pregnancy after IVF is usually diagnosed by measuring the level of hCG in serum (in the mother's blood) shortly after a missed menstrual period. For the purposes of measuring success rates, such a clinically determined pregnancy must be confirmed by ultrasound with the visualization of a fetal sac, a miscarriage with tissue diagnosis, or an ectopic pregnancy. All other measures are now considered biochemical pregnancies and do not count in pregnancy success rates using IVF.

Advanced Reproductive Technologies Related to IVF

Micromanipulation-Assisted Fertilization

Micromanipulation-assisted fertilization is primarily used to treat severe male-factor infertility but can also overcome some egg defects. There are three micromanipulation methods available to circumvent fertilization disorders. In the first method, an opening is made in the zona pellucida, or shell, of the egg. The opening can be made mechanically by partial zona dissection (PZD), or zona slitting; chemically by zona drilling; or, less commonly, by using laser technology. The hole in the zona pellucida allows sperm to have access to eggs without having to penetrate the zona pellucida. The second technique is known as subzonal insertion (SUZI or SZI), in which the zona is completely bypassed and viable sperm are injected directly into the subzonal (or perivitelline) space of the egg under the zona pellucida.

The most recent development in assisted-fertilization technologies is intracytoplasmic sperm injection (ICSI), in which a single viable but immobilized sperm is injected directly into the ooplasm, or core, of the egg. In this way, most causes of fertilization failure are circumvented, whether due to abnormalities in sperm, zona pellucida, or the ova membrane (oolemma). ICSI has virtually superseded the previous micromanipulation technologies and is now the method of choice for assisted fertilization. It has completely changed the field of IVF and has revolutionized the treatment of male-factor infertility.

Micromanipulation-Assisted Hatching

As the mammalian embryo develops, the zona pellucida thins. At the blastocyst stage, the embryo hatches from the zona and implants in the uterine wall. It has been suggested that after IVF the hatching process is compromised and that some embryos may not hatch successfully. Abnormalities of the zona pellucida and failure to hatch may be induced by ovarian stimulation and/or culture conditions. Some ova may be inherently poor and, although able to fertilize, are less likely to develop, hatch, and implant.

Deficiencies in the hatching process can be overcome by breaching the zona pellucida. The technology is known as micromanipulation-assisted hatching and, like micromanipulation-assisted fertilization, can be performed several ways: PZD, zona drilling with acidic Tyrode's medium, or laser technology. Hatching is believed to be most successful when performed on eight-cell embryos. Assisted hatching improves pregnancy rates in older women, women with elevated FSH, and women who have had repeated implantation failures. It enhances implantation rates for embryos with thick zonae, retarded development, and/or severe fragmentation.

Embryo Cryopreservation

Human embryos at the pronuclear and early cleavage stages have been successfully cryopreserved (frozen) using several cryoprotectants (suspension fluids): 1-, 2-propanediol, or dimethylsulfoxide. Glycerol is the cryoprotectant of choice for blastocysts (slightly older embryos). The methods involve slow cooling and are referred to as "equilibrium" freezing techniques. Intracellular water is drawn out of cells, which then freezes extracellularly. Cryoprotectants protect cells from lethal formation of intracellular ice. With the methods most widely used today, approximately 70 percent of embryos can be expected to survive freezing and thawing. Embryo survival is related to embryo quality. Embryos with even blastomeres (cellular components) and no evidence of acellular fragments have better survival rates than do poor-quality embryos. Pregnancy rates are comparable to those with standard IVF.

Rapid-freezing techniques have been developed to cryopreserve human embryos. The concentrations of cryoprotectant are much greater than for slow-freezing methods. Cells experience extensive dehydration, and the water is replaced by very high levels of cryoprotectant. The cryoprotectant solution vitrifies (forms a glasslike substance) when cooled rapidly and does not form ice. High survival and pregnancy rates have resulted.

The process of IVF is changing rapidly as more technologies become available. Micromanipulation techniques can be used to overcome severe male-factor infertility and to assist in implantation of embryos with impaired hatching mechanisms. Supernumerary embryos can be cryopreserved, stored, and transferred at a later date. The scope of IVF can be expected to continue to broaden as scientists find new ways to overcome infertility.

FOR FURTHER READING

American Fertility Society/Society for Assisted Reproductive Technology. 1994. "Assisted Reproductive Technology in the United States and Canada: 1992 Results Generated from the American Fertility Society/Society for Assisted Reproductive Technology Registry." *Fertility and Sterility* 62: 1121–1128.

Cohen, Jean. 1993. "Assisted Reproductive Management in Women Aged 40 and Over." *Assisted Reproductive Reviews* 3: 141–145.

Conn, P. M., and W. F. Crowley Jr. 1991. "Gonadotropin-Releasing Hormone and Its Analogues." *New England Journal of Medicine* 4: 1–9.

Devroey, P., et al. 1994. "Recombinant Follicle Stimulating Hormone." *Assisted Reproduction Reviews* 4: 2–9.

Friedler, S., L. C. Giudice, and E. J. Lamb. 1988. "Cryopreservation of Embryos and Ova." *Fertility and Sterility* 49: 743–764.

Gutierrez A., et al. 1994. "In Vitro Fertilization in Infertile Patients with Endometriosis." *Assisted Reproduction Reviews* 4: 162–171.

Katayama, P. 1994. "Assisted Hatching: The Current Status and Future Protection." *Assisted Reproduction Reviews* 4: 33–38.

Leykin, L. 1994. "In Vitro Fertilization/Embryo Transfer and Luteal Phase Support." *Assisted Reproduction Reviews* 4: 134–147.

Mortimer, D. 1994. *Practical Laboratory Andrology.* New York: Oxford University Press.

Roseboom, T. J., and J.P.W. Vermeiden. 1995. "Evaluation of Embryo Scoring Systems and Their Value in Predicting IVF Outcome." *Assisted Reproduction Reviews* 5: 53–59.

Scott, R. T., Jr., and G. E. Hofmann. 1995. "Prognostic Assessment of Ovarian Reserve." *Fertility and Sterility* 63: 1–11.

Sharma, V., et al. 1988. "An Analysis of Factors Influencing Establishment of a Clinical Pregnancy in an Ultrasound-Based Ambulatory in Vitro Fertilization Program." *Fertility and Sterility* 49: 468–478.

Tournaye, H., et al. 1992. "Comparison of in Vitro Fertilization in Male and Tubal Infertility: A 3-Year Study." *Human Reproduction* 7: 218–222.

Van Steirteghem, A. C., et al. 1993. "Intracytoplasmic Sperm Injection." *Assisted Reproduction Reviews* 3: 160–163.

Wood, Carl, and Alan Trounson. 1989. *Clinical in Vitro Fertilization.* 2nd ed. London: Springer-Verlag.

thirty-eight

In Vitro Fertilization—Historical Development

ROBERT GORE-LANGTON AND SUSAN DANIEL

Early Developments

The treatment of infertility due to occluded or nonfunctional fallopian tubes originated over a century before the birth of the first test-tube baby, Louise Brown (1978). The earliest recorded attempt to surgically repair obstructed tubes was by Tyler Smith in 1849. Although at that time the physiological role of the fallopian tubes was known, the concepts that fertilization involved penetration of the ova by a single sperm and that the genetic material of both parents was joined were not understood. At the end of the nineteenth century and with growing interest in the development of organ transplantation, physicians from both the United States and Europe attempted to overcome tubal infertility by grafting ovaries below the obstruction either in the oviduct or in the uterine cavity. They had limited success: Of the five patients reported treated, three became pregnant; however, only one patient delivered an infant. Shortly afterward, ovarian-graft technology was improved by developing methods to preserve blood supply. This technology was primarily used to treat premature ovarian failure and was seldom used to overcome infertility. At the same time that ovarian-graft methods were being developed, the foundations of endocrinology were being established.

In Vitro Fertilization Before
Robert Edwards and Patrick Steptoe

The first documented attempt to fertilize mammalian ova outside the body was made in 1878, but the experiment failed. In 1890, Walter Heape described an embryo-transfer technique: He flushed fertilized rabbit ova from oviducts and transferred them to surrogate mothers. In the 1930s others succeeded in producing live rabbit young by in vitro fertilization (IVF) using the transfer of early embryos into the oviduct. At about the same time it was learned that human ovulation occurs at the midpoint between two menstrual cycles. Shortly afterward (1937) a new method for detecting ovulation in women—laparoscopy—was created (early versions of the laparoscope were described in 1920 and 1921). The missing link was the method for retrieving mature ova for fertilization in a culture vessel. Ovulated human ova, both fertilized and unfertilized, were removed from fallopian tubes during surgery during the 1930s. There were some attempts made to fertilize some of these ova in vitro, and success was reported in 1946 and 1948, although there was some doubt as to the validity of the claim. Studies on IVF and early embryo development began shortly afterward. None of this work, however, was motivated by a desire to overcome infertility.

Robert Edwards and Patrick Steptoe:
The First Pregnancy and Baby

The geneticist Robert Edwards became involved in the study of human ova maturation and fertilization in vitro around 1960, and in 1968 he met the gynecologist and obstetrician Patrick Steptoe at a meeting of the endocrinological and gynecological section of the Royal Society of Medicine in London. It was then that they joined in a collaborative project to develop IVF as a fertility procedure by collecting ova from preovulatory ovarian follicles in women undergoing ovariectomies or hysterectomies. It was not until ten years later that Louise Brown was born.

At the time that Edwards and Steptoe began their work, rapid advances were being made in reproductive physiology. The discovery of capacitation (the process of sperm fertilizing an egg) in the rabbit was published in 1951. Contributions to improved embryo culture and transfer techniques in mice and rabbits were made in the later 1950s and early to middle 1960s. Methods for the collection of ova from mice were developed between 1955 and 1959, and at the same time fertilization of rabbit ova in vitro was demonstrated. It was with this knowledge that Edwards and Steptoe recovered ova by laparoscopy from human follicles as close to the time of ovulation as possible, mixed them with sperm, and achieved fertilization. The first pregnancy from IVF and embryo transfer occurred in 1975 but was ectopic. Louise Brown was conceived in November 1977 and born on July 25, 1978. With this event began a new era in the history of assisted reproduction.

Significant Developments in IVF Since 1978

IVF was developed using natural ovulatory cycles. Experience in domestic species with hyperovulation was soon applied to humans by the Australian vet and scientist Alan Trounson. With increased follicular development, more ova (eggs) were collected and fertilized and more embryos transferred. The result was an improved pregnancy rate compared to that for IVF in natural cycles.

Eggs for IVF were initially recovered by aspiration of follicles at laparotomy or by the laparoscopic method pioneered by Steptoe. Ultrasound-guided (usually transvaginal but sometimes transvesicular) ova retrieval is preferred today, since it can be performed as an outpatient procedure using gentle sedation and a local anesthetic. Ultrasound-guided egg retrievals are more cost- and time-effective than the earlier procedures that required the use of general anesthetics and operating rooms. Women and their partners can be together during the egg retrieval and generally leave the clinic within a few hours of the procedure.

Cryopreservation of human cells has a relatively short history. Sperm were the first human cells to be successfully cryopreserved, by Chris Polge in 1949, and over the years, methods for freezing sperm have changed very little. Cryopreserved sperm were first used clinically in 1954, and now frozen sperm are used routinely for donor insemination in IVF. In 1983, Trounson reported the first human pregnancy to result from a cryopreserved eight-cell embryo (using dimethyl sulfoxide as a cryoprotectant). Since then, embryo freezing has become an integral part of IVF. In 1985, a method for freezing blastocysts (slightly older embryos) using glycerol was developed, and a year later a method using 1, 2-propanediol as cryoprotectant was developed for early-cleavage-stage embryos. Methods for freezing eggs have not been as successful as those for embryos and sperm. In 1986 a pregnancy from cryopreserved eggs that were subsequently inseminated in vitro, fertilized, and transferred was reported. Most scientists have concerns about egg cryopreservation because disruptions occur during cooling and could lead to genetically abnormal eggs.

The fertilization rate after IVF for couples with male-factor infertility is considerably lower than that for couples with other types of infertility, and micromanipulation-assisted fertilization has completely revolutionized the treatment of male-factor infertility through IVF. Partial zona dissection (PZD), in which the opening is made mechanically, was described in 1989. Successful fertilization using subzonal insertion (SUZI or SZI) was reported in 1987. It is somewhat more invasive than PZD. The zona pellucida is completely bypassed by injecting viable sperm directly into the subzonal (or perivitelline) space. The most recent development in assisted fertilization is intracytoplasmic sperm injection (ICSI). The first pregnancies using this method were reported in 1992; since then, ICSI has become the most significant development in the field of assisted-reproduction technology since the birth of Louise Brown.

Future Developments

The field of assisted-reproductive technologies has experienced explosive growth and development since Edwards and Steptoe started their collaboration. Future developments are likely to include improved methods of hyperovulation, methods for maturing eggs in culture to avoid hyperovulation completely, improved culture conditions for gametes and embryos, methods to select embryos most likely to implant and embryos devoid of genetic abnormalities, and ways to enhance uterine receptivity.

FOR FURTHER READING

Cohen, J., et al. 1992. *Micromanipulation of Human Gametes and Embryos*. New York: Raven Press.

Edwards, Robert, and Patrick Steptoe. 1980. *A Matter of Life*. London: Hutchinson.

Fredericks, C. M., J. D. Paulson, and A. H. DeCherney. 1987. *Foundations of in Vitro Fertilization*. Washington, D.C.: Hemisphere.

Iritani, A. 1991. "Micromanipulation of Gametes for in Vitro Assisted Fertilization." *Molecular Reproduction and Development* 28: 199–207.

Lenz, S., J. G. Lauritsen, and M. Kjellow. 1981. "Collection of Human Ova for in Vitro Fertilization by Ultrasonically Guided Follicular Puncture." In *Follicular Maturation and Ovulation*. Amsterdam: Excerpta Medica Foundation.

Trounson, Alan, and Carl Wood. 1984. *In Vitro Fertilization and Embryo Transfer*. Edinburgh: Churchill-Livingstone.

Wolf, D. P., R. M. Brenner, and R. L. Stouffer. 1993. *In Vitro Fertilization and Embryo Transfer in Primates*. New York: Springer-Verlag.

thirty-nine

Ovarian Suppression by GnRH Agonists

ANDRÉ LEMAY

Egg Maturation and Female Sex Hormones

The human ovaries have two main roles: the release of an egg each month and the secretion of sex hormones responsible for the differentiation and function of the uterus and vagina. These functions are principally controlled by two hormones, FSH (follicle-stimulating hormone) and LH (luteinizing hormone). These two chemical regulators come from the pituitary gland, located at the base of the brain. At the time of the menses, FSH and LH initiate the stimulation of a cohort of eggs. The eggs are surrounded by granulosa cells that secrete the female sex hormones, the estrogens, principally estradiol. The secretion of estradiol is responsible for the proliferation of the endometrium, the tissue lining the uterine cavity. After a few days, one follicle among the cohort becomes dominant and the others regress. At ultrasonic examination it can be seen as a small cyst containing fluid, and at maturation it has an average diameter of two centimeters and protrudes from the surface of the ovary. At midcycle, a surge of LH and FSH triggers ovulation: the rupture of the follicle and the release of the egg. Following ovulation the cells of the follicle form a yellow cyst (corpus luteum) that still secretes estrogens and in addition releases large amounts of progesterone. This second type of female sex hormone is required for the maturation of the endometrium and implantation of a fertilized egg. In the absence of implantation, the corpus luteum cannot

TABLE 39.1 Clinical Utilities of Ovarian Suppression by GnRH Agonists

Symptoms	Condition	GnRH Agonist Administration
Early sexual development	Idiopathic precocious puberty	Alone
Failure to conceive	Infertility related to tubal obstruction or otherwise unexplained	Pre–in vitro fertilization (IVF) Controlled ovarian hyperstimulation with hMG and hCG
Chronic pelvic pain	Endometriosis proven by laparoscopy	Short-term treatment ≤ 6 months
		Preoperative (3–6 months) Long-term treatment >6 months plus add-back of replacement hormones
Abnormal uterine bleeding	Myomas (fibroids)	Preoperative (3–6 months) Long-term treatment >6 months plus add-back of replacement hormones
Male type hairiness	Polycystic ovarian disease	Long-term treatment >6 months plus add-back of replacement hormones

last more than fourteen days, and its degeneration leads to menstrual uterine bleeding. The usual length of this cycle is twenty-eight days.

A dysfunction in the menstrual cycle can lead to clinical problems such as heavy irregular uterine bleeding, no ovulation (anovulation), and excess or abnormal hair growth (hirsutism). These symptoms are frequently related to numerous small cysts at the periphery of the ovaries (polycystic ovarian disease; see Table 39.1). Other gynecological conditions such as endometriosis and myomas, also called fibroids, which occur during the reproductive period and regress at menopause, are also related to sex hormones of the menstrual cycle. The possibility to selectively suppress the development of a follicle and female sex hormones with the recent advent of GnRH (gonadotropin-releasing hormones) agonists has allowed new strategies for the management of these frequent and chronic infections.

GnRH Agonist Structure and Formulations

GnRH (previously named LHRH for luteinizing hormone–releasing hormone) is a hormone released from the hypothalamic area of the brain. It stimulates the release of both LH and FSH. Its composition and structure as a chain of ten amino acids were discovered in 1971 by Andrew Schally and Roger Guillemin, who received the Nobel Prize for this important contribution to medicine. Chemists have synthesized large numbers of GnRH agonists or derivatives that cause greater and more prolonged stimulation of gonadotropins than do naturally occurring GnRH. There is no allergic reaction to these discrete modifications of the native molecule, and GnRH agonists can be administered in large doses or over extensive periods of time.

GnRH agonists cannot be given orally, since these small molecules are rapidly destroyed by the digestive enzymes. In initial studies they were administered by nasal spray two or three times daily or by subcutaneous injection once daily. In the late 1990s formulations were developed permitting a monthly subcutaneous injection of a small implant or an intramuscular injection of a suspension of microcapsules.

The initial effect of a GnRH agonist is a maximal and sustained release of LH and FSH, replacing the normal pulsatile release with a massive discharge of hormones. During such stimulation, the cells secreting LH and FSH rapidly become resistant to subsequent stimulation for several hours, and repetitive administration of GnRH produces a progressive inhibition of both LH and FSH hormones (see Figure 39.1). This inhibition leads to a low gonadal hormone secretion like that in the menopausal state, yet the inhibitory effect is rapidly reversible following cessation of treatment. The possibility of putting the reproduction axis at rest, at will, for a defined duration has now been put to use in several gynecological situations.

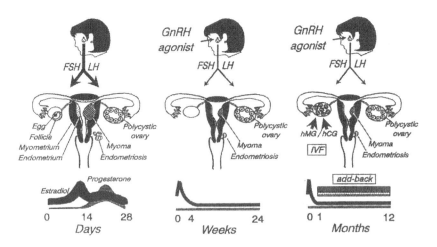

FIGURE 39.1 GnRH Analogs and the Female Hormonal Cycle

Clinical Utilities of Ovarian Suppression by GnRH Agonists

Since the late 1980s, it has become clear that GnRH agonists are useful to control secretions of LH and FSH and to correct abnormal gynecological conditions related to female and male sex hormone production in women. Alternatively, GnRH agonist suppression can be used to prepare the ovaries for controlled hyperovulation in in vitro fertilization (IVF). GnRH agonists can also be combined with other medications to improve their efficacy and limit their side effects.

Idiopathic precocious puberty occurs occasionally in young girls presenting with early pubic hair, breast development, and uterine bleeding between ages five and nine. One major consequence of precocious puberty is short stature due to early fusion of long-bone growth plates with their shafts. Most often there is no evidence of an underlying cause indicating a premature activation of the reproductive cycle. Until the advent of GnRH agonists, progesterone derivatives were effective in slowing breast and genital development and in preventing menstruation in most cases. However, they have not been successful in preventing early bone fusion. Most studies with GnRH agonists have shown a reduction in linear growth rate and a decreased progression in bone maturation during treatment. Further longitudinal studies are required before the effect of GnRH agonist therapy on final adult height is fully known. No adverse effects have been reported with long-term GnRH agonist suppression in children.

For IVF, the use of GnRH agonists suspends all normal reproductive hormonal activity and allows the administration of hMG (human menopausal gonadotropins, purified from the urine of menopausal women) to synchronize the development of multiple follicles (see Figure 39.1). Final maturation is achieved by an injection of hCG (human chorionic gonadotropin, a hormone similar to LH and purified from the urine of pregnant women) before egg retrieval for IVF. The degree of multiple-follicle growth is one of the most important factors in successful IVF trials; therefore the use of agents that allow for more control of follicle development and an increased number of available eggs is highly desirable. Randomized studies, controlled open trials, and reports on large series of patients all show the superiority of the combination of GnRH agonist with exogenous hMG and hCG in terms of pregnancy rate and live birth rate. Various schedules have been developed, and nearly all IVF programs are now using GnRH agonists.

Endometriosis, the development of glands similar to those lining the uterine cavity but on the organs or the layer of cells (peritoneal membrane) covering the pelvic cavity (see Figure 39.1), is the most frequent cause of severe pelvic pain at the time of menstruation, between menstruation, and during sexual intercourse. Endometriosis is also associated frequently with infertility. The identification of this disease is made by laparoscopy. A laparoscopy is also done for otherwise unexplained pelvic pain or infertility and for the diagnosis of a pelvic mass. The true incidence of endometriosis in the general population is still unknown, but it is estimated to be as frequent as 2–5 percent. Ovarian suppression by GnRH agonists for three to six months rapidly alleviates pain and causes a marked reduction of the lesions as evaluated by a second laparoscopy at the end of the treatment. In moderate and severe cases, GnRH agonist treatment can be administered preoperatively in order to facilitate surgery. The various formulations of GnRH agonists have been approved in most countries for the treatment of this condition.

Myomas or fibroids, benign tumors of the myometrium, or muscle part of the uterus, are frequently associated with abnormal uterine bleeding and are the most common indication for the surgical removal of the uterus (hysterectomy). Medicinal treatments for uterine leiomyoma have also been sought, but no treatment other than GnRH agonists has given consistent results in the treatment of myomas. GnRH agonists have the unique ability to reduce grossly (by up to half) the volume of uterine myomas. A major drawback of GnRH agonists is that volume reduction is only temporary. Regrowth of the tumor three to six months after therapy stops is the rule.

Commonly, GnRH agonists are used before removing the uterus or the tumor. They correct anemia, decrease the operative blood loss, and reduce the need for blood transfusion. Also, preoperative therapy with GnRH agonists may allow the surgeon to perform less aggressive surgery; for example, the uterus can be removed through the vagina rather than an abdominal incision. Alternatively, if a woman wishes to keep her uterus, the tumor(s) can be more easily removed in isolation after treatment with GnRH agonists. Sufficient shrinkage of the tumor can also allow its removal by endoscopy through the abdominal wall (laparoscopy) or the cervix (hysteroscopy).

Polycystic ovarian syndrome is characterized by an exaggerated secretion of LH, which leads to excessive secretion of male gonadal hormones from the theca cells surrounding the multiple small cysts found typically at the periphery of the ovaries. Elevated androgen levels cause an increase in hairiness in women at sites that are characteristic for males (superior lips, chin, breast, midline of the abdomen, and pubis). This condition is frequently associated with obesity, irregular or absent menses, and infertility. Several studies have indicated that GnRH agonists are effective in reducing excess hair after six months of medication. However, there is no evident change in the appearance of the multiple cysts in the ovaries, and there is normally a rapid recurrence of the symptoms of hair growth and irregular bleeding after cessation of treatment. No long-term treatments have been conducted with GnRH agonists alone because of the potential adverse effects of the prolonged suppression of female sex hormones.

Adverse Effects and Safety in GnRH Agonist Treatment

The side effects of GnRH agonist treatment are menopausal-like symptoms related to very low levels of estrogens in the blood. The main symptoms are hot flashes, vaginal dryness, headache, emotional lability, and fatigue. It is well known that after menopause there is a progressive increase in blood cholesterol, atherosclerosis, and coronary heart disease. One concern is that similar changes would occur following ovarian suppression by GnRH agonists. Fortunately, the deprivation of estrogens does not have a deleterious effect on blood cholesterol and other lipids during treatment with GnRH agonists.

The main potential drawback of ovarian suppression with GnRH agonist therapy is accelerated bone loss. New and sensitive techniques to measure bone density have revealed a rapid decrease in bone mineral content. At the level of the lumbar spine, results indicate an average bone loss of 1 percent per month in young women (average twenty-five years old) treated for endometriosis. This observed bone loss is faster than the well-accepted rate of 3 percent for the first year of menopause.

The change in bone density appears readily reversible after discontinuation of treatment. However, only a few studies have reported a complete recovery at the level of the spine six months after therapy stops. It appears that new bone formation takes more time than bone loss and that one year would be required for bone recovery in the majority of treated patients. The delay in bone recovery following GnRH agonist treatment might be meaningful, especially for young women in whom bone mass increases until their third decade. Rapid bone demineralization prevents the prescription of GnRH agonists for over a six-month period. Because the question of recovery is not clear, there are serious concerns about cumulative bone loss with repeated or prolonged periods of exposure.

GnRH Agonists with Addition of Steroidal and Nonsteroidal Agents

Gynecological conditions such as endometriosis and myomas are chronic problems often requiring prolonged or repeated treatments. Concerns about bone loss with GnRH agonist treatment prompted recent studies on hormonal replacement. The use of a synthetic progesterone substitute alone appears unsatisfactory, since large doses are required to prevent bone loss. A high dose of a progesterone substitute induces detrimental changes in blood cholesterol. Several regimens, not unlike the usual hormonal replacement for menopausal women, have been proposed using various combinations of natural estrogens and synthetic progesterone substitutes in small amounts. Current information bearing on the utility of this approach is still sparse. However, the effectiveness of the GnRH agonist on endometriosis and fibroids is preserved, and most of the side effects related to estrogen deprivation are suppressed and palliated. Bone loss appears to be prevented. Bone loss can be totally prevented by biphosphonates, a new class of drugs that has been developed for the treatment of osteoporosis.

Other reports have shown the potential utility of combining GnRH and addback hormones for polycystic ovarian disease, premenstrual syndrome, and abnormal uterine bleeding. There are opportunities in ovarian suppression with GnRH to design specific and effective hormonal regimens for these conditions. In these regimens, hormonal substitution is not restricted to small doses. Prospective clinical studies will have to be carried out to establish the long-term effectiveness and safety of the GnRH agonist addback strategies.

FOR FURTHER READING

Adashi, E. Y. 1994. "Long-Term Gonadotrophin-Releasing Hormone Agonist Therapy: The Evolving Issue of Steroidal 'Add-Back' Paradigms." *Human Reproduction* 9: 1380–1397.

Barbieri, R. L. 1993. "GnRH and GnRH Analogues: Applications in Gynecology." *Clinical Obstetrics and Gynecology* 36: 615–636.

Lemay, A., E. S. Surrey, and A. J. Friedman. 1994. "Extending the Use of Gonadotropin-Releasing Hormone Agonists: The Emerging Role of Steroidal and Nonsteroidal Agents." *Fertility and Sterilization* 61(1): 21–34.

Polan, M. L., and M. R. Henzl. 1993. "The Clinical Use of GnRH Superactive Analogues." *Infertility and Reproductive Medicine: Clinics of North America* 4(1).

Shaw, R. W., and J. C. Marshal. 1989. *LHRH and Its Analogues: Their Use in Gynaecological Practice.* Toronto: Butterworth.

forty

Human Pituitary Hormones and Creutzfeldt-Jakob Disease

LYNETTE DUMBLE

Following experiments in the 1940s and 1950s, pituitary glands from human cadavers were found to contain growth hormones and gonadotropin, which could, respectively, overcome short stature and infertility. By the mid-1960s, clinical programs had attracted government sponsorship in Australia, Canada, France, the United Kingdom, New Zealand, and the United States. All programs with the exception of the French one were abruptly halted in 1985, when four young adults—one in the United Kingdom and three in the United States—who had been exposed to human pituitary growth hormone (hGH) injections more than a decade earlier suddenly died within months of each other from a brain illness known as Creutzfeldt-Jakob disease (CJD). CJD is a rare illness affecting less than one per million in the majority of world regions; this cluster of CJD deaths raised concerns that an estimated 20,000 to 30,000 recipients of human pituitary hormones around the world would contract the disease. Based on the assumption that the purity of the hormone-extraction process accounted for the absence of a single case of hGH-related CJD in France to 1985, the government-sponsored program continued unabated in that country. In 1989, by which time the number of French children at risk of growth-hormone-related CJD had practically doubled, the first French child came down with CJD. In 1993, some French doctors faced manslaughter charges, and by 1996 France was home to half of the world's 100-plus cases of pituitary-hormone-related CJD. Contrary to the predictions of health authorities and medical experts, CJD tragedies are not confined to hGH-treated children. By 1997 five infertile women, all exposed during infertility treatment in Australia to a hormone also taken from human pituitary glands, hPG, had contracted CJD.

Creutzfeldt-Jakob Disease

Unheard of in humans before two German physicians, Creutzfeldt and Jakob, independently reported sporadic cases in the 1920s, CJD remains an illness that defies cure. Warning symptoms emerge only after a prolonged incubation period, during which the agent of CJD turns the brain into the spongelike mass that accounts for the disease being originally classified as a spongiform slow virus disorder. Death may be a welcome escape from the extreme muscular jerks of CJD, which silently eats away at the brain over years, robbing its victims of all means of communication: sight, speech, hearing, the comprehension of language, and the ability to write.

Unlike sporadic CJD, which tends to occur in the late fifth or sixth decade of life, human-pituitary-hormone-related CJD has appeared at an earlier age. The mean age of the five Australian women contracting CJD from hPG was only forty-five years when their neurologic symptoms emerged, and children treated with hGH have died of CJD without entering their teens. Additionally, the prominent early features of dementia and brain abnormalities measured by electroencephalograph in sporadic CJD are frequently absent from pituitary-hormone-related CJD, and whereas sporadic CJD frequently has a chronic clinical phase persisting over years, hPG/hGH-related CJD has a rapidly progressive course that generally brings death within months.

These and other subtle differences between pituitary-hormone-related CJD and other forms of the disease may account for the belated recognition of some cases of pituitary-hormone-related CJD. To date, known examples of escaped diagnosis include the pneumonia-attributed death of a sixteen-year-old hGH-treated girl in the United States in 1979. Upon a reexamination of her medical history and brain histology in 1986, it was confirmed that she had contracted CJD. For two years before CJD was recognized in one woman from South Australia, the same institution where she was treated for physiological (neurologic) problems and had been treated for infertility with hPG twelve years earlier persisted in diagnosing her problem as a psychiatric one. A Western Australian hPG-treated woman was misdiagnosed with multiple sclerosis when her CJD manifested in 1988 subsequent to her 1976 infertility treatment. This woman's diagnosis was changed to degenerative/demyelinating illness before her death in 1989; in 1993, a government investigation into deaths in human-pituitary-hormone recipients recognized her CJD features and acknowledged that she had been another CJD victim of the program. It has been widely speculated that the connection between the CJD of a Melbourne woman living in the United Kingdom and her hPG infertility treatment would not have been made had it not been for the coincidence that a member of the Oxford medical team treating her had had experience during his neurological training with a case of hPG-related CJD in South Australia.

Nature and Transmissibility of CJD

The precise agent of transmissible spongiform encephalopathies such as CJD remains unidentified but is referred to as a "prion," or a protein with atypical viral characteristics. The original lesson about the infectious nature of this group of brain diseases came from a 1934 vaccine catastrophe in the United Kingdom in which scrapie (mad sheep disease) developed in almost 5,000 out of 18,000 lambs within two years of their immunization against louping-ill virus infection. Scientists have been able to determine that the 1934 vaccine serum was prepared from a number of lambs whose dams subsequently developed scrapie. Because of a series of interprofessional feuds, the data on scrapie passing vertically from ewes to their lambs and horizontally from lamb to lamb by virtue of the vaccine injections did not appear in the scientific literature, and thus was kept from international view, for fifteen years.

Some thirty years after the catastrophe in the United Kingdom, Carlton Gadjusek performed his Nobel Prize–winning experiments to demonstrate the transmissibility of human brain diseases across species, in this case between laboratory rodents and primates. By 1975, two neuroscientists from Yale University in the United States, Laura and Eli Manuelides, had demonstrated that injections of human blood, like injections of brain taken from kuru and CJD victims, transmitted the disease across the species barrier to laboratory animals. Their prophetic, but unheeded, message implied that blood was the vehicle that carried the agent of CJD around the body until it chanced upon a hospitable residence like the brain. In other words, the blood route was identified as a key element in the transmission of CJD from a primary host to a secondary one. CJD is distinct from infections such as influenza that are caused by an airborne virus but similar to AIDS and hepatitis B, which are caused by blood-borne viruses. This means that recipients exposed to human-pituitary-gland-hormone injections, or to blood or organ transplants from a donor with CJD, risk becoming secondary CJD hosts once contagious material enters their bloodstream.

Overall, the implications of the Manuelides experiments escaped the international consortium involved in human pituitary hormones programs. British scientist and scrapie expert Alan Dickinson was the only scientist to follow this line of research, though by 1986 he admitted in his published results that attempts to filter the CJD agent out of the human pituitary between 1978 and 1982 were unsuccessful. During this period, CJD was increasingly recognized as a contagious illness; instances of suspected human-to-human transmissions through accidental cross-infections via surgical instruments, transplanted corneas, and dura mater grafts appeared in the medical literature. There were also reports of CJD deaths among histology technicians, pathologists, surgeons, and nurses, all of which served to increase awareness of CJD as an occupational hazard.

Women and Exposure to CJD During Infertility Treatments

A 1976 report coauthored by the Australian Pituitary Advisory Committee and the Australian Department of Health hailed the treatment of anovulatory infertility with hPG as one of the therapeutic milestones in gynecology but stipulated that hPG would be provided if only anovulation was the sole reason for infertility. Yet in what clearly amounted to a breach of regulatory guidelines, another 1976 report appearing in the same issue of the same medical journal indicated hPG administration to ovulatory women with total tubal destruction who were in the process of being conditioned for in vitro fertilization (IVF). To this day, it remains unclear how many women were exposed to hPG in IVF practices and whether they, like human-pituitary-hormone-treated infertile men and Turner's syndrome girls, are included in the government's tally of 2,100 official pituitary-hormone recipients.

In addition, unlike with growth-hormone-treated children, whose years of biweekly to daily injections made it impossible for pediatricians to avoid the detailed record keeping that came with government sponsorship, women's gonadotropin injections usually lasted for less than six months. As a result, there was frequently leftover gonadotropin that infertility specialists could inject into new candidates without going through the bureaucratic application process to renew hormone supplies, and thus government records of women exposed to pituitary gonadotropin were incomplete. In Australia in the face of a 1997 Senate inquiry, the Federal Health and Family Services Department admitted that 190 of the 2,100 validated recipients of human hPG and hGH remained untraced by the department. It also revealed that the total number at risk of CJD from the Australian program was between 2,600 and 2,700; between 500 and 600 additional recipients, undoubtedly the overwhelming majority being infertile women, had been exposed to the hormones in the absence of government approval.

Similarly, in countries other than Australia, there have been systematic efforts to downgrade the significance of women exposed to human pituitary hormones. In 1988, within three years of the first cases of pituitary-growth-hormone-related CJD, the National Institutes of Health in the United States prematurely assumed that the short-term nature of the gonadotropin treatment precluded any risk of contracting CJD and set about shredding the records of infertile women treated by some 250 American gynecologists over the previous fifteen years. Similar records had also been shredded in the United Kingdom, so when news of pituitary-gonadotropin-related CJD in Australia hit the headlines in Britain in 1993, British authorities were in no position to answer consumer inquiries. One came from a thirty-two-year-old woman whose mother had received five pituitary gonadotropin injections in the 1960s and had died of CJD in 1975 when aged fifty-five. Officially, 300 infertile British women were exposed to pituitary gonadotropin, but medical literature from British infertility circles that dates back to the 1960s indicates that the number was probably much larger. Although the risk of gonadotropin-related CJD to Australian and, to a lesser extent, British women has reached the media, the issue has scarcely been raised in North America and the rest of Europe.

Although the uneven distribution of health care worldwide has restricted human pituitary programs to North America, Europe, and Australasia, Third World children and women did not altogether escape exposure to CJD. A medical report in 1991 linked the CJD death of a young Brazilian man, along with five young New Zealand men and women, to childhood treatment involving pituitary growth hormone obtained from the United States. Also, the fate of women in Mexico City whose breasts were injected with American pituitary hormones in an experiment to increase the volume of milk in lactating mothers (some already pregnant again) is unknown.

Public Health Repercussions of Risky Medicine

Although the concept of blood-transfusion-related CJD was initially and openly dismissed by many public health authorities, by 1987, all American and New Zealand registered recipients of pituitary growth hormone had been advised not to donate blood and organs. It took until 1992 for Australian and British blood banks and transplant programs to follow suit with the result that the Australian and British populations were exposed to the risk of secondary CJD transmission for five years longer than their American and New Zealand counterparts. Also, despite the claim that blood-transmitted CJD is unproven in humans, actions between 1995 and 1998 indicate that authorities have finally opened their minds to the public health implications of the Manuelides experiments. Canadian authorities spent Can$15 million in 1995 to withdraw pooled plasma already in the process of being transfused to thousands across the country on the grounds that it contained a donation from a man who had subsequently died of CJD. Similarly, in 1996, New Zealand authorities, under the weight of public pressure, finally agreed to quarantine blood products that had been contaminated by a donation from a CJD-infected donor. British blood banks also increased their precautionary measures with an extended questioning routine designed to screen out donations from parents, siblings, and children of CJD victims.

British microbiologist Steven Dealler estimates that CJD-infected blood may reach as many as 60,000 recipients each year, but the lengthy incubation time preceding CJD symptoms increases the difficulty of linking a blood-transfusion recipient's CJD with a donor source. Also, it is possible that secondary CJD in a transfusion recipient may appear years in advance of the primary CJD in a blood donor. CJD was found in a liver-transplant recipient even though the liver donor had been cleared. The disease was traced back to a CJD-like illness in one of the blood donors. The problem of detection is made worse by the inaction of government and medical authorities, which has placed the public at risk of CJD from uninformed hGH and hPG recipients who unwittingly spread the disease to others via blood donation. Similarly, the possibility that women treated with hPG may have transmitted CJD to their children has been widely overlooked. There are currently no public initiatives (medical or governmental) to investigate whether some women's deaths from CJD in the 1990s were due to their infertility pituitary hormone treatments in the 1960s, 1970s, and 1980s. According to the frequent reports of these cases in the medical journals, these women died a decade younger on average than women with sporadic CJD.

Legal Responses to Human-Pituitary-Hormone Programs

A landmark High Court ruling in the United Kingdom on July 21, 1996, deemed that the Department of Health had been negligent in permitting the hGH treatment of short-statured children up until 1985 given that there had been warnings as early as 1977 that the hormone was possibly contaminated with CJD. Whereas this ruling indicated the culpability of health officials and pediatric endocrinologists and physicians, reproductive endocrinologists and gynecologists who administered CJD-infected hormones to infertile women went unnoticed. The High Court restricted its judgment to the clinical use of hGH and did not include the use of the fertility hormone hPG. The production of both took place during the same time and under the umbrella of a single program that was designed to simultaneously extract gonadotropin and pediatric growth hormone from a pool of human pituitary glands. Gonadotropin and growth hormone are equally prone to pituitary hormone CJD contamination.

Early in 1997, the Australian government refused to provide compensation for the lifelong anxiety suffered by those who know they may contract CJD. On the eve of a test case involving one affected woman and estimated to cost the government Aus$1 million, it settled the case out of court. Later the government extended the offer of legal expenses plus financial compensation to surviving families if CJD appeared in any recipient of human pituitary hormones. Since then, a Senate committee has recognized the cold comfort of the government handout and has also recommended payouts for proven psychological trauma from contending with the possibility of CJD over a lifetime.

FOR FURTHER READING

Billette de Villemeur, T., et al. 1996. "Creutzfeldt-Jakob Disease from Contaminated Growth Hormone in France." *Neurology* 47: 690–695.

Cooke, J. 1998. *Cannibals, Cows and the CJD Catastrophe*. Milson's Point, Australia: Random House.

Dumble, L. 1996. "Brain-Dead Imperialism: Manmade Creutzfeldt-Jakob and Mad Cow Disease." *Third World Resurgence* 75: 21–24.

Lacey, R. W., and S. F. Dealler. 1994. "The Transmission of Prion Disease: Vertical Transfer of Prion Disease." *Human Reproduction* 9: 1792–1796.

Lyons, W. R., C. H. Li, and N. Ahmad. 1968. "Mammotrophic Effects of Human Hypophysial Growth Hormone Preparations in Animals and Man." In A. Pecile and E. E. Müller, eds., *Growth Hormone: Proceedings of the First International Symposium on Growth Hormone*. Amsterdam: Excerpta Medica Foundation.

Manuelidis, L. 1994a. "Dementias, Neurodegeneration, and Viral Mechanisms of Disease from the Perspective of Human Transmissible Encephalopathies." *Annals of the New York Academy of Sciences* 724: 259–281.

Manuelidis, L. 1994b. "The Dimensions of Creutzfeldt-Jakob Disease." *Transfusion* 34: 915–928.

Morgan, J. 1996. "Blood to Be Screened for CJD." *British Medical Journal* 313: 441.

forty-one

In Vitro Fertilization— Culture Media

ROBERT GORE-LANGTON AND
SUSAN DANIEL

Most of the culture media used in human in vitro fertilization (IVF) were first developed for laboratory rodents and domestic species and modified for use in humans. As with the mouse, many human embryos experience a developmental block in vitro. In the human, the incidence of developmental arrest increases markedly between the four- and eight-cell stages. The block in vitro corresponds to the stage at which the embryonic genome is activated (the embryo acquires its own genetic code). Unlike with other species, cultured human embryos have an initial growth rate similar to that of embryos in vivo. One division occurs approximately every twenty-four hours after fertilization for about six days. There is great variability, however, between embryos from different couples and even among embryos from a single couple. It is generally accepted that embryos with the highest cleavage rate are those most likely to implant. The difficulty in obtaining human eggs and embryos for research has resulted in limited information regarding their metabolic requirements in culture, and although significant advances have been made, deficiencies still exist in providing suitable media for human IVF and embryo culture.

Media for IVF and Early Embryo Culture

There are three general types of media used for human IVF: simple, balanced salt solutions; complex media; and physiological fluids. Simple, balanced salt solutions contain two components, salts and energy substrates (glucose, pyruvate, and lactate). The most widely used solutions are Earle's balanced salt solution (EBSS), modified T6, and human tubal fluid (HTF), which is formulated to simulate the chemical composition—in particular, potassium ion concentration—of fallopian tube fluid. These media contain bicarbonate and require an atmosphere of 5 percent carbon dioxide to maintain an acceptable pH level of 7.4. At room conditions, their buffering capacity is inadequate, and media containing phosphate or the acid HEPES must be used. Complex culture media such as Menezo B_2 or B_3 (same as B_2 but contains a protein supplement) and Ham's F10 contain amino acids, nucleic acid precursors, and vitamins in addition to salts and energy substrates. Amniotic fluid obtained from amniocentesis has been used successfully for human IVF and embryo culture. However, when compared with the use of T6, pregnancy rates were not improved.

There are no studies that conclusively support the superiority of one medium over all others. In one study, human tubal fluid was reported to yield higher pregnancy rates than T6. It was suggested that the superiority of HTF was due to a higher potassium concentration than that of T6. However, in a larger controlled trial, no difference was found between HTF and T6 in pregnancy rates after IVF. More recently, a modification of HTF lacking glucose and phosphate ions was reported to yield a higher implantation rate than the standard formulation of HTF. This finding is in agreement with work in laboratory rodents. Glucose is not required for early embryo development, and its inclusion in culture medium is detrimental.

Menezo B_2 yields a superior fertilization rate and improved embryo development when compared with EBSS; however, pregnancy rates do not differ between the two media. The standard formulation of Ham's F10 contains hypoxanthine, which inhibits mouse embryo development. Its omission from Ham's F10 enhances early human embryo development. Complex media also contain other components known to be detrimental to mouse embryo development under some conditions. These include essential amino acids, nicotinamide, and transitional metals (iron and copper). The impact of these components on human embryos is unknown.

Media for Blastocyst Development

The nutritional requirements of early-cleavage-stage (two- to eight-cell) embryos and later stages (morula to blastocyst) differ. Eggs and early embryos (two- to eight-cell stages) require the substance pyruvate to develop; later-stage embryos require glucose. As mentioned, research in laboratory rodents has shown that early embryo development is improved in media devoid of glucose. The same may be true in humans.

Limited development of blastocysts occurs in simple media; however, continued development fails. Blastocysts expand and then collapse and degenerate. More complex formulations are required. Minimum essential medium (MEM), the alpha modification of MEM, and Ham's F12 and CZB (the designation assigned by the authors who first described the formulation) have all been reported to provide superior developmental support for the blastocyst stage. Supplementation of medium with serum is also beneficial.

Protein Supplements

Culture media for human IVF are usually supplemented with protein; it is unlikely, however, that protein is required for early embryo development. The advantage of protein is that it facilitates embryo handling by preventing adherence to plastic or glass surfaces. The type of protein used to supplement culture media varies widely. Maternal and fetal cord serums were the first protein supplements used for IVF, and maternal serum is commonly used today. Collection and preparation require great care and are laborious. Blood must be drawn separately from each female patient, since pooling and sharing of serum are strongly discouraged to prevent transmission of blood-borne infections. Serum can also be toxic to embryo development or contain sperm antibodies that inhibit fertilization.

Albumin (usually with other serum proteins present) is an alternative to serum. It is readily available from commercial sources, and the effort required for preparation is minimal. However, since albumin is derived from pooled human blood samples or from other species (usually cows), extensive screening and appropriate decontamination precautions are critical for patient safety. Some batches of albumin have been found to be toxic to embryo development. Each batch requires toxicity testing.

Problems with protein supplements can be eliminated by excluding them from media preparations used for egg and embryo culture. Media devoid of protein have been shown to support early embryo development and have been used successfully in IVF.

Other Culture Conditions

There is no standardized culture method for human IVF. Culture systems include microdrops of medium with oil overlay or medium in test tubes, culture dishes, or multiwell culture trays. Culture media for IVF can be equilibrated with either 5 percent carbon dioxide, 5 percent oxygen (low oxygen tension), and 90 percent nitrogen or 5 percent carbon dioxide in air (ambient—20 percent—oxygen tension). Temperature is maintained at thirty-seven degrees Celsius. Equilibration of medium with carbon dioxide is important to regulate pH levels, and incubator gas is humidified to reduce evaporation and regulate carbon dioxide levels. Some laboratories prefer using low illumination or yellow light. There are advantages and disadvantages to all these different culture systems, and there is no clear evidence that any one set of conditions is superior to the others.

Coculture Technology

Fertilization and early embryo development occur in the fallopian tube (oviduct). Tubal fluid provides a complex and dynamic environment that is absent in vitro. Coculture technology was developed to overcome deficiencies in culture media and to mimic conditions in the fallopian tube by incubating ova, sperm, and embryos with monolayers of somatic feeder cells. Coculture enhances human embryo quality, improves embryos' development in vitro, and improves pregnancy rates after IVF.

The beneficial effects of coculture are not species-specific or specific to any particular cell type or tissue origin of the feeder cells. Improved results have been reported using human oviductal cells, fetal bovine (cow) uterine fibroblasts, bovine oviductal epithelium, Vero cells, and autologous cumulus cells, endometrial cells, and granulosa-lutein cells. Autologous coculture systems have the advantage that viral screening is not necessary. Feeder cells from other species and humans require rigorous screening and subculturing to reduce the risk of disease transmission.

Somatic feeder cells are believed to improve embryo development by secreting embryotrophic factors (positive conditioning). Once these factors have been identified, they can be added to standard IVF media formulations, and the need to coculture will be eliminated. The feeder cells may also act by removing or metabolizing deleterious agents in IVF culture media (negative conditioning).

Quality Control in the IVF Laboratory

Good quality control in the IVF laboratory is essential to maintain acceptable fertilization and pregnancy rates. All culture media, plasticware, and other material that come into contact with gametes or embryos must be nontoxic. Tests for toxicity include mouse embryo development, human sperm survival, rodent IVF, and monolayer cell cultures. These tests are useful in identifying serious toxicity problems, and at least one should be used to screen media and materials before use in IVF. More subtle toxicity problems that reduce embryo viability are often much more difficult to identify. Tests in which cell proliferation is measured (in mouse embryos and other types of cell culture) are very sensitive and may be able to detect subtle toxicity problems.

The purity of the water used in the preparation of culture media is extremely important. The source of water varies widely, including rainwater distilled multiple times and city water treated by reverse osmosis and multiple distillations. The most commonly used method for water purification is reverse osmosis followed by ultrafiltration and passage through a pyrogen filter. Considerable care is required to maintain ultrafiltration systems, and routine maintenance is critical.

All other aspects of the IVF laboratory require strict quality control. Incubators must be routinely cleaned and sterilized. Temperature and carbon dioxide levels must be closely monitored. Adequate humidification is essential. All glassware in contact with culture media must be washed and sterilized using the tissue culture method. Washing procedures should include soaking in dilute acid solution, sonication, and thorough rinsing in ultrapure water. When detergents are used, they must be completely removed by proper rinsing procedures. Dry-heat sterilization is commonly used for human IVF. Ethylene oxide can also be used, but adequate venting is necessary to remove all traces of gas. Autoclaving is not recommended, and irradiation should not be used on some plastics. Sterile technique is essential to avoid contamination of the culture system with microorganisms. Yeast and fungi are common contaminants known to have detrimental effects on gametes and embryos.

Conclusion

Fertilization and early embryo development occur in the fallopian tube, and culture systems for IVF have attempted to mimic this environment. However, due to the inaccessibility of reproductive tract fluids for analysis and the dynamic nature of the tubal environment, only moderate success has been achieved. Nevertheless, human IVF has had a remarkable history and has experienced incredible growth since the birth of the first IVF baby in 1978. In vitro fertilization has become an accepted therapeutic procedure for coping with many types of infertility and is continuing to broaden in scope. Future developments will depend on media formulations and culture conditions that have been improved to meet the metabolic requirements of eggs and embryos.

FOR FURTHER READING

Bongso, A., et al. 1995. "Coculture Techniques for Embryonic Stem Cell Production." *Assisted Reproduction Reviews* 5: 106–114.

Fredericks, C. M., J. D. Paulson, and A. H. DeCherney. 1987. *Foundations of in Vitro Fertilization*. Washington, D.C.: Hemisphere.
Wolf, D. P., R. M. Brenner, and R. L. Stouffer. 1993. *In Vitro Fertilization and Embryo Transfer in Primates*. New York: Springer-Verlag.
Wood, Carl, and Alan Trounson. 1989. *Clinical in Vitro Fertilization*. 2nd ed. London: Springer-Verlag.

forty-two

In Vitro Maturation and Ova Freezing

KATHY MUNRO

Scientists have been studying the physiology and cell processes of human ova (eggs) since the 1920s; however, it was not until 1938 that the first successful in vitro maturation studies were performed with human ova. During the early 1930s scientists discovered that mature ova were most likely to be found in women between the twelfth and fifteenth days of the menstrual cycle. By the mid-1930s they had discovered that the maturation of these ova occurs within the follicle prior to ovulation. By 1939 it had been observed that fully grown, follicle-free ova mature spontaneously if placed in a culture. This was an important breakthrough because it meant that scientists were no longer dependent on mature ova formed in vivo (in the body). It was now possible to produce mature ova from the much larger pool of immature ova.

Following this discovery the focus then moved from using the less accessible ova matured in vivo to using in vitro–matured human ova. A new phase of research thus began in which scientists attempted to achieve successful fertilization in a culture medium. During the 1950s further work was undertaken on the fertilization status of ova to obtain a better understanding of human follicular ova before and after exposure to sperm in vitro. In the 1960s Robert Edwards and Patrick Steptoe (the same scientists who in 1978 managed the first IVF baby) documented for the first time the stages of maturation in the nucleus of human ova. This research was then used as the foundation for other studies to improve the success rates of the in vitro fertilization experiments that were under way at this time. It was during this phase that doubts began to emerge about the effectiveness of maturing and subsequently fertilizing ova, because the initial success rates were very low. Researchers turned to other strategies for developing in vivo protocols for the production of mature ova within multiple follicles through hormonal stimulation. This pioneering work for the establishment of hormone-stimulation protocols is used in assisted reproduction today.

By the 1970s the focus had turned to the factors in the women themselves that might influence the number of ova that could be retrieved, matured, and fertilized. Research during this period uncovered that as a woman aged, the number of ova retrieved declined. It was also during this time that scientists established that ova would mature only if they were retrieved just prior to or immediately after ovulation. This period in the history of the development of in vitro maturation therefore focused most heavily on improving the conditions and success rates for the procedure.

Almost all this pioneering work on human ova maturation was possible because of the practice of harvesting ova from ovaries obtained after they had been removed from women who had undergone clinically indicated oophorectomies (the surgical removal of the ovary) or hysterectomies. However, a considerable transfer of technology has also occurred from the fields of veterinary science and animal husbandry (in particular with cows from abattoirs).

During the 1980s, work continued on enhancing the number of ova that could be matured using the previously mentioned techniques. This research also laid the foundation for more extensive explorations of the relationship of hormones such as estrogens, androgens, and progesterones to the maturation of ova. Many of these studies involved exposing ova to differing concentrations and combinations of these hormones in culture media to establish how their maturation was affected. During the 1970s and 1980s other research was also under way to develop cryopreservation (freezing) techniques for use with ova before and after fertilization. With the increased use of hyperovulatory drugs with infertile women during this period, greater numbers of ova were produced and fertilized than could be transferred during any IVF cycle. Cryopreservation research enabled surplus embryos to be frozen by the method previously outlined and then stored for later use.

The first birth following the freezing of human embryos was recorded in Melbourne, Australia, in 1984. Although this achievement gained considerable attention at the time and has since been widely applied in the clinical context, the development of alternative methods (such as freezing ova) has continued because so many legal and ethical issues have arisen from freezing embryos. For a long time freezing ova was not successful because the ovum is the largest cell in the body and the ice crystals that formed during freezing invariably ruptured the delicate cell membrane. However, in 1986, scientists from the Flinders Medical Center in Adelaide, South Australia, reported that they had developed a method that allowed for the freezing and thawing of unfertilized human ova. Doctors were originally worried that the chemicals used to protect the ova while frozen might cause some harm to them and to any embryos developed from them. When scientists sought permission to test this theory using human eggs and the institutional ethics committee refused, the researchers moved to Asia so that they could continue their work.

Rationale for in Vitro Maturation and Ova Freezing

Scientists have argued that in vitro maturation and ova freezing are beneficial because they allow women with life-threatening illnesses such as cancer to become mothers. These techniques allow women to store their own ova for later use before undergoing procedures such as radiation therapy or chemotherapy that might reduce their fertility. In vitro maturation and ova freezing require women to undergo only a limited amount of hyperovulation prior to egg harvesting and help relieve the effects of women's whole bodies being repeatedly subject to the ovarian stimulants that have been associated with health risks such as breast cancer and birth defects. In vitro maturation and egg freezing also mean that the woman has to undergo only one laparoscopy rather than one during every IVF cycle. These techniques also have the potential to make IVF much cheaper and therefore accessible to many more people.

A less conventional rationale for the development of in vitro maturation and ova freezing has been that it allows women to take their own eggs when they are young, store them, and have them implanted later in life when their fertility has declined. Some scientists argue that in vitro maturation represents a significant improvement on the previous techniques of hyperovulation and embryo freezing because it involves the retrieval of an egg before it is ripened, thereby overcoming a range of ethical problems associated with the storage and disposition of embryos. A number of scientists have supported the technique because they believe it provides a means of preserving the genetic material of endangered primate species.

Concerns and Criticisms Associated with in Vitro Maturation and Ova Freezing

For many years, research scientists in the field of reproductive technology have expressed frustration with the lack of ova available as experimental material. Although these scientists have promoted the view that the demand for donor ova is generated by infertile women, there is significant evidence suggesting that the demand is driven by clinicians and, more particularly, scientific researchers. By providing more embryos, reproductive technologies such as in vitro maturation now move the research beyond the context of infertility and into that of genetic engineering.

Existing policy frameworks in key countries such as Australia, Canada, the United Kingdom, and the United States recognize that research with ova and fertilized ova has been and remains inseparable from the development of IVF and embryo transfer. However, there is very little attention paid to the increasingly interdependent relationship between in vitro maturation research and genetic-screening techniques. Although most countries have laws and policies founded on the belief that it is undesirable to deliberately create embryos as research material, it is now possible to obtain an unlimited supply of embryo research material using in vitro–matured ova without interfering with existing regulations relating to embryos.

Some feminists have argued that with the increased availability of ova as experimental material, the commodification of women has expanded and there is a further fragmentation of women's reproductive capacities and experience. These technologies, in effect, now allow men to use women—their bodies, their skills, their commitment, their feelings—until they can produce a perfect, genetically linked baby.

Owing to the focus of ethical debates around the sanctity of the embryo as the beginning of human life, a greater emphasis has been placed on the importance of recording and monitoring details and practices surrounding the fertilization of gametes. There has been much less attention paid to the need to monitor the impact of these procedures on the women who are subjected to the procedures prior to fertilization. Ova banking, like most other forms of ova donation, requires that women undergo invasive procedures in order to donate their reproductive material, procedures that are vastly more hazardous than the act of masturbation required to obtain gametes from men. Furthermore, at present very little is known about the long-term safety of in vitro maturation and immature ova cryopreservation techniques for women receiving donated ova or for the offspring produced.

One of the more disturbing implications of in vitro maturation is the potential in its application to harvest ova from aborted fetuses and cadavers. Serious consideration must be given to the effect on children created from rejected fetal tissue and whether the emotional experimentation involved is acceptable. The use of the ova of aborted fetuses also raises the question of whether the woman who carries the fetus should be the one to consent to the donation of any of its tissue. This technique has also been criticized because it can help women delay childbearing until after menopause in order that they may pursue careers and still have children who are biologically related. Some critics note that this indefinite extension to the childbearing phase of women's lives is an onerous prospect and exaggerates the already excessive pronatalist views toward women in our community. Also, women's reproductivity becomes a secondary issue in the face of commercial enterprise and is managed to fit the priorities of the market.

The use of these techniques to preserve the genetic material of endangered species has also been challenged as a technological fix after the event rather than an integrated solution to preserve or protect the habitats of these species. In general terms, the issues associated with the development of in vitro maturation technologies are only just beginning to emerge with the incremental expansion of their application within the clinical context.

FOR FURTHER READING

Bartels, D. 1988. "Built-In Obsolescence: Women, Embryo Production, and Genetic Engineering." *Issues in Reproductive and Genetic Engineering* 1(2): 141–152.

Bequaert Holmes, Helen. 1992. "To Freeze or Not to Freeze: Is That an Option?" In Helen Bequaert Holmes, ed., *Issues in Reproductive Technology.* New York: Garland.

"Frozen Eggs Find Ethical Favour in Australia . . . But Iced Embryos Make Money in the U.S." 1986. *New Scientist* 110(1505): 22.

Kaufman, Mellissa L., Tresa Nelson-White, and Catherine Racowsky. 1994. "Human Ova Recovered from Oophorectomised Ovaries: A Historical Review with Present Day Applications for Assisted Reproduction." *Assisted Reproduction Reviews* 4(4): 183–191.

Munro, Kathy. 1994. "In Vitro Maturation: Ethical, Legal and Regulatory Issues." *Alternative Law Journal* 19(2): 94–95.

National Action Committee on the Status of Women. 1988. *The New Reproductive Technologies: A Handmaid's Tale*. Ottawa: Canadian Communications Group.

Toth, T. L., et al. 1992. "Cryopreservation of Immature Primate Ova Collected from Unstimulated Ovaries." *Abstracts of the Scientific Oral and Poster Sessions, Annual Meeting of the American Fertility Society*, S177.

forty-three

In Vitro Fertilization and Male-Factor Infertility

MICHELLE A. MULLEN

A common clinical standard describes the male factor as significant when a couple fails to conceive naturally and repeat semen analysis demonstrates one or more of the following: concentration of sperm cells less than 20 million per milliliter, progressive forward motility less than 50 percent, or greater than 50 percent abnormal forms. Natural pregnancies may occur when the analysis of semen shows poor results, and infertility may persist when semen parameters are near normal. What is clear is that oligozoospermia (very few sperm cells) is highly associated with infertility, and azoospermia (no sperm cells) is absolutely associated with infertility (true sterility).

The causes of male-factor infertility or subfertility are poorly understood. Primary testicular dysfunction may be caused by disease of the testes as a result of infection, trauma, serious medical illness, genetic abnormality, radiation, or chemical toxicity from drugs or environmental agents such as pesticides. Hypothalamic or pituitary disease may also contribute to subfertility in the male. Medical management of male infertility may involve surgical repair of varicocele, administration of luteinizing hormone, or administration of antibiotics. The extremely limited results of these interventions in most cases have led to increasing interest in the application of IVF (in vitro fertilization and variants such as GIFT) for the "treatment" of male infertility. This use of IVF involves the treatment of a healthy female partner for male infertility and raises complex ethical, social, and feminist concerns.

Differential Gradient Methods and IVF

Discontinuous high-density gradients have been used with some success to prepare semen for fertilization in vitro. The methods involve layering different concentrations of high-density gradient in a test tube, overlaying semen, then centrifuging briefly. The gradients separate sperm cells on the basis of morphological characteristics and motility, permitting harvest of the layer containing sperm cells with normal appearance and forward progression in cases of mild to moderate male factor. Successful pregnancies have been achieved, although pregnancy rates remain at least half those of optimum IVF.

Micromanipulation

When semen quality is extremely poor, attempts have been made to enhance the possibility of fertilization by the manipulation of ova in vitro. Such manipulations require removal of the cumulus oophorus (cells adherent to the ovum) by washing the ovum in dilute enzyme and then gently drawing the ovum through a narrowed pipette to shear off excess cells. Various manipulations may then be made to the zona pellucida (sturdy outer layer of the ovum) to facilitate sperm cell penetration. In one method, the ovum is held by a micromanipulator under microscopic visualization and a closed-tip needle is used to cut a hole in the ovum.

Another approach entails chemical drilling by localized application of acid Tyrode's solution to create a "drill hole"; no clinical pregnancies have been reported using this method. Partial zona dissection (PZD) uses special micromanipulation instruments to hold the ovum and to create a series of gaps in the zona pellucida. Prepared sperm cells are then added to the culture wells with the ovum. PZD has been used with microinjection of five to ten sperm cells into the perivitelline space (near the "egg yolk"). Recently, intracytoplasmic sperm injection (ICSI) has been used to inject a single sperm cell directly into the human ovum.

Indications

Discontinuous-gradient approaches and medical management of the male partner may result in pregnancies where the male factor is mild or moderate in severity. Still other approaches may be attempted for special cases of male infertility; for example, electro-ejaculation was used to collect sperm cells from a quadriplegic man for IVF, resulting in a successful pregnancy. The literature also reports an attempt to microinject sperm aspirated (by needle biopsy) from a male with obstructive azoospermia; this attempt did not result in a successful pregnancy.

Results

Established IVF programs report a range of results for fertilization of 70–85 percent and clinical pregnancy rates of 10–20 percent where male-factor infertility is not the main indication for IVF treatment. When discontinuous gradients for semen preparation are used in conjunction with IVF, fertilization rates range from 30 to 50 percent with a less than 10 percent clinical pregnancy rate. The results with ovum micromanipulation are much poorer: No pregnancies have been reported using acid Tyrode's zona drilling, and only one clinical pregnancy has been reported with zona cutting. Fertilization rates from using micromanipulation may be quite high; unfortunately there is a very high incidence of polyspermia (entry of more than one sperm) and failure of embryo cleavage (further development). Many centers experimenting with these techniques report no pregnancies. Pregnancy results for the ICSI technique, however, may soon rival those of conventional IVF.

Risks

The use of IVF for male-factor infertility carries a variety of risks. The materials used in the manipulation of sperm in vitro are thought to be inert, and apparently normal embryo development and children have resulted from such conceptions. The use of such materials is entirely novel, however, and risks of long-term effects on children thus conceived cannot be known at present. Micromanipulation of the ovum may cause damage to the cell, preventing embryo development or causing cell death. The most common risk to micromanipulated ova is polyspermia—fertilization by more than one sperm cell. Disruption of the zona pellucida clearly damages those mechanisms that normally prevent entry of more than one sperm cell. Currently researchers are investigating methods of removing excess pronuclei from polyspermic ova. Survival and cleavage rates are very low for this procedure.

Generally, fertilization and pregnancy rates using such techniques are extremely limited, and the decision to pursue such treatment requires an extensive process of counseling and informed consent. At this time, micromanipulation techniques for male-factor infertility are better considered as clinical experimentation rather than treatment. Also, these techniques may contribute to even greater psychosocial stress for couples.

The advent of each new micromanipulation method brings new hope to couples, but the results are anything but encouraging. These technologies raise important feminist issues: The medical "problem" lies with the male partner, but it is the female partner who undertakes the risks associated with ovarian stimulation, ovum retrieval, and the possibility of early abortion or multiple pregnancy. The possibility that ovarian-stimulation drugs may increase risk for ovarian cancer in susceptible individuals adds a further dimension of clinical, ethical, and social concern, especially when these techniques are used with normally fertile women.

FOR FURTHER READING

Chang, S. Y. 1991. "A Clinical Pregnancy After a Simple Method of Zona Cutting, Cryopreservation, and Zygote IntraFallopian Transfer." *Fertility and Sterility* 55: 420–422.

Fishel, S., et al. 1991. "Presentation of Six Pregnancies Established by Sub-Zonal Insemination (SUZI)." *Human Reproduction* 6: 124–130.

Garrisi, G. J., et al. 1990. "Clinical Evaluation of Three Approaches to Micromanipulation-Assisted Fertilisation." *Fertility and Sterility* 54: 671–677.

Hyne, R. V., et al. 1986. "Pregnancy from in Vitro Fertilisation of Human Eggs After Separation of Motile Spermatozoa by Density Gradient Centrifugation." *Fertility and Sterility* 45: 93–96.

Iritani, A. 1991. "Micromanipulation of Gametes for in Vitro Assisted Fertilization." *Molecular Reproduction and Development* 28: 199–207.

Leeton, J., et al. 1991. "Successful Pregnancy Using Donor Ova Fertilised in Vitro by Spermatozoa Obtained by Electro-Ejaculation from a Quadriplegic Husband." *Human Reproduction* 6: 384–385.

Loriaux, T. C. 1991. "Male Infertility: A Challenge for Primary Health Care Providers." *Nurse Practitioner* 16: 38–45.

Malter, H. E., and J. Cohen. 1989. "Partial Zona Dissection of the Human Oocyte: A Nontraumatic Method Using Micromanipulation to Assist Zona Pellucida Penetration." *Fertility and Sterility* 51: 139–148.

Olar, T. T., et al. 1990. "Fertilization of Human Ova by Microinjection of Human Sperm Aspirated from the Caput Epididymis of an Individual with Obstructive Azoospermia." *Journal of in Vitro Fertilization and Embryo Transfer* 7: 160–164.

Silber, S. J. 1989. "The Relationship of Abnormal Semen Parameters to Male Fertility." *Human Reproduction* 4: 947–953.

Wittemer, C., et al. 1991. "A Case of Human Pregnancy After Microinjection of Capacitated Sperm into the Perivitelline Space." *Journal of in Vitro Fertilization and Embryo Transfer* 8: 222–224.

forty-four

Gamete Intrafallopian Transfer (GIFT)

RICHARD T. HULL

Fertilization typically takes place high in the fallopian tube, near the point where the ovum enters the tube after leaving the ruptured follicle. From this point, passage down to the uterus usually takes two or three days. It now seems that lower points are less optimal for fertilization either because the chances for implantation in the wall of the uterus are decreased as the time of passage to the uterus is shortened or because unknown factors reduce the chances of fertilization in the lower tubal regions.

Female infertility often is the result of scarring of the fallopian tubes subsequent to infection by a sexually transmitted disease. In such cases it is not possible for the ovum to pass down the tube or for sperm to reach it. Fallopian tubes can sometimes be repaired so as to reopen them, permitting normal fertilization to occur. However, because such surgical procedures often involve removal of the scarred section and reconnection of the open ends of the fallopian tube, there may be insufficient tube for reconnection or the tube may be so shortened that it is more difficult for the ovum to pass from the ovary into the tube. Sometimes the upper portions of fallopian tubes are missing due to malformation or surgical removal as a part of treatment for cancer or other diseases.

History and Procedure

In vitro fertilization (IVF) was developed to circumvent persistent tubal blockage. The procedure's complexity and expense prompted researchers to seek other ways to assist conception. In May 1982, the British journal *Lancet* reported the first pregnancy resulting from inserting ova and sperm through the cervix directly into the uterus. This was followed by another new fertility procedure, announced in 1983: low tubal ovum transfer, or LTOT. Simply put, it involved a laparoscopy on the woman immediately prior to predicted ovulation to retrieve one or more ova (eggs), the relocation of the ova so as to circumvent the area of tubal damage, and then intercourse with the ova in place in the lower portion of the tube in the hopes that fertilization would take place.

To Catholic moralists, LTOT had several advantages over IVF. It did not involve a decision whether to implant or discard the embryo; in fact, the embryo was not manipulated at all. Fertilization would take place in vivo in the normal manner rather than artificially in vitro, and masturbation to obtain sperm was not involved. This procedure appeared to most Catholic commentators to be morally permissible, analogous to a diabetic person's daily dose of insulin that bypasses the defective insulin-producing gland. Practically, however, LTOT did not work; no pregnancies resulted when LTOT was employed in sixty-five cycles of forty women over twenty-three months despite the earlier optimism generated by results in studies with monkeys. A different procedure, tubal ovum transfer (TOT), soon replaced LTOT.

In TOT, the ovum was placed as high as possible in the tube. Such placement restricted its application to women whose fallopian tubes were not damaged. Ova were taken from the woman's body, and the sperm were collected during intercourse by means of a perforated sheath. Sperm and ova were then combined and inserted into the upper region of the tube. The acronym was later changed to TOTS (tubal ovum transfer with sperm) to reflect the differences in treatment of sperm between LTOT and the new technique.

During the time between the inauguration of LTOT and TOT, Ricardo Asch and associates introduced a technique similar to TOT/TOTS, which they gave the acronym GIFT (for gamete intrafallopian transfer). With GIFT, semen was obtained from the husband through masturbation two hours before laparoscopy and removal of ova, ova were incubated to permit some additional maturation, and sperm and ova were placed in a catheter separated by air to prevent in vitro fertilization. The catheter tip was inserted into each fallopian tube and a mixture of ova and sperm was delivered into each. A twin pregnancy resulted the first time the procedure was used. Variations on the technique, involving frozen or donated sperm or the use of laser repair of tubal blockage and GIFT in a single procedure, were subsequently developed.

GIFT and TOTS require at least one healthy fallopian tube. IVF, where fertilization occurs in vitro, does not. With GIFT and TOTS, some of the elements of normal conception occur; the manipulations are to assist sperm and ova to reach the right place together. Sperm are collected in a manner compatible with some sperm reaching the ovum naturally; because there is at least one healthy tube, ova are manipulated in a manner compatible with an ovum reaching the tube naturally. Hence, as no barriers exist to natural conception provided the means of collecting ova and sperm are approved, some forms of GIFT and TOTS appear to be consistent with Catholic doctrine. However, as GIFT often involves sperm obtained through masturbation rather than in intercourse, its practice often is at odds with such doctrine.

Complications

GIFT and the associated alternatives have a number of possible complications. One recent study of 1,000 pregnancies achieved chiefly through IVF and GIFT reports that 1 of every 100 pregnancies involves multiple-sited or heterotopic pregnancies—that is, concomitant pregnancies either within the uterus or in the fallopian tubes or the abdominal cavity (also called ectopic pregnancies). Pregnancies outside the uterus almost never develop to term and almost always pose grave risks to the mother. Presumably, the process of injecting ova and sperm into the upper reaches of the fallopian tubes either washes them back into the abdominal cavity or delays their normal passage into the uterus sufficiently that the stage of implantation is reached in the tube; also, sperm may bypass the transferred ova and encounter an ovum just at the point of, or just after, follicular release. The technique often involves insertion of multiple ova with sperm into each fallopian tube (if both are intact). That multiplicity, together with the likelihood of additional ova ripening under the influence of luteinizing hormone surges both at the time of, and after, retrieval of ova, can result in multiple concomitant intrauterine pregnancies.

GIFT is a strictly physical manipulation; it can be employed with ova and sperm from any source and so can be used both as a form of artificial insemination from a donor and as a form of ovum donation. Indeed, the acronym GIFT is suggestive of gamete donation. Donor gametes provide a special problem for Catholic and some non-Catholic moralists in that the child is denied a perceived right to be conceived and brought into the world within the institution of marriage.

Because GIFT does not require extracorporeal incubation, it is substantially cheaper than IVF, but it does involve drug therapy (to stimulate multiple ovarian follicles) and laparoscopic (and possible other) surgery to obtain the ova and sometimes to repair the fallopian tubes. In one 1987 survey, success was obtained on average in 29 percent of cases (ranging from 10 to 56 percent depending on the type of infertility) at an average cost of $3,500. Those studying the likely directions of cost containment in health care see high-technology infertility services at risk of exclusion from both national and private insurance coverage because they are generally limited to otherwise healthy individuals not experiencing life-threatening illness. Thus such services are likely to remain, as they are generally now, available only to those who can afford them.

Couples seeking high-technology infertility services have often invested years of effort and expense to achieve pregnancy. As fertility services offer greater technological intervention in pursuit of the couple's goal, many couples report increasing anxiety, obsessive preoccupation, and disruption of other activities and responsibilities. That technology offers such a low probability of success at such a high personal and financial price raises deep questions about the rationality of the pursuit of such technological fixes, confounding our understanding of the protective role of the traditional requirement of informed consent. Finally, as infertile couples have traditionally been the chief pool of likely adoptive parents and as the world already holds a vast number of orphans and abandoned and unwanted children, the need to transform infertile couples into parents by reproductive technology raises important social questions about the prioritization of genetic lineage.

FOR FURTHER READING

Bartels, Dianne M., et al., eds. 1990. *Beyond Baby M: Ethical Issues in New Reproductive Techniques.* Clifton, N.J.: Humana.

Cahill, Lisa Sowle. 1996. "The New Birth Technologies and Public Moral Argument." In *Sex, Gender and Christian Ethics.* New York: Cambridge University Press.

Catholic Church. Congregation pro Doctrina Fidei (Congregation for the Doctrine of the Faith). 1987. *Instruction on Respect for Human Life in Its Origin and on the Dignity of Procreation.* Boston: Pauline Press.

Jones, Howard Wilbur, ed. 1988. *In Vitro Fertilization and Other Assisted Reproduction.* New York: New York Academy of Sciences.

Kaplan, Lawrence J., and Rosemarie Tong. 1996. *Controlling Our Reproductive Destiny: A Technological and Philosophical Perspective.* Cambridge: MIT.

Peters, Ted. 1996. *For the Love of Children: Genetic Technology and the Future of the Family.* Louisville, Ky.: Westminster John Knox Press.

Pope John Center. 1987. *Reproductive Technologies, Marriage and the Church.* Braintree, Mass.: Pope John Center.

U.S. Congress, Office of Technology Assessment. 1988. *Infertility: Medical and Social Choices.* Washington, D.C.: U.S. Government Printing Office.

Wildes, Kevin William, ed. 1997. *Infertility: A Crossroad of Faith, Medicine, and Technology.* Boston: Kluwer Academic.

forty-five

In Vitro Fertilization—Risks

MICHELLE A. MULLEN, JUDITH LORBER, AND LINDA S. WILLIAMS

Various risks or negative effects are known to be associated with different aspects of in vitro fertilization (IVF); still others have been hypothesized but are unproven. These risks may be physical, psychosocial, economic, legal, or ethical and pose various burdens for different "players"—women and men seeking treatment, care providers, and children born as a result of IVF.

Risks to Women

IVF tests and interventions focus almost exclusively on the female body even when infertility results from a male factor, so women carry the greater proportion of burden and risks. There are physical risks to women in addition to the numerous side effects related to the use of drugs with IVF and related procedures. Ovum retrieval may result in bleeding and infection, and when general anesthesia is used, another serious risk is involved: Early pregnancy wastage (spontaneous abortion) is high in IVF patients.

In terms of psychological effects, many women report experiences of depression, futility, and loss of control, and research indicates that women experience greater depression and anxiety than do their partners when treatments fail. Also, when multiple gestations result from IVF, "selective reduction" of pregnancy may be offered. Although reduction is generally successful in limiting the number of gestational sacs (embryos), the decision to undergo selective abortion may be extremely difficult for patients to reconcile with efforts to achieve pregnancy.

Risks to Children Conceived with IVF

A high prevalence of multiple births is associated with IVF. This type of birth tends to result in premature delivery (less than thirty-seven weeks gestational age) and low birth weights. Some 30 percent of IVF infants are born weighing less than two and a half kilograms. Birth-defect rates in IVF children appear to echo those in the general population, although long-term follow-up is required. Psychosocial and intellectual development in these children has been studied and appears, at the very least, normal. High scores on psychometric development scales have been attributed to exceptional parental motivation ("wantedness") and generally high socioeconomic status. Long-term effects as a result of IVF conception are not known. Future issues, particularly when donor gametes or donor embryos are involved, may arise. As in adoption, there may be demand for a uniform policy that both protects donors and permits children to discover details of their genetic history.

Risks to Couples

Infertility places substantial burdens on couples: Feelings of inadequacy, guilt, depression, futility, and loss of control are common. Infertility often necessitates explaining childlessness and treatment demands to the outside world: friends, relatives, employers, and insurance companies. Traditional psychiatric concepts of depression and alienation may be inadequate and inaccurate in describing the experiences of couples undergoing infertility therapy, and it has been suggested that new methods be developed both to diagnose and to implement stress therapy for this population. The purpose of such methods would be to provide appropriate intervention while avoiding stigmatizing psychiatric labels.

Gender-specific diagnosis of the cause of infertility may lead to different types and degrees of emotional response. One study has shown that women tend to react in much the same way to a diagnosis of infertility regardless of the gender specificity of the diagnosis. By contrast, men tend to experience a significantly deeper negative emotional response in terms of depression, feelings of inadequacy, and low self-esteem when a male-specific diagnosis is made. Different gender experiences of infertility may contribute to feelings of alienation and relationship breakdown. Finally, stress associated with infertility therapy may actually contribute to a poor outcome. The nature of psychogenic subfertility is poorly understood, but recent research into psychoendocrinological stress responses suggests these may affect the outcome of interventions such as IVF.

To infertile women and to heterosexual couples whose procreative difficulties have an unknown cause or are due to fertility problems of both partners, new procreative technologies often represent a valuable physiological, psychological, and social resource. When the cause is clearly with the male, however, the woman may feel coerced into treatment; she is the partner who undergoes the greater part of these procedures. This imbalance in the demands of treatment for male infertility can create psychological difficulties in the relationship.

There are a variety of stresses associated with the IVF process itself. The "emotional roller-coaster" that patients describe for all infertility treatment is exacerbated by the high rate of failure in IVF. The most difficult time for both partners is usually the wait to see if a pregnancy will actually ensue after embryo transfer. When it does not (in the majority of cases), grieving occurs. Couples who present themselves for infertility treatment often have sexual dysfunction. Ironically, the pressure that results from potential examination or examination of the dysfunction sometimes eradicates the problem, causing the common phenomenon of "waiting list" pregnancies. The male partner often is unable to masturbate to ejaculation on demand. Other sources of stress are the procedures of surgical laparoscopy and embryo transfer and the high cost of treatment.

IVF clients use a variety of coping mechanisms that allow them to feel in control. Couples have reported some success with acupuncture, meditation, and a focus on nutrition during IVF trials. Disclosure to relatives and friends that the couple is undergoing IVF usually brings social and emotional support. However, couples are usually more reluctant to admit problems with infertility when the man is physiologically unable to inseminate than when the woman is unable to conceive. For some couples, pursuing adoption concomitantly helps to relieve the stress of the likely failure of IVF.

However, adoption is also an imperfect alternative. The only children who can be adopted quickly, easily, and cheaply through public adoption agencies in most developed countries are older, nonwhite, or disabled, and most couples do not want to adopt these children. Private adoption, which is legal in many places, offers couples a better chance of adopting the type of child they desire, but this route to parenthood can also be difficult, uncertain, and expensive. The realities of adoption in turn encourage continued attempts at IVF.

It is reasonable to assume that the continued importance of the biological tie between parent and child, as well as the current lack of adoptable babies in most countries where IVF is practiced, will ensure that the demand for IVF remains high. However, unless IVF success rates increase dramatically, it can also be expected that infertile couples will continue to seek adoption in the event of actual or expected IVF failure. The relationship between IVF and adoption will remain complex with most IVF couples seeking adoption simultaneously in their determined quest to finally become parents.

Willingness to undergo repeated trials of IVF is explained in a number of ways. IVF can be an alternative for fertile or infertile women who require but cannot get their husband's consent for adoption or artificial insemination. It is also rationalized as an appropriate approach by women who want their present partner's child or to restore their own or their partner's self-esteem. Research focusing on infertile women has shown that the existence of advanced infertility technologies sets up its own imperative and that IVF use can become almost addictive. The discourse on infertility and the new reproductive technologies frames personal narratives in terms of social loss, biological pressures, and hope regarding technological advances. Hence "doing IVF" is often an obligatory rite of passage not only to try to have a child but also to protect against social stigmatization and to prove that one is involuntarily childless. The woman whose male partner is infertile has an additional burden of exoneration—to be held blameless for *his* inability to have a biological heir.

Risks to Health Care Providers

High-tech medicine stresses not just patients and families but health care providers as well. Each step in IVF is essential to a positive outcome; thus there is little or no margin for staff error, be it physician selection of the hyperovulation regimen, nurse administration of gonadotropins, or the handling of gametes and embryos by laboratory staff. Further, infertile patients experience and share much grief with their caregivers, and the relatively low success rates compound this experience for service providers.

Advanced infertility technologies also raise difficult ethical and social questions for caregivers, and dissent among team members can arise when they hold different values. One case report cites the difficulties encountered by an infertility team when both partners in a couple seeking infertility treatment proved to be HIV positive. Despite counseling about transmission, the couple remained adamant in their wish for aggressive treatment. The team members finally decided that they would provide diagnostic tests but no active management because of the ethical uncertainty. Recognizing and respecting different values held by patients can also be extremely difficult, and there is evidence that providing treatment to patients with different cultural values poses a serious problem. One study has shown that patients and different caregivers perceive patient physical and emotional stress differently: Nurses tended to rate patient distress higher than did physicians, and older nurses and physicians rated patient distress lower than did their younger colleagues. These results may suggest not only that differences exist between physicians' and nurses' perceptions of patient distress but that both groups are subject to diminished sensitivity over time. A final problem area for both caregivers and patients is when and how to approach decisions to discontinue treatment. There are no guidelines for either caregivers or patients to help them decide when further treatment is futile, and this lack represents a grave challenge to both.

The risks associated with IVF hold implications at many levels. For patients and caregivers, the weight of these risks ought to form an integral part of the informed-consent process. These risks also underscore the need for vigilance in registry data, in the development of practice guidelines, and in the calculations required for social evaluation of the safety and efficacy of IVF practices. These issues remain at the core of the ongoing discussion and debate over IVF.

FOR FURTHER READING

Berg, B. J., and J. F. Wison. 1990. "Psychiatric Morbidity in the Infertile Population: A Reconceptualization." *Fertility and Sterility* 53: 654–661.

Blenner, J. L. 1991. "Health Care Providers' Treatment Approaches to Culturally Diverse Infertile Couples." *Journal of Transcultural Nursing* 2: 24–31.

Demyttenaere, K., et al. 1991. "Coping, Ineffectiveness of Coping, and Psychoendocrinological Stress Responses During in Vitro Fertilization." *Journal of Psychosomatic Research* 35: 231–243.

Greenfeld, D., M. P. Diamond, and A. H. DeCherney. 1988. "Grief Reactions Following in Vitro Fertilization Treatment." *Journal of Psychosomatic Obstetrics and Gynaecology* 8: 169–174.

Koch, L. 1990. "IVF—An Irrational Choice?" *Issues in Reproductive and Genetic Engineering* 3: 235–242.

Kopitzke, E. J., et al. 1991. "Physical and Emotional Stress Associated with Components of Infertility Investigation: Perspectives of Professionals and Patients." *Fertility and Sterility* 55: 1137–1143.

Lorber, J., and L. Bandlamudi. 1993. "The Dynamics of Marital Bargaining in Male Infertility." *Gender and Society* 7: 32–49.

Morin, N. C., et al. 1989. "Congenital Malformations and Psychosocial Development in Children Conceived by in Vitro Fertilization." *Journal of Pediatrics* 115: 222–227.

Nachtigall, R. D., et al. 1992. "The Effects of Gender-Specific Diagnosis on Men's and Women's Response to Infertility." *Fertility and Sterility* 57: 113–121.

Newton, C. R., et al. 1990. "Psychological Assessment and Follow-Up After in Vitro Fertilization: Assessing the Impact of Failure." *Fertility and Sterility* 54: 879–886.

Reading, A. E., and J. Kerin. 1989. "Psychologic Aspects of Providing Infertility Services." *Journal of Reproductive Medicine* 43: 861–871.

Sandelowski, Margarete. 1993. *With Child in Mind: Studies of the Personal Encounter with Infertility*. Philadelphia: University of Pennsylvania Press.

Smith, J. R., et al. 1991. "Infertility Management in HIV Positive Couples: A Dilemma." *British Medical Journal* 302: 1447–1450.

Williams, Linda S. 1992. "Adoption Actions and Attitudes of Couples Seeking in Vitro Fertilization." *Journal of Family Issues* 13(1): 99–113.

forty-six

Counseling

KEN DANIELS

For individuals and couples who cannot have the children they desire, there are considerable psychosocial implications. These implications will be experienced at the personal, interpersonal (family and wider networks), and social levels. As a result of the growing recognition of these psychosocial implications, counseling services associated with reproduction are being provided. However, most of these services tend to be associated with the new reproductive technology programs that have developed to respond to infertility. Counseling services for individuals and couples during and after infertility diagnosis and while they are considering treatment options also need to be provided.

Components and Models of Counseling

The word "counseling" means different things to different people. In an attempt to clarify the various components of counseling, the Asche Committee (1985), dealing with issues emerging from developments in reproductive technology in Australia, noted that counseling often refers to at least three activities: information-giving and discussion, support and therapy, and selection/screening. Four types of counseling are identified in the British report of the King's Fund Centre Counselling Committee (1991): information, "implications support," and therapeutic counseling. The Australian National Bioethics Consultative Committee's *Issues Paper on Infertility Counselling* (1990) also lists four components: information, decisionmaking, support, and "therapeutic." The various components identified by these committees and papers refer to quite different functions, and it is clear that much of the confusion among health professionals in the field, as well as between consumers and professionals, can be traced to the lack of clarity concerning the different aspects of counseling.

Infertility counseling literature for the most part concentrates on the emotional and relationship needs of individuals and couples. Surprise, denial, anger, isolation, guilt, grief, and, finally, resolution are seen as common responses to infertility and reproduction technology treatments. Some counseling experts liken infertility to a death—the loss of the ability to biologically parent. Others describe infertility as a series of losses: of potential children, social role, and self-esteem. In response, grief work has been widely used by infertility counselors, as has crisis intervention. Crisis theory sees the experience of infertility as an unexpected, disruptive, and emotionally hazardous event resulting in symptoms such as anxiety, disorganization, distractibility, moodiness, unpredictability, and fatigue followed by a prolonged period of preoccupation with the crisis event and obsession with infertility. The therapeutic role of the social worker or counselor has been defined as guiding clients through the tasks of resolution, in particular, dealing with the onset of intense emotions; addressing issues concerning body image, self-esteem, and sexuality; deciding on parenthood as a life goal; and choosing a life plan that includes an alternative to having a biological child.

Psychoanalysis has been used by some workers, usually psychiatrists, although this approach may be most useful where infertility is compounded with existing psychopathology. Obviously this model relates to the therapeutic component of counseling and, due to its nature, is not likely to be used extensively in a busy reproductive technology practice. (That is not to say that some concepts and insights from the psychoanalytic model will not be found in individual counselors' practices.) The behavioral model is also used by counselors. In particular, relaxation techniques are used with many individuals who have become anxious about treatment procedures. Little research has been undertaken in this area, however, and much of the literature is based on assumptions.

The Wider Role of the Counselor

Counseling models have as their starting point the individual and the couple; hence the previously noted emphasis on the psychological and emotional. However, the issues and needs of the individual or couple are social as well as psychological in nature, and consideration must be given to the social end of the psychosocial continuum, including the impact of infertility and treatments on relationships with extended family and friends, interactions with the clinic team, social attitudes, and social policy and legislative frameworks. Counselors have a potential role in each of these areas. They are uniquely placed to work with family issues and difficulties that emerge between a couple and clinic staff, sometimes playing the role of advocate. They become involved in ongoing work or consultation with support groups, assist in the team development of the staff, and contribute a psychosocial perspective to the policy and ethical debates that surround reproductive technologies.

Selection and Counseling

The Asche Committee (1985) identified selection/screening as one of the components of infertility counseling. It argued that because concern for the welfare of the future child is paramount and substantial community resources are involved, a selection/screening process for couples entering assisted-conception programs is justified. The National Bioethics Consultative Committee's view (1990) is that "screening and assessment should be kept entirely separate from counselling and should not be performed in the same place, at the same time, or by the same person as counselling." The involvement of infertility counselors in the area of selection and screening is obviously controversial. It means that the counselor takes on a control function, which is uncomfortable for some. This is the area where the psychological and the psychosocial models come into sharpest contrast. The psychological perspective tends to focus on the infertile couple or individual as the client, whereas the psychosocial looks beyond the couple to the child who may be born as a result of reproductive technologies.

FOR FURTHER READING

Asche Committee. 1985. *Creating Children: Report of the Family Law Council of Australia.* Canberra: Australian Government Publishing Service.

Australian National Bioethics Consultative Committee. 1990. *Issues Paper on Infertility Counselling Australia.* Canberra: Australian Government Publishing Service.

Batterman, R. 1985. "A Comprehensive Approach to Treating Infertility." *Health and Social Work* 10(1): 46–54.

Berg, B. J., and J. F. Wilson. 1991. "Psychological Functioning Across Stages of Treatment for Infertility." *Journal of Behavioral Medicine* 14: 11–26.

Daniels, K. R. 1993. "Infertility Counselling—The Need for a Psychosocial Perspective." *British Journal of Social Work* 23(5): 501–515.

Daniluk, J. C. 1988. "Infertility: Intrapersonal and Interpersonal Impact." *Fertility and Sterility* 49: 982–990.

Edelman, R. J. 1990. "Emotional Aspects of in Vitro Fertilization Procedures: Review." *Journal of Reproductive and Infant Psychology* 5: 63–70.

Ellis, J. 1982. "Infertility as an Emotional Crisis: The Role of Counselling." *Patient Management* (September): 57–64.

Hammer Burns, L., and S. Covington. 1998. *Infertility Counselling: A Comprehensive Handbook for Clinicians.* New York: Parthenon.

King's Fund Centre Counselling Committee. 1991. *Counselling for Regulated Infertility Treatments.* London: King's Fund Centre.

Naish, S. 1994. *Counselling People with Infertility Problems.* Rugby, U.K.: British Association for Counselling.

United Kingdom. 1990. *Human Fertilisation and Embryology Act, 1990.*

Valentine, D. P. 1986. "Psychological Impact of Infertility: Identifying Issues and Needs." *Social Work in Health Care* 11(4): 61–69.

forty-seven

Selection and Assessment for Treatment

KEN DANIELS

Not all couples or individuals who wish to utilize advanced infertility technologies can do so. Access may be restricted by what can be termed global factors. These include resource allocation and funding for the technologies, the availability of information to couples experiencing infertility, cost, geography, and gender. Access may also be restricted by selection. It is frequently the providers of the services who determine access; they decide who will gain admissions to their programs. In effect, the medical profession is privileged to decide who is fit for parenthood by the simple act of determining who is eligible for infertility services. In terms of gender, most of the specialists working in this field are male, which may affect access for single women and lesbians.

Selection may also be examined in terms of the formal and informal criteria applied. Within the former are the legislative guidelines that have been propagated. Knoppers and LeBris, in their comprehensive international survey of committee and commission reports and legislation (1991), found a consensus that access to fertilization techniques should be limited to heterosexual married couples or those living in stable unions. Marital status is the most prominent factor in selection.

The Warnock Report, produced in the United Kingdom (Warnock Committee 1984), states that it is immoral to allow a child to be created through assisted reproduction when the child is not destined to be cared for by both a mother and a father in a stable heterosexual relationship. Current British legislation (the Human Fertilisation and Embryology Act, 1990) supports this philosophy. Similarly, laws in Israel (1987), France (1988), Denmark (1987), and two states in Australia (Victoria 1984; South Australia 1988) either limit or give priority of access to married or cohabiting couples. In the United States, some clinics limit their IVF services to married couples, although there is nothing in the law that prohibits unmarried individuals from using reproductive technologies, and such a prohibition may in fact be unconstitutional when state monies are involved. In some countries legislation is absent, but a consensus exists among practitioners to limit access to DI and IVF services on the basis of marital status. Under Sweden's (1984) law on donor insemination a doctor must ascertain the couple's psychosocial circumstances as well as ensure that they are both medically fit. A doctor can refuse to perform DI, but the couple can complain to the National Board of Health and Welfare if they feel the decision is unjust.

In addition to these laws and formal guidelines, programs themselves may restrict access using their own criteria. These are sometimes imposed by hospitals' boards of management or their ethics committees, but most are developed by the program staff—either individuals or teams. The Australian National Bioethics Consultative Committee (NBCC) has summarized (1991) criteria followed recently by some clinics, and these include requirements that participants be some or all of the following: married (or less often, de facto married) heterosexuals; in a "stable" relationship; under an age limit (for prospective mothers and, less often, fathers); childless; and medically and psychologically healthy. Clinics may also limit services to those couples with a certain minimum duration of infertility, the "right" motivations for wanting a child (e.g., not because of social pressure or the need to save an ailing marriage), and no history of child abuse by either partner. In addition, they may require couples to attend counseling in order to discuss fully their feelings about infertility and to consider alternatives to assisted reproduction, such as adoption or childlessness.

Advanced infertility procedures involve issues far beyond those a doctor normally deals with in most other areas of medicine. The underlying issue of access and selection is whether criteria should be determined by public and social policy or by the couple or individual and a health professional, normally a doctor. Arguments for the public policy approach are based on the belief that there are social consequences and an aggregate impact on society arising from who is accepted into reproductive technology programs. Such consequences will manifest particularly through the children conceived, and society is seen to be the protector of the needs and rights of such children. A second point is that public policy implications stem from the use of public health funds either to provide these services or to fund research that has led to these services.

The private contract model is reinforced by notions of private enterprise, confidentiality, and the freedom of the individual to choose. Support for this model comes from UN and European conventions stating that reproduction is a right of every man and woman. State interference with this model is seen to be tantamount to an infringement of the individual's basic right to reproduce or, more accurately, the right not to have one's reproductive decisions overridden.

All the commissions and committees of inquiry set up by governments and professional bodies have addressed the issue of access, and in particular, the criteria that should be used by health professionals. A number of these bodies have sought submissions from the public or been involved in public consultations. However, it would be appropriate to summarize the position on access as being one in which the public has not really had a chance to make a major contribution. Three major issues need to be addressed: Should access to reproductive technologies be restricted? If so, on what basis should decisions concerning access be made? Who should make these decisions?

FOR FURTHER READING

Asche Committee. 1985. *Creating Children: Report of the Family Law Council of Australia.* Canberra: Australian Government Publishing Service.

Australia. National Bioethics Consultative Committee. 1991. *Access to Reproductive Technology: Final Report for the Australian Health Ministers.* Canberra: Australian Government Publishing Service.

Blank, R. H., 1990. *Regulating Reproduction.* New York: Columbia University Press.

Daniels, K. R., and K. Taylor. 1993. "Formulating Selection and Assessment Policies for Assisted Reproduction." *Social Science and Medicine* 37: 1473–1480.

Denmark. 1987. "Law No. 353 on the Establishment of an Ethical Council and the Regulation of Certain Forms of Biomedical Research." Reprinted 1988 in *International Digest of Health Legislation* 39: 95.

France. 1988a. "Decree No. 88-328 Concerning the Report of the National Commission on Medicine and Reproductive Biology." *International Digest of Health Legislation* 39: 647.

France. 1988b. "Law No. 88-1138 Pertaining to the Protection of Persons Subject to Biomedical Research." Reprinted 1989 in *International Digest of Health Legislation* 40: 109.

Israel. 1987. "The Public Health (in Vitro Fertilization) Regulations of 1987." *International Digest of Health Legislation* 38: 779.

Knoppers, B. M., and S. LeBris. 1991. "Recent Advances in Medically Assisted Conception: Legal, Ethical and Social Issues." *American Journal of Law and Medicine* 17(4): 329–361.

New Zealand. Department of Justice. Law Reform Division. 1985. *New Birth Technologies: An Issues Paper on AID, IVF and Surrogate Motherhood.* Wellington: New Zealand Government Printer.

Stephenson, P. A., and M. G. Wagner. 1991. "Turkey-Baster Babies: A View from Europe." *Milbank Quarterly* 69(1): 45–50.

Sweden. 1986. "Act on Insemination of 1984: Law No. 1140, December 20, 1984." *International Digest of Health Legislation* 37: 272.

United Kingdom. 1990. *Human Fertilisation and Embryology Act, 1990.*

Victoria, Australia. 1984, 1987. *Infertility (Medical Procedures) Act.* Melbourne: Government Printer.

Warnock Committee. 1984. *Report of the Committee of Enquiry into Human Fertilisation and Embryology.* London: Her Majesty's Stationery Office.

Western Australia. 1986. *Report of the Committee Appointed by the Western Australian Government to Enquire into the Social, Legal and Ethical Issues Related to in Vitro Fertilization and Its Supervision.* Perth: Government Printer.

forty-eight

Egg Donation

ERICA HAIMES

Egg (ovum or oocyte) donation involves the transfer of an egg from one woman to help another woman conceive a child. This practice occurs when the recipient either cannot produce her own eggs (for example, because of early menopause or treatment for cancer) or when a genetic disorder might be passed on to the child if her eggs are used. The first birth of a baby conceived from a donated egg occurred in 1984 in Australia. This is a complex procedure for all parties and is particularly invasive for the donor, as it is she who must undergo hyperovulation and egg retrieval. The menstrual cycles of both donor and recipient have to be artificially coordinated. The donor receives hormones to stimulate her ovaries to produce extra eggs, and these eggs are then collected, either under general anesthetic using laparoscopy or more commonly through a variety of ultrasound techniques. A range of side effects has been reported in donors undergoing all of the above. Donation also makes demands on a donor's time, energy, and emotions.

Success rates of 40–47 percent have been reported, but it is not clear whether these figures refer to the number of pregnancies achieved or the number of live births. Egg donation is available in the United States, the United Kingdom, Australia, New Zealand, Spain, and Israel; but several countries, such as Austria, Ireland, Japan, and Sweden, prohibit its use even though each allows a variety of other assisted-conception techniques. In Germany, egg donation is allowed only in exceptional circumstances. In Sweden, it has been argued that egg donation goes against the natural process of life.

Egg donation raises many difficult issues, particularly the recruitment of donors and the use of known donors. Originally eggs were donated by women undergoing infertility treatment who were producing more eggs than could be used immediately in their own treatment. However, as embryo-freezing techniques improved, these women could store their fertilized eggs for their own later use, so other sources of eggs were needed. Concern has been expressed that women have been offered inducements, such as cheaper sterilizations, in exchange for donating eggs. To avoid the exploitation of the poor and based on the assumption that poor women are likely to be unhealthy, some programs buy eggs only from "healthy" donors. An increasingly common system is to ask women receiving donated eggs to recruit donors either for their own direct use or to add to a group of anonymous donors for all women on the program.

The case for women receiving eggs from known donors rests on the general shortage of donors and the view that relatives or friends have a strong altruistic desire to help someone they know. The case against rests on fears of undue pressure on relatives, on possible conflict between the genetic and carrying mothers, and on the confusion for the child growing up with blurred family relationships. No consistent legislation has emerged on this point. In the United Kingdom the woman giving birth to the child is legally defined as the mother regardless of whether the child was conceived using a donated egg. Few other countries have formally legislated in this area, though it would appear that Western Australia's *Human Reproductive Technology Act* (1991) follows, by default, the British legislation. In the United Kingdom, this position holds for surrogacy cases as well, although if the commissioning parents have donated one or both sets of gametes, they can apply for a parental order to allow them to be treated legally as the child's parents.

FOR FURTHER READING

Ahuja, K., and E. Simons. 1996. "Anonymous Egg Donation and Dignity." *Human Reproduction* 11: 1151–1154.

Englert, Y. 1996. "Ethics of Oocyte Donation Are Challenged by the Health Care System." *Human Reproduction* 11: 2353–2355.

Haimes, E. 1993. "Issues of Gender in Gamete Donation." *Social Science and Medicine* 36(1): 85–93.

Morgan, D., and R. Lee. 1991. *Blackstone's Guide to the Human Fertilisation and Embryology Act, 1990*. London: Blackstone Press.

Power, M., et al. 1990. "A Comparison of the Attitudes of Volunteer Donors and Infertile Patient Donors on an Ovum Donation Programme." *Human Reproduction* 5(3): 352–355.

Raoul-Duval, A., H. Letur-Konirsch, and R. Frydman. 1992. "Anonymous Oocyte Donation: A Psychological Study of Recipients, Donors and Children." *Human Reproduction* 7(1): 51–54.

Sauer, M., and R. Paulson. 1992. "Oocyte Donors: A Demographic Analysis of Women at the University of Southern California." *Human Reproduction* 7(5): 726–728.

Saunders, D., and F. Garner. 1996. "Oocyte Donation Using 'Known' Donors: It May Seem the Convenient Answer But Who Pays?" *Human Reproduction* 11: 2356–2357.

United Kingdom. 1990. *Human Fertilisation and Embryology Act, 1990.*

Western Australia. 1991. *Human Reproductive Technology Act.*

forty-nine

Surrogacy

LAURA M. PURDY AND
HELEN BEQUAERT HOLMES

Definitions

"Surrogate" has long meant "substitute, a person acting in place of another," but of late it has been widely used to denote surrogate motherhood (surrogacy for short), a usage coined by Noel Keane and Dennis Breo in their 1981 book *The Surrogate Mother*. What, in relation to surrogacy, does "mother" or "motherhood" come to mean?

Before the age of infertility technologies, a mother played three roles: (1) she provided half the genetic material for an embryo, (2) she gestated an embryo into a newborn child, and (3) she typically nurtured that child until it was ready to leave home. However, Keane and Breo use the term "surrogate" for women who perform the first two roles and, for a fee, hand the child over for the third role to a woman who, in most cases, is connected to the child only as a partner to the man who provided sperm for conception.

Some have attempted to replace "surrogate" and "surrogacy" with other terms, such as "contract pregnancy," "intrauterine adoption," and, as in the report of the Canadian Royal Commission on New Reproductive Technologies (1993), "preconception arrangements." And as reproductive technologies have evolved and individuals have devised new twists, categories of surrogacy other than those described by Keane and Breo have appeared and include the following:

1. Natural Surrogacy. Here the surrogate provides half the genetic material and gestates the embryo. She has sexual intercourse with the partner of the woman who will raise the child. The best known example is the

story in Genesis of the slave Hagar, who slept with Abraham, husband of Sarah. Other examples are provided in the popular novel *The Handmaid's Tale* by Margaret Atwood. Natural surrogacy is probably relatively rare; in any case, few would publicize it, as it may well involve morally or legally questionable sexual acts.

2. Low-Tech Surrogacy. This is also called donor-insemination surrogacy, genetic gestational surrogacy, or traditional surrogacy. The surrogate again provides half the genetic material and gestates the embryo but receives sperm from the partner of the woman who will raise the child via artificial insemination. Low-tech surrogacy is by far the most common form. It is accessible to any woman who can obtain sperm from a male, although insemination carried out by the medical establishment is often limited to married, heterosexual women.

3. High-Tech Surrogacy. In this situation, also called IVF surrogacy, gestational surrogacy, or total surrogacy, the surrogate only gestates the embryo. Sophisticated medical intervention is needed to remove the egg from another woman (the one providing half the genetic material), who in most cases intends to raise the child.

4. Egg Donation. Also called genetic surrogacy, this type of surrogacy is seldom perceived as such.

5. Surrogate Embryo Transfer, or SET. This variant of egg donation, sometimes called embryo flushing, is also seldom seen as surrogacy. The surrogate's egg is fertilized by artificial insemination with sperm from the partner of the woman who hopes to gestate the embryo and raise the child. The resulting embryo is flushed out of the surrogate's uterus (uterine lavage) and transferred into the other woman. This method is little used because of extremely low rates of embryo recovery and complications for the surrogate with the procedure.

Clinical Techniques

Low-tech surrogacy requires only that the woman's fertile period be determined and that she be inseminated with viable sperm. Anyone can do it with a wide-mouthed syringe (the "turkey baster" method); medical personnel do it with untreated semen, washed semen, or (preferably and more commonly) semen tested and found to be HIV negative.

High-tech surrogacy is far more problematic. It requires first that the reproductive cycles of egg provider and carrying mother be synchronized. Each clinic may have a different method. Often both women are given hormonal analogs (sometimes the Pill) to stop their cycles and then get one or another of the various regimens of fertility drugs to induce ovulation. In some clinics the egg provider's cycle is synchronized to the other woman's natural cycle. The cycle is monitored by frequent blood tests and ultrasound; at the right moment, ovulation is induced with human menopausal gonadotropin. Then, a physician removes eggs by laparoscopy or vaginal aspiration and adds sperm to them in a laboratory dish. He or she then transfers any resulting embryos to the surrogate's uterus, timed two or three days after her luteinizing hormone surge. If implantation is successful, the surrogate then carries the pregnancy to term. The IVF variants GIFT and ZIFT (zygote intrafallopian transfer) may also be used. In 1989, after thirty-three stimulation cycles, a U.S. team reported five live births, a 15 percent success rate.

History, Issues, and Critiques

History

The current version of low-tech surrogacy came to public notice in the mid-1970s; it is widely believed that in the two decades since, over 4,000 babies have been born by this method. Apparently most surrogacy arrangements are carried through to the satisfaction of the contracting parties, although a series of cases gone awry has presented the public with a disturbing picture of the pitfalls of this practice. For example, although enthusiastic about her experience as a surrogate mother in 1980, by 1987, Elizabeth Kane, together with another surrogate mother, Mary Beth Whitehead, asked the U.S. Congress to make surrogacy arrangements a federal offense. Whitehead provided the egg for and gestated the child known as Baby M. Her attempt to keep the baby resulted in a widely reported legal custody battle in 1987. Another publicized instance of low-tech surrogacy gone wrong involved Judy Stiver, who contracted to bear a child with Alexander Malahoff. The baby was born with microcephaly and placed in foster care; neither party would initially accept custody. However, when the baby's father turned out to be Stiver's husband, the Stivers accepted the baby. Another problem is unstable family relations. Again in the United States, Elvira Jordan refused to give up for adoption the baby she had borne for Robert Moschetta when she learned that he and his wife were divorcing. That situation in turn led to a three-party custody suit.

The first public report of a high-tech surrogacy was in the United States. Surrogate mother Shannon Boff gave birth in 1986 to Shira, whose picture appeared on the cover of the June 1987 *Life Magazine*. Australia's first was Baby Alice, born in May 1988 in a sister-sister surrogacy. Also noteworthy is the South African case of a woman who bore triplets for her daughter, whose uterus was missing. One estimate is that by January 1991 eighty live births had occurred via high-tech surrogacy, about forty of them in California.

In 1986 in Beverly Hills, California, the Center for Surrogate Parenting, with several satisfied surrogate mothers, launched the National Association of Surrogate Mothers. In 1987 the association prepared a brief supporting the commissioning couple in the Baby M case. In 1987 the Foundation for Economic Trends in Washington, D.C., started the National Coalition Against Surrogacy with a core group of surrogates who had changed their minds as well as feminists who had supported Whitehead.

Selection Issues

Clients. Surrogacy can provide babies for men without access to a woman and for women who are infertile or unwilling to undergo pregnancy. In practice, clinics have generally limited reproductive services to married couples where the woman is infertile, thus excluding single men and women, gay couples, and women who, for whatever reason, do not wish to be pregnant. Advocates for high-tech surrogacy such as the physician Eugene Sandberg encourage developing this method for women with missing uteruses, women for whom pregnancy would be a hazard, women who carry defective genes, or DES daughters with uterine abnormalities.

The Surrogate Mother. Unresolved issues include whether surrogates should be anonymous or known to commissioning couples and whether relatives or friends make the best surrogates or should never be surrogates. For high-tech surrogacy, some clinics require couples to find their own surrogates and to make all legal arrangements beforehand. Alternatively, most surrogacy brokers ask clients to select from their lists of interviewed candidates and then allow surrogates, their spouses, and commissioning couples to meet each other.

A major issue in the choice of surrogates is the possible exploitation of disadvantaged women, which usually plays a role in cases that go to court. An Office of Technology Assessment survey (U.S. Congress 1988) on surrogacy in the United States indicated that although typical surrogates were white, they were not highly educated and 53 percent came from households with incomes of only $15,000 to $30,000 a year.

Social and Ethical Issues

Surrogacy raises many overlapping issues regarding potential harm to children, to the family, to society at large, and to women in particular. Possible physical harm to children would arise as an issue only for the more high-tech versions of surrogacy that involve IVF, frozen embryos, or egg donation. Most critics seem more concerned with possible psychological harm to both the children resulting from surrogacy and the existing children of the surrogate mother. The former may be disturbed at the thought that their mothers gave them away or accepted money for them; the latter may wonder if they themselves might be given away or sold. There is some disagreement about whether these are serious concerns.

Traditionalists worry about the impact of reproductive technologies such as surrogacy on the family and on society as a whole. Some believe that it is wrong to separate sex, reproduction, and child rearing and that doing so will destroy the family. Others believe that surrogacy constitutes baby-selling and the further commodification of human relationships. An additional source of concern is the many practical difficulties inherent in new social arrangements. Finally, some opponents wonder whether it can be moral to create new children in this way when people could take existing children into their homes.

Unique to high-tech surrogacy is the fact that two biological mothers—the gestating and the genetic—can be different persons. If these mothers are sisters, a mingling of aunt and mother roles is not unusual; if they are mother and daughter, we then may have a grandmother of a child being also a mother to that child and a mother who is also a sister to that child. No children of these arrangements are yet old enough for us to learn whether these situations (as well as those involving unrelated or anonymous surrogates) contribute to children's genealogical bewilderment.

Legal Issues

Surrogacy involves several different kinds of legal issues. The lowest-level questions are whether specific acts and approaches are compatible with existing law and, in the United States, with the Constitution. However, the answer to these types of questions is determined to some extent by the general paradigm within which the issue is considered. Despite the recent flourishing of new arrangements and the new technologies that support them, the problem is not a dearth of relevant law but rather competing bodies of existing law. For example, contract law, laws against selling babies, and adoption law are among the bodies of law relevant to surrogacy; judges and legislatures may also develop new laws. Determining which to use is not solely a legal issue but a policy issue that requires thorough moral examination.

The central question for low-tech surrogacy is the status of the contract between the surrogate and the expected child rearers. Some argue for a strict interpretation of contract law; others point out that the demand for specific performance seems inappropriate in such cases. Others—and this position reflects most of the law so far enacted on the subject, both at the state level in the United States and in other countries—believe that a surrogacy contract is, or should be, unenforceable. Indeed, in the context of baby-selling law, such contracts may well be criminal. A second major issue is whether baby-selling law prohibits payment to surrogates or whether the U.S. Constitution would ban such prohibition on the basis of the Fourteenth Amendment.

High-tech surrogacy adds still other problems. The fundamental legal issue here is how to make the genetic parents the legal parents of the child. Since in the common law of most countries the person who gave birth to a child is presumed to be the mother, genetic parents may have no inherent rights to that child. In the United States the Uniform Parentage Act, adopted by some eighteen states, holds that a child's relationship to its natural mother may be established by proof of her having given birth to the child. Thus in those states, genetic parents involved in high-tech surrogacy must go on to adopt the child; in other states the genetic father can get parental rights through a blood test, and then only the rearing or genetic mother needs to adopt.

The *Johnson v. Calvert* case illustrates the California situation and the legal quagmires that form when a high-tech surrogate wants rights to her child. At a 1990 hearing and shortly afterward in a superior court trial, Orange County judge Richard N. Parslow Jr. disregarded California's revision of the Uniform Parentage Act. He removed all custody and visitation rights from surrogate Anna Johnson, who wanted to keep her baby boy, and he gave them instead to the genetic parents, Mark and Cristina Calvert. A year later in an appeals court decision, Judge David Sills affirmed Parslow's decision. This example of privileging a genetic connection is troublesome because Johnson was poor and on welfare, a black native American, and had evidently been untruthful at times with the Calverts, medical personnel, the welfare department, and her own lawyer.

In some countries (Australia, for example) the situation has other complexities. Adoption among relatives may not be permitted unless it is clear that no money has changed hands, because persons over forty are not allowed to adopt (and contracting couples are frequently over forty) and because adoption laws may require a couple at the top of the waiting list to get the next available child. One issue peculiar to Australia (in the state of Victoria) arises from sections of its Infertility (Medical Procedures) Act (Victoria, Australia 1984) that declare that none of the procedures listed therein may be used on fertile women. Since a surrogate is ordinarily fertile, these sections, in effect, have made high-tech surrogacy illegal.

Feminist Critiques

Feminists have generally been critical of surrogacy. Many liberal and socialist feminists believe that the practice could promote feminist values but that to do so it must be carefully regulated. Radical feminists believe that it harms women and should be prohibited. Central to the liberal case is the importance of women's freedom to control their bodies and lives; the arguments against surrogacy are held to be inadequate to undermine the case for it, and it is argued that regulation can protect women's most important interests. Limiting women's right to contract to use their bodies is alleged to be paternalistic because of the underlying assumption that they are incapable of making informed choices about the risks. Such paternalism seems especially contradictory in light of similar risks women are expected to assume in routine childbearing and in the workplace. Liberals also draw attention to the possible benefits of surrogacy to women and children. Infertile women or those with health risks can raise children genetically related to their loved ones, as can gay men. The suffering caused by infertility is reduced, and although the desire for genetically related children may be irrational, satisfying it often brings much happiness. Children borne by healthy women are also less at risk of health problems such as prematurity, and surrogacy might also be used to avoid genetic disease carried by the rearing mother. Low-tech surrogacy could be the easiest method of achieving these aims, uses the fewest medical resources, and potentially can be controlled by women.

Radical feminists deny most of these points or argue that they are outweighed by the disadvantages of surrogacy for women. These feminists contend that surrogacy is predicated on and promotes the social inferiority of women and that it nourishes the stereotype of women as valuable only for their biological role in perpetuating the species. Furthermore, although new reproductive arrangements may seem to add to women's choices, they actually constrict those choices. In particular, these technological fixes draw attention away from underlying social injustices and trap women in a male-dominated medical enterprise with a poor track record of attention to women's needs and rights. Radical feminists also believe that these arrangements and technologies may well increase the exploitation of those already socially disadvantaged by reason of race or poverty and that the infertility of some, painful though it may be, is not sufficient reason to run that risk.

FOR FURTHER READING

Andrews, Lori B. 1989. *Between Strangers: Surrogate Mothers, Expectant Fathers and Brave New Babies*. New York: Harper and Row.

Anna J. v. Mark C. 1991. Ct. of App., 4th App. Dist., no. G01022, decided October 8.

Canadian Royal Commission on New Reproductive Technologies. 1993. *Proceed with Care: Final Report of the Royal Commission on New Reproductive Technologies*. Ottawa: Canadian Communications Group.

Field, Martha. 1990 (1988). *Surrogate Motherhood: The Legal and Human Issues.* Cambridge: Harvard University Press.

Gostin, Larry, ed. 1990. *Surrogate Motherhood: Politics and Privacy.* Bloomington: Indiana University Press.

Holmes, Helen Bequaert. 1992. "Contract Pregnancy: An Annotated Bibliography." In Helen Bequaert Holmes, ed., *Issues in Reproductive Technology: An Anthology.* New York: Garland. Also published in 1994, New York: New York University Press.

Johnson v. Calvert. 1990. Cal. Supr. Ct., Orange Co., Dept. 11, no. X633190, October 22.

Keane, Noel, and Dennis Breo. 1981. *The Surrogate Mother.* New York: Everest House.

"Politics of Surrogacy Contracts." 1990. *Politics and the Life Sciences.* Special issue 8(2): 147–220.

Purdy, Laura. 1989. "Surrogate Mothering: Exploitation or Empowerment?" *Bioethics* 3: 18–34.

Sheean, Leon A., et al. 1989. "In Vitro Fertilization (IVF)–Surrogacy: Application of IVF to Women Without Functional Uteri." *Journal of in Vitro Fertilization and Embryo Transfer* 6(3): 134–137.

"Surrogate Motherhood." 1988. *Law, Medicine, and Health Care* 16(1–2).

U.S. Congress. Office of Technology Assessment. 1988. "Legal Considerations: Surrogate Motherhood." In *Infertility: Medical and Social Choices.* Washington, D.C.: U.S. Government Printing Office.

Victoria, Australia. 1984 (amended 1987, 1991). *Infertility (Medical Procedures) Act.*

fifty

"Baby M" Surrogacy Case

SHARYN ROACH ANLEU

In the United States on February 6, 1985, Mary Beth Whitehead and William Stern entered into a contract in which she agreed to be inseminated with his sperm, become pregnant, and then, following the baby's birth, relinquish her maternal rights and give the child over to him. Mr. Whitehead was a party to the contract but Elizabeth Stern, William's wife, was not, presumably to avoid legal prohibitions on baby-selling. The contract provided that "Mary Beth Whitehead understands and agrees that in the best interests of the child, she will not form or attempt to form a parent-child relationship with any child or children she may conceive, carry to term and give birth to ... and shall freely surrender custody to William Stern" (Supreme Court of New Jersey 1988: 1265). The contract refers to Mary Beth Whitehead as the "Surrogate" and William Stern as the "Natural Father." Stern paid $7,000 to the Infertility Center of New York, the brokers of this arrangement, and $10,000 to Mary Beth.

After the birth on March 27, 1986, Mary Beth realized that she could not part with the baby, who became known as Baby M. At first, she did relinquish the baby, but the following day she went to the Sterns and asked to have the baby for one week. After emotional scenes, the Sterns agreed. Mary Beth did not return Baby M but informed the Sterns that she had decided to keep the child. The father, Stern, responded by obtaining a court order directing the mother, Whitehead, to return the infant to him. Instead the Whiteheads, with the baby, left for Florida, where Mary Beth's parents lived. Almost three months later Stern located them through a private detective, the police forcibly removed Baby M, and in January 1987 Stern commenced court action, seeking enforcement of the surrogate parenting contract. Widespread media attention surrounded these events.

The case was first heard by Judge Sorkow in the Superior Court of New Jersey. The bulk of the testimony from thirty-eight expert and lay witnesses sought to determine the parenting arrangements most compatible with the child's best interests. Although Judge Sorkow warned that "this court must not manage morality or temper theology" (Superior Court of New Jersey 1987: 1138) his judgment relied heavily on psychiatrists' assessments that reflected values about good mothers and appropriate parenting. The judgment compares the "fitness"—in terms of education, income, family situation, and behavior—of the Whiteheads and the Sterns to be the parents of Baby M. The Sterns were presented as economically well off, rational, middle class, and reasonable people who sought a child, whereas the Whiteheads were viewed as financially insecure, disorganized, working class, and unstable.

Judge Sorkow observed that as Stern was the sole surviving member of his family, most of whom perished in the Holocaust, "the desirability of having his own biological offspring became compelling . . . , thus making adoption a less desirable outcome" (Superior Court of New Jersey 1987: 1139). Elizabeth Stern decided not to risk complicating her diagnosed multiple sclerosis by becoming pregnant. Both Sterns had doctorates; William was a research scientist and Elizabeth, a practicing pediatrician. The Whiteheads had minimal education. Richard worked as a driver, and Mary Beth had a series of part-time sales-assistant jobs after leaving school. In 1983 they had filed for bankruptcy.

The judge spent considerable time assessing Mary Beth's personality, her behavior toward the baby, and the appropriateness of her actions after the birth. Based on the psychiatrists' reports, he found she was "impulsive," "unreliable," "manipulative," "use[d] her children for her own ends," "lie[d] under stress," and was "unable to separate her own needs from those of the child." Judge Sorkow concluded:

> The judgement-making ability of Mrs. Whitehead is sorely tested. One outstanding example was her decision to run away in the face of a court order. . . . She is a woman without empathy. She expresses none for her husband's problems with alcohol and her infusion of her other children into this process, exposing them rather than protecting them from the searing scrutiny of the media, mitigates against her claim for custody. She is a good mother for and to her older children. She would not be a good custodian for Baby M. (Superior Court of New Jersey 1987: 1168–1170)

Judge Sorkow found that a valid and enforceable contract existed; neither party had a superior bargaining position, as each "had what the other wanted." Accordingly the court ordered specific performance of the surrogate parenting agreement and compelled delivery of the child to the biological father and the termination of the biological mother's parental rights. Mary Beth Whitehead appealed this decision.

Throughout this judgment two sets of criteria were used: The Whiteheads could do nothing right and the Sterns could do nothing wrong. The judge castigated Mary Beth for using the news media to have her concerns and plight heard but made no comment regarding the Sterns' use of litigation. He viewed Mary Beth's "flight" to Florida and refusal to relinquish the child as selfish, unlike the Sterns' desire for a child. Biological contribution was sufficient to make William Stern the father with full parental rights; it was not sufficient for Mary Beth Whitehead. Judge Sorkow imbued contract law with considerable power and did not consider the public interest.

On February 3, 1988, the Supreme Court of New Jersey held that the surrogacy contract was invalid and unenforceable, thus illegal. Chief Justice Wilentz, delivering the judgment of the court, indicated that the payment of money to a surrogate mother conflicts with prohibitions on baby-selling and is potentially degrading to women. He stated: "We have no doubt whatsoever that the money is being paid to obtain an adoption and not, as the Sterns argue, for the personal services of Mary Beth Whitehead" (1240). Moreover, the contract violated state policy that "the rights of the natural parents are equal concerning their child, the father's right no greater than the mother's." The court acknowledged Mary Beth's maternal rights but awarded custody to William Stern, arguing this would be in the best interests of the child. Again, it was persuaded by the testimony "contrasting both the family life of the Whiteheads and the Sterns and the personalities and characters of the individuals." As Mary Beth had visitation rights, the situation was analogous to court-ordered parental arrangements following a divorce.

Although the New Jersey Supreme Court found commercial surrogacy arrangements illegal, it left the way open for voluntary agreements without payment wherein the birth mother could change her mind and assert her parental rights.

FOR FURTHER READING

Harrison, Michelle. 1987. "Social Construction of Mary Beth Whitehead." *Gender and Society* 1: 300–311.

Superior Court of New Jersey. 1987. "In the Matter of Baby M, a Pseudonym for an Actual Person." 217 N.J. Super. 313, 525 A.2d 1128, March 31.

Supreme Court of New Jersey. 1988. "In the Matter of Baby M, a Pseudonym for an Actual Person." 109 N.J. 396, 537 A.2d 1227, February 3.

fifty-one

World Health Organization Report on the Place of In Vitro Fertilization in Infertility Care

PATRICIA A. STEPHENSON WITH
MARSDEN G. WAGNER

In vitro fertilization (IVF) and related technologies have revolutionized reproductive medicine. Much has been written in the scientific and popular press about the social, medical, legal, and ethical aspects of these technologies. However, until recently, little consideration has been given to the question of the appropriate application of these technologies within an integrated system of social and medical services for the prevention and management of infertility in the global community.

Most governments in the industrialized world have developed elaborate systems for evaluating drugs before their introduction on the market, but typically no such systems apply to medical technologies. To determine what is and is not an appropriate application of medical technology, one requires information on its effectiveness, safety, costs, and benefits. This type of evaluation, using scientifically acceptable methods, is lacking for new reproductive technologies despite the fact that they are now in widespread use. Their true value has not been determined; nor have the risks associated with such treatment been assessed adequately. No attempt has been made to determine the need for services in specific populations, to assess the effectiveness of the new reproductive technologies compared with other technologies designed to restore fertility, or to exhaust the possibilities of preventing infertility in the first place.

Health care policymakers are beginning to ask these questions. In order to further the development of sound policy decisions, the World Health Organization (WHO) Regional Office for Europe held a meeting in June 1990 entitled "The Place of in Vitro Fertilization in Infertility Care." The meeting was attended by sixteen participants from ten countries representing the following disciplines: sociology, psychology, epidemiology, health services research, economics, medicine, journalism/media, law and ethics, and public policy.

The participants agreed that the discussion would be guided by the principles for health care outlined in the targets for global health by the year 2000 and by the principles of human rights outlined in the Helsinki Declaration. It was acknowledged that infertility is a social construct. The participants accepted WHO's definition of infertility as the failure to conceive after at least two years of unprotected intercourse; thus this definition encompasses both sterility and subfertility. However, since the social consequence of infertility, involuntary childlessness, is the chief concern of infertile men and women and may or may not be remedied by the health services, the starting point for the meeting was an examination of all infertility in the community and all care options, both social and medical. The following recommendations were agreed on by consensus. They are taken from the summary report of the meeting (World Health Organization 1990).

1. Each country needs to determine the prevalence of primary and secondary infertility by gender and cause.
2. Each country needs to assess the availability of medical and social options for infertile women and men.
3. Each country needs to determine the proportion of the infertile population, choosing the various social (i.e. adoption, fostering, voluntary childlessness) and medical options (i.e. IVF, other medical treatments).
4. There is a need for research on the preventable causes of infertility, including the role of environmental factors, workplace hazards, iatrogenic causes, sexually transmitted diseases, and emotional factors.
5. The effectiveness of infertility prevention programs needs careful evaluation.
6. Each country needs to assess the social options available to infertile people, including counselling services, barriers to these options, and inequities in access to these options.

The Place of In Vitro Fertilization in Infertility Care

7. Research is needed on the attitudes of the general public and of infertile women and men towards medical and social options. Such research should also assess the cultural and social meaning of infertility.
8. Further proliferation of new IVF centres and expansions of IVF services should not occur until countries have determined the need for infertility services, the priority for infertility services within all human services, and the priority for the various social and medical options for infertile women and men.
9. The role of industry and commercial interests in IVF should be documented including industry's role in funding IVF research and its involvement in service provision. This information should be available to the public.
10. Governments should consider limiting the number of IVF treatment cycles per woman.
11. Governments should consider limiting the indications for IVF.
12. According to the European Society of Human Reproduction and Embryology, the hazards of pregnancy increase and success rates drop for women over the age of forty who undergo IVF. Governments should consider limiting eligibility for IVF to women of forty years of age and under.
13. Infertile individuals must have full information on the availability, risks and effectiveness of all social and medical options for the management of infertility. They must then, in turn, have free choice of the use of these options.
14. Counselling should be available to infertile people. Interested individuals should be encouraged to seek help prior to contact with any type of infertility service. Infertile people may also be referred to mutual aid groups for support before, during, and after pursuing social or medical options.
15. Counselling services and mutual aid groups must be independent of social and medical programs for the management of infertility. Funding for these services should not come from clinics or industry.
16. There is a need for a standard definition of the effectiveness of IVF. The best definition for the purposes of evaluation and health planning is the number of live births per 100 treatment cycles.
17. The effectiveness, short-term safety, and cost of IVF must be scientifically determined through multi-centered, randomized, clinical trials. As a treatment for a given cause of infertility, IVF should be compared with other medical options and with no treatment.
18. Case-control studies are needed to evaluate the short-term and long-term risks of ovulation induction and other procedures.
19. Until there is an adequate appraisal of the risks of ovulation induction and other IVF procedures, countries should take steps to limit exposure of women and their offspring:
    —more stringent guidelines on the indications for ovulation induction should be developed

- limits should be placed on the number of artificially stimulated cycles (both within and outside of IVF) that women undergo
- ovulation stimulation protocols should be as simple as possible
- for selected women, natural cycle IVF may be a preferable option
- the practice of ovulation induction for the purposes of timing pregnancy or regulating the menstrual cycle should be discontinued
- the practice of ovulation induction in normally ovulating women for the sole purpose of ova donation should be discontinued
- social options should be promoted
- prevention programs can be implemented

20. All clinics should follow the guideline set out by the European Society of Human Reproduction and Embryology that limits the number of eggs or embryos transferred during an IVF treatment cycle to no more than three.
21. Governments should set priorities for infertility research and make available funding and other support.
22. Evaluation of the direct and indirect costs of IVF and related technologies is an essential part of rational planning. To calculate the costs of one IVF birth, one must include the costs of drugs, materials, and human resources for all treatment cycles, successful and failed, for all women enrolled in the program. IVF pregnancies require more high-risk obstetrical care and IVF babies more often require neonatal intensive care, so the costs of these services must be included as well. The proportion of the overall costs of IVF paid by government sources, private insurance sources, and out-of-pocket payments by clients should also be determined. IVF costs then need to be compared with the costs of other forms of infertility care, both medical and social.
23. Through surveys or other means, the priority that the public at large assigns to infertility management vis-à-vis other social and health services [should be] determined so that the appropriate proportion of all health and social resources can be allocated to infertility.
24. Following this, the public and policy makers [should] decide on the priority to be given to each option, social and medical, for the management of infertility. This allows the appropriate proportion of the resources for infertility to be allocated to prevention (research and services), social options (research and services), conventional medical and surgical options (research and services), and IVF and related technologies (research and services).
25. As IVF and related technologies require knowledge and skill far beyond that of normal medical and gynecological training, the certification of providers must be tied to thorough training and demonstrated skill. Each IVF center must have at least one such certified provider who assumes direct responsibility for certain crucial steps such as dispensing ovulation induction drugs, evaluating potential new clients, evaluating clients wishing to repeat cycles, and training and supervising other clinic personnel.

26. There should be mandatory reporting of all IVF cycles as a basis for quality assurance. Such population based registries would also provide sampling frames for research and data for ongoing assessment of the costs and benefits of IVF. Additionally, record linkage of IVF registries with birth defects and cancer registries may provide useful data for monitoring adverse effects of treatment.
27. The monitoring and audit of IVF centers must be done by a team, the majority of members having no direct involvement in providing IVF. Sanctions for noncompliance with established standards should include closing the center. The results of the monitoring and audit should be available to the public.
28. Ethical considerations in infertility need to focus first on the services provided (including equity, screening procedures, honesty of information, and the rights of women and men), not just on the egg, embryo, and fetus.
29. Service systems for infertility need mechanisms that provide for community participation in the planning and monitoring of these services including their ethical aspects. The mechanism must ensure that the nature of the services, including ethical issues, reflects the opinion of the entire community and is not dominated by service providers. Various models are available but generally include a local group of unbiased, well-informed people, preferably having at least 50 percent women and a majority of lay people, whose selection is independent of the service providers. In addition, a similarly constituted group at national level is usually necessary. The mandates for these groups may be broader than infertility services, to include other types of health service. In some countries it is important for the mechanism to be given full weight of the law, with regulatory powers given to the national group to monitor and enforce the law, with the assistance of local groups. Whatever model is used, these groups must be accountable to the public, and their deliberations should be available.
30. Because it is against international law to discriminate against individuals on the basis of personal, racial or social characteristics, countries should commit themselves, as an integral part of the provision of all infertility services, to a policy of nondiscrimination:
    —by ensuring that access to these services is not based on inappropriate use of irrelevant personal characteristics such as race, sexual preference, or social economic or marital status
    —by providing appropriate mechanisms for the monitoring and review of access and screening decisions
    —by establishing an accessible and appropriate forum, with decision making and enforcement powers, for individuals seeking review of access decisions
31. In order to monitor the equity and ethical aspects of IVF services, centers should be required to report the demographic and social characteristics of clients. This information should be available to the public.

32. In every IVF center, activities that are primarily for the purpose of developing or contributing to general knowledge need to be labelled as research and clearly differentiated from activities that are primarily for the purpose of enhancing the well-being of an individual client. There should be no incentives for clients to participate in research (for example, by providing remuneration to clients who agree to participate in research or moving them to the top of the waiting list for treatment). Similarly, there should be no incentives for women seeking sterilization to agree to undergo ovulation induction for the purpose of ovum donation. Clients who participate in research must be fully informed as to its nature, purpose, and conditions, and as to their rights as research subjects.

FOR FURTHER READING

United Nations. *1948 Universal Bill of Human Rights*. UNdocA/811. New York: United Nations.

World Health Organization Regional Office for Europe. 1985. *Targets for Health for All*. Copenhagen: WHO-EURO.

World Health Organization Regional Office for Europe. 1990. *Summary Report: Consultation on the Place of in Vitro Fertilization in Infertility Care*. Copenhagen: WHO-EURO (EURI/ICP/MCH 122 S 7139r).

fifty-two

Advanced Infertility Technologies and Occupational Environments

H. PATRICIA HYNES

Reproductive technologists have declared infertility to be the reproductive crisis of industrial countries, and population and environmental organizations have claimed overfertility to be the major environmental crisis of the developing countries. The two crises appear divergent; yet women in industrial and nonindustrial countries alike are subjected to reproductive strategies with common characteristics. These include an emphasis on reproductive technologies rather than prevention of infertility, reduction of the complex issue of human reproduction to women's reproductivity with some women being construed as being too infertile and others overly fertile; and a sexual politics whereby a male-dominated medical profession defines the problem of overfertility and underfertility as a female "deficiency" and then exposes women to risk-laden biomedical techniques and chemicals. For women in both the industrialized and increasingly polluted West and the rural but rapidly urbanizing South, the physical and social environments in which they live and within which reproduction takes place have historically been overlooked.

A growing number of studies have focused on environmental factors, including the occupational environment, that may cause or be implicated in infertility and other reproductive disorders such as spontaneous abortions. Two factors, in particular, have contributed to this new research interest. First, women are entering the workforce in unprecedented numbers. In some industries, notably electronics, the majority of assembly-line workers are women, and most are of childbearing age. Second, more women demand the same manufacturing, assembly, and repair jobs as men but are also asking managers and company physicians for information about the reproductive hazards of chemical and physical agents in the workplace. Some industries, prodded by these events and the specter of liability, are undertaking epidemiological studies of reproductive impacts within the industry. Likewise, women health researchers in public health agencies and universities are advocating for and undertaking research under the broad umbrella of environmental factors and fertility. The research demonstrates the risks of many toxic industrial chemicals to women's and men's fertility. A recent study was conducted on the chemical exposure of firefighters, and it was found that many combustion agents, including benzene and the aldehydes, have adverse reproductive effects in animals and, in some cases, in humans. Male and female animals alike are affected and can transfer dangerous effects to the embryo.

In California's Silicon Valley, about 75 percent of the production workers are women with at least 40 percent of these being Hispanic and Asian. Typically, women working in the manufacturing of computer chips have higher rates of miscarriage and lower rates of fertility, most likely caused by glycol ethers used as solvents in the process. Other studies (in the United States and Europe) indicate that males produce less than a quarter of the sperm than did the average Western male of the early twentieth century. The period of the sperm-quality comparison studies coincides with the rapid rise in industrialization and the introduction of tens of thousands of synthetic chemicals into consumer products and the environment. PCBs, a flame retardant found in foam mattresses, and three kinds of insecticide- and fungicide-like chemicals have been identified in semen. Also, recent IVF studies of contaminated semen fertilizing eggs and subsequent implantation offer the first indications that higher levels of chlorinated organics in semen reduce fertility.

Similarly, in the dental profession, evidence of reproductive disorders from exposure to occupational use of nitrous oxide has been found among women and the wives of male dentists. Specifically, chair-side assistants and wives of dentists tend to suffer increased spontaneous abortions, and children born to chair-side assistants typically have higher rates than usual of congenital abnormalities.

Lead is, perhaps, the best studied reproductive toxin, affecting both men and women. Battery-making is the most hazardous (women of childbearing age are normally prohibited) and the largest of lead industries since the nineteenth century. Current studies on males exposed to lead at such occupational levels correlate malformed sperm, decreased sperm activity, and a decrease in sperm motility with the high level of lead in their blood. Studies of male lead workers in storage battery plants also found a higher rate of sterility and miscarriage than in the control groups. An exhaustive survey of literature on the occupational exposure of lead reveals that men exposed to lead at levels considered acceptable in the industry are likely to suffer significant reproductive harm.

Recently the Massachusetts Department of Public Health and the University of Massachusetts Occupational Health Program conducted the first systematic study of U.S. corporate policy regarding reproductive hazards in the workplace. Two major findings are consistent with the history of the lead industry on reproductive toxicity. First, the use of reproductive hazards was high, but overall knowledge of reproductive hazards was low. Fewer than half of all companies provided any information on reproductive hazards to employees. Second, although companies varied widely in their policies regarding reproductive hazards, those that had policies focused on women. Nearly 20 percent restricted the work of women on the grounds of potential reproductive risks. Of the companies with a known reproductive hazard, 54 percent had no reproductive policy. Where there was a policy, the focus was on pregnant women.

The recent findings of environmental risks to fertility in the industrial environment contrast with U.S. public environmental and workplace policy, with actions taken by industry, and with the focus of the new reproductive technology industry. Reproductive toxicity testing has traditionally not been required by the government in toxicity determinations of new chemicals or in regulating workplace exposures. Consequently, we lack reproductive toxicity data to set exposure limits for workers in the workplace. When data do exist, reproductive effects have been considered only on the fetus, implying that the mother exclusively transfers toxins to the fetus and is not affected herself. This stance also results in fetal protectionist policies that remove or bar women from the workplace.

The majority of recently tested chemicals in the workplace have adverse reproductive effects in males and females. Further, more agents have been shown to be toxic to male reproductive processes than to female reproductive processes. Despite evidence that male fertility is impaired by environmental toxins, the new reproductive technologies are designed and practiced exclusively on women. Crucial potential prevention of reproductive toxicity and infertility is thus overlooked, and women are further exposed to risks in the one-sided treatment of both infertility and overfertility.

FOR FURTHER READING

Blinch, Russell. 1992. "Pregnant Microchip Workers Face Risk." *Boston Globe* (December 4): 73–75.
Commonwealth of Massachusetts. 1989. *Family, Work, and Health.* Boston: Commonwealth of Massachusetts.
Elkington, John. 1985. *The Poisoned Womb: Human Reproduction in a Poisoned World.* New York: Viking Press.
Feichtinger, W. 1991. "Environmental Factors and Fertility." *Human Reproduction* 6(8): 1170–1175.
Klein, Patricia Vawter. 1987. "For the Good of the Race: Reproductive Hazards from Lead and Exclusionary Policies Toward Women." In Barbara Drygulski, ed., *Women, Work and Technology.* Ann Arbor: University of Michigan Press.
Markoff, John. 1992. "Miscarriages Tied to Chip Factories." *New York Times* (November 12): 1, D2.
McDiarmid, Melissa, et al. 1991. "Reproductive Hazards of Fire Fighting II: Chemical Hazards." *American Journal of Industrial Medicine* 19: 447–472.
Raymond, Janice G. 1993. *Women as Wombs.* San Francisco: Harper.
Rudolph, Linda, and Hanna Swan. 1986. "Reproductive Hazards in the Microelectronics Industry." *State of the Art Reviews: Occupational Medicine* 1(1): 135–143.
Yagiela, John A. 1991. "Health Hazards and Nitrous Oxide: A Time for Reappraisal." *Anesthetic Progress* 38: 1–11.

fifty-three

Informed Consent and Advanced Infertility Technologies

FRANÇOISE BAYLIS

The key elements of informed consent are competence, disclosure, understanding, voluntariness, and authorization. An informed consent is an intentional choice by a competent person made with an understanding of the nature and consequences of available options. This understanding presumes appropriate disclosure of relevant information and suggests the need, in some cases, for education and counseling. Further, an informed consent is a choice that is neither coerced nor manipulated. It is a choice not subject to influences such as force, fraud, deceit, duress, overreaching, or other ulterior forms of constraint or coercion. And finally, informed consent finds its expression in the authorization of another to proceed with a particular intervention.

The text includes passages from Françoise Baylis, "Assisted Reproductive Technologies: Informed Choice," in *New Reproductive Technologies: Ethical Aspects,* vol. 1 of *Research Studies of the Royal Commission on New Reproductive Technologies* (Ottawa: Canadian Communications Group, 1993). Reproduced with the permission of the minister of Public Works and Government Services Canada, 1997.

Competence

Health care providers must not proceed with a diagnostic, therapeutic, or research intervention without an informed consent from a competent patient or research participant (or surrogate decisionmaker). The ethical basis for this requirement is the principle of respect for persons. This principle requires that persons deemed incompetent be offered appropriate protection and that decisions on their behalf be made in their best interests. It further requires that the wishes of competent persons be respected. Competent persons have the right to make autonomous decisions about their participation in treatment or research.

Competence determinations are intended to ascertain whether an individual is capable of deliberation and choice, and ideally there should be particular attention to (1) the person's capacities at the time of decisionmaking, (2) the nature of the decisionmaking task, and (3) the context in which the decision is being made. For example, the capacity to understand relevant information can be intermittent or fluctuating. Also, though a person may not be capable of managing her financial affairs, it doesn't follow that she can't make health care decisions. And though she may not be able to make difficult health care decisions beyond her comprehension (i.e., decisions where the information to be understood and the harms and benefits to be weighed are complex), she may be capable of giving or withholding her informed consent to simple, low-risk interventions with clear medical benefit.

Disclosure

Persons presumed competent (i.e., capable of understanding and deliberating) need adequate information about available options and associated consequences so as to make choices consistent with their preferences (needs, values, life goals, etc.) At minimum, they need information about their medical status, the nature and objectives of available options, the nature and probability of the known and possible consequences (harms and benefits) of the options, and any other information that may help them to make a choice. In this last category, persons considering the use of advanced infertility techniques or new reproductive technologies (NRTs) will need additional information about the qualifications of the team members and the costs involved. As well, prospective patients and research participants should be told that they may ask questions at any time, that confidentiality and privacy will be respected, and that consent is always revocable.

It is particularly important that full disclosure be given as to the nature and objectives of the various NRT technologies. For example, in vitro fertilization (IVF) would usually be described as a process that involves controlled ovarian hyperstimulation, ova retrieval, semen collection, and fertilization of the ova outside the body, followed by embryo transfer. In explaining controlled ovarian hyperstimulation, a medical practitioner would identify the drugs that are used to stimulate follicular growth, suppress ovarian function, and induce ovulation. In relation to ova retrieval, the use of transvaginal follicular aspiration or laparoscopy is explained. With semen collection, the topic for discussion is masturbation and the need to abstain from ejaculation two to three days before producing a semen sample. More than a description of the technology is required, however, for an adequate understanding of its nature. For example, information about the likely impact of an IVF cycle on daily living is imperative. The social, psychological, and practical aspects of the intervention are as important as the medical ones. Moreover, individuals should also know whether IVF is a therapeutic or research intervention.

Whereas some NRTs clearly fall within the realm of clinical practice, others are more accurately described as clinical research and still others as innovative or nonvalidated practice. The primary objective of NRTs as clinical practice is to benefit infertile individuals (to help them have genetically or biologically related children). There is reasonable evidence of some clinical NRTs' safety and efficacy and some measure of professional consensus as to their therapeutic merit. Other NRTs are in the realm of clinical research, the primary objective of which is to generate and validate new knowledge. The target population in this case is larger and includes infertile and fertile individuals as well as gametes and embryos. The evidence of safety and efficacy of such technologies is lacking, and there is no professional consensus as to their therapeutic merit. Examples include preimplantation genetic diagnosis, sperm sorting, and ova freezing. Finally, some NRTs are neither pure therapy nor research. Their objective is to benefit infertile couples, but there is no (or limited) evidence of safety and efficacy. There is strong belief, however, on the part of some members of the profession that there are therapeutic merits to the proposed intervention. IVF for unexplained infertility and noncommercial preconception (surrogacy) agreements are examples.

Understanding

Informed decisionmaking for both research and therapy begins with, but requires more than, the disclosure of information. If the decisionmaking process is to culminate in a choice to authorize or refuse a particular intervention, the decisionmaker must be able to understand and assess the information disclosed so as to make a choice consistent with personal life goals, objectives, values, and beliefs. From the perspective of most infertile persons, the potential benefit of IVF is the birth of a genetically and/or biologically linked (healthy) child. Thus a critical consideration in assessing the harm-benefit ratio of IVF is the likelihood of having a child as a result of the technology. For this reason, a realistic assessment of the success rates of IVF is particularly relevant. There is often much confusion, however, regarding the definition of "success." There are biochemical pregnancy rates, clinical pregnancy rates, and take-home-baby rates. These rates are available per cycle, per ova retrieval, and per embryo transfer. These rates also vary from clinic to clinic, from year to year, and for different patient populations (the cause of infertility and age of the female partner are important variables). Effective communication, education, and counseling are needed to promote adequate understanding that, arguably, could be greatly enhanced by providing people with the information they most want, namely the likelihood of a live birth.

Voluntariness

An informed consent must be voluntary. The requirement here is that the decision to pursue a particular course of action not be coerced or manipulated. One concern with NRTs that applies to both fertile and infertile individuals is the risk that they will be pressured by their physicians or family members and friends seeking infertility treatment to donate, trade, or sell their gametes for therapeutic or research purposes. A second concern is that women may be pressured by their partners to avail themselves of technologies that will provide their partners with genetically related children when such women might prefer to use a different technology, pursue adoption, or accept child-free living. A third, broader concern is with the socially constructed nature of women's desire for children. Young girls and women are socialized to believe that they will not be fulfilled until they have "their own" children, and this pervasive pronatalism pressures many women into motherhood. In a context where childlessness remains socially unacceptable and where women's identity is still very much defined in terms of motherhood, agreeing to infertility treatment is not necessarily an expression of free choice.

Legal Requirements

Legislation and case law on various aspects of informed consent (for treatment and research) vary among jurisdictions. Typically, the law addresses both procedural and substantive questions of consent, such as who decides and on what basis. As well, the law may set out the scope of adequate disclosure (i.e., what must be told to patients and research participants).

Beyond Informed Consent

For many, the moral acceptability of NRTs turns on informed consent. The view is that if the persons consenting to the use of a particular technology fully understand the situation and freely choose to proceed, no one should interfere with their use of NRTs. This view is criticized by others who believe that informed consent is not possible because NRTs are inescapably coercive. These technologies are presented as "the only hope" and so there is no choice. More generally, it is held that disadvantaging social and medical conditions necessarily constrain choice. Still others argue that informed consent is not the only concern in assessing the ethical acceptability of NRTs. They argue that there is no such thing as the right to have a child and that NRTs promote the commodification of children and the continued oppression of women. For these and other reasons they maintain that the pursuit of certain reproductive technologies can legitimately be thwarted in the interest of protecting the vulnerable and promoting certain social values.

FOR FURTHER READING

Baylis, Françoise. 1993. "Assisted Reproductive Technologies: Informed Choice." In *New Reproductive Technologies: Ethical Aspects*. Vol. 1 of *Research Studies of the Royal Commission on New Reproductive Technologies*. Ottawa: Canadian Communications Group.

Beauchamp, Tom. 1997. "Informed Consent." In Robert M. Veatch, ed., *Medical Ethics*. 2nd ed. Boston: Jones and Bartlett.

Faden, Ruth, and Tom Beauchamp. 1986. *A History and Theory of Informed Consent*. New York: Oxford University Press.

Katz Rothman, Barbara. 1989. *Recreating Motherhood*. New York: W. W. Norton.

Lauritzen, Paul. 1995. "What Price Parenthood?" In Joseph H. Howell and William F. Sale, eds., *Life Choices: A Hastings Center Introduction to Bioethics*. Washington, D.C.: Georgetown University Press.

Lippman, Abby. 1991. "Prenatal Genetic Testing and Screening: Constructing Needs and Reinforcing Inequities." *American Journal of Law and Medicine* 17(1–2): 15–50.

Robertson, John. 1994. *Children of Choice: Freedom and the New Reproductive Technologies*. Princeton: Princeton University Press.

Sherwin, Susan. 1992. "New Reproductive Technologies and Paternalism." In *No Longer Patient: Feminist Ethics and Health Care*. Philadelphia: Temple University Press.

fifty-four

Legislation— United Kingdom

DEBORAH LYNN STEINBERG

In 1990, after an eight-year legislative process begun in 1982 with the Warnock Committee—established to inquire into the development of new reproductive technologies in the United Kingdom—the Human Fertilisation and Embryology (HFE) Act was passed. The main purpose of the act was to establish regulatory principles and standards and a statutory regulatory agency for in vitro fertilization (IVF) and related practices.

The act provides definitions and guidelines for a number of IVF and related issues including the status and treatment of embryos and gametes; the legitimation and prohibition of certain practices; the establishment of a licensing system and a statutory authority; and the legal definition, status, and rights of parents. Additionally, the act contains a provision for the amendment of the Surrogacy Arrangements Act of 1985 (extending the prohibition of commercial surrogacy arrangements), as well as an amendment of the 1967 Abortion Act (reducing the upper time limit of legal abortion from twenty-eight to twenty-four weeks except in cases of danger to the mother's life or where the fetus is diagnosed as carrying genetic or congenital damage). The central argument made in favor of the reduction in the upper time limit for legal abortion was that fetal viability, due to advances in neonatal technology, is now possible at an earlier stage. In British law, fetuses are "persons" when they can be said to be viable. The law previously assumed viability at twenty-eight weeks; with the passage of the HFE Act, fetal viability is assumed at twenty-four weeks. Both the provision allowing abortions later than twenty-four weeks in cases of suspected congenital defect and the provision approving IVF-related embryo research in order to develop genetic diagnostic and prevention techniques validate genetic eugenic practices in principle. The act raises no questions about the issues of genetic screening or eugenic practices either in principle or, beyond calls for record keeping and working under a license, in practical terms.

Critical Perspectives

The HFE Act represents a significant development in the history of state intervention into medical scientific practices and is consistent with the direction taken in most developed countries to regulate new reproductive technologies (NRTs). Of the many critical points that can be made about the legislation, perhaps most important are those revolving around the issues of medical scientific accountability and women's reproductive rights, health, and well-being (both in and outside the context of IVF treatment).

As a whole, the HFE Act provides for the establishment of medical scientific accountability to the British state for NRTs (principally, IVF and related practices). Indeed, most of the act's provisions are devoted to the establishment of procedures through which that accountability will be exercised and a complex bureaucracy that administers those procedures. In so doing, the act appears to provide a mechanism for controlling NRT practices and practitioners, keeping those practices within "reasonable" and "acceptable" bounds. Ostensibly, the act provides a challenge to and erosion of long-standing self-regulation in the professions of medicine and science.

However, close examination of the act's provisions reveals that it is organized around and substantively protects the medically and scientifically defined agenda for NRT practices. Indeed, the act structurally provides for the continuation of the better part of professional self-regulation. First, aside from making it illegal to perform all existing NRT practices without a license, the act validates nearly all of them. The list of prohibited procedures includes those that at the time the act was passed were not practiced (e.g., interspecies embryo transfer) or were not yet possible (nuclear transfer, a method of cloning). Moreover, there are a number of loopholes that would seem to prevent successful prosecution under the act. For example, practitioners who have violated the act can argue that they were acting with intent to follow the law or were acting under the orders of a "person responsible" for a clinic (i.e., usually a license holder). Moreover, although the act requires the establishment of a code of practice, it is not a criminal offense to violate that provision. At worst, a practitioner may lose the right to hold a license, but this matter is entirely at the discretion of the statutory authority. Finally, the main avenue of medical scientific accountability is through the submission of written reports (both practitioners' own and those of government representatives who periodically visit and review clinics). Although the act does require that practitioners provide information to their patients, what this should consist of is not enumerated but rather left to the discretion of practitioners. Ultimately, then, the act establishes a form of medical and scientific accountability upward to the state hierarchy rather than downward to patients (women) and laypeople more generally. Substantively, the act both validates existing medical scientific principles and protocols in relation to NRTs and conscripts these principles and practices into the apparatus of the state. In effect, IVF practitioners are conscripted as agents of the state, and the state becomes a secondary agent of IVF practices.

Besides its validation of professional power and practices, the HFE Act holds significant (and in some ways unprecedented) implications for women's health and reproductive rights both within and outside the IVF context. First, there are a number of significant omissions in the act. Of these, most notable perhaps is the near-total omission of specific reference to women even though the IVF practices in question can be performed only on women. Moreover, nowhere in the act are there any provisions establishing treatment standards with respect to women's health. Indeed, insofar as NRTs affect women, the act substantially disregards questions of potential dangers to women's health or reproductive rights.

Mentions of women in the act are equally, if not more, problematic. For example, when women are not implicitly covered by gender-neutral terminology (e.g., "gamete donors," "persons"), they are described as undergoing treatment with a man. In both cases, there is implied a false equivalency between the experiences and positions of women and men in relation to NRTs. The HFE Act revolves around embryo- (and science-) centered concerns rather than women's health or reproductive rights. Nearly all provisions, including administrative ones, are organized around establishing a special status for in vitro embryos. Most important among these are the categorical distinction made in the act between IVF treatment and IVF research (on embryos)—though both involve the same treatment of women—and the legitimation of IVF (embryo) research up to fourteen days' development. With respect to the latter decision, the act establishes that embryos in general have a special status but for the first fourteen days cannot be seen as persons. The act lays down a strong basis for arguing that after fourteen days, embryos have full personhood rights—a potential precedent that could endanger women's reproductive autonomy and the future of women's access to legal abortion.

The act's reduction of the upper time limit of legal abortion to twenty-four weeks also has negative implications. In the United Kingdom, with progressive cuts to the National Health Service budget, increasing numbers of women are forced to have later abortions due to long waiting lists. Moreover, practitioners are not likely to perform terminations after twenty-two weeks (or even earlier) so as not to risk breaking the law. It seems inevitable that the reduction in the upper time limit will make it more difficult, if not impossible, for many more women to terminate their pregnancies.

The HFE Act establishes a number of additional precedents that threaten women's reproductive rights. Chief among these is its definition of pregnancy: A woman is not to be treated as carrying a child until the embryo is implanted. This definition has two important implications. First, the unprecedented use of the term "child" for fetus in a legislative context implicitly establishes a basis for arguing the legal personhood of embryos after implantation has been diagnosed. Second, the unprecedented use of implantation as an index of pregnancy means that the state and medical scientific authorities have legal jurisdiction over embryos during the period between embryo transfer and implantation. In other words, the state and practitioners have legal rights over women's bodies through their legal rights over women's embryos.

Another precedent established within the HFE Act concerns the establishment of male reproductive rights over IVF embryos (as an extension of their rights over their gametes). This provision could set a precedent for arguing that men should have such rights over embryos in any context; for example male consent may be required for women to terminate their pregnancies. To establish male reproductive rights over sperm once sperm is incorporated in an embryo and part of a woman's body is to establish male reproductive rights over women. In addition, a number of the act's provisions are aimed at regulating the reproduction of nuclear families. This is reflected in the terminology of IVF "couples," the establishment of a strict patrilineal framework for record keeping, the definitions of legal parenthood around the prerogatives of marriage, and, perhaps most pointedly, in the suggested restriction of access to IVF treatment to married women. Although not precisely binding, the act's strong injunction to practitioners on this matter states that women should not be treated with IVF unless account has been taken of the welfare of any child who may be born—including the need of that child for a father.

In sum, the HFE Act elaborates a regulatory framework for NRTs that establishes a number of potentially devastating consequences for women's reproductive health and rights. These include the general linguistic erasure of women in the NRT context; the lack of provision for standards aimed to protect women's health and rights; and the establishment of standards for the protection of embryos, medical scientific progress, male reproductive rights, patrilineality, and the heterosexual nuclear family—all at the expense of women's autonomy over their bodies and reproductive decisionmaking. In establishing these principles, the act lays the basis for eroding women's reproductive rights more generally, having potential adverse effects for women who will never undergo the procedures in question.

FOR FURTHER READING

Daniels, Cynthia R. 1995. *At Women's Expense: State Power and the Politics of Fetal Rights*. Cambridge: Harvard University Press.

Degener, Theresia. 1990. "Female Self-Determination Between Feminist Claims and 'Voluntary' Eugenics, Between 'Rights' and 'Ethics.'" *Issues in Reproductive and Genetic Engineering* 3(2): 87–100.

Faulder, Caroline. 1985. *Whose Body Is It? The Troubling Issue of Informed Consent*. London: Virago.

Feinman, Calrice, ed. 1992. *The Criminalization of a Woman's Body*. New York: Harrington Park Press.

McNeil, Maureen, Ian Varcoe, and Steven Yearley, eds. 1990. *The New Reproductive Technologies*. London: Macmillan.

Morgan, D., and R. Lee. 1991. *Blackstone's Guide to the Human Fertilisation and Embryology Act 1990*. London: Blackstone Press.

Steinberg, Deborah Lynn. 1991. "Adversarial Politics: The Legal Construction of Abortion." In Sarah Franklin et al., eds., *Off-Centre: Feminism and Cultural Studies*. London: Harper Collins/Routledge.

Steinberg, Deborah Lynn. 1997. *Bodies in Glass: Genetics, Eugenics, Embryo Ethics*. Manchester: Manchester University Press.

United Kingdom. 1990. *Human Fertilisation and Embryology Act, 1990*.

United Kingdom. 1992–1995. *Human Fertilisation and Embryology Authority Reports*. London: Her Majesty's Stationery Office.

Warnock Committee. 1984. *Report of the Committee of Enquiry into Human Fertilisation and Embryology*. London: Her Majesty's Stationery Office.

Warnock, Mary. 1985. *A Question of Life: The Warnock Report on Human Fertilisation and Embryology*. Oxford: Basil Blackwell.

fifty-five

Legislation— The Netherlands

MARTA KIREJCZYK

In the Netherlands the first baby conceived by means of in vitro fertilization (IVF) was born in 1983. Since then, the use of IVF has rapidly increased. The prevailing liberal social climate and the changed attitudes toward procreation among Dutch women contributed greatly to this rapid growth. From the early 1970s onward, the use of contraceptives became more widespread and effective. The rates of abortion and teenage pregnancies are lower and decreasing. Women systematically postpone childbearing to a later age (in 1995, the age of women giving birth to their first baby was on average twenty-eight and a half years), the number of children born per woman has decreased considerably, and the proportion of women who choose not to bear children at all is on the increase (in 1990, some 15 percent of women born in 1950 had had no children). The idea of planned parenthood is firmly rooted in Dutch society. At the same time, many women who fail to become pregnant during the period they have chosen usually request immediate medical intervention. The number of so-called impatient consults for IVF is increasing.

In the Netherlands the provision of IVF through the health care system is regulated by the 1989 ministerial decree Planningsbesluit IVF, which introduced licensing for the IVF laboratories operating in the hospitals offering IVF programs. In order to be eligible for an IVF license, a hospital has to fulfill a number of requirements that must guarantee the quality of the medical service. The requirements include the necessary qualifications of the medical-scientific staff and organizational arrangements that permit twenty-four-hour functioning of the clinic. In an official document (protocol), the hospital must indicate the medical grounds for IVF, the procedure followed during the treatment, and the rules regarding the handling of gametes and embryos. A yearly minimum of 150 IVF cycles per licensed hospital is required, and each IVF program must achieve a minimum success rate of 10 percent (calculated as a ratio between the number of pregnancies lasting for twelve weeks or more and the number of hormonal stimulations of ovulation).

By 1991, twelve hospitals (eight academic and four general) had been licensed for IVF. Each of them is allowed to collaborate with a maximum of four nonlicensed hospitals in a "transport IVF" arrangement. Under that arrangement, the first stages of the treatment (stimulation of ovulation and egg retrieval) are performed in a nonlicensed hospital. The fertilization and embryo transfer are carried out in a licensed one. In 1996, the number of treatments performed in more than thirty hospitals running an entire IVF program or parts of it approached 12,000. Women are usually not in the program for more than three cycles. Though in the early days, tubal occlusion was considered the only indication for IVF, currently IVF is being applied to other forms of infertility, such as endometriosis, unexplained infertility, and male infertility. The application of IVF to male infertility is particularly disturbing, since it requires healthy and fertile women to go through a hazardous medical procedure in order to alleviate the consequences of the infertility of her partner. In the Netherlands, male infertility as the sole indication occurs in approximately 30 percent of all IVF treatments. The IVF centers greatly differ with regard to the range of indications for IVF and the actual rate of success. According to the authoritative opinion of the Health Council, the effectiveness of IVF is unquestionable for one indication only: blocked fallopian tubes.

During 1994, the licensed IVF clinics began performing intracytoplasmic sperm injection (ICSI). By 1995 the number of ICSI treatments had risen to 1,500. In view of the suspicion that ICSI in combination with microsurgical epididymal sperm aspiration and testicular sperm extraction would result in an increased rate of genetic defects in offspring, a voluntary moratorium on these extraction techniques was proclaimed in 1996 by the professional organizations of gynecologists and clinical embryologists.

The handling of gametes and embryos is not yet regulated by law. Sperm donation is widely accepted and practiced. An estimated 600–800 women yearly are impregnated with the aid of artificial insemination with donated sperm. Egg and embryo donations are not prohibited but take place only sporadically. In the ministerial regulation of 1989, provisions were made to prevent commercialization of the sperm, egg, and embryo donations and of surrogate motherhood (the latter occurs very sporadically in the Netherlands). Since 1993, commercial surrogacy has been forbidden by law. Embryo research is not yet regulated by law. Formally, each research proposal involving embryos is subject to compulsory approval by the National Ethics Committee. In 1988, however, the parliament called for a moratorium on embryo research pending the outcome of the legislative process. No cases of breaching the moratorium have been reported.

The costs of medical services for approximately 65 percent of the Dutch population are covered by a public insurance system, the so-called Sick Funds Insurance. During the 1980s, only a limited number of IVF procedures were subsidized from this public insurance system. However, since 1989, the Sick Funds Insurance covers the costs of IVF treatments of up to three cycles per pregnancy and puts no restrictions on the type of medical indication for IVF. Private health insurance coverage of IVF costs varies; some include, others exclude, IVF from their policies.

For acceptance to the IVF program, there are no formal or legal restrictions regarding women's conjugal relationships. In practice, however, IVF is usually limited to women living in heterosexual relationships. In 1995 half the licensed clinics running the full IVF program did not accept lesbian women for treatment and only one clinic accepted single women.

A long-standing topic in the feminist critique of IVF is the question of detailed and documented warnings about the health hazards inherent in the IVF procedure. Only since the beginning of the 1990s has this problematic side of IVF been publicly discussed by medical practitioners and health care policymakers. The adverse effects now recognized by the medical profession include those associated with hyperstimulation of ovulation, an increased rate of multiple and complicated pregnancies requiring hospital treatments, more frequent ectopic pregnancies and cesarean sections, a high risk of miscarriage and premature labor, a high (25 percent) incidence of multiple births with a third of the babies being severely underweight at birth, and the increased chance of the occurrence of neural tube defects. Medical authorities have called for restraint but not for the abandonment of the IVF procedure altogether.

FOR FURTHER READING

Haan, G., R. van Steen, and F. Rutten. 1989. *Evaluatie van In-vitro-fertilisatie*. Maastricht: Rijksuniversiteit Limburg.

Kirejczyk, Marta. 1996. *Met Technologie Gezend? Gender en de Onstreden Invoering van in Vitro Fertilisatie in de Netherlandse Gezondheidszorg*. Utrecht: Jan van Arkel.

Netherlands Gezondheidsraad (Health Council). 1992. *Jaaradvies Gezondheidszorg 1991*. The Hague: Gezondheidsraad.

Netherlands Gezondheidsraad (Health Council). 1997. *Het Planningsbesluit IVF.* The Hague: Gezondheidsraad.

Netherlands Minister of Justice and Minister of Welfare, Health and Culture. 1988. *Notitie Kunstmatige Bevruchting en Draagmoederschap.* The Hague: SDU Vitgevers.

Netherlands Ministry of Welfare, Health and Culture (WVC). 1989. "Planningsbesluit in Vitro Fertilisatie." *Staatscourant* 146 (July 31): 6–7.

Te Velde, E. R. 1991. *Zwanger Worden in de 21ste Eeuw: Steeds Later. Steeds Kunstmatiger.* Utrecht: Rijksuniversiteit Utrecht.

fifty-six

Legislation—France

JEAN COHEN

France has played a large part in the development of new reproductive technologies (NRTs). Two French teams took part in the pioneering meeting at Bournhall in 1983, along with one English, one U.S., and two Australian teams. There are approximately 150 NRT centers in France. They make approximately 40,000 in vitro fertilization (IVF) attempts per year. Most of the centers participate in the national registry FIVNAT (which in French stands for IVF National). In 1996, the national pregnancy rate per transfer was 26 percent and per cycle, 20.5 percent.

Since July 29, 1994, France has adopted the Loi de bioéthique covering NRTs. The law covers insemination with husband or with donor semen, IVF (including ICSI), embryo research, and antenatal (prenatal) diagnosis. With the exception of insemination, NRTs may be performed only in licensed centers under the responsibility of a recognized practitioner. Licensing is granted for five years by the Ministry of Health after notification from the National Committee of Reproduction Medicine, Biology, and Antenatal Diagnosis. This committee is composed of practitioners proposed by their representative organizations, experts, lawyers, and representatives of relevant administrative and professional bodies and family associations. All accredited infertility clinics are required to present an annual report of activities to the minister of health.

NRTs are intended to remedy medical infertility. Both partners seeking this service must be alive (some surviving spouses may hold the stored gametes of their deceased spouse), of reproductive age, and married or able to prove cohabitation of two years. They must give written consent after receiving precise counseling. Single mothers and homosexual couples are excluded. The certificate must be kept in the files of the clinic doing the procedure.

Under French law, IVF, ICSI, and embryo freezing are permitted. The number of embryos that can be transferred is not specified. Selective reduction is not mentioned. Embryo freezing and storage may be requested by the parents for a period of up to five years. The law is silent on the use of stored, frozen embryos in cases where communication with the couple is lost because of divorce, death, or other circumstances. Difficulties in determining the status of these embryos can be anticipated. There are currently 6,000 frozen orphan embryos awaiting a decision.

Concerning gamete and embryo donation, the recipient couple must obtain an order by joint declaration before a judge or solicitor. Both partners are legally responsible for the child. Those who donate gametes must have had children, and no payment is granted. Anonymity is mandatory, and gametes may be obtained only through an agreed center (bank). Advertising is forbidden. Negative biological analysis for HIV, hepatitis, cytomegalovirus (CMV), syphilis, and other diseases must be obtained, and donor gametes are quarantined for six months before use. As a result of these complicated procedures, embryo donation is very rare. Also, there is a lack of donors. Donors cannot be IVF patients, IVF surrogacy is not allowed, and all experimentation on embryos is forbidden. Preimplantation genetic diagnosis (PID) is theoretically allowed but only in authorized centers. Since the enactment of the law in 1994, no center has been authorized to practice PID.

After evaluation of its application, the present law will be subjected to further examination by Parliament within a maximum of five years from its enactment (by 1999). All French NRT teams respect this law, but many practitioners want to modify it somewhat. Practitioners typically call for permission to undertake embryo research within ethical guidelines. The current situation does not permit any embryo research in French labs. Practitioners also seek permission to provide PID. Currently, French patients are sent to Belgium or the United Kingdom for this service. Practitioners also believe that the common-law certificate should not be the doctor's responsibility and that implantation should be permitted in case of death of the father. Finally, it is felt that the law needs to clarify menopausal women's right of access to ova donation. Currently the law stipulates only that eligible women must be of a "reproductive age."

In France, one-half of the NRT centers are public and the other half are private. French social security reimburses four IVF attempts per couple, including ovulation stimulation, egg collection, and laboratory workup. If a couple is treated in a public center, they do not pay anything (except for special procedures such as embryo freezing). If a couple is treated in a private center, they may have to pay the difference between the doctors' fees and social security reimbursement. The waiting lists do not exceed two to three months in public hospitals.

FOR FURTHER READING

France. 1994. *Loi de bioéthique.*

fifty-seven

Legislation—Australia and New Zealand

SHARYN ROACH ANLEU

Australia

Some Australian states have enacted legislation to regulate new reproductive technologies (NRTs), seeking to arbitrate between or reflect the diverse viewpoints and interests surrounding these technologies. The public and highly controversial nature of debates around this legislation stems from several factors. Australia has been the location of many of the major world NRT developments, resulting in widespread local and international media coverage. The research monies have derived largely from commonwealth government–funded grants. Medibank, the national health scheme, provides partial insurance for the procedures and, as part of the national budget, is amenable to public scrutiny. As a result, church leaders, feminists, medical scientists, and right-to-life activists have all participated vigorously in debates at conferences, in the news media, and at public hearings. The governments of each state and the commonwealth have responded by establishing committees to investigate the ethical, moral, social, and legal implications of new reproductive technologies.

The Federal Parliament has not legislated in this area, although there was an unsuccessful attempt to pass the Human Embryo Experimentation Bill in 1985, and the government established the National Bioethics Consultative Committee in 1988, which was disbanded in 1991. Three states have passed statutes regulating artificial insemination, gamete donation, in vitro fertilization (IVF) and related procedures, and embryo experimentation and storage. The statutes also specify access to reproductive technology programs, require that participants receive counseling, and emphasize informed consent. Four states have outlawed commercial surrogacy, and all states and territories have amended "status of children" legislation to remove parental rights and obligations from gamete donors and to recognize the recipient couple as the legal parents.

Victoria

In 1982 the government of Victoria established the multidisciplinary Committee to Consider the Social, Ethical and Legal Issues Arising from IVF. The committee produced an interim report recommending legislation authorizing hospitals to offer IVF programs. The report suggested that programs be limited to situations in which the gametes derive from husbands and wives and that the embryos subsequently be transferred to the wife. The first major report advised that donor gametes and donor embryos be available in IVF programs, and a second report recommended that the freezing of embryos formed in an IVF program be permitted. Most of the committee members agreed that destructive, nontherapeutic embryo research be limited to "excess" embryos produced by patients in an IVF program and that embryos not be allowed to develop beyond fourteen days after fertilization. Embryos formed with the original intention that they be transferred to a woman for implantation but ultimately not used for that purpose become excess or spare. The committee also suggested the establishment of a standing review and advisory body to examine and report on all matters in the scientific and medical management of infertility.

The Victorian government passed the Infertility (Medical Procedures) Act in 1984, which prohibits IVF except for the purposes of implanting the embryo in a woman's uterus, outlaws cloning, and prohibits embryo freezing unless implantation will be carried out later. It requires couples to receive counseling by approved counselors and to provide written consent before undergoing IVF regardless of whether donor gametes are involved. The act specifies that donated gametes (ova and sperm) can be used only when there is infertility or when it is "reasonably established" that an "undesirable" hereditary disorder could be transmitted. Donation is without payment except for the reimbursement of any expenses incurred, and donors and their spouses must also provide written consent and receive counseling.

The legislation restricts the procedures to married women, defined to include any woman "living with a man as his wife on a bona fide domestic basis although not married to him." The woman must also be "unlikely to become pregnant as the result of a procedure other than a fertilization procedure." The act provides the medical profession with a monopoly on the application of the new reproductive technologies even though some of the techniques, especially artificial insemination, do not entail sophisticated medical skills. IVF must occur in approved hospitals. Approved hospitals must keep records, and nonidentifying information may be disclosed to donors and patients. Finally, the legislation established the Standing Review and Advisory Committee on Infertility (SRACI), consisting of a philosopher, two medical practitioners, two religious representatives, a social worker, a legal practitioner, and a teacher. The functions of this committee are to advise the health minister on techniques for alleviating infertility and to consider and approve experimental procedures.

An unusual aspect of this legislation is the provision of criminal penalties for noncompliance. Failure to conform with the provisions relating to the manipulation of embryos outside the human body could result in imprisonment for four years or 100 penalty points (calculated at Aus$100 per point), and deviation from the informed-consent and counseling requirements carries a one-year prison sentence or twenty-five penalty points. These penalties have led to the coining of the term "white-coat crime," although to date there have been no prosecutions.

The most contentious aspects of the act deal with embryo experimentation. The act was amended in 1987 and further changes were recommended in 1991. The 1984 law prohibits "experimental procedures" (other than those approved by the SRACI), defined as research on an embryo of a kind that would cause damage to the embryo, would make the embryo unfit for implantation, or would reduce the prospects of a pregnancy resulting from the implantation of the embryo. Moreover, ova shall not be fertilized outside a woman's body except for the purposes of implantation. The act does not define "embryo"; nor does it refer to spare embryos or specify time limits on experimentation. In 1995, new legislation—the Infertility Treatment Act—was passed that bans destructive research on embryos.

The first major test of the 1984 legislation occurred in 1986 following a research proposal involving the deliberate fertilization of human ova for the purposes of destructive research. The research entailed the surgical microinjection of sperm into ova (eggs) and sought to obtain information about male infertility. The SRACI was deadlocked with half the members deciding that the proposal did not require their consent. These members agreed with the medical scientists that the product of the conjunction of a sperm and an ovum is not an embryo until syngamy, when the chromosomes fuse, about twenty to twenty-four hours after fertilization. The other four members decided that the section of the legislation requiring the implantation of all embryos prohibited the research. Ultimately the committee approved the experiment.

The SRACI recommended an amendment to the legislation enabling the formation of presyngamous embryos for the purposes of destructive, nontherapeutic experimentation in research projects designed to assist the alleviation of infertility provided that gametes be obtained only from infertile couples participating in an IVF program. Such an amendment was made in 1987, and the act now allows "fertilization of a human ovum from the point of sperm penetration prior to but not including the point of syngamy," although the Infertility (Medical Procedures) (Amendment) Act 1987 did not specify a time period. Although the committee can consider applications for embryo formation for research, such embryos will not be transferred to a woman's uterus for implantation if experimentation indicates chromosomal abnormality.

A second test of the legislation occurred in January 1989 when the committee approved an "embryo biopsy" experiment on eggs not becoming fertilized twenty-two hours after insemination. The proposed research entailed removing a single cell from the dividing "embryo" in order to identify which embryos were chromosomally normal before implantation. The usual practice is to discard all late-fertilizing eggs due to the high risk of miscarriage or birth defect. The committee approved the procedure and specified that the embryos used in the tests be "spare" or "left-over" and not specially created for experimentation. Considerable controversy, especially in local news media, about the legality and morality of such experimentation subsequently emerged. The government placed a moratorium on the embryo-biopsy experiment and ordered the SRACI to instigate an inquiry and seek public consultation.

The inquiry discerned four different interpretations of the legislation: It permits destructive, nontherapeutic experimentation in untransferred embryos; it permits such experimentation only up to but not including syngamy; it implies a difference between spare or excess embryos that can reasonably be transferred and those that cannot (due to abnormality, for example); and some embryo experimentation may be a form of cloning and is thereby prohibited. The majority of the committee agreed that destructive experiments on embryos created originally for the purpose of transfer to a woman in the course of treatments should be permitted, subject to its approval. However, disagreement existed on whether the act should provide a definition of "embryo." Some members thought that the expression should be left to interpretation and determination in the light of developing scientific knowledge and the community's acceptance of that knowledge. Others proposed a definition that included any or all of the stages of embryonic development from the point of sperm penetration to the formation of the primitive streak around fourteen days after penetration.

South Australia

Less controversy has surrounded the legislation in South Australia, where relatively few issues have been enshrined in the law. Following a government inquiry that reported in 1987, the Reproductive Technology Act was passed in 1988. Many of the issues that the Victorian law codifies, the South Australian legislation delegates to the Council on Reproductive Technology, which the legislation established. The council consists of nominees from two South Australian universities, two medical practitioners, a religious representative, a member of the Law Society, and five people nominated by the state minister for health. The legislation provides that the council should, as far as practicable, be constituted of equal numbers of men and women. The act also establishes a licensing system whereby a person must not carry out an artificial fertilization procedure except in pursuance of a license granted by the Health Commission, the penalty for breach being Aus$10,000.

The functions of the council include the formulation and review of a code of ethical practice regarding artificial fertilization procedures and experimentation with human reproductive material. The legislation requires that this code include prohibitions on embryo flushing, provide that any persons on whose behalf an embryo is stored must have the right to decide how the embryo is to be dealt with, restrict the storage of embryos to ten years, and prohibit the prolongation of culturing a human embryo outside the human body beyond the stage of development at which implantation would normally occur.

The South Australian Health Commission (a state government department) determines the conditions of and grants licenses to persons carrying out artificial fertilization procedures; noncompliance carries a Aus$10,000 penalty. A license is subject to a condition prohibiting research that may be detrimental to an embryo. Licenses also must contain a condition preventing the application of artificial fertilization procedures except for the benefit of married couples (includes cohabitation relationships of longer than five years) where infertility is apparent or a risk of the transmission of a genetic defect exists. The council also advises the health minister on the conditions of licenses authorizing artificial fertilization procedures; formulates license conditions dealing with research; and carries out and promotes research into infertility, including the social consequences of reproductive technology.

Western Australia

Western Australia's Human Reproductive Technology Act (1991) is similar to the South Australian statute, as it establishes a licensing system and sets up the ten-member Western Australian Reproductive Technology Council. An individual or corporate body must obtain a license in order to store eggs, sperm, and embryos, and a practice license enables the carrying out of any "artificial fertilization procedure" (defined to include artificial insemination and IVF) and any approved research project.

The Technology Council's major tasks include developing a code of practice, offering advice to the government on reproductive technology and licensing matters, and considering and approving (where appropriate) research proposals. Unlike the other two state statutes, the Western Australian law defines "embryo" and "fertilization," presumably to avoid the difficulties encountered by the Victorian legislation. It also provides that the council approve experiments only when satisfied that the procedures are intended to be therapeutic for an egg or embryo and that, according to scientific and medical knowledge, detriment to any egg in the process of fertilization or any embryo is unlikely.

New Zealand

The level of public comment, inquiry, and legislative activity regarding assisted conception has been much lower in New Zealand, where the government has left most issues of regulation, record keeping, and access to the medical profession. The Department of Justice produced an "issues" paper for public discussion in 1985, but the only legislative change has been a 1987 amendment to the Status of Children Act deeming gamete donors not to be the legal parents. In 1993 the government established a national three-person ethics committee to investigate the emerging issues.

Conclusion

Despite the various arguments made vis-à-vis reproductive technologies, the legislation passed in Australia tends to focus primarily on the status of the extracorporeal human embryo, the assumed importance of (heterosexual) marriage as the basis for family formation, and the need to control the kinds of experiments medical scientists undertake. There has been little legislative attention to the interests of women, who are overwhelmingly the patients in reproductive technology programs, or to the possibilities for reproductive autonomy in this context. Moreover, as the federal government has declined to legislate in this area (although it could under its corporations power, for example), serious problems emerge regarding the absence of a uniform legal approach among the state jurisdictions.

FOR FURTHER READING

Henaghan, Mark. 1992. "New Zealand: Regulating Human Reproduction." In Sheila A.M. McLean, ed., *Law Reform and Human Reproduction*. Aldershot: Dartmouth.

New Zealand. 1969 (amended 1987). *Status of Children Act*.

South Australia. 1988. *Reproductive Technology Act*.

Victoria, Australia. 1982. *Interim Report of the Committee to Consider the Social, Ethical and Legal Issues Arising from in Vitro Fertilization*. Melbourne: Victorian Government Printer.

Victoria, Australia. 1983. *Report on Donor Gametes in IVF*. Melbourne: Victorian Government Printer.

Victoria, Australia. 1984. *Report on the Disposition of Embryos Produced by in Vitro Fertilization*. Melbourne: Victorian Government Printer.

Victoria, Australia. 1984 (amended 1987, 1991). *Infertility (Medical Procedures) Act*.

Victoria, Australia. 1995. *Infertility Treatment Act*.

Victoria, Australia. Standing Review and Advisory Committee on Infertility (SRACI). 1990a. *Review of "Post-Syngamy" Embryo Experimentation: An Information Paper*. Melbourne: Victorian Government Printer.

Victoria, Australia. Standing Review and Advisory Committee on Infertility (SRACI). 1990b. "Part I: Background and Legislation." In *Report to the Minister for Health on Matters Related to the Review of "Post-Syngamy" Embryo Experimentation*. Melbourne: Victorian Government Printer.

Victoria, Australia. Standing Review and Advisory Committee on Infertility. 1991. "Part III: Recommendations for Amendment of the Infertility (Medical Procedures) Act 1984." In *Report to the Minister for Health on Matters Related to the Review of "Post-Syngamy" Embryo Experimentation*. Melbourne: Victorian Government Printer.

Western Australia. 1991. *Human Reproductive Technology Act*.

fifty-eight

Legislation—Canada

ANNETTE BURFOOT
(WITH ADVICE FROM HEALTH CANADA)

In an effort to respond to scientific advances in reproductive and genetic technologies and to the profound social, ethical, legal, and health questions they raise, the Canadian government established the Royal Commission on New Reproductive Technologies in 1989. The commission submitted a comprehensive report, *Proceed with Care*, in 1993 that outlined 293 far-reaching recommendations for legislation. These recommendations are divided into three broad areas of concern: the need to prohibit problematic reproductive and genetic technology practices, the need to regulate and manage these technologies at a national level, and the need to focus on infertility prevention as a health issue.

In July 1995, the Canadian government called for a voluntary moratorium on nine new reproductive technologies (NRTs) that caused serious social and ethical concerns. This moratorium included a request to medical and research communities to refrain from using sex selection for non-medical purposes, commercial preconception or surrogacy arrangements, ectogenesis, and the cloning of human embryos. The moratorium was designed as an interim measure until legislation was put in place. The Advisory Committee on the Interim Moratorium on Reproductive Technologies was established by the Canadian government in January 1996. This committee, currently called the Advisory Committee on New Reproductive and Genetic Technologies, continues to provide feedback to the government on managing the technologies.

The Processing and Distribution of Semen for Assisted Conception Regulations, part of the Food and Drugs Act, came into effect in June 1996. This set of regulations established uniform national standards to decrease the risk of infectious disease transmission through semen when used in assisted conception. Canadian doctors and sperm banks were given the responsibility to properly screen donors and semen, to keep records of the distributed semen, and to stop distribution and investigate when semen is suspected of being infected with a sexually transmitted disease.

The government of Canada tabled its first piece of comprehensive legislation on NRTs on June 14, 1996. The intent of the Human Reproductive and Genetic Technologies Act (Bill C-47) is to protect Canadians from unsafe and unethical uses of technology in the area of human reproduction. It prohibits cloning, interspecies reproduction, germline genetic engineering, the use of ova from fetuses and cadavers for human reproduction, sex selection for other than medical uses, ectogenesis, IVF for embryo research, mediated and paid surrogacy, and the purchase and sale of human gametes. It provides for appropriate consent with assisted-reproduction procedures and research with human gametes. It provides for a national level of regulation of human reproduction and genetic procedures. The discussion paper *New Reproductive Technologies: Setting Boundaries, Enhancing Health* was released in conjunction with Bill C-47. It proposes a regulatory framework for the management of other NRTs (such as donor insemination) and for reproductive health in general (including infertility preventative measures). The paper also proposes national regulatory guidelines, a national registry of donors and their offspring, and national licensing measures and standards.

Due to a call for a federal election in 1997, Bill C-47 failed to proceed to a parliamentary vote. The legislative process had to begin again under the newly formed government. As of 1999, the voluntary moratorium remained in effect, and Canada was without legislation or enforceable national regulations and standards for NRTs. Health Canada developed the Framework for Action on Sexual and Reproductive Health in 1998 with the participation of other federal departments as well as provincial, territorial, and nongovernment representatives. The intent of this initiative is to improve the sexual and reproductive health of Canadians, including the prevention of infertility.

FOR FURTHER READING

Canada. 1993. *Proceed with Care: Final Report of the Royal Commission on New Reproductive Technologies.* Vols. 1, 2. Ottawa: Canadian Communications Group.

Canada. 1996. *Bill C-47: The Human Reproductive and Genetic Technologies Act.* First reading, June 14.

Canada. Health Canada. 1988. *Framework for Action on Sexual and Reproductive Health.* Ottawa: Canadian Communications Group.

Canada. Health Canada. 1996. *New Reproductive and Genetic Technologies: Setting Boundaries, Enhancing Health.* Ottawa: Canadian Communications Group.

fifty-nine

Legislation— The United States

ANNE DONCHIN

The United States has lagged notably behind most countries in governmental regulation of new reproductive techniques. Yet congressional interest has been evident since Congress established the National Commission for the Protection of Human Subjects of Biomedical and Behavioral Research in 1974, the year the first request came to the National Institutes of Health (NIH) to fund research on embryos. Because the commission limited its scope to fetuses after implantation and took embryo research to be "difficult and divisive," it recommended establishment of the Ethics Advisory Board (EAB) to review specific funding proposals. This recommendation was adopted as a Department of Health and Human Services (DHHS) regulation stipulating prior EAB review and approval before federal funding of any in vitro fertilization (IVF) proposal. The board convened in 1978, and though it was designed to be a standing body, the DHHS disbanded it in 1980 and so violated its own regulation. The board survived just long enough to issue its first report in 1979 and approve one research protocol before a new federal administration came to office under Ronald Reagan, who was committed to the view that human life begins at conception and opposed to any practice remotely viewed as threatening to prenatal life. In 1988 the DHHS announced plans to revive the board, but the Bush administration declined to sign the revised charter.

Other congressional attempts to create bodies to regulate reproductive research fared no better. The Biomedical Ethics Advisory Committee, created in 1985, was mandated to consider human genetic engineering and fetal research. The committee, structured along partisan, pro-choice, antiabortion lines, deadlocked over the choice of a chair and expired in 1989 before issuing any reports. A de facto moratorium on federally supported embryo research remained in effect until President Clinton took office and Congress nullified the federal regulations requiring EAB approval for embryo research. In 1994 the NIH established the Human Embryo Research Panel to establish guidelines. Shortly after the panel issued its report, President Clinton opposed one of its most controversial recommendations and directed that no federal funds be used for projects that involved creating human embryos expressly for experimentation. The NIH set up a review group to develop detailed rules and evaluate specific projects, but after a Republican majority gained control of Congress in 1994, the moratorium was reinstated. In 1996 President Clinton created the new nonstatutory National Bioethics Advisory Commission, which by 1999 had issued only one report: *Cloning Human Beings* (1997). The report recommended continuation of the Clinton administration's moratorium on the use of federal funds for human-cloning research and the call for a voluntary private moratorium. It also endorsed federal legislation to prohibit the use of somatic cell nuclear transfer techniques to create children, at least until adequate human subject protection had been established.

Since the early 1980s, clinics offering IVF and related techniques have proliferated and been uninformed by any systematic research to validate the techniques practiced on patients or to monitor embryo manipulation. The only federal agency to protect patient interests has been the Food and Drug Administration, which is concerned principally with the safety and efficacy of products. It exercises no control over the provision of medical services or privately funded research. As commercial venture capital enterprises offering reproductive services burgeoned, the focus of congressional concern turned to the protection of patients undergoing IVF. They were, in effect, research subjects, since the procedures performed on them have never been subject to controlled trials. Congressional committees conducted hearings in 1984, 1988, and 1989 and collected data on clinic success rates with the intent of preparing legislation to establish uniform reporting standards for all clinics. Concurrently, in response to consumer complaints about false and misleading clinic advertising, the Federal Trade Commission brought charges against several clinics that overstated results or misled consumers about the likelihood of achieving birth after using their services. In 1992, federal legislation was finally passed requiring fertility clinics to provide pregnancy success rates in a standardized format to the DHHS. Data would be published and distributed to the public on request. A model program would be developed for the inspection and certification of laboratories that handle embryos, and procedures would be established to report inspections to the DHHS. However, the American Society for Reproductive Medicine (ASRM, formerly American Fertility Society) effectively exercised its influence in shaping the legislation to ensure that laboratory inspectors had no authority over the clinical practices of physicians. The selection, screening, and matching of ova donors and recipients were categorized as a "medical service" beyond the reach of systematic regulation. The Center for Disease Control was given two years to implement the legislation, but no funds were appropriated within that time span. Hence patients utilizing these services still need to exercise considerable vigilance in checking out the success rates and credentials of particular facilities. There is no assurance that once they have selected a clinic they will receive only nonexperimental procedures, be provided with full information, or be offered counseling of any kind.

At the state and local levels, the policing of services and procedures varies considerably from state to state. The only authority monitoring the development of new techniques is likely to be the local hospital institutional review committee, which often includes in its membership colleagues of the researcher who is requesting project approval. The lack of uniform standards has an immediate effect in states that require private health insurance companies to reimburse for fertility services. In some states, reimbursement is contingent on adherence to the guidelines for IVF/GIFT programs established by the ASRM. But not all states mandating insurance coverage place even these limitations on the facilities used or the qualifications of service providers. Since publicly funded insurance excludes fertility services, women lacking both substantial personal resources and private insurance have no access even to the most basic infertility workup. In the wake of fertility clinic scandals disclosed in 1995, the ASRM released a statement in November of the same year reconsidering its former opposition to compulsory regulation of the fertility industry and endorsing consideration of an independent licensing authority to oversee and validate the clinical practice of assisted reproduction.

FOR FURTHER READING

Bonnicksen, A. L. 1990. *In Vitro Fertilization: Building Policy from Laboratories to Legislatures.* New York: Columbia University Press.

Green, R. M. 1994. "At the Vortex of Controversy: Developing Guidelines for Human Embryo Research." *Kennedy Institute of Ethics Journal* 4(4): 345–356.

United States. 1992. *The Fertility Clinic Success Rate and Certification Act of 1992.*

United States. 1994. *Human Embryo Research Panel Report.* Bethesda, Md.: National Institutes of Health.

U.S. Congress. Office of Technology Assessment. 1988. *Infertility: Medical and Social Choices.* Washington, D.C.: U.S. Government Printing Office.

U.S. Congress. Office of Technology Assessment. 1993. *Biomedical Ethics in U.S. Public Policy—Background Paper.* OTA-BP-BBS-105. Washington, D.C.: U.S. Government Printing Office.

U.S. Department of Health, Education and Welfare. 1979. *Report and Conclusions: HEW Support of Research Involving Human in Vitro Fertilization and Embryo Transfer.* Washington, D.C.: U.S. Government Printing Office.

U.S. House of Representatives. 1989. *Hearings Before the Subcommittee on Regulation, Business Opportunities and Energy of the Committee on Small Business.* No. 101-5 (March 9). Washington, D.C.: U.S. Government Printing Office.

U.S. House of Representatives. 1992. *Hearing Before the Subcommittee on Health and the Environment of the Committee on Energy and Commerce.* No. 102-120. Washington, D.C.: U.S. Government Printing Office.

U.S. National Bioethics Advisory Commission. 1997. *Cloning Human Beings—Reports and Recommendations.* Vol. 1. Rockville, Md.: National Bioethics Advisory Commission.

sixty

Legislation—Germany

ANNE WALDSCHMIDT

The German Embryonic Protection Act (EPA) came into force in 1991 and is seen as one of the most restrictive regulations worldwide for embryonic research. The EPA is a criminal law and is intended to counter the improper manipulation of human embryos. However, it permits artificial insemination within a marriage or partnership, sperm donation for single women and lesbian partnerships, the eugenic selection of sperm donors, and quality control of sperm. Also protected by the law are sperm banks; artificial insemination and embryo transfer without medical indications; research using embryonic germline cells and entire embryos with no capacity for development; dead embryos; and the cryopreservation of germline cells, pronuclei, and embryos. Related areas remain legally unresolved, such as genome analysis and its diverse areas of application as well as human genetic engineering as so-called somatic gene therapy.

The EPA forbids the following activities: the production of pronuclei and embryos for research purposes, research using embryos that are "surplus" to reproductive medicine and have a "capacity for development," the use of embryos for nonmedical purposes (for example, for commercial or industrial exploitation and research), preimplantation diagnosis, cloning as well as chimeric and hybrid formation, surrogate motherhood, and sex selection of sperm. There is no provision in the act, however, for the implementation of these restrictions, and the act is intended only to deter improper actions by doctors and scientists. All other involvement (e.g., on the part of surrogate mothers, egg donors, sperm donors, clients, and mediators) is exempt from legal sanctions. The act imposes a prison sentence of between one and five years or fines. Prison sentences without probation are an option for repeat offenders in particularly serious cases. The legislation expresses confidence that doctors and scientists will act responsibly, and it appears to serve mainly to reassure the public. To this effect, there is the provision that only physicians may perform artificial insemination. Thus those who actually ought to be controlled by the law acquire monopoly power over the practice of the sanctioned procedures.

At the core of the EPA is Germany's constitutionally guaranteed protection of human dignity; yet the only protection to which the EPA makes reference is that of the embryo. Potential offenses against the fundamental rights of women do not receive any consideration whatsoever. Thus the act is in full agreement with the prevailing legal discussion on reproductive medicine and abortion, which obscures the issues of women's human dignity. A pregnant woman is no longer seen as a complete human being who creates life but as a fetal environment that poses a potential threat to the embryo under protection. The EPA gives rise to an extension of the embryo's sphere of protection. According to paragraph 218 of the criminal code, which regulates abortion in Germany, the embryo is protected by the state from the moment it is implanted in the womb, and according to paragraph 8, Section 1 of the EPA, the fertilized egg is already regarded as an embryo from the moment of cell union. At this time it becomes an independent legal entity. This definition has significant implications for women. The newly formalized legalization of the beginning of life separates the embryo from the woman, and there is now no limit to the extent to which the woman is responsible for the legally protected entity in her body.

There is also further male bias evident in the legislation in that the EPA permits the use of microinjection on fertile women in order to treat male infertility. The EPA forbids the technique only when its use is not for procreation, a measure intended to prevent the possible genesis of embryos for research purposes only. But women also need protection from unnecessary, painful, and extremely risky medical operations.

The EPA makes a rather weak attempt at preventing the killing of multiple embryos in the womb. The act limits to a maximum of three the number of embryos that can be transferred back to the woman. There are, however, no regulations pertaining to the production and extraction of egg cells. These cells are harvested from women's bodies for surplus embryos and future research. The EPA also adopts Germany's prevailing view on freedom of research, and numerous exceptions contained in the act provide loopholes for embryo researchers. The act defines an "embryo" as a "fertilized, human egg cell, capable of development from the moment of cell union." Also protected by the act are cells with full potential (those able to divide and develop into an individual) and pronuclei (cells that exist from the moment of penetration and introduction of sperm into an egg cell until cell union). According to the EPA, all embryos should be considered capable of development in the first twenty-four hours unless the fertilized egg cell does not develop beyond the unicellular stage. Beyond that, the act offers no exact definition of capacity for development; it even includes the deep-freezing of germ cells and embryos. Nothing stands in the way of such preservation provided that the storage of surplus embryos can be medically warranted and performed by a doctor.

The EPA also allows unencumbered research on germ cells. It regulates the use of germ cells and permits their artificial change only when it is certain that fertilization and transmission will not follow. Though at present the execution of germline therapy will be prosecuted under the act, research into its development will not. This opens the door to future research into gene transfers in germlines. The legislation also lacks a clear prohibition of germ cell therapy.

Legislation has remained steadfast in only one area: Despite fierce protest from the medical profession, an indirect ban on preimplantation diagnoses of embryos was passed. The EPA should also prevent the deliberate generation of clones as well as the splitting of embryonic cells capable of development for purposes of research and diagnosis. Nevertheless, various loopholes remain. Although exploitative embryonic research is prohibited, "noninvasive" observational diagnosis and examination of embryos from the in vitro stage to the moment of transference to a woman for the purpose of pregnancy are not. Furthermore, dead embryos or embryos classified as "not having the capacity to develop" may be researched without limits.

The EPA is also controversial in that it gives legislative approval to eugenic measures. It enables the selection of sperm on the basis of gender when this serves to protect the child from a muscular dystrophy, Duchenne-type, or similarly serious sex-linked, hereditary illness. Aside from Down syndrome, which can already be avoided with prenatal diagnostics, muscular dystrophy has become the next potentially preventable handicap. Thus a catalog of potentially eradicable embryos—based on their hereditary diseases—will be gradually introduced and sanctioned.

Public financing plays a decisive part in the development of reproductive technology. Diagnoses, methods of treatment, and medical techniques that are lucrative are most likely to be selected by doctors who stand to gain from them. These points were included in another law discussed by Parliament in emergency proceedings, passed in 1990, and made retroactive to 1989. This so-called KOV Amending Law guarantees the financing of reproductive technology by legal medical insurance but limits insemination treatment, in vitro fertilization, and GIFT to spouses. Sperm donation from a third party is not permitted. A recommendation from a medical doctor who will perform the measure himself or herself must be provided by the married couple seeking the treatment. Furthermore, only fully equipped practices and doctors to whom the authorities have granted a permit for the treatment will be publicly funded. Moreover, the procedure must have an adequate chance of succeeding and is limited to four attempts. The criterion for success is pregnancy, not live births; in this way failure rates are kept down.

This legislation has failed in terms of ensuring the safety of patients. The assessment and appraisal of its consequences have only just begun; they comprise enormous social and individual dangers, including control and exploitation of women, denial of their fundamental rights, numerous serious health threats for women and their children, eugenics and discrimination against the disabled and ill, and the exploitation of embryonic cells for dubious scientific purposes.

In light of legislation that supports embryonic research, the EPA is only a halfhearted ban on such research with a simultaneous sanctioning of reproductive medicine and germline research and can be seen as the appeasement of both researchers and those who want to "protect" life. Moreover, legal changes and concessions to the EPA are already on the horizon. There are indications that in the case of cancer research, a loosening up of general bans against embryo and genetic research will become possible. Last, the EPA marginalizes women and treats them as natural resources and experimental fields. Its basis in support of human dignity becomes highly questionable when the worth of women is disregarded in contrast to that of the embryo.

FOR FURTHER READING

Academy for Ethics in Medicine. 1989. *Position on the Announcement of the Law for Embryonic Protection to the Legal Committee of the German Bundestag*. Bonn: N.p.

Beier, Henning. 1989. "The International Development of Reproductive Medicine and Research into Human Embryos." In *The Central Commission of the Federal Chamber of Physicians for the Protection of Ethical Principles and Reproductive Medicine, Embryonic Research and Gene Therapy: Work and Experience Report 1988*. Point 2.4. Cologne: N.p.

Central Commission of the Federal Chamber of Physicians for the Protection of Ethical Principles and Reproductive Medicine, Embryonic Research and Gene Therapy. 1988. *Work and Experience Report 1988*. Cologne: N.p.

Germany. 1990."1990 Embryonic Protection Act: Act for the Protection of Embryos." *Official Bulletin of the Federal Government* 1: 2746.

Germany. 1990. *Decisions of the German Parliament in Matters Relating to Laws: Law on the Nineteenth Amendment of Accomplishments in Accordance with the Federal Law of Precautions and of Further Alterations in Provisions Pertaining to Social Laws* (KOV-Amending Law). Federal file 314/90.

Germany. Faction of the Green Party in the Bundestag, ed. 1990. *Reproductive Technology, Embryonic Research, and Legal Regulation: Position of the Faction.* Bonn: N.p.

Germany. Federal Minister for Justice. 1986. *Discussion Proposal for a Law for the Protection of Embryos* (Embryonic Protection Act). Bonn: N.p.

Germany. Federal Minister for Justice. 1989. *Speaker's Outline for Law for the Protection of Embryos* (Embryonic Protection Act). Bonn: N.p.

Germany. Federal Minister for Work and Social Order. 1990. *Speaker's Outline for a Law on the Nineteenth Amendment of Accomplishments in Accordance with the Federal Law of Precautions and of Further Alterations in Provisions Pertaining to Social Laws* (KOV-Amending Law). Bonn: N.p.

Germany. Federal-Provincial Working Group on Genome Analysis. 1990. *Final Report.* Bonn: N.p.

Germany. Federal-Provincial Working Group on Reproductive Medicine. 1988. *Final Report.* Bonn: N.p.

Germany. German Bundestag. 1989a. *Outline of the Law for the Protection of Embryos* (Embryonic Protection Act). Law Proposals of the Federal Government. 11th Electoral Period. Federal file 11-5460. Bonn: N.p.

Germany. German Bundestag. 1989b. *Outline of a Law for the Regulation of Problems in Human Artificial Insemination and Human Germ Cell Operations.* Law Proposals from the Faction of the SPD. 11th Electoral Period. Federal file 11-5710. Bonn: N.p.

Germany. German Bundestag. 1990a. *Final Petition from the Faction of the Green Party/Alliance 90 Regarding the Outline for the Law of Embryonic Protection.* 11th Electoral Period. Federal file 11-8179. Bonn: N.p.

Germany. German Bundestag. 1990b. *Final Recommendations and Report from the Legal Committee a) on the "Outline for the Law for Embryonic Protection" Submitted by the Federal Government (File 11-5460), b) on the Federal Government's Instruction "Cabinet Report on Human Artificial Insemination" (File 11-1856) and c) on the Petition of the SPD Faction "Chances and Risks in the Usage of New Methods of Artificial Insemination and Human Germ Cell Operations (File 11-1662).* 11th Electoral Period. Federal file 11-8057. Bonn: N.p.

Klein, Renate, ed. 1989. *The Business with Hope. Experiences with Reproductive Technology.* Berlin: Orlanda Frauenverlag.

von Bülow, Detlev. 1989. "Outline for the Law of the Protection of Embryos—Legal Limits for the Freedom of Research." In Max Planck Society, ed., *Respect for Nascent Life.* Munich: Selbstverlag.

Waldschmidt, Anne. 1991. "The Embryo as a Legal Entity—Woman as a Fetal Environment: The New German Laws on Reproductive Engineering and Embryo Research." *Issues in Reproductive and Genetic Engineering* 4(3): 209–222.

Waldschmidt, Anne. 1992. "'L'éprouvette éprouvée' or 'Test Tube Under Test.'" Report on the International Conference to Critically Assess Reproductive Engineering, Paris, June 28–29, 1991. *Issues in Reproductive and Genetic Engineering* 5(1): 75–77.

Part Five

Reproductive and Genetic Science

Advanced infertility technologies have given rise to a new era of reproductive science and genetic engineering. In vitro fertilization (IVF) allows for the externalization and manipulation of reproduction at the cellular and genetic level, which in turn allow genetic research and engineering. The main focus of these activities is on increasing our understanding of human, genetic development at the embryonic stage. The rationale for the research is often construed in terms of improved genetic health through screening and treatment (engineering) of preimplanted embryos. Although experimental and often highly controversial, reproductive and genetic science proceeds with little effective resistance. Genetic and reproductive science, as it stands today, raises a host of issues concerning the status of the embryo, reproductive autonomy in the face of routinized screening, the extent to which we should allow doctors and scientists to control life, and eugenics.

Fetal tissue has been used since the 1950s in viral research and vaccination development. More recently, brain stem cells from aborted fetuses have been used in the treatment of diabetes, neural defects, and degenerative diseases. Largely because of the intense controversy surrounding the status of the fetus within abortion debates, little is made known of this practice. Fetal tissue transplant also serves as the precedent for contemporary embryo research and genetic engineering.

IVF presents the scientific community with a new research material, an entire human being contained within a few cells up to fourteen days old. The possibility of researching on the much younger conceptus than an aborted fetus and a preimplanted entity arose once IVF turned to hyperovulation protocols that generated more embryos than were used in infertility techniques. This notion of "spare" embryos remains controversial and has drawn considerable criticism from a variety of perspectives including those who maintain that life begins at conception and that no human life should be violated or killed by research. Feminists criticize an emphasis on embryos that obliterates and denigrates woman's role in reproduction and assumes women as a natural source for embryo harvesting. General public concern tends to focus on the prospect of an unbounded science going too far in the manipulation of life at such an early stage of development.

There are also a host of legal issues raised by the prospect of human life as a microscopic speck in labs, undergoing investigations and being stored for future use in research and infertility techniques. The most prominent issue is whether to accord the tiny cellular mass rights of personhood. Some emphasize the mass's human potential and seek to protect it as such. Others, particularly those with a stake in embryo research, emphasize the embryo as just another part of a well-established scientific and medical research agenda in the interests of human well-being. (This controversy is further complicated by the fact that the object of scrutiny is so small in stature and hence difficult to identify and track yet deemed so large in terms of human potential.) Feminists assert a central role for women's reproductive rights, as women are the most involved in the reproductive process from which embryos are taken. Finally, related to the legal conundrums over embryo status is the notion of truly informed consent in such a highly technical area.

Cloning is a good example of the kind of social and political dispute that embryo genetic research and development generate. Although reproduction as it is commonly understood in developed countries is typically regarded as a private affair, the manipulation of people at the fundamental level of development, where their very being may be determined, has become the source of widespread public concern. Indeed, it is chiefly the public fear of the unrestricted genetic engineering of humans that prompted legislation to regulate advanced infertility techniques providing embryos for research. Recent successes with cloning have renewed this concern about research boundaries. Ectogenesis, the development of an embryo to term without a woman, is another area—mostly of scientific curiosity rather than medical accomplishment—likely to attract public interest and draw criticism from feminists concerned about the diminishing role women are already given in the new reproductive technology context.

Meanwhile, genetic screening of people and embryos throughout various stages of development promotes a heightened concern with genetic disability. Adults are potentially subject to a form of biological surveillance that can adversely affect their employment; children can be identified as potential health problems and as such run the risk of losing state support for their health and other care costs. Parents come under pressure to abort fetuses with genetic predispositions for illness, and in some social contexts simply for being female. With advanced infertility techniques, the selection of desirable genetic traits can be performed before implantation of the embryo. Without any clear status, these embryos become both a source of social development in terms of experimentation in the name of the public good and a source of public concern as new markers of scientific and medical interventions are set.

Partly due to the public concern for truly informed consent and partly to avoid issues of coercion, many advanced infertility procedures are now accompanied by genetic counseling. However, neither this type of informational assistance nor the practice of genetics addresses broader social and political issues such as the reinforcement of existent patterns of discrimination against the disabled and a new form of eugenics. The history of eugenics in Nazi Germany is a poignant and important indicator of how this type of discrimination works. Even more disturbing is that the conjunction of refined abilities to determine human potential with notions of therapeutic reproductive intervention makes eugenic selection easier and publicly more acceptable.

sixty-one

Fetal Tissue Research and Applications

MICHELLE A. MULLEN

The use of electively aborted human fetal tissue in research and therapy such as transplantation raises tempting clinical possibilities and a variety of social, ethical, and legal issues. Much of the debate over the technologies has been generated by antiabortionists who view them as complicit with abortion and hence morally repugnant. Advocates of fetal tissue research and therapy include scientists, clinicians, and patient populations that may benefit from the use of human fetal tissues. Recent research indicates that the practices may raise important feminist issues in respect of the medical management of women considering abortion, consent to donation of fetal tissues, and the potential for competition between a perceived need for fetal tissues and the availability of new, earlier abortion methods such as the abortifacient pill (RU-486).

Properties of Fetal Tissue

When compared with other sources of human tissue for research and transplantation, human fetal tissues exhibit distinct biological characteristics, including an enormous capacity for growth and functional differentiation. They are also highly resistant to oxygen deprivation and easy to transplant, usually as a suspension of cells injected into the target organ. Finally, immature fetal cells provoke little or no immune response in the host. This is extremely important, since graft rejection is the biggest obstacle to successful clinical outcome in any transplant procedure. Electively aborted fetal tissue is the technically preferred source, since tissues from spontaneous abortion or ectopic pregnancy are frequently contaminated by infection, genetic defect, and cell death.

Commercial Uses

Human fetal tissue has been used for many decades in viral research, in the development of vaccines, and in the testing of efficacy and teratogenicity (malformation-causing properties) of new pharmaceutical products. In the 1950s, the Salk polio vaccine was developed using human fetal tissues in culture. Today, human fetal tissues are used in viral research involving human influenza virus, hepatitis B virus, the measles virus, and human immunodeficiency virus (HIV). Recently, preliminary research using pig fetal tissue has been undertaken to examine the use of fetal connective tissue and cartilage in dermal injection for soft-tissue filling of the face (plastic surgery).

Clinical and Therapeutic Uses

Fetal tissue transplant is currently under investigation for use in a wide variety of conditions. Some are extremely rare; others are common and growing health concerns, especially in aging populations. Considerable research has been undertaken to examine the efficacy of the transplant in type-1 ("juvenile," or insulin-dependent) diabetes and in Parkinson's disease (a progressive, debilitating neurological condition). Results of treatment of type-1 diabetes are limited but pose particular concerns in terms of supply, since pancreatic cells of sixteen to twenty weeks' gestation are required and over 90 percent of elective abortions take place in the first trimester. Parkinson's disease is characterized by tremors, muscular rigidity, and slowness and is thought to reflect deterioration of the brain's dopamine-producing cells. Various drug therapies are used to moderate symptoms, but the disease is progressive and eventually all therapies fail. Fetal tissue transplantation for Parkinson's disease involves the injection of immature fetal brain tissue into the recipient's brain, and there is growing evidence that the transplant will prove an important aid, if not cure, for the disease. This procedure has been suggested as a treatment for Alzheimer's disease, another common, serious degenerative disease. Finally, fetal tissue transplant may hold promise in the treatment of certain leukemias when matched donors for bone marrow transplant cannot be found.

Fetal tissue transplant has also been tested in a host of rarer diseases characterized by impaired or absent immune systems: DiGeorge's syndrome, severe combined immunodeficiency disease (SCID, or "the boy in bubble" disease), and inherited metabolic storage disorders. Still other uses for the practice are under consideration, including for AIDS and in the treatment of a peculiarly twentieth-century menace, radiation poisoning. This last application was used in the treatment of certain victims of the Chernobyl accident, although long-term follow-up is not available.

Social and Ethical Issues

The debate over the use of electively aborted fetal tissue has been dominated by protest and lobbying from antiabortionists; more recent research raises a broader set of concerns, particularly with regard to women. A survey of gynecologists and family doctors in Canada indicates that fetal tissue transplant may pose a conflict of interest for practitioners who both counsel women considering abortion and collect fetal tissues at the time of abortion. In the study, 85 percent of subjects agreed with the use of aborted tissues for transplantation, and over 90 percent agreed that the decision to undergo abortion should be separate from any decision to donate fetal tissue. However, 30 percent agreed that the method or timing of abortion might be altered to optimize "harvest," 10 percent that donation could be offered to a woman undecided about abortion, and over one-third that a woman who undergoes abortion cedes rights to make decisions about the use of the conceptus materials. Twenty percent of subjects did not agree that the woman's safety must be foremost if abortion technologies are altered to improve tissue collection. Such data not only have important implications in the development of public policy and professional guidelines around fetal tissue transplant, they raise important questions about how women who undergo abortion are viewed and consulted and to what degree they are respected by physicians providing their health services.

FOR FURTHER READING

Crombleholme, T. M., et al. 1991. "Transplantation of Fetal Cells." *American Journal of Obstetrics and Gynecology* 164(1): 218–230.

Freed, C. R., et al. 1992. "Survival of Implanted Fetal Dopamine Cells and Neurologic Improvement 12–46 Months After Transplantation for Parkinson's Disease." *New England Journal of Medicine* (327): 1549–1555.

Gale, R. P. 1987. "Fetal Liver Transplantation in Aplastic Anemia and Leukemia." *Thymus* 10(1–2): 89–94.

Gale, R. P., and Y. Reisner. 1988. "The Role of Bone Marrow Transplants After Nuclear Accidents." *Lancet* 1(8677): 923–925.

Goldsobel, A. B., et al. 1987. "Bone Marrow Transplantation in DiGeorge Syndrome." *Journal of Pediatrics* 3(1): 40–44.

Gustavii, B. 1989. "Fetal Brain Transplantation for Parkinson's Disease: Technique for Obtaining Donor Tissue." *Lancet* 1(8637): 565.

Hansen, J. T., and J. R. Sladek. 1989. "Fetal Research." *Science* 246(4931): 775–779.

Huisjes, H. J. 1984. "Spontaneous Abortion." In *Current Reviews in Obstetrics and Gynecology*. No. 8. Edinburgh: Churchill Livingstone.

McGourty, C. 1989. "Ban on Use of Fetal Tissue to Continue." *Nature* 342(6246): 105.

Mullen, M. A., and F. H. Lowy. 1992. "Physician Attitudes Towards Aborted Fetal Tissue Transplantation in Parkinson's Patients: Policy Implications." *Clinical and Investigative Medicine* 15, supp. 4: A13.

Numazaki, K., et al. 1989. "Replication of Measles Virus in Cultured Human Thymic Epithelial Cells." *Journal of Medical Virology* 27(1): 52–58.

Ochiya, T., et al. 1989. "An in Vitro System for Infection with Hepatitis B That Uses Primary Fetal Hepatocytes." *Proceedings of the National Academy of Sciences of the United States of America* 86(6): 1875–1879.

Phipps, P. H., et al. 1989. "Rapid Detection of Influenza Virus Infections in Human Fetal Lung Diploid Cell Cultures." *Journal of Infection* 18(3): 269–278.

Touraine, J. L., et al. 1987. "Fetal Tissue Transplantation, Bone Marrow Transplantation, and Prospective Gene Therapy in Severe Immunodeficiencies and Enzyme Deficiencies." *Thymus* 19(1–2): 75–87.

sixty-two

Embryo Research

PATRICIA SPALLONE

Since the 1970s, embryologists and human geneticists have placed great importance on and have applied much of their research funding to understanding developmental processes, for example, how a fertilized egg becomes a biologically complex human being. They examine the chains of genetic events that lead to the development of distinct tissues and organs in the growing organism. The thinking is that genes may determine which of two alternative paths of development is followed. To rationalize this research scientists argue that the knowledge gained from genetic research on the human embryo will lead to a more comprehensive assault against genetically caused diseases. The technological advances that have allowed this research are in vitro fertilization (IVF) and genetic engineering. The former provides scientists access to embryos outside the woman's body and under laboratory conditions; the latter provides the research tools for studying the genes and related processes.

Embryo Testing and Screening

In November 1986, about thirty scientists and clinicians met at the CIBA Foundation (now known as the Novartis Foundation) in London to discuss whether it was possible to diagnose genetic conditions in two-day-old human embryos. They decided that it was, due to IVF procedures already established in advanced infertility practices. Meanwhile, researchers in the bioengineering industry and academia were perfecting techniques to detect specific genes or enzymes (the chemicals genes make) in embryo cells. They found that they could remove a single cell from a mouse embryo at the eight-cell stage and use this cell for genetic tests without harming the embryo itself. Other methods for testing embryo quality were also being developed, including a method that bypasses the embryo by testing biochemicals in the liquid surrounding the embryo in the laboratory dish.

Human embryo experimentation using these and other methods quickly followed animal studies. By 1988, a commercially available gene probe was used to determine sex in seven experimental human embryos at the University of Edinburgh; other tests were tried on some 400 two-day-old human embryos at the Hammersmith Hospital in London before being offered to couples at risk of passing on inherited conditions such as cystic fibrosis and the sex-linked illness hemophilia. Since then many more genetic probes have been under development. These probes indicate a range of genetic configurations from those that cause serious disease to those that play a role in common nonthreatening traits such as sex, weight, and hair color.

Experimental embryos used in developing genetic probes have mostly been provided by IVF in advanced infertility programs, although by the early 1990s it was possible, albeit more controversial, to use eggs from aborted female fetuses for both IVF and experimentation. Certain ethical issues of embryo research attracted public attention, such as the rights of embryos raised by those sympathetic to antiabortion arguments. Also controversial is the creation of embryos solely for research. These challenges are usually measured against arguments for healthy children, that is, children free of genetic-linked disease. In contrast with the pro-embryonic life arguments, feminist scholars are concerned with embryo screening research in that the apparent increase in choice in one area (to screen for genetic disease) restricts choice in another area (women may be expected to undergo screening and to abort when deemed necessary). They also argue that expectations regarding what is a normal baby are changing: Those born with an impairment arrive in an atmosphere of heightened critical views of illness and impairment. Today there is greater awareness that public attitudes toward the creation and use of embryos are complex and ambiguous. Although many people accept limited, medical uses of human embryos, the public is not necessarily wholly comfortable with such practices.

Manipulating Reproduction

Embryo genetic testing or screening (also known as preimplantation diagnosis) is an example of the new possibilities in genetic intervention brought about by reproductive embryo research. Another, though as yet much more controversial and untried, is the gene manipulation of embryos. Early scientific arguments for the gene manipulation of embryos include that from the leading British embryologist Ann McLaren, who maintains that in the long run it is not enough to provide a "cellular crutch" for genetically defective embryos so that they may survive and reproduce. McLaren sees hope in recombinant DNA techniques (genetic engineering technology) coupled with methods of gene transfer in that they may eventually allow the replacement of defective genes with normal counterparts. If this treatment could be carried out on the newly fertilized egg, genetically defective individuals would be able to reproduce without transmitting their abnormality to future generations. This view supports genetic engineering as the only effective treatment of genetic defects. However, such a possibility raises a certain level of ethical concern, shared by governments and some scientists and medical practitioners: Genetic changes to embryos not only concern the organism directly involved but also may affect future generations as altered genetic states are reproduced. Most national and state reports of the 1980s placed a moratorium or ban on genetic alterations to germline cells, egg cells, sperm cells, and fertilized eggs (embryos) because these genetic changes would be inherited by future generations. These same reports allow genetic manipulation of the other type of body cells (somatic cells), manipulation that affects only the organism directly involved.

The term "gene therapy" was coined to refer to the genetic engineering of human cells for some medical reason, but it is interesting that the term is often used for *any* genetic manipulation of human cells. The acceptance of somatic gene therapy was based on the assumption that changes to the somatic cells in a child or adult would not affect the germline (the series of cells that become egg and sperm and are reproduced in future generations). Also, there is a medical scientific argument that gene therapy is no different from other forms of high-tech medicine. Yet uncertainties and new problems with gene therapy have arisen. The distinction between somatic and germline cells has been criticized by some health consumer organizations and women's groups who claim that important ethical considerations have been bypassed. Although scientists have evidence that genetic changes to somatic cells do not migrate to the germline cells, there is a chance that the reproductive system can be affected. Also, acceptance of somatic gene therapy is likely to influence future discussions of germline therapy. Some researchers argue that if gene therapy of body (somatic) cells is acceptable, society should also accept alterations to the hereditary genetic makeup (germline cells).

FOR FURTHER READING

CIBA Foundation. 1986. *Human Embryo Research: Yes or No.* London: Tavistock.
McLaren, Anne. 1986. "Reproductive Options, Present and Future." In C. R. Austin and R. V. Short, eds., *Manipulating Reproduction*. Cambridge: Cambridge University Press.

Spallone, Patricia. 1989. *Beyond Conception: The New Politics of Reproduction.* London: Macmillan; South Hadley, Mass.: Bergin and Garvey.
Spallone, Patricia. 1992. *Generation Games: Genetic Engineering and the Future for Our Lives.* London: Women's Press; Philadelphia: Temple University Press.
United Kingdom. Department of Health. 1992. *Committee on the Ethics of Gene Therapy.* January, Cm 178. London: Her Majesty's Stationery Office.
Wheale, Peter, and Ruth McNally. 1988. "Technology Assessment of a Gene Therapy." *Product Appraisal* 3(3): 199–204.

sixty-three

Embryo Research—Legal Issues

SHARYN ROACH ANLEU

The status of the embryo is highly contested, and little agreement exists among medical scientists, religious leaders, feminists, right-to-life advocates, lawyers, philosophers, and policymakers on the moral significance of fertilization. A major problem for the law in this area is the rapidity of scientific experimentation and the production of new knowledge and technological procedures. The level of disagreement about the status of the embryo means that any laws and legal definitions will be to some extent arbitrary, pragmatic, and the focus of continual controversy.

The legality of embryo experimentation varies enormously. In some countries, for example, Germany, legislation completely bans embryo research. Others, including three Australian states and the United Kingdom, have passed statutes allowing experimentation under limited circumstances and with time constraints. In the United States, the disbanding of the Ethics Advisory Board has meant that there is no federal funding for embryo research. Commentators suggest that the questions around embryo research are too closely tied to abortion debates and that conservative governments during the 1980s were unwilling to countenance such research. In addition, a number of U.S. states have fetal research laws that could be used to prohibit research on human embryos. For example, a 1986 Louisiana law treats an embryo created through in vitro fertilization (IVF) as a juridical person who is owed a duty of care.

The Status of the Embryo

Does a human embryo outside the body have rights or special qualities that warrant legal protection or at least recognition? Are such rights tantamount to personhood? Is human life synonymous with a right to life? What kinds of experiments, if any, should the law allow? What form of regulation should exist? Until what time should experimentation be possible? Who determines the disposal of embryos—the couple from whom the gametes derive, the medical scientists, or the law?

The existence of human embryos in laboratories and their storage by freezing (cryopreservation) have stimulated widespread calls for the regulation of medical scientists' experimental activities and for the law to accord some respect or protection to embryos. However, the nature of such respect or the kinds of legal protection sought are unclear. Some critics seek total legal prohibition against embryo experimentation, arguing that it is destructive of human life and equivalent to the murderous activities of Nazi scientists during World War II. These critics argue further that the embryo is distinctively human and has a right to life—that is, a right to be implanted and a chance to be born—whereas destructive research would deny those rights. Others advocate prohibition because of the detrimental consequences for women from whose bodies large numbers of ova are obtained via invasive procedures and hormonal stimulation. Typically, medical scientists emphasize the importance of experimentation for alleviating infertility and advocate some embryo experimentation without legal intervention. For law the pivotal questions are (1) whether to allow embryo experimentation, (2) where to draw the line between acceptable and unacceptable experimentation, and (3) what kinds of prohibitions to adopt.

Common law traditionally does not recognize a conceptus or fetus as having any legally protected rights until after birth and complete separation from the mother's body. Neither a pregnant woman nor the resulting child can avail themselves of criminal or tort law to remedy any damage or harm sustained to the fetus in utero. Statutes criminalizing abortion or prohibiting pregnancy termination in certain circumstances modify this common-law position. Recent judicial decisions and some state legislation, notably in the United States, allow that harm to an embryo in utero that adversely affects the child born can support a tort claim for medical negligence or wrongful birth.

Courts and legislatures have been reticent to legally define the beginning of life. In *Roe v. Wade* (1973), the U.S. Supreme Court held that the word "person," as used in the Fourteenth Amendment, does not include the unborn and therefore it did not need to resolve the difficult question of when life begins. However, in a widely publicized U.S. case dealing with the custody or future of frozen embryos after the divorce of the parents, *Davis v. Davis v. King* (1989), a Tennessee circuit court viewed the embryo as a person. It decided that human life did begin at the moment of conception and that the traditional common-law doctrine of *parens patriae* (often expressed as the "best interests of the child doctrine") applies to in vitro children in the same way it has applied to newborns of married couples in domestic relations cases in Tennessee. The decision that custody of the embryos be awarded to Mrs. Davis was overturned on appeal.

Although the law tends not to view the embryo as possessing personhood rights, neither has it accepted that the embryo is property that can be possessed, controlled, or transferred. The Committee to Consider the Social, Ethical and Legal Issues Arising from in Vitro Fertilization set up in Victoria (Australia) disagrees that the couple whose embryo is stored owns or has dominion over that embryo. It rejects the use of such concepts as property or ownership when considering an individual and genetically unique human entity, that is, an embryo. Nevertheless, the report suggests that the couple whose gametes form the embryo should have rights to decide whether to donate the embryo, to have it stored, or to make it available to IVF research—but not to sell or casually dispose of it.

One of the first attempts to criminalize embryo experimentation occurred in Australia with the introduction in 1985 of a private member's bill in the Senate (upper house) of the Commonwealth Parliament. The proposed Human Embryo Experimentation Act sought to prohibit any experimentation that was not primarily undertaken for a benefit that would enable development of the human embryo's full human potential. Thus the bill proscribed any research that would lead to the destruction of embryos. The bill was referred to a Senate select committee for inquiry and public consultation. Adopting the Declaration of Helsinki's distinction between medical research, where the aim is diagnostic or therapeutic for a patient, and purely scientific research, the Senate committee concluded that the respect due to the embryo commencing at fertilization necessitated its protection from destructive, nontherapeutic experimentation. (It did not recommend the bill's passage because of its reliance on the criminal law as the sole method of regulation and enforcement.)

When Does an Embryo Come into Existence?

A legal definition of the embryo must be formulated in order to regulate embryo experimentation. Such a definition is contingent on whether fertilization is an event or a process and whether marker events can be identified. In the past, fertilization has been viewed as an event, but the development of medical technology indicates that there is no single moment when conception occurs. Determining the legal consequences of fertilization and attaching significance to any particular stage of development have proven extremely difficult. The British Warnock Report (Warnock 1985) observes that although timing of the different stages of development is critical, once the process has begun, no aspect of the continuous developmental process is more important or significant than another. However, the meaning or scope of the term "fertilization" is imprecise. Does fertilization occur when the sperm has entered the egg, when the two sets of genetic material fuse, or at some other point? These questions demanded a legal response in Victoria (Australia) when medical scientists proposed an experiment involving the microinjection of a single sperm into an egg. In 1987, after much debate and concern that medical scientists deliberately produce embryos for destructive research, the Victorian legislation was amended to permit experimental procedures involving the fertilization of a human ovum from the point of sperm penetration prior to, but not including, syngamy (when a distinct embryonic genetic code forms).

Coincidentally, despite the Warnock Report's emphasis on the continuous nature of fertilization and embryo development, it concluded that the formation of the primitive streak—a groove that develops in the embryonic disc—about fifteen days after fertilization marks the emergence of an individuated embryo and is the last stage at which twinning of the conceptus might occur. Before this occurs, the dividing cells are labeled "pre-embryos," a new concept. Until that point, it argued, certain research is acceptable. The report's recommendation that embryos not be used as research subjects beyond fourteen days after fertilization is enshrined in the United Kingdom's Human Fertilisation and Embryology Act (1990). The American Fertility Society, which promulgates the major set of ethical guidelines regarding embryo research in the United States, relies on the term "pre-embryo" to describe the entity existing before the development of the genetically distinct individual "embryo." It advises that in the absence of specific legislation, gamete providers have primary decisionmaking authority regarding pre-embryos and that such decisions involve a person's liberty to procreate. The society also recommends research not be allowed beyond the fourteenth day of postfertilization.

Should Embryos Be Created Specifically for Research Purposes?

One of the most controversial moral and legal aspects of embryo research is which embryos, if any, can be used. Critics maintain that if permitted, scientists would produce as many embryos as they needed, thus reducing the level of respect or responsibility vis-à-vis those embryos. Further, they argue, the aims of experimentation would broaden from infertility research to genetic manipulation. On the other side, scientists express frustration that the scarcity of embryos hampers their ability to do the IVF research necessary to improve its success rates.

A focus of this debate has been on the status of "spare," "surplus," or "extra" embryos that result from IVF procedures. The questions emerge of what to do with such embryos and who decides. In Australia, the Victorian legislation, for example, does not permit the creation of embryos specifically for research purposes. Proposed Canadian legislation includes the same provision. However, in practice, embryos are developed in vitro with the intention to implant, as required by law, but end up in research without violating legislation. Medical scientists can easily create excess embryos, and disproving their initial intention to implant those embryos would be very difficult. Moreover, why should the intention of either medical practitioners or their patients alter the moral and legal status of entities that are in all other respects identical? Opponents of IVF use the problematic distinction between spare and specially created embryos to argue that embryo research be prohibited, whereas medical scientists use the same information to argue that it should be legal to produce embryos specifically for infertility research. Finally, the overwhelming focus of scientists, critics, and policymakers on the status of the embryo-for-research diverts attention from the risks taken by women who undergo the hormonal stimulation and surgical procedures used to obtain the eggs. Despite the active lobbying of feminists, the legislation tends not to reflect their concerns.

In conclusion, the central legal issue regarding embryo experimentation has been defining the special protection or respect owed to the embryo. Although courts and legislatures generally do not assign personhood to the embryo-conceptus, they have developed specific guidelines and regulatory regimes attesting to its special status. Formulating that special status is difficult, however, and depends on the power and influence of particular interest groups to have their point of view or moral stance codified into law.

FOR FURTHER READING

American Fertility Society. 1990. *Ethical Considerations of the New Reproductive Technologies*. Birmingham, Ala.: American Fertility Society.

Andrews, Lori B. 1986. "The Legal Status of the Embryo." *Loyola Law Review* 32: 357–409.

Australia. Senate Select Committee on the Human Embryo Experimentation Bill, 1985. 1986. *Human Embryo Experimentation in Australia*. Canberra: Australian Government Publishing Service.

Blank, Robert H. 1990. *Regulating Reproduction*. New York: Columbia University Press.
Davis v. Davis v. King. 1989. Fifth Jud. Ct., Tennessee, E-14496, September 21.
Roe v. Wade. 1973. 410 U.S. 113.
United Kingdom. 1990. *Human Fertilisation and Embryology Act, 1990*.
Victoria, Australia. Committee to Consider the Social, Ethical and Legal Issues Arising from in Vitro Fertilization. 1984. *Report on the Disposition of Embryos Produced by in Vitro Fertilization*. Melbourne: Victorian Government Printer.
Warnock, Mary. 1985. *A Question of Life: The Warnock Report on Human Fertilisation and Embryology*. Oxford: Basil Blackwell.

sixty-four

Cloning Technologies

ROBIN WOODS

Somatic Cells and Gametes

To appreciate the techniques involved in cloning one must understand the differences between the two cell types, somatic cells and gametes (or germline cells), and the two types of cell division, mitosis and meiosis. The bulk of the human body consists of somatic cells that contain two copies of each chromosome (a threadlike structure that carries the genes) and that are called diploid. In humans the somatic cells contain twenty-three pairs of chromosomes (forty-six in total). One member of each chromosome pair comes from the mother and the other from the father. The chromosomes carry the genes that determine the characteristics of each individual. The genes too come in pairs, one from the mother and one from the father.

Somatic cells divide by a type of cell division known as mitosis (see Figure 64.1). Before a cell can divide it must grow and duplicate its chromosomes. During the first part of the cell cycle, the G1 phase, the cell just grows. During the next stage, the S phase, the chromosomes are duplicated, but the duplicates, known as sister chromatids, remain attached to each other. In the G2 phase the cell grows again and prepares to divide. Finally, during the M phase, or mitosis, the cell divides, and the two sister chromatids of each chromosome separate, one passing to each of the two daughter cells. The daughter cells each have 46 chromosomes and are genetically identical. Some cell types, for example, nerve cells, do not divide. They pass from the G1 phase into a dormant phase known as G0.

The second type of cell, the gametes, are the eggs and sperm. The cells that give rise to the eggs are known as primary oocytes, and those that

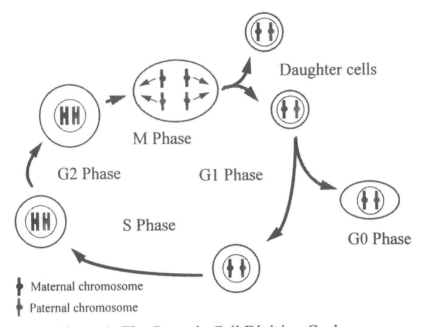

Figure 1 The Somatic Cell Division Cycle

give rise to the sperm are known as primary spermatocytes. These cells are diploid. The gametes are formed by a type of cell division known as meiosis, which occurs only in the testes and ovaries (see Figures 64.2 and 64.3). Prior to meiosis each chromosome duplicates to give two sister chromatids, which remain attached to each other. During the first cell division of meiosis, the maternal and paternal members of each pair of chromosomes come together and exchange sections of DNA between nonsister chromatids. The cell then divides, but the sister chromatids remain attached to each other. The maternal sister chromatids go to one of the new daughter cells, and the paternal sister chromatids go to the other. The twenty-three different maternal and paternal chromosomes (sister chromatid pairs) separate independently, so the daughter cells receive a mixture of maternal and paternal chromosomes.

The cells formed by this first division have only twenty-three chromosomes, but each chromosome is composed of two chromatids. A second division follows. This time the cell divides, and the chromatids of each chromosome separate to the daughter cells as they did in mitosis. Thus in meiosis, the cell divides twice, but the chromosomes divide only once with the result that the four products of meiosis are haploid (possess half

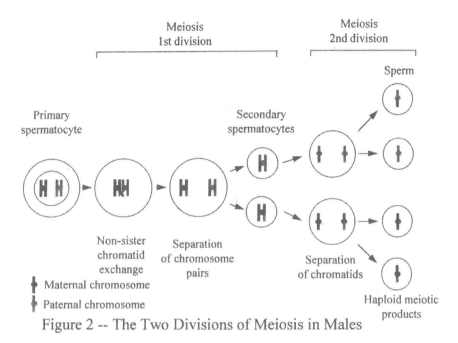

Figure 2 -- The Two Divisions of Meiosis in Males

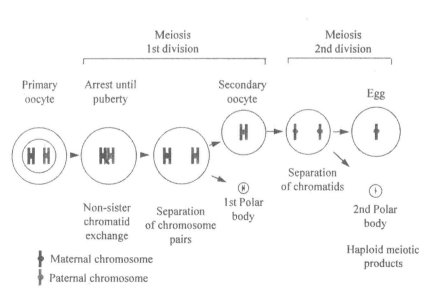

Figure 3 -- The Two Divisions of Meiosis in Females

the diploid, or normal, number of chromosomes found in somatic cells). They contain only twenty-three chromosomes, and they have only one copy of each gene. The exchange of genetic material between the nonsister chromatids of each maternal and paternal pair of chromosomes during the first division of meiosis, coupled with the independent separation of the twenty-three pairs of chromosomes, means that each of the gametes formed by meiosis is genetically different. The fusion at fertilization of gametes with different combinations of maternal and paternal chromosomes and genes means that except for identical multiple births, each human being is genetically unique.

The outcome of meiosis is quite different in males and females. In males the production of sperm begins at puberty, and all four products of meiosis develop into functional sperm (see Figure 64.2). In females only one product of meiosis becomes a functional egg (see Figure 64.3). Meiosis begins during the development of the ovaries in the fetus but is arrested at the stage of chromosome pairing. The dormant meiotic cells, or primary oocytes, remain in this state until the onset of puberty. Then at each ovulation phase of the menstrual cycle, one primary oocyte completes the first division of meiosis. This division produces one small cell, the first polar body, which degenerates, and one large cell, the secondary oocyte. The secondary oocyte, which has twenty-three duplicated chromosomes, halts in the second division of meiosis until stimulated to continue by the entry of a sperm (see Figure 64.4). The second meiotic division is also unequal. The small cell forms the second polar body, which degenerates, and the larger one becomes the egg, or ovum. Fusion of the egg nucleus with the sperm nucleus, both with twenty-three chromosomes, forms a diploid zygote with forty-six chromosomes (twenty-three pairs). The diploid zygote then divides by mitosis to form the embryo.

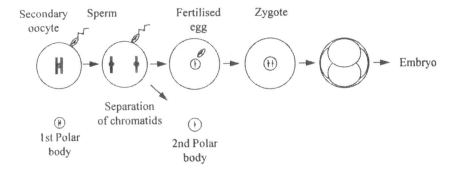

Figure 4 -- Fertilisation and the Zygote

Cloning

Natural Clones and Embryo Splitting

Clones are genetically identical copies of an organism. In humans and other mammals, identical twins (and higher multiples) are natural clones. The cells formed from the first two or three divisions of the fertilized egg can develop into separate embryos (see Figure 64.5). The frequency of multiple identical births in humans, cattle, sheep, and goats is increased by ovulation-inducing agents and by in vitro fertilization (IVF) procedures. Clones of domesticated animals can also be produced by embryo splitting. In this procedure, the cells of a very early embryo are separated from each other and implanted into surrogate mothers. Embryo splitting yields a limited number of clones and has not been widely used in animal breeding. For both natural clones and those obtained by embryo splitting, the characteristics of the clones are predictable only within certain limits. Animal breeders select specific parents, but the progeny are the products of the random processes of meiosis and fertilization.

Cloning by Nuclear Transplantation

The only way to obtain an exact copy of an adult organism with specific genetic characteristics is to clone it by nuclear transplantation. This procedure involves the removal of the nucleus from an unfertilized egg and its replacement with a nucleus from a somatic cell of the selected adult organism. The first successful nuclear transplantation experiments were carried out with frogs' eggs. These experiments demonstrated the feasibility

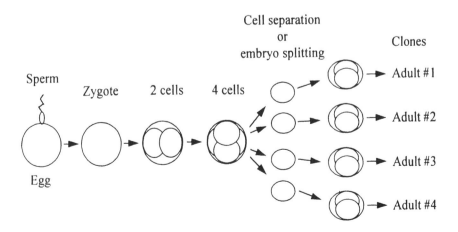

Figure 5 -- Origin of Clones by Cell Separation or Embryo Splitting

of nuclear transplantation, but the age of the transplanted nuclei affected the outcome. Nuclei from tadpole cells supported normal development; nuclei from frog cells did not. In the early 1980s, experiments with mice gave similar results: Only nuclei from the very early embryos supported normal development. In adult animals, the genetic material in the nuclei of differentiated cells has been modified so that certain genes are activated and others, such as the genes for embryonic functions, are inactivated. Some of these changes result from methylation, a specific chemical modification of the genetic material. The patterns of methylation present in the sperm and the egg are passed on to the zygote nucleus at fertilization but are erased after the first few cell divisions of the embryo. As development and differentiation proceed, the patterns are reset.

Cloning Sheep by Nuclear Transplantation

Nuclear transplantation technology has been developed furthest with sheep. In experiments with sheep, somatic cells are fused with enucleated eggs (secondary oocytes that have had their nuclei removed). This procedure is illustrated in Figure 64.6. The somatic cell provides a diploid nucleus to replace the diploid zygote nucleus that would result from fertilization. Ewes are induced to hyperovulate by the administration of human chorionic gonadotropin hormone. The unfertilized eggs (secondary oocytes) are collected and enucleated with a micropipette (a small glass tube). An enucleated egg and a somatic cell are fused by a series of electrical pulses, and the resulting "reconstructed" embryos are transferred to the uterus of a recipient ewe. After several days, the embryos are recovered and checked by microscopic examination. If they are develop-

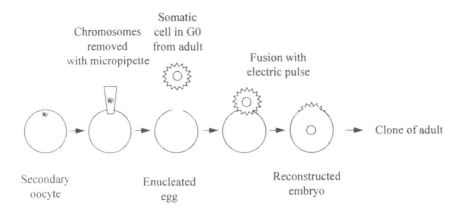

Figure 6 -- Cloning by Nuclear Transplantation

ing normally, they are reimplanted into secondary recipient ewes. Alternatively, the implanted embryos can be left in place and monitored by ultrasound.

In 1986, Steen Willadsen reported successful nuclear transplantation experiments in sheep with donor cells obtained from eight- or sixteen-cell embryos. However, these cells were young enough to have developed into embryos by embryo splitting. In 1996, Keith Campbell and colleagues demonstrated nuclear transplantation with cells obtained by microdissection from normal nine-day-old sheep embryos. The cells were grown in tissue culture for a number of generations. They showed some degree of differentiation at the time they were used in the nuclear transplantation experiments. They synthesized keratin, a cellular component typically found in skin cells. The cultured cells were transferred to a tissue culture medium lacking growth factors—that is, chemicals that stimulate growth and cell division. The absence of growth factors in the medium caused the cells to become dormant and enter the phase of the cell cycle known as G0 (see Figure 64.1). It seems that when cells are arrested in the G0 phase, the methylation patterns of the genetic material associated with differentiation are at least partially reversed. In effect, this demethylation allows the genetic material in the transplanted nucleus to behave as if it were "young" again! However, the clones produced in this experiment were not clones of an adult animal.

In February 1997, Ian Wilmut and others at the Roslin Institute reported, in the scientific journal *Nature*, the first clone of an adult mammal. Dolly, a Finn Dorset lamb, was the product of a nuclear transplantation experiment in which a cell derived from an adult sheep was fused with an enucleated egg. Cells from an udder of a pregnant Finn Dorset ewe were grown in culture and starved of growth factors to induce them to enter the G0 phase. A total of 277 cultured udder cells were fused to enucleated eggs obtained from Scottish Blackface ewes. Twenty-nine of the fusions developed in surrogate mothers to the early-embryo stage and were then transferred to secondary recipient ewes. The result was one live lamb. Dolly looked like the Finn Dorset ewe that provided the udder cell, and her DNA contained sequences characteristic of the cultured udder cells.

Applications of Cloning Animals by Nuclear Transplantation

One of the aims of the research project that resulted in Dolly was to extend the use of domestic animals as sources of biological pharmaceuticals. Currently, the pharmaceutical industry uses bacteria, yeast, and animal cells expressing specific human genes for the production of a number of pharmaceuticals. The gene coding for human insulin was cloned and introduced into bacteria over a decade ago. The human insulin synthesized by bacteria is more effective and results in fewer adverse reactions than insulin obtained from pigs or cattle. If sheep clones produced by nuclear transplantation are derived from a cell line that carries a human gene for a biologically active protein such as insulin and the gene has been engineered so that it will be expressed in mammary tissue, then the milk of the mature ewes should contain human insulin. If the nuclear transplantation technique can be applied to cattle, the potential for production of specific biopharmaceuticals on an industrial scale can more readily be realized. The production of insulin from milk is likely to be cheaper and easier than that from bacterial cultures. In August 1997, the same scientific team that created Dolly reported the successful nuclear transplantation of fetal skin cells carrying a human gene into enucleated eggs. The five lambs that resulted are not clones of an adult, but they are potentially important for the production of biological pharmaceuticals.

It is likely that nuclear transplantation cloning into other mammals with cell lines carrying specific human genes will play an important role in the study of human diseases. Mice have already been genetically engineered so that they carry the mutant forms of the genes responsible for a number of human diseases, but they do not necessarily show the same disease symptoms as do humans. Cloning by nuclear transplantation will broaden the range of species that can be used for such research, and the results may be more directly relevant to human pathology.

Nuclear transplantation also promises to be of considerable value in improving the "performance" of domesticated animals. Cell lines established from the "best" animals could be used to derive flocks or herds of clones that would be genetically identical and all have the desired traits for high-performance characteristics.

Prospects for Human Cloning

The techniques used to produce Dolly could theoretically be applied to humans. However, the induction of hyperovulation, the recovery of the secondary oocytes, the implantation of the reconstructed embryos, and the assessment of embryonic development would be time consuming, invasive, and expensive. There are also concerns with respect to the development of the embryo. The chromosome numbers of cells grown in tissue culture are unstable. Deviations from the normal complement of forty-six chromosomes in humans can have serious consequences. For example, embryos with one too many or one too few of most of the human chromosomes do not survive. In the cell line that was used to clone Dolly, a few of the cells did not have the normal sheep chromosome complement of fifty-four. A second concern relates to the age of the cells used for transplantation. The human life span is genetically limited. Cells obtained from a human fetus grow in culture for about fifty-five divisions and then die. Cells obtained from an adult human die after fewer divisions. Dolly is the clone of a seven-year-old ewe. She appears to be a normal lamb, but we do not know how she will develop. Was she born with seven-year-old cells or did the demethylation in the early embryonic cell divisions reset the clock to zero?

FOR FURTHER READING

Campbell, K.H.S., et al. 1996. "Sheep Cloned by Nuclear Transfer from a Cultured Cell Line." *Nature* 380: 64–66.

Forbes, L. S. 1997. "The Evolutionary Biology of Spontaneous Abortion in Humans." *Trends in Ecology and Evolution* 12: 446–450.

Pennisi, E. 1997. "Transgenic Lambs from Cloning Lab." *Science* 277: 631.

Roslin Institute Home Page. http://www.ri.bbsrc.ac.uk/cloning.

Solter, D. 1996. "Lambing by Nuclear Transfer." *Nature* 380: 24–25.

Stewart, C. 1997. "An Udder Way of Making Lambs." *Nature* 385: 769–771.

Willadsen, S. M. 1986. "Nuclear Transplantation in Sheep Embryos." *Nature* 320: 63–65.

Wilmut, I., et al. 1997. "Viable Offspring Derived from Fetal and Adult Mammalian Cells." *Nature* 385: 810–813.

sixty-five

Cloning—Ethics

LAURA SHANNER

Human cloning was first widely discussed in the 1970s as a result of rapid advances in genetics. However, because human cloning did not appear to be imminent, the topic quickly disappeared from public view. The appearance of Dolly, the cloned sheep, in 1997 unexpectedly made human cloning more realistic. The ethical implications of human cloning have since been revisited.

Risks of Human Cloning

As with most emerging technologies, concerns about safety provide the most obvious ethical grounds for caution. Somatic cell nuclear transfer (SCNT), required to clone an existing person, poses a risk in passing on mutations in the source cell's DNA, which could result in unexpected anomalies. In addition, cloned offspring might also be born with a cellular age equivalent to that of the genetic progenitor and would have a reduced overall life span. As with all in vitro technologies, cloning raises concerns about physical damage to the embryo and health risks for women who undergo ovulation induction and surgical egg retrieval.

Although research may settle these worries about safety, several more abstract issues may be harder to resolve. A primary concern involves individuality. Although naturally occurring identical siblings sometimes feel that being a twin undermines their unique identities, they generally seem unharmed by having a natural clone. However, although most of us are not greatly bothered by the notion that one other identical person might exist, many people become uneasy with the idea of batches of identical persons. Sets of clones might come to be viewed as types rather than as individuals.

If the point of cloning is to ensure precisely identical offspring, the endeavor is likely to fail in unexpected ways. The personal cost to the clone for failing to live up to specific (and perhaps unrealistic) expectations could be devastating. Mutations in the source cell DNA, and even the mitochondria provided by the recipient egg, may prevent SCNT from producing a fully identical clone. Clones created by embryo cleavage may be gestated by different women or at different times, and cogestating multiple siblings will experience variations in uterine position, nutrition, and growth. Later, environmental influences and life events will cause further deviations from identical roots.

Today, ethical discussions about families often invoke the notion of choice. Whereas we might choose whether to have children, we cannot (yet) choose the specific children to have. Natural twins and segmented embryos gestated at the same time may be genetically identical, but their specific combination of traits remains the unchosen outcome of meiosis and fertilization. Delayed transfer of frozen embryo segments and SCNT, however, allow the production of a nearly identical copy of a known—and chosen—individual. Genetic testing allows us to reject certain offspring, and gene replacement may allow us to instill chosen specific traits. Cloning would allow us to choose specific offspring with known traits, thus replacing the ethics of unchosen family (genetic) relations with an ethic of control.

Issues with Cleaving Embryos

Embryo segmentation and cryopreservation would allow identical siblings to be born to different mothers or at different times, perhaps even in different generations. Our social and legal structures concerning generations and family relationships would be disrupted by such practices. It is not yet clear whether such an upheaval would be ethically unacceptable or an improvement on current norms.

Transferring copies of an embryo known to have developed into a healthy child might improve IVF success rates and would be particularly attractive to families at risk of a genetic disease. Identical embryos might also be transferred to several different women in a controlled experiment to document the effects of genetics and environment on development. The value of improving fertility treatments or resolving the nature-nurture debate would have to be weighed against the physical, psychological, and social risks of cloning.

Issues with Cloning Adults

Dolly the sheep heralds the possibility of cloning human adults, which is distinct from making identical sets of offspring who are only partly genetically related to biological parents. Assuming that the physical risks of the procedure are overcome, several important social structures would be called into question. The mother and father of someone who is cloned would have the same genetic relationship to the clone as they do to the progenitor. Would the progenitor's parents therefore become parents of yet another child (the clone) without their knowledge and consent, or would they become grandparents to their offspring's identical offspring? If DNA from one female is inserted into an egg of another and gestated by yet another woman, the clone will have as many as three biological mothers. Other questions arise: Who is the father? Would a cloned male be the father or twin of his clone? And who is the mother? How would such relationships differ when the genetic progenitor is a child, an adult, or a deceased individual? How ought matters of custody, child support and protection, and inheritance be resolved?

Reasons to Undertake Cloning

The most frequent cloning scenarios in science fiction involve the resurrection of a great leader or thinker, a plot to re-create a tyrant to march toward world dominance, a narcissistic desire to multiply oneself, or the desire to copy oneself to share the load of a busy schedule. More plausible motives in the real world include the desire to replace a deceased loved one. However, all of these plans, real and imaginative, would fail because the clones would first appear as newborn infants rather than the fully developed individual who inspired the cloning. Due to environmental influences and minor mutations, the clones might never behave exactly like the progenitor. Further, clones would each have a separate consciousness rather than a shared awareness with the progenitor. They would therefore lack the memories that would make the clones most useful to their creators, and it would remain impossible for one person to be in two places at once.

Clones might be produced for organ or tissue transplants. Freezing embryo segments for relatively rapid development would work only for tissues such as bone marrow and skin due to the extensive time needed to grow organs to a size suitable for transplant. There is controversial precedent for bearing additional offspring in order to procure bone marrow for an existing child, so bearing the child's clone would seem to raise no substantially different ethical questions. Sacrificing the life of a clone to retrieve vital organs, however, would clearly undermine the clone's rights.

Any clone of a human would be human and as such should be entitled to the full protection of human rights and moral standing. A question not commonly asked that underlines a cloned person's human rights is Would the progenitor be equally willing to sacrifice himself or herself if the clone experienced life-threatening complications first? More promising circumstances for cloning include the relief of infertility, avoidance of severe genetic anomaly, or assistance in reproduction for single adults or homosexual couples. In each of these cases, we must compare the risks and benefits of cloning to alternative reproductive options, including the option of not having children at all.

Parents who suffer the heartbreaking death of a young child might wish to have that child cloned. Although it is understandable that grief inspires a multitude of coping strategies and beneficent attempts to provide relief, this one seems particularly counterproductive. The truth of the child's death cannot be erased by having another child. The parents would seem more likely to remain in the denial stage of grief if "the same" (genetically identical) child took the deceased child's place. It is not clear why a clone would be a better child than a different second child, especially if the death occurred in infancy before most distinctive traits were revealed. Clones would also seem more likely than other later children to suffer from the expectations to be just like the lost sibling, and they would bear the load of the parents' grief.

Most suggested justifications for cloning focus on the clone's usefulness to others, but any ethical assessment of the techniques must also consider the situation from the clone's perspective. Would cloning create a fair distribution of opportunities and burdens? How will we resolve complex new structures of family relationships and generations in ways that support the clone's personal development and integration into the community? Can we ensure that clones will be treated as self-directed individuals, or will they face unreasonable expectations generated by their identical siblings, progenitors, and others? Whereas we might find it attractive to create a clone, how many of us would want to be a clone?

FOR FURTHER READING

"Cloning Human Beings: Responding to the National Bioethics Advisory Commission's Report." 1997. *Hastings Center Report*. Special issue 27(5): 6–22.

Fletcher, John. 1974. *The Ethics of Genetic Control*. New York: Doubleday.

Humber, James M., and Robert F. Alexander, eds. 1998. *Biomedical Ethics Reviews: Human Cloning*. London: Humana.

Kass, Leon. 1972. "Freedom, Coercion and Asexual Reproduction." In J. Katz, ed., *Experimentation with Human Beings*. New York: Russell Sage Foundation.

Kolata, Gina. 1997. *Clone: The Road to Dolly and the Path Ahead.* New York: William Morrow.

Robertson, John. 1994. "The Question of Human Cloning." *Hastings Center Report* 24(2): 6–14.

Silver, Lee. 1997. *Remaking Eden: Cloning and Beyond in a Brave New World.* New York: Avon.

U.S. National Advisory Board on Ethics in Reproduction. 1994. "Report on Human Cloning Through Embryo Splitting: An Amber Light." *Kennedy Institute of Ethics Journal* 4(3): 251–282.

U.S. National Bioethics Advisory Commission. 1997. *Cloning Human Beings.* Rockland, Md.: N.p.

sixty-six

Preimplantation Genetic Diagnosis

ANDREA L. BONNICKSEN

In vitro fertilization (IVF) clinics in North American and European countries have added to their service options the diagnosis of microscopic human eggs and embryos for genetic anomalies. In preimplantation genetic diagnosis (PGD), genes associated with serious disorders are detected before implantation and pregnancy. Preimplantation diagnosis is an alternative to prenatal (fetal) testing for couples who would not terminate a pregnancy but who are at high genetic risk for passing on such disorders as Tay Sachs disease or cystic fibrosis to their offspring. Embryo diagnosis is an early step in a line of practices that may one day include the genetic correction of embryos.

There are several types of PGD. In the embryo biopsy, a single cell from a four- to eight-cell externally fertilized egg is removed and examined. The embryo itself is transferred to the woman's uterus for a possible pregnancy only if the biopsied cell is free from the DNA sequence associated with the disease in question. In the trophectoderm biopsy, cells surrounding the multicell and older (but still microscopic) embryo are examined. This procedure leaves the cells of the inner embryonic mass intact, but successful implantation rates appear to be lower when embryos are transferred at this later stage. In polar body analysis, technicians examine the first polar body of the unfertilized egg. In situ hybridization is used to identify female and male embryos in order to transfer only female embryos to women at risk for passing a sex-linked genetic disease, such as

Duchenne muscular dystrophy, to their sons. Successful implantations following the sexing of embryos and births after embryo biopsy have been increasingly reported.

Supporters regard PGD as a beneficent alternative to prenatal testing and pregnancy termination. They see it as an incremental advance in genetic testing that poses no significant ethical problems and that opens the door to understanding genetic disease. It is seen as a service to high-risk couples who want another child but who would not terminate a pregnancy if they were to discover that the fetus carried a genetic disease. It also holds promise as a technique for identifying in embryos chromosomal abnormalities such as that associated with Down syndrome.

Critics regard PGD as significantly different from prenatal testing because it prepares for the correction of disease-linked genes in embryos. They see it as an expensive technique that is offered before systematic studies have demonstrated its safety and accuracy. Pronatalists voice concerns about the number of embryos that will be lost in PGD research projects and in the selective nontransfer of affected embryos. Feminists who argue that IVF compartmentalizes reproduction and reduces women's control over conception and gestation note that PGD further dissects reproduction, subjects women to more research as questions of safety and reliability are worked out, and involves a new set of women—those who are fertile—in the emotional and physical stresses of IVF.

The momentum for PGD is building, and the number of healthy births is increasing, although questions about safety and efficacy remain to be worked out. Studies on animals have demonstrated a range of potential manipulations, such as births following the biopsy and freezing of embryos. Studies showing frequencies of chromosomal and genetic abnormalities in human sperm, eggs, and embryos create a rationale for testing. It is not unreasonable to expect PGD eventually to be routinely offered to couples trying IVF under the supposition that if the embryo is available, it can easily be tested for selected disorders before transfer to the uterus.

National and subnational governments have introduced embryo research laws that may have an impact on PGD. The German Embryo Protection Act (1990), for example, restricts PGD. The British Human Fertilisation and Embryology Act (1990), in contrast, creates a licensing authority and code of practice that allow research on PGD. Several U.S. states have enacted restrictive embryo research laws, although their constitutionality has not been tested.

Although PGD improves genetic testing by allowing diagnosis at the earliest stages of the reproductive process, it is a gateway to controversial applications. Detecting genetic abnormalities in embryos sets the stage for attempts to correct these flaws, which, theoretically, will be permanently encoded in the reproductive line of descendants. Such control gives a new degree of power to humans, it raises the prospect of unexpected side effects, and it creates the temptation to correct an array of nonmedical traits. Among the clinical questions raised are: Should clinicians offer PGD to couples worried about conceiving a child with a disorder but who are not at high genetic risk? Should they offer PGD for moderate as well as serious genetic disorders? Should tests that are less than 100 percent accurate be offered? Among broader, societal questions are Who will benefit economically from PGD? Who decides who has access to PGD? Should primary responsibility for overseeing PGD lie in the clinics, professional associations, or public agencies? Is PGD truly an alternative that is less burdensome than prenatal diagnosis?

FOR FURTHER READING

Beier, H. M., and J. O. Beckman. 1991. "Implications and Consequences of the German Embryo Protection Act." *Human Reproduction* 6: 607–608.

Grifo, J. A., et al. 1994. "Healthy Deliveries from Biopsied Human Embryos." *Human Reproduction* 9: 912–916.

Handyside, A. H., et al. 1990. "Pregnancies from Biopsied Human Preimplantation Embryos Sexed by Y-Specific DNA Amplification." *Nature* 344: 768–770.

Handyside, A. H., et al. 1992. "Birth of a Normal Girl After in Vitro Fertilization and Preimplantation Diagnostic Testing for Cystic Fibrosis." *New England Journal of Medicine* 327: 905–909.

Pergament, E., and A. L. Bonnicksen. 1994. "Preimplantation Genetics: A Case for Prospective Action." *American Journal of Medical Genetics* 55(1): 80–84.

Rothman, B. K. 1992. "Not All That Glitters Is Gold." *Hastings Center Report* 22: S11–S15.

Simpson, J. L., and S. A. Carson. 1992. "Preimplantation Genetic Diagnosis." *New England Journal of Medicine* 327: 951–953.

Trounson, A. L. 1992. "Preimplantation Genetic Diagnosis—Counting Chickens Before They Hatch?" *Human Reproduction* 7: 583–584.

United Kingdom. "Human Fertilisation and Embryology Act 1990." 1991. *International Digest of Health Legislation* 42: 69–85.

Verlinsky, Y., E. Pergament, and C. Strom. 1990. "The Preimplantation Genetic Diagnosis of Genetic Diseases." *Journal of in Vitro Fertilization and Embryo Transfer* 7: 1–5.

sixty-seven

Genetics—Discrimination

REGINA H. KENEN

The diffusion of genetic testing can lead to the misuse of findings, placing those being tested at risk for possible psychological trauma, stigmatization, and discrimination. This happened in the 1970s when unaffected carriers of the sickle-cell trait were sometimes denied employment and life insurance because sickle-cell disease and sickle-cell trait were confused. This risk broadens as diagnostic technology becomes more sophisticated and additional gene-based tests for susceptibilities and carrier states are developed.

Although behavioral genetics has recently gained respectability, it still has a high potential for abuse. Investigations into genetic components for mental illness, aggression, alcoholism, intelligence, and homosexuality—the findings of which are portrayed in the media as a "crime gene" or an "alcoholic gene" or a "gay gene"—further stigmatize minority groups.

Through the fruits of genetic research, physicians will be able to detect more of the relatively few individuals who have fairly uncommon diseases and an increasingly large number of individuals who bear higher-than-average risks for more common conditions such as colon, prostate, and breast cancer; cardiovascular disease; and Alzheimer's disease. In the late 1990s packages of multiple and simultaneous genetic tests became widely available. Combined with a growing social concern with the role of genetics in disease, these tests could lead to various forms of discrimination against those with genetic conditions, particularly those in targeted populations. In addition, using statistical models, insurance companies and employers will try to determine which groups of individuals are at higher or lower risk for future use of health facilities based on their purported genetic heritage even though they cannot precisely identify specific individuals within these groups who will develop the diseases in question.

The National Center for Human Genome Research through the Ethical, Legal and Social Implications (ELSI) program, the Department of Energy in the United States, and the worldwide Human Genome Organization are very much aware of these problems and have studied questions of fairness in the use of genetic information pertaining to the criminal justice system, the educational system, adoptions, and the military. In addition, privacy and confidentiality of genetic information are of prime concern, particularly with respect to ownership and control of genetic information, consent to disclosure, and use of genetic information. The Equal Opportunity Commission has interpreted the Americans with Disabilities Act to include discrimination against genetic carriers. A large number of U.S. state legislatures have passed genetic privacy and nondiscrimination laws, and the U.K. has created the Human Advisory Commission to consider consequences of developments in human genetics in relation to public health, insurance, patient care, and employment.

The intersection of two powerful revolutions—the information-systems revolution and the biomedical revolution—has resulted in the development of parallel sets of norms, one set protecting the privacy of personal information and another protecting citizens' rights of access to public information. Concern for the right of genetic privacy has been expressed in many countries, and they have handled the issue in slightly different ways. For example, the Federal Republic of Germany has invoked constitutional principles that lead to a "right of informational self-determination," and the United States has applied the principles of medical ethics to genetic screening. These intents are noble, but the reality, according to a March of Dimes–sponsored survey of the U.S. public, is that invasion of personal privacy is becoming subtly acceptable.

Geneticists estimate that every one of us has four to eight recessive deleterious genes. The carrier label, however, cannot be applied to individuals carrying potentially mutant genes that have not yet been identified. Recent developments in genetic technology and the ability to identify carriers of a large number of genetic diseases change definitions of health and ability and put an increasing number of people at risk for erroneous interpretations by others, stigmatization, and discrimination regarding employment, insurance, and health care.

FOR FURTHER READING

American Medical Association Council on Ethical and Judicial Affairs. 1998. "Multiple Genetic Testing." *Hastings Center Report* 28(4): 15–21.

Andrews, L., and A. Jaeger. 1991. "Confidentiality of Genetic Information in the Workplace." *American Journal of Law and Medicine* 17: 75–108.

Bartels D., B. Leroy, and A. Caplan, eds. 1993. *Prescribing Our Future, Ethical Challenges in Genetic Counselling.* Hawthorne, N.Y.: Aldine de Gruyter.

Bowman, J., and R. Murray. 1990. *Genetic Variation and Disorder in Peoples of African Origin.* Baltimore, Md.: Johns Hopkins University Press.

Davis, J. 1993. "Reproductive Genetic Testing: State of the Art/Science." In Mark Evans, E. J. Thomas, and K. Rothenberg, eds., *Proceedings of NIH Working Group on Reproductive Genetic Testing: Impact on Women.* New York: S. Karger and Basel.

Faden, R., and N. Kass. 1993. "Genetic Screening Technology: Ethical Issues in Access to Tests by Employers and Health Insurance Companies." *Journal of Social Issues* 49: 75–88.

Holtzman, N. 1989. *Proceed with Caution: Predicting Genetic Risks in the Recombinant DNA Era.* London: Johns Hopkins University Press.

Hubbard, R., and E. Wald. 1993. "Inherited Tendencies: Behaviors." In *Exploding the Gene Myth.* Boston: Beacon Press.

Kevles, D., and L. Hood, eds. 1992. *The Code of Codes: Scientific and Social Issues in the Human Genome Project.* Cambridge: Harvard University Press.

Lippman, A. 1991. "Prenatal Genetic Testing and Screening: Constructing Needs and Reinforcing Inequalities." *American Journal of Law and Medicine* 17: 15–50.

U.K. Working Party of the Clinical Genetics Society. 1994. "The Genetic Testing of Children." *Journal of Medical Genetics* 31: 785–797.

U.S. Congress, Office of Technological Assessment. 1990. *Genetic Monitoring and Screening in the Workplace.* Washington, D.C.: U.S. Government Printing Office.

U.S. Congress, Office of Technological Assessment. 1992a. *Cystic Fibrosis and DNA Tests: Implications of Carrier Screening.* Washington, D.C.: U.S. Government Printing Office.

U.S. Congress, Office of Technological Assessment. 1992b. *Genetic Tests and Health Insurers: Results of a Survey.* Washington, D.C.: U.S. Government Printing Office.

U.S. National Center for Human Genome Research. National Institutes of Health. 1991. *The Ethical, Legal and Social Implications of Human Genome Research: Preparing for the Responsible Use of New Genetic Knowledge.* Washington, D.C.: U.S. Government Printing Office.

Wiesel, T. 1994. "Genetics and Behavior." *Science* 264: 1647.

sixty-eight

Genetic Counseling

DOROTHY C. WERTZ

Genetic counseling is a medical service that provides relevant information about patients' genetic status and psychological and social support for individuals and families with genetic disorders. Those seeking counseling are usually referred by their physicians for one or more of the following reasons: There is a family or personal history of genetic disorder, a woman over the age of thirty-five is pregnant or considering pregnancy, the parents have a child with a genetic disorder, the woman has a history of multiple miscarriages of unknown origin, or the parents have been exposed to toxic substances. The majority are women having prenatal diagnosis for advanced maternal age, which in most industrialized countries is considered to be over the age of thirty-five. Many of the rest are parents of children with genetic conditions. Those in counseling are usually most interested in getting information that will help with reproductive decisions. Many are also interested in learning about the effect of a genetic disorder on family life, costs of raising a child with a genetic disorder, and education and treatment for the affected family member. About 70 percent of the time, those receiving counseling are a couple seen together.

Counselors may be physicians or those with doctorates, postgraduate training, or medical board certification in genetics or, in the United States and Canada, professionals with a special two-year master's degree in genetic counseling from one of twenty-seven special programs. Programs also exist in Australia, South Africa, and the United Kingdom. Most physician-counselors are pediatricians with a thorough knowledge of genetics who may or may not have clinical training in the psychosocial aspects of counseling. There are about 5,000 doctoral-level geneticists worldwide; about 50 percent are women.

Approximately 1,700 master's-level counselors practice in North America; about two-thirds are certified by the American Board of Medical Genetics or the American Board of Genetic Counselling. They have training in counseling psychology but are not psychotherapists. Most master's-level counselors are white women between the ages of thirty and forty-five. Most work in hospital clinics under medical supervision; some work in commercial laboratories. Solo or group practice is rare for genetic counselors at any level. In the United States, the National Society of Genetic Counsellors serves as the professional organization for those at the master's level. In some places, such as the United Kingdom and South Africa, genetic nurses, who constitute an emerging specialty, provide some of the counseling.

Genetic counseling in its modern form began after World War II. In 1947 Sheldon Reed coined the term to replace earlier terms from the 1930s, such as "genetic hygiene" and "genetic advice," which sounded too eugenic. Genetic counseling was supposed to be nondirective, providing medical and genetic information on which patients could base their own decisions. In 1974, a committee of the American Society of Human Genetics (ASHG) set forth the following goals of genetic counseling:

- helping individuals and couples understand their options and the present state of medical knowledge so that they can make informed decisions,
- helping individuals and couples adjust to and cope with their genetic problems,
- removing or lessening patient guilt or anxiety,
- helping individuals and couples achieve their parenting goals,
- preventing disease or abnormality,
- improving the general health and vigor of the population, and
- reducing the number of carriers of genetic disorders in the population.

Studies in the United States and worldwide found that almost 100 percent of genetics professionals subscribed to the first five goals; smaller majorities subscribed to the last two, more "eugenic," goals.

Most genetics professionals worldwide say that they will refuse to make decisions for patients; but in practice and outside English-speaking nations, much counseling after prenatal diagnosis is directive. As with any medical service, there are problems in communication. One study of typical counseling sessions of forty-five to sixty minutes found that in only 26 percent of cases did both professional and patient become aware of what the other most wanted to discuss. These were largely white, well-educated patients. Communication with minority groups is more difficult, as about half do not keep their appointments. Also, counselors may have difficulty explaining genetic disorders in different cultural, religious, and socioeconomic contexts. Finally, professional counselors recognize the difficulty in providing truly nondirective counseling.

FOR FURTHER READING

Fraser, F. Clarke. 1974. "Genetic Counselling." *American Journal of Human Genetics* 26: 636–639.

Kessler, Seymour. 1992. "Psychological Aspects of Genetic Counselling. VII: Thoughts on Directiveness." *Journal of Genetic Counselling* 1: 9–18.

Rapp, Rayna. 1988. "Chromosomes and Communication: The Discourse of Genetic Counselling." *Medical Anthropology* 2: 143–147.

Reed, Sheldon. 1974. "A Short History of Genetic Counselling." *Social Biology* 21: 332–339.

Sorenson, James R., Judith P. Swazey, and Norman A. Scotch. 1981. *Reproductive Pasts, Reproductive Futures: Genetic Counselling and Its Effectiveness.* New York: Alan R. Liss.

Wertz, Dorothy C. 1997. "Society and the Not-So-New Genetics: What Are We Afraid Of? Some Future Predictions from a Social Scientist." *Journal of Contemporary Health Law and Policy* 13: 299–346.

Wertz, Dorothy C., and John C. Fletcher. 1988. "Attitudes of Genetic Counsellors: A Multinational Survey." *American Journal of Human Genetics* 42: 592–600.

Wertz, Dorothy C., John C. Fletcher, and John J. Mulvihill. 1990. "Medical Geneticists Confront Ethical Dilemmas: Cross-Cultural Comparisons Among 18 Nations." *American Journal of Human Genetics* 46: 1200–1213.

sixty-nine

Ectogenesis

DAVID N. JAMES

The word "ectogenesis" was coined in 1924 by the British biologist J.B.S. Haldane. It refers to the prospect of growing a human fetus to term totally outside a woman's womb. The development of in vitro fertilization to treat infertility, combined with ever more sophisticated neonatal intensive care of premature babies, makes development of an artificial womb seem possible. Researchers in Japan have recently developed the means to keep goat and lamb fetuses that are near full gestation alive ex utero.

But should ectogenesis be further developed? Peter Singer, a prominent Australian bioethicist, and Deane Wells, a member of the Australian Parliament, defend ectogenesis as both a way to save aborted fetuses and a way to treat infertility. Many writers, including Singer and Wells, connect ectogenesis with abortion. Assuming that the right to an abortion is a right to be free of an unwanted pregnancy, not a right to the death of one's fetus, the idea is that ectogenesis would make it possible to reconcile survival of the fetus with the right to abortion on demand. Thus, many believe, ectogenesis resolves the conflict between a woman's right to choose abortion and her fetus's right to life by allowing both to be exercised.

The main problem with this argument may be seen once abortions and fetal transplants are clearly distinguished. Over 90 percent of abortions are performed in the first trimester of pregnancy using vacuum aspiration. The aspirator uses suction to extract the fetus, which at this point in pregnancy is just a few centimeters long. Such an early abortion is safe, but the fetus does not emerge intact from the uterus. A fetal transplant would be more like a cesarean section than a first-trimester vacuum-aspiration abortion: It is an elaborate surgical procedure aimed at the delicate removal of the fetus from the mother's placenta and its transfer and attachment to an external machine. Unlike an early abortion, a fetal transplant requires general anesthesia and surgery within the uterus with all the risks of medical complications that accompany such an invasive procedure.

The moral right at issue here is the right to choose which medical procedures one undergoes based on a full disclosure of relevant risks. This right to informed consent is ultimately grounded in the patient's autonomy. Autonomy guarantees the right to choose a less risky and invasive abortion over a more risky and invasive fetal transplantation based on one's own judgment of the foreseeable risks. Since many, perhaps most, women would choose not to undergo more risky fetal transplants, it is mistaken to suppose that in general the right to abortion could ever be reconciled with the survival of fetuses through ectogenesis. The social and financial costs of this proposal would also be staggering. Current newborn intensive care often costs over $100,000 per baby, and it is safe to assume that ectogenesis would cost more. Fetal transplants on the same scale as current abortions in developed countries—1.5 million annually in the United States, for example—would quickly result in a need for orphanages and related social services to care for the hundreds of thousands of new unwanted ectogenetic children who would be born every year.

The second major argument for developing this technology is that ectogenesis would provide an improvement over surrogate motherhood to enable infertile couples to have children. Conflicts over child custody, the behavior of the surrogate, her feelings of attachment to the baby she bears, and her complex emotional and legal relationship to the adoptive parents would no longer cause problems because there would no longer be a human surrogate.

Despite these advantages, a broader look at the social context reveals the weakness of this argument. Defenders of ectogenesis most often define infertility as a medical problem and then proceed to discuss the solution to this problem solely in medical terms. But adoption of existing orphaned or unwanted children allows couples to satisfy their desire to nurture. Adoption enriches the lives of the adopted children, relieves society of the expense of their care, and promotes the goal of limiting the population.

It might be objected that too few children are available for adoption to make for a workable option. The shortage of adoptive babies has led to long waits and more stringent requirements facing prospective adoptive parents. Yet the number of children available is not an eternal given but is responsive to policy choices. For one thing, there are already large numbers of older children and handicapped, nonwhite, and Third World infants available for adoption. Of course, adopting these children often requires support for their special needs. But insofar as education, counseling, and civil law can do so, we could try to make adoption of these already living children administratively simpler, less expensive, and socially more normal instead of trying to increase the supply of young, white, healthy babies.

Feminists have focused attention on ectogenesis as representing more than just health risks to women. Ectogenesis could imply that pregnancy is merely a collection of bodily processes and thus undermine women's reproductive labor. The procedure also seems to downgrade women's natural biological capacities by suggesting that the way to treat infertility is to remove reproduction from women's bodies completely.

FOR FURTHER READING

James, David N. 1987. "Ectogenesis: A Reply to Singer and Wells." *Bioethics* 1: 80–99.

Lupton, M. L. 1997. "Artificial Wombs: Medical Miracle, Legal Nightmare." *Journal of Medical Law* 16(3): 621–633.

Murphy, Julien S. 1992. "Is Pregnancy Necessary? Feminist Concerns About Ectogenesis." In Helen Bequaert Holmes and Laura Purdy, eds., *Feminist Perspectives in Medical Ethics*. Bloomington: Indiana University Press.

Singer, Peter, and Deane Wells. 1985. *Making Babies: The New Science and Ethics of Conception*. New York: Charles Scribner's Sons. First published in 1984 as *The Reproductive Revolution: New Ways of Making Babies*. Oxford: Oxford University Press.

Wells, Deane. 1987. "Ectogenesis, Justice and Utility: A Reply to James." *Bioethics* 1: 372–379.

Yasufuku, M., et al. 1998. "Arterio-Venous Extracorporeal Membrane Oxygenation of Fetal Goat Incubated in Artificial Amniotic Fluid (Artificial Placenta): Influence on Lung Growth and Maturation." *Journal of Pediatric Surgery* 33(3): 442–448.

seventy

Genetic Screening and German-Based Eugenics— Old and New

ANNE WALDSCHMIDT

Eugenics in World War II Germany

German history has taught us, in a particularly brutal way, that the social stigmatization, ostracism, and institutional segregation of people with disabilities can end in eugenic-based abuses. Since the industrial revolution, the physically and mentally disabled, the psychologically ill, and other similarly challenged persons have been socially stigmatized; this treatment has included systemic abuse and routine institutionalization. Those who lived in institutions separate from their families were typically defenseless in the face of so-called scientific and political agendas.

The segregation of people with disabilities into custodial institutions prior to 1933 was an important prerequisite for the eugenic measures of "racial hygiene" perpetrated by the German National Socialists. It permitted the National Socialists to seize inmates without hindrance and to transport them to large camps where the disabled were eventually murdered. Shortly after the Nazis rose to power, they began immediately and systematically to eradicate persons designated as social liabilities, "unworthy of living." They began with programs of forced sterilization in order to prevent people with disabilities from procreating. Later they murdered designated disabled people under the guise of so-called euthanasia.

As early as the first half of 1933, a committee of experts for population and racial policy was set up by the Ministry of the Interior. It was their task to draw up legislation and regulations that would make forced sterilization legal. The result was the notorious Law for the Prevention of Hereditarily Ill Future Generations, which was brought into effect in 1934. From that point onward, forced sterilization was permitted on individuals who had been diagnosed with the following illnesses: congenital mental deficiency, schizophrenia, manic-depressive psychosis, hereditary epilepsy, Huntington's disease, grave physical deformity, and severe alcoholism.

In the years that followed, the opportunities to carry out forced sterilization increased at a rapid rate. The measures that at first affected primarily the institutionalized disabled and ill were, as of 1935, carried out on healthy family members as well. Furthermore, in that same year, it became permissible to perform forced abortions on women up until their sixth month of pregnancy, a procedure that was also combined with forced sterilization. Eventually, male castration was also included under the law, and in 1936, the use of X rays and radium rays, both highly controversial, health-endangering methods of operation, became approved procedures of sterilization and castration. Meanwhile, circulars were published in which the terms "hereditary suffering" and "mental deficiency" were used to address the worth of the affected with regard to the national community as well as his or her productivity. Within such parameters, virtually anyone could be forcibly sterilized. By the end of the war, at least 300,000 people had become victims of the Law for the Prevention of Hereditarily Ill Future Generations. In the early 1940s, a second phase of the eugenic policy to limit and eradicate people with disabilities began—its purpose was to provide a "final solution" to the disabled question.

The first victims of this phase were newborn children. A secret bill passed by the Ministry of the Interior in August 1939 required midwives and doctors to report the birth of all "misshapen figures." The Berlin Committee for the Scientific Registration of the Hereditarily or Inherently Handicapped inspected these reports and passed them on to medical experts. Its recommendations then led to the admission of these "scientifically interesting cases" to thirty special children's homes. There, the children were subjected to medical experiments and were often killed in the process.

Shortly after the beginning of this child "euthanasia" program, the political and bureaucratic guidelines for the nationwide eradication of all disabled and hereditarily ill persons were established. The program was set in motion by an informal authorization by Hitler addressed to Reichsleiter Bouhler and his consultant on health policy. It was deliberately backdated to September 1, 1939—the first day of World War II. By the end of 1939, questionnaires demanding information regarding individual patients, their type of illness, length of stay, and productivity were sent out to the directors of all institutions. These served as registration forms and were then screened by three expert doctors who determined the fate of each individual. In accordance with their decisions, lists bearing the names of patients to be transferred were sent back to the institutions. Those intended for euthanasia were taken to the extermination facilities in inconspicuous gray buses under the cover of a company claiming to serve the public need for transportation of the sick.

The authorities went to great lengths to keep these murders of the disabled secret. Nevertheless, the population became alarmed, and isolated instances of resistance surfaced. On August 3, 1941, this resistance culminated in a significant sermon delivered by the bishop of Münster, Graf von Galen, who openly criticized the regime's euthanasia program. Three weeks later, as a result of a verbal directive given by Hitler, the program was terminated. Despite this, euthanasia continued among psychiatric patients, people with tuberculosis, "racially undesirable" children, forced-labor convicts, and "unproductive" concentration camp inmates. The extermination camps were the scene of cruel and sadistic experimentation carried out by doctors and scientists. The number of those murdered in the name of "racial hygiene" is estimated to be between 100,000 and 275,000.

Eugenics Today

Can history be repeated? The large institutions that were starting points for the extermination programs of the National Socialists still exist. During the past fifty years, in Germany as well as globally, the system of segregating the disabled has not been dismantled. To the contrary, it has been expanded with only superficial improvements. Despite the efforts of integration and independent living programs, handicapped persons continue to be subjected to special treatment in all aspects of life from separate kindergartens and schools to special education measures, segregated workshops for the handicapped, specially made living quarters at the edge of the city, and segregated recreational facilities.

In Germany, the trend since the beginning of the 1970s in the segregation of persons on the basis of their physical "quality" can be seen in the establishment of human genetic counseling. Today, almost every large city has an advisory bureau for human genetics, generally affiliated with universities. Increasing numbers of established doctors offer their services for genetic consultation and screening. Since 1974, such consultations have been financed by standard medical insurance. Since 1976, eugenic evidence has been sufficient ground for granting an abortion, and prenatal examinations are now routine for pregnant women over the age of thirty-five. The diagnosis of disability means, in the majority of cases, prenatal death.

An important difference between yesterday's eugenics and today's human genetics is the earlier lack of knowledge and techniques regarding prenatal selection. At the time of Hitler's final solution, methods of embryonic examination did not exist. The analysis of the amniotic fluid (amniocentesis), the first invasive method for the examination of fetal cells in the uterus and the study of chromosomes, was developed only in the 1950s and 1960s. Today, prenatal diagnostics are routine, and findings indicating illness almost always result in the abortion of the screened fetus. Thus abortion on the grounds of eugenic indication is now widely accepted. It appears that the earlier in a lifetime that eugenic selection occurs, the more it will be openly accepted. Here is where we encounter the difficult question of whether the abortion of "abnormal" unborn children can be compared with the killing of disabled adults as it was practiced by the National Socialists during the war. This is not to say that abortion and National Socialist mass murder should be considered equal; a woman's individual decision—although made under social pressure—is much different from the program of murder carried out by a totalitarian state. There is, however, a similarity: In both cases, a life-or-death decision is made based on arbitrary evaluations of the worth of the lives of individual human beings.

First developed at the end of the nineteenth century, the improvement of human genetic makeup, initially the science of eugenics and later the German National Socialists' program of "racial hygiene," does indeed have much in common with today's human genetics. Both sciences research human hereditary diseases, and the knowledge acquired by both has always been aimed at the prevention of these diseases. So-called sick genes must be diminished and healthy ones propagated. Human genetic advising, prenatal screening, and genome analysis today belong to the standard corpus of medical services offered and are conducted by doctors on a regular basis. Eugenic measures have been redefined as treatment and therapy. Those working in human genetics argue that as medical doctors they strive only to prevent individual suffering and do not take into account any eugenic politics. They draw a sharp contrast between the state-run population policy implemented against the wishes of those affected by it and today's human genetic counseling and diagnostics at the request of patients themselves. A survey conducted by the German Parliament in 1992 showed that genetic testing during pregnancy was approved by 47 percent of those questioned and only 21 percent of respondents were worried about the dangers of human genetic counseling and diagnostics.

Opposition to Genetic Screening

Persons with disabilities have been among the first to speak out against genetic counseling and screening, arguing that modern human genetic practices implicitly negate their right to life. Like so many other protest movements, the West German disabled persons movement developed during the 1970s, when people with physical and mental handicaps first spoke out against their subordination to "professional helpers." They began to form their own groups throughout West Germany and even behind the walls of institutions and segregated facilities. Self-help was their key concept.

There also emerged something entirely new: the so-called *Krüppelgruppen* (cripple groups). The starting point for these associations, unlike that of previous self-help groups, was the state of disability itself, not the specific causes of the impairment. Regardless of whether the disability was due to a work-related accident or genetic makeup, the common factor uniting all these people was their segregation from society. The *Krüppelgruppen* were the origins of the German independent-living movement of people with disabilities that emerged in the 1980s and is, at present, very strong and successful. It develops antidiscrimination policies and supports civil rights for all people with disabilities.

Society typically singles out and marginalizes the disabled. Handicapped people, in turn, see themselves as being discriminated against by the exclusionary attitudes of those around them. Members of the independent-living movement argue that society must fully accept persons with disabilities into the mainstream. They demand radical changes in living standards for all people with disabilities on the premise of rights, not charity. Services available to people with disabilities were—and still are, to a large extent—based on the concepts of disability as deficiency and abnormality. The abilities and talents of people with disabilities are often ignored, robbing them of a sense of social purpose and vision. Also, being disabled is not a static condition that can never be modified or developed. "Disability" is actually a social construct produced by complex human interactions and through sociopolitical discourse. When encountered every day, it becomes a permanent life experience and part of the individual's identity. Being disabled means being considered economically and socially inferior, that is, being defined as inefficient and unable to survive in a competitive and individualistic society.

Women, Disabilities, and Genetic Screening

To live as a disabled woman in Western society means being exposed to many different forms of discrimination. Because of their ability to conceive and bear children, women with disabilities have experiences to which men, whether disabled or not, cannot relate. Nor can nondisabled women relate; disability as a way of life is often so foreign to them that they sometimes reject it in others. Also, a disabled woman is far more likely to be unemployed than a disabled man or a nondisabled woman. It is often impossible for the disabled woman, however, to fall back on the standard female alternative of a career as a spouse, housewife, and mother. Most disabled women are not considered attractive enough in the normative sense to be serious contenders as future wives. Moreover, there is usually doubt about whether they are mobile enough or psychologically and physically strong enough to function as housewives and mothers. Finally, society has difficulty accepting that such women may have childbearing capabilities, and this attitude has resulted in a kind of childbearing "prohibition" for the disabled.

Herein lies one of the reasons for the independent-living movement's opposition to genetic counseling and screening. If disability is a socially constructed problem, then the idea that the problem must be solved by eliminating the problematic person before birth is hard to buy, especially by women with disabilities. Yet medical doctors tend to reinforce this childbearing "prohibition," and often their message is unmistakable: Disabled women should not bring disabled children into this world. As a result, women with disabilities were one of the first targets of genetic screening and counseling in the interests of preserving a healthy, "qualitatively functional" population. This is just one example of how genetic consultation with its implied birth preferences and prohibitions can affect women by controlling reproductive behavior and sexuality. This form of counseling may at its deepest level be not only handicapping but misogynist.

Conclusion

In both the early science of eugenics with its political applications in World War II Germany and the contemporary genetic science, the principle of selection plays an important role. But whereas formerly only those already born were subject to evaluations of their quality, today the unborn are judged as well. Decisions that at first glance appear to be purely medical emerge, upon closer examination, as socially based. Since 1945 there have been extensive scientific developments in the field of human genetics. Gene technology has revolutionized its methods and contributed greatly to the acquisition of knowledge. However, despite modernization and the perfection of methods in the study of human genetics, there is strong reason to doubt that scientific gains have been matched by gains in ethical and social awareness.

FOR FURTHER READING

Bayertz, Kurt. 1987. *Gene Ethics: Problems in the Technicalization of Human Reproduction*. Reinbek: Rowohlt.
Ewinkel, Carola, et al., eds. 1985. *Disabled by Gender—Specific Characteristic Female: A Book About Disabled Women*. Munich: AG Spak.
Germany. Bureau of the German Parliament for the Assessment of Technical Advancements. 1992. *Survey for Gene Technology and Genome Analysis*. Bonn: N.p.
Germany. Ministry for Youth, Family and Health, ed. 1979. *Genetic Counselling. A Model Attempt by the Federal Government in Frankfurt and Marburg*. Bonn/Bad Godesberg: Eigenverlag.
Kaupen-Haas, Heidrun, ed. 1986. *The Grip on the Population: Actuality and Continuity in Nazi Population Policy*. Vol. 1 of *Writings of the Hamburg Foundation for Twentieth Century Social History*. Nördlingen: Greno.
Klee, Ernst. 1983. *Euthanasia in the NS State: The "Extermination of Unworthy Lives."* Frankfurt am Main: Fischer.
Müller-Hill, Benno. 1984. *Deadly Science: The Segregation of Jews, Gypsies and the Mentally Handicapped, 1933–1945*. Reinbek: Rowohlt.
Schindele, Eva. 1990. *Glass Uteri. Prenatal Diagnosis: Curse or Blessing?* Frankfurt am Main: Fischer.
Schroeder-Kurth, Traute, ed. 1989. *Medical Genetics in the Federal Republic of Germany: An Inventory with Political, Medical and Ethical Concepts and Patient-Group Opinions*. Frankfurt am Main and Munich: Schweizer.
Sierck, Udo, and Nati Radtke. 1984. *The Charitable Mafia: From the Hereditary Health Report to Human Genetic Counselling*. Hamburg: Eigenverlag.
Waldschmidt, Anne. 1992a. "Against Selection of Human Life—People with Disabilities Oppose Genetic Counselling." *Issues in Reproductive and Genetic Engineering* 5(2): 155–167.
Waldschmidt, Anne. 1992b. "Human Genetic Counselling Today—An Instrument of Selection?" In Anne-Dore Stein, ed., *Quality of Life Instead of Quality Control in Human Life*. Berlin: Marhold Edition in the Scientific Publishing House Volker-Spiess.
Weingart, Peter, Jürgen Kroll, and Kurt Bayertz. 1989. *Race, Blood and Gene: The History of Eugenics and Racial Hygiene in Germany*. Frankfurt am Main: Suhrkamp.
Wunder, Michael, and Udo Sierck, eds. 1982. *They Call It Care: The Disabled Between Extermination and Opposition*. Berlin: Verlagsgesellschaft Gesundheit.

About the Editor and Contributors

Rona Achilles is coordinator of family planning research for the Department of Public Health in Toronto. She worked as a consultant for the Canadian Royal Commission on New Reproductive Technologies and has written extensively on the psychosocial issues surrounding donor insemination.

Marjorie Altergott is research associate at the University of Illinois and a visiting faculty member at DePaul University in the School for New Learning. Her area of research includes midwifery policy and infant feeding.

Sharyn Roach Anleu is associate professor of sociology at the Flinders University of South Australia. Her teaching areas include the sociology of law, deviance, and criminology. Her current research investigates the local regulation of medical science, and the role of guilty pleas in the Australian criminal justice system. She has published on women in law, the legal profession, feminist legal theory, surrogacy, and deviance and has just completed *Law and Social Change* (forthcoming).

Françoise Baylis is associate professor in the Office of Bioethics Education and Research, Faculty of Medicine, and the Department of Philosophy at Dalhousie University. Her research is supported by grants from Associated Medical Services, Toronto, and the Dean's Development Fund, Dalhousie University.

Andrea L. Bonnicksen is professor in the Department of Political Science, Northern Illinois University. She was a Rockefeller Foundation fellow at the Institute for the Medical Humanities, University of Texas. Her research interests include reproductive and genetics policy. She is a member of the Ethics Committee of the American Society for Reproductive Medicine. Her publications include *In Vitro Fertilization—Building Policy from Laboratories to Legislatures* (1989) and, articles in the *Journal of Law, Medicine, and Ethics, The Hastings Center Report, Cambridge Quarterly of Health Care Ethics*, and *Politics and the Life Sciences*.

Richard Boroditsky is associate professor, Department of Obstetrics, Gynecology, and Reproductive Sciences at the University of Manitoba, and head of the University Section of Gynecology. He has lectured widely and published extensively on sexuality education and clinical research in the areas of family planning and menopausal management. He is chair of the Social and Sexual Issues Committee of the Society of Obstetricians and Gynecologists of Canada and was president of Planned Parenthood Manitoba and chair of the Manitoba Section of District VI of the American College of Obstetricians and Gynecologists.

James J. Boulton is clinical professor in the Department of Obstetrics and Gynecology at the University of Alberta. He is also head of the Department of Obstetrics and Gynaecology at the Grey Nuns Hospital in Edmonton, Alberta.

Annette Burfoot is associate professor of sociology at Queen's University, Kingston, Ontario. Her areas of teaching and research include women and reproductive technologies, feminist theory, popular culture of the body, and the sociology of science and technology. She has published widely on national policy initiatives in reproduction, the popular representation of women in science fiction film, and the social impact of biotechnology.

Joan C. Callahan is professor of philosophy and director of Women's Studies at the University of Kentucky, where she teaches ethics, social and political philosophy, and feminist theory. In addition to a number of articles in these areas, she has published *Ethical Issues in Professional Life* (1988); *Preventing Birth: Contemporary Methods and Related Moral Controversies*, with James W. Knight (1989); *Menopause: A Midlife Passage* (1993); and *Reproduction, Ethics, and the Law: Feminist Perspectives* (1995).

Douglas T. Carrell has worked in the area of human infertility for the past nineteen years. He is currently director of the Andrology and in Vitro Fertilization Laboratories at the University of Utah School of Medicine and also director of the Andrology and in Vitro Fertilization Laboratories at Abbott Northwestern Hospital in Minneapolis, Minnesota. His major areas of research interest include sperm fertilization and the acrosome reaction, abnormalities of sperm morphology, and human in vitro fertilization.

Mary Anne Coffey is a freelance editor and researcher. Her academic interests include alternative family forms, reproductive technologies old and new, and feminist organizational structures. She has a personal and political interest in the changes women activists have made in union structures and bargaining goals.

Jean Cohen is a gynecologist and obstetrician and director of the Centre de Stérilité at the Hôpital de Sèvres since 1974. He has served as president of the Société Française de Gynécologie, the European Society of Human Reproduction and Engineering (ESHRE), the Société Française pour l'Etude de la Stérilité, and the International Federation of Fertility Societies (IFFS). He has written numerous medical articles and textbooks and made many instructional films in the area of gynecology with an emphasis in assisted conception.

Susan Daniel was awarded a postdoctoral fellowship from the Medical Research Council (Canada) in 1985 to work at the Jackson Laboratory, Bar Harbor, Maine. In 1987, she became the manager and technical services scientist in the In Vitro Fertilization Program at University Hospital, London, and is scientific director for the Embryology and Andrology Laboratories at the Montgomery Fertility Institute/Center for Reproductive Medicine and Genetics, Suburban Hospital.

Ken Daniels is associate professor and former head of the Department of Social Work, University of Canterbury, Christchurch, New Zealand. He has been researching, writing, and counseling in the area of assisted reproduction since 1978.

Anne Donchin is associate professor of philosophy and former director of Women's Studies at Indiana University/Purdue University in Indianapolis. She teaches and writes principally in the areas of medical ethics and feminist philosophy (preferably in combination). For the past several years her interests have focused predominantly around feminist reworkings of bioethical theory and social and ethical issues underlying debates about new reproductive technologies. She is a founding coordinator of the International Network on Feminist Approaches to Bioethics and coeditor (with Laura Purdy) of *Embodying Bioethics: Recent Feminist Advances* (1999). She is currently completing a manuscript titled *Procreation, Power, and Personal Autonomy: Feminist Reflections*.

About the Editor and Contributors

Lynette Dumble is senior research fellow, Department of History and Philosophy of Science, University of Melbourne and coordinator of the Global Sisterhood Network. She is a medical scientist whose research publication subjects include human and animal organ transplantation, immunobiology, medical ethics, and women's health. She was senior research fellow in the University of Melbourne's Department of Surgery at the Royal Melbourne Hospital (1970–1997) and visiting professor (surgery) at the University of Texas in Houston (1991–1994).

Robert Gore-Langton is a recipient of a Career Scientist Award from the Ontario Ministry of Health and a principal investigator in the Medical Research Council Interdisciplinary Research Group in Reproductive Biology. In 1991 he joined University Hospital in London, Ontario, to establish a clinical research program in micromanipulation and preimplantation diagnosis. He is senior staff scientist in the Department of Pediatrics, Division of Genetics, of Georgetown University, working within the Diagnostic Development Branch of the National Center for Human Genome Research. His current research includes cellular and molecular aspects of oocyte and embryo development, preimplantation genetics, and new reproductive technologies.

Erica Haimes is professor of sociology in the Department of Social Policy, University of Newcastle, United Kingdom. She has conducted research into health care, adoption, and various aspects of assisted conception. She is currently writing a book on identity and changing family forms. She has previously published articles on gamete donation, donor anonymity, and the policy aspects of assisted conception. She is coauthor (with Noel Timms) of *Adoption, Identity and Social Policy* (1985), and coeditor (with Ken Daniels) of *Donor Insemination: International Social Science Perspectives*(1998).

Helen Bequaert Holmes is facilitator for the Center for Genetics, Ethics and Women, Amherst, Massachusetts, and the founder and a former coordinator for the international network Feminist Approaches to Bioethics. She has published on sex selection, in vitro fertilization, and the genome project. She is editor of *Issues in Reproductive Technology I: An Anthology* (1992), coeditor with Betty B. Hoskins and Michael Gross of *The Custom-Made Child? Women-Centered Perspectives* (1981), and coeditor with Laura Purdy of *Feminist Perspectives in Medical Ethics* (1992). She has researched feminist assessment of reproductive technologies in the United States, New Zealand (as a Fulbright scholar), and the Netherlands.

Richard T. Hull is professor emeritus of philosophy, State University of New York at Buffalo and executive director, Texas Council for the Humanities (Austin). He is a past president of the American Society for Value Inquiry. He has edited several books: *Ethical Issues in the New Reproductive Technologies* (1990); *A Quarter Century of Value Inquiry* (1993); W. H. Werkmeister's *Martin Heidegger on the Way* (posthumous publication, 1996); *Presidential Addresses of the American Philosophical Association, 1901–1910* (1998); *Presidential Addresses of the American Philosophical Association, 1911–1920* (1998). He is the author of numerous articles and chapters on medical ethics, philosophy of medicine, nursing ethics, and philosophy of mind.

H. Patricia Hynes is professor of public health at Boston University School of Public Health and director of the Urban Environmental Health Initiative. She works on issues of urban environment, feminism, and environmental justice. She is author of *The Recurring Silent Spring* (1989), *EarthRight* (1990), and *Taking Population out of the Equation: Preformulating I=PAT* (1993). Her current work, *A Patch of Eden* (1996), a book on community gardens in inner cities and their potential for social justice and urban ecology, won the 1996 National Arbor Day Foundation Book Award.

David N. James was associate professor of philosophy at Old Dominion University, Norfolk, Virginia. His publications include articles in bioethics (with a special focus on reproductive technology), business ethics, moral theory, aesthetics, and social philosophy. He coedited a book on ethical problems in university sports, *Rethinking College Athletics*, in 1991, and he authored two audiotapes in the 1995 Great Moral Issues series from Knowledge Products, one on abortion and one on euthanasia. He is recently deceased.

Regina H. Kenen is professor in the Department of Sociology at Trenton State College of New Jersey. Her publications include *Pregnancy at Work* (1998) and *Reproductive Hazards in the Workplace* (1993).

Marta Kirejczyk is associate professor in gender and technology at the Department of Philosophy of Science and Technology at the University of Twente in the Netherlands. Her present research focuses on the connection among the women's movement, the development of new reproductive technologies, and policymaking in the Netherlands. She is author of *Met Technologie Gezond?* (1996).

Rosalind Ekman Ladd is professor of philosophy at Wheaton College in Massachusetts and lecturer in pediatrics at the Brown University Medical School. She serves on three hospital ethics committees and has published a number of articles in medical ethics. She is coauthor with E. N. Forman of *Ethical Dilemmas in Pediatrics: A Case Study Approach* (1991; reprinted 1996).

Paul Lauritzen is professor of religious studies and director of the Program in Applied Ethics at John Carroll University in Cleveland, Ohio. He is the author of *Pursuing Parenthood: Ethical Issues in Assisted Reproduction* (1993).

André Lemay is a certified endocrinologist and medical biochemist with subspecialty training in reproductive endocrinology. Scholar of the Medical Research Council of Canada, he was among pioneers in the clinical applications of GnRH agonists. His main activities are related to clinical and basic research concerning mainly endometriosis and hirsutism and sex hormone replacement therapy.

Abby Lippman is professor of epidemiology and biostatistics at McGill University. She is widely published in feminist health, the social sciences and medicine, and the social impact of new reproductive and genetic technologies.

Judith Lorber is professor emerita of sociology at Brooklyn College and the Graduate School, City University of New York. She is the author of *Gender Inequality: Feminist Theories and Politics* (1998), *Gender and the Social Construction of Illness* (1997), *Paradoxes of Gender* (1994), and *Women Physicians: Careers, Status and Power* (1984). She has published numerous articles on gender, women as health care workers and patients, and sociological aspects of the new procreative technologies. She was founding editor of *Gender and Society*, past chair of the Sex and Gender section of the American Sociological Association, and received the 1996 ASA Jessie Bernard career award.

Elizabeth Mathiot-Moen focused in her research, publications, and teaching on social demography, reproductive politics, population planning, women and development, and grassroots development theory and strategy. Research sites included energy boom-and-bust communities in western Colorado and the Madurai area of Tamilnadu, India. Elizabeth Mathiot-Moen died suddenly in 1993.

Michelle A. Mullen is assistant professor in the Departments of Obstetrics and Gynaecology and Health Administration at the University of Toronto. She is author of a variety of publications on reproductive technologies, ethics, and public policy and acted as a consultant to the Canadian Royal Commission on New Reproductive Technologies.

Kathy Munro is principal policy officer with the Legislative Projects Unit of Queensland Health. She has also worked in women's health issues in service delivery and policy development for various state governments in Australia. In 1990, Kathy was awarded an ANZAC fellowship to travel to New Zealand to study the outcomes of *Inquiry into Allegations Concerning the Treatment of Cervical Cancer at National Women's Hospital and into Other Related Matters.*

Christine Overall is professor in the Department of Philosophy at Queen's University, Kingston, Ontario. She is the author of *Ethics and Human Reproduction: A Feminist Analysis* (1987), *Human Reproduction: Principles, Practices, Policies* (1993), and *A Feminist I: Reflections From Academia* (1998). She is editor, with William Zion, of *Perspectives on AIDS: Ethical and Social Issues* (1991).

Claire D. F. Parsons has since 1983 been undertaking research in the public health arena as a medical social scientist. She has worked in developing countries of the Pacific and Southeast Asia as well as Australia. She has a strong interest in women's health, risk perception, HIV/AIDS, multiculturalism and health, and primary health care in general. She was involved in the Women and AIDS community development program, which is conducting a trial of a model for a family-based infectious diseases (including HIV/AIDS) care program in Thailand. She has numerous publications in the area of public health and in 1998 shifted her focus to update her knowledge of clinical settings.

Susan P. Phillips is associate professor of family medicine at Queen's University in Kingston, Ontario. She is the author of numerous academic articles on women's health, medical education, and sexual harassment. Her clinical work includes sexual health and family planning.

Laura M. Purdy is a bioethicist at the University of Toronto Joint Centre for Bioethics and the Toronto Hospital, and is professor of philosophy in the University of Toronto Philosophy Department and at Wells College. Most of her research has been in applied ethics, particularly reproductive ethics. She is coeditor with Helen Bequaert Holmes of *Feminist Perspectives in Medical Ethics* (1992) and with Anne Donchin of *Embodying Bioethics: Recent Feminist Advances* (1999). She is author of *In their Best Interest: The Case Against Equal Rights for Children* (1992) and *Reproducing Persons: Feminist Issues in Bioethics* (1996).

Sue Rosser is director of the Center for Women's Studies and Gender Research and professor of anthropology at the University of Florida–Gainesville. She has written five books, edited two collections, and written over eighty journal articles on the theoretical and applied problems of women and science. Her three most recent books are *Women's Health: Missing from U.S. Medicine* (1994), *Teaching the Majority* (1995), and *Re-engineering Female Friendly Science* (1997).

Robyn Rowland is a social psychologist, professor in Women's Studies, and former head of the School of Social Inquiry at Deakin University, Victoria, Australia. She was a member of the Asche Committee on Reproductive Technology, whose report *Creating Children: A Uniform Approach to the Law and Practice of Reproductive Technology in Australia* (1985) was tabled in Federal Parliament and formed the basis of the establishment of the National Bioethics Consultative Council. She has lectured in Britain, Ireland, Europe, and the United States on these issues. Robyn Rowland has published widely in scholarly journals on reproductive technology and is a contributor to many books in this area including *Test-tube Women: What Future Motherhood?* (1984) and *Made to Order: The Myth of Reproductive and Genetic Progress* (1987). Her latest book is *Living Laboratories: Women and Reproductive Technology* (1992; reprint 1993).

Sheryl Burt Ruzek is professor of health education at Temple University, Philadelphia. She is the author of books and articles on women's health issues and medical technologies. In addition to serving on the U.S. Food and Drug Administration Obstetrics and Gynecology Devices Panel and the Philadelphia Health Department Maternal and Infant Health Advisory Council, she edits the Health, Society and Policy Series (with Irving Zola) for Temple University Press.

S. Nan Schuurmans is regional program clinical director of the Women's Health Program for the Capital Health Authority in Edmonton, Alberta. She is also assistant clinical professor at the University of Alberta, Edmonton, and is past president of the Society of Obstetricians and Gynaecologists of Canada (SOGC).

Laura Shanner is an associate professor in the John Dossetor Health Ethics Centre and the Department of Public Health Services at the University of Alberta. She has served on a Canadian Federal Ministry of Health discussion group to refine regulations regarding embryo research and is a coordinator of the International Network of Feminist Approaches to Bioethics. Her main interests include multidisciplinary approaches to genetic and reproductive technologies, pregnant embodiment, and bioethics education.

Patricia Spallone worked for twelve years as a biochemist at the University of Pennsylvania School of Medicine in Philadelphia, Pennsylvania. Since 1985, she has been working in England as a freelance researcher and writer on women's health and social issues in science and technology, primarily on reproductive technology and genetic engineering. Her books include *Generation Games: Genetic Engineering and the Future for Our Lives* (1992), *Beyond Conception: The New Politics of Reproduction* (1989), and (coedited with Deborah Lynn Steinberg) *Made to Order: The Myth of Reproductive and Genetic Progress* (1987). She also has worked as a volunteer in women's health provision.

Deborah Lynn Steinberg is lecturer in the Department of Sociology at the University of Warwick. She has published since 1986 on the new reproductive technologies and her major works include *Bodies in Glass: Genetics, Eugenics, Embryo Ethics* (1997), (coedited with Debbie Epstein and Richard Johnson), *Border Patrols: Policing the Boundaries of Heterosexuality* (1997), and (coedited with Patricia Spallone) *Made to Order: The Myth of Reproductive and Genetic Progress* (1987).

Patricia A. Stephenson is health services researcher/health systems analyst with a particular interest in women's health care. She has served on the faculty at the University of Washington. Currently, she lives in Sweden, where she works as the managing editor of the *European Journal of Public Health* and serves as a consultant health systems analyst directing field projects for several international agencies.

Ellen 't Hoen is one of the cofounders of DES Action the Netherlands and its coordinator for ten years. She is presently international coordinator at the independent French drug and therapeutics journal *La Revue Prescrire* and the coordinator of the International Society of Drug Bulletins (ISDB).

Nahid Toubia is the first woman surgeon in Sudan. She has worked as an associate for women's reproductive health at the Population Council in New York and is currently assistant professor in clinical public health at Columbia University. She is founder and president of RAINBO (Research, Action, and Information Network for the Bodily Integrity of Women). She publishes widely on issues of women's health, gender inequities, and human rights, particularly in Africa and the Middle East.

Nancy Tuana is professor of philosophy at the University of Oregon. She is author of *The Less Noble Sex: Scientific, Religious, and Philosophical Images of Woman's Nature* (1993) and *Woman and the History of Philosophy* (1992) and editor of *Feminist Interpretations of Plato* (1994) and *Feminism and Science* (1989). She is currently coeditor with Laurie Shrage of *Hypatia: A Journal of Feminist Philosophy*.

Ronald L. Urry directed the Andrology Laboratory at the University of Rochester School of Medicine. He was director of the andrology and in vitro fertilization laboratories at the University of Utah until his recent death. He was the author of numerous papers and chapters dealing with clinical human infertility and a pioneer in the fields of clinical human andrology and in vitro fertilization.

Vicki Van Wagner has worked as a community midwife in Toronto since 1980. Her work as a midwife has included active involvement in the work of the Association of Ontario Midwives towards the legal recognition of midwifery and with the College of Midwives of Ontario in the development of midwifery regulation. She acted as director of the Ryerson Polytechnic University Midwifery Education Program (Toronto) from 1993 to 1998 and continues to work as a faculty member in the program. Her research interests include community-based midwifery practice and midwifery education.

Marsden G. Wagner is a long-serving consultant on human reproduction for the World Health Organization (WHO). He was the convenor of two WHO consensus conferences (Brazil in 1985 and Trieste in 1986) on appropriate birth technology. His publications include *Pursuing the Birth Machine* (1994), and he edited, with Patricia A. Stephenson, *Tough Choices* (1993).

Anne Waldschmidt is a social scientist and has been active for many years in both the women's movement and the independent-living movement of people with disabilities. She was also a scientific consultant for the Green Party/Alliance 90 in the field of genetic and reproductive technologies. She was assistant professor at the University-Polytechnical Institute of Siegen and is now doing research at the University of Dortmund. She completed a research project on the history of human genetics in Germany since 1945 (published in *The Subject in Human Genetics: Expert Discourses on Programme and Conception of Human Genetic Counselling 1945–1990* [1996]).

Dorothy C. Wertz, a social scientist, specializes in ethics, genetics, and the impact of new reproductive technologies on society. Her publications include *Lying-*

In: *A History of Childbirth in America* (1989), *Ethics and Human Genetics: A Cross-Cultural Perspective* (1989), and over fifty articles in scientific journals. She is conducting a thirty-seven-nation survey of geneticists' and patients' ethical views.

Emma Whelan is a Ph.D. student in the Department of Sociology and Anthropology at Carleton University, Ottawa. Her current research examines the efforts of women's health groups to develop knowledge claims about endometriosis, gynecologists' responses to those efforts, and the resulting reconfiguration of the expert-lay divide in medical knowledge.

Linda S. Williams works in the area of social and ethical aspects of genetics and biotechnology. She has researched women and their husbands seeking in vitro fertilization in Ontario, has completed a study on legislation and guidelines on infertility treatments in seven countries while a consultant to Canada's Royal Commission on New Reproductive Technologies, was a member of the Sociology Department of Trent University in Ontario, has worked with Health Canada as a policy analyst, and was a member of the team formulating the government's response to the Royal Commission.. She has written numerous journal articles, book chapters, and monographs, including an analysis of the human rights implications of new reproductive technologies for the Canadian Human Rights Commission.

Robin Woods is professor of biology at the University of Winnipeg, Canada. He taught in the Department of Genetics, Sheffield University, from 1962 to 1976. He was chair of the Department of Biology, University of Winnipeg, from 1977 to 1987. He is also professor in the Department of Human Genetics at the University of Manitoba. His research is in the molecular biology of yeast.

Index

Abortifacient (abortifacient effects or pill), 100, 129, 333. *See also* Abortion, as contraceptive; RU–486
Abortion, 43, 61, 57, 101, 128, 145, 250, 333, 335, 376
   access to (on demand, right to) , 61, 124, 127, 300, 370–371
   as contraceptive, 62, 92, 99–100
   debate, 100, 329, 341. *See also* Antiabortionists; Feminists; Prochoice; Right to life
   ethics of, 122–124, 125–127
   forced (pressure to undergo), 103, 301, 374
   law, (criminalizing abortion, illegal abortion), 122, 125, 129, 324–325, 342
   and prenatal testing (amniocentesis, chorionic villus sampling), 23, 194, 200, 201, 195
   rate (percent), 126, 303, 334, 370
   spontaneous, 60, 105, 120, 147, 185, 195, 255, 277, 284, 290, 334. *See also* Miscarriage
   time limit, 298–299, 301
   techniques (induced abortion), 118–120
   See also Feminist critiques; Reproductive autonomy; Rights; RU–486
Adoption, 38–40, 61, 125–127, 161, 256, 257–258 266, 296, 365, 371-372
AID. *See* Donor insemination
AIDS, 87, 149, 168, 231, 335. *See also* HIV
AIH. *See* Artificial insemination, by husband
Alternative insemination. *See* Artificial insemination, self insemination
Amenorrhea, 81, 95, 106, 109. *See also* Infertility; Menstruation
Amniocentesis, 24, 51, 77, 147, 190, 193–196, 198, 201, 204, 237, 376. *See also* Abortion, and prenatal testing; Prenatal diagnosis; Sex selection
Anesthesia, 64–65, 70–72, 118–119, 133, 151, 255, 371. *See also* Cesarian section; Labor, and analgesia
Antiabortionists (antiabortion, antiabortion arguments), 333, 335, 338. *See also* Prochoice; Pronatalists; Right to life
Antisepsis, 70, 76–77. *See also* Infection; Sepsis
APGAR score, 72
Aristotle, 1, 5–11. *See also* Ovum, theories of; Sperm, theories of
Artificial infant feeding, 15–18, 21, 83–91
   and baby (infant) formula, 2, 60, 80, 85–87, 89, 90. *See also* Nestlé
   and consumer advocacy groups, 89–90
   and nonindustrialized countries, 88–89
   See also Breastfeeding; Infant feeding technologies
Artificial insemination, 51, 145–147, 149–152, 174, 177, 180–183, 204, 208, 253, 273, 304, 312, 324

by husband (artificial insemination homologous) (AIH), 149–151, 154, 156, 160
techniques, 150–152
risks, 152
See also Catholic church; Donor insemination; Legislation
Artificial insemination by donor. *See* Donor insemination
Artificial insemination by husband. *See* Artificial insemination, by husband
Asch, Ricardo, 252. *See also* Australia and New Zealand, The Asch Committee; Gamete intrafallopian transfer
Assisted conception, 36–41, 145, 181, 184, 207, 210, 318. *See also* In vitro fertilization; Legislation, of in vitro fertilization
Atwood, Margaret, 53, 56–57
Australia and New Zealand, 39, 71, 86, 155, 158, 161, 210, 229, 232–235, 243, 245, 261, 266, 269–270, 277, 310–316, 341, 343–345, 367, 370
The Asch Committee (Report), 261, 263
The Human Reproductive Technology Act (Western Australia), 270, 315
Infertility (Medical procedures) Act (Victoria), 277, 311
Infertility treatment Act (Victoria), 312
Status of Children Act (New Zealand), 315

Baby formula. *See* Artificial infant feeding, and baby formula
Baby M, 47, 48, 209, 274–275, 280–282. *See also* Sorkow, Harvey; Stern, William; Surrogacy; Whitehead, Mary Beth
Behavioral genetics, 364
Birth, 21, 37, 59–60, 75, 77, 80, 133, 139–143, 145, 147, 209, 270, 296, 321, 342. *See also* Labor; Midwifery; Premature birth; Wrongful birth
Birth control. *See* Contraception; Contraceptives
Birth defect, 179, 244, 287, 313. *See also* Genetic abnormality
Birth mother, 47–48, 155, 282. *See also* Maternity; Surrogacy
Birth rate , 225. *See also* In vitro fertilization, success of; Pregnancy rate
Birth technologies, 59–62, 63–73, 75–77
Blocked (nonfunctional or scarring of) fallopian tubes, 211, 218, 251, 304. *See also* Gamete intrafallopian transfer; Infertility, female; In vitro fertilization
Blue baby. *See* Erythroblastosis fetalis
Breastfeeding, 15–22, 59, 79–81
and decline in rate, 16, 19–20, 60, 83–84, 89–90
See also Artificial infant feeding; Infant-feeding technologies; Milk banking; Nestlé; Women's health groups
Breech birth (deliveries), 73, 75. *See also* Labor
Brown, Louise, 207, 218–221. *See also* Edwards, Robert; In vitro fertilization; Steptoe, Patrick

Cadavers, 9, 229, 245, 318. *See also* Donation, ovum
Canada, 37, 64, 71, 112, 116, 142, 150, 155, 158, 168, 205, 210, 229, 245, 317–318, 335, 367,
Canadian Royal Commission on New Reproductive Technologies, 167, 272, 317–318
See also Legislation
Cancer (carcinoma), 31, 32, 38, 51, 60, 81, 94–95, 100–101, 105–107, 111–112, 120, 152, 181, 185–186, 188–190, 244, 250, 269, 364. *See also* Women's health groups
Cancer drugs, 135
Cancer research, 33, 327

Castration, 374
Catholic church (Catholic moralists, Catholics), 3, 42–44, 115, 252-253
  Instruction on the Respect for Human Life in Its origin and on the Dignity of Procreation, 42
CECOS. *See* Donation, and The French Federation of Centers for Cryopreservation of Eggs and Sperm
Cephalopelvic disproportion (narrowing of pelvis), 65–66, 72. *See also* Forceps
Cervical cap, 96–97. *See also* Contraception, barrier methods of
Cesarean section, 60, 64, 66, 67, 69–73, 77, 100, 120, 128, 132, 141, 305, 370
  rate, 71, 77, 141, 305
  See also Antisepsis; Birth technologies; Infection; Informed consent; Labor; Sepsis
Chamberlen, Peter (Chamberlen family), 65–66, 75. *See also* Forceps
Childbearing prohibition, 378
Childlessness, 126, 256, 266, 284, 296,
Children (child), 38–41, 49, 54, 105, 114–117, 123–124, 126–127, 130–131, 135, 147–148, 179, 199–201, 230, 233–235, 245, 249, 255–256, 275–278, 297, 330, 359, 371–372, 378. *See also* Donor insemination, and children
Chloroform. *See* Labor, and analgesia
Chorionic villus sampling, 77, 190, 194–196, 198, 204. *See also* Abortion, and prenatal testing; Amniocentesis; Prenatal diagnosis; Sex selection
Clitoridectomy, 115. *See also* Female genital mutilation
Clomid. *See* Clomiphene citrate
Clomiphene citrate (clomid), 205, 212. *See also* Hyperovulation
Clones, 55, 326, 351, 356–359. *See also* Cloning; Dolly; Legislation, of cloning
Cloning, 27, 55, 330, 347–355, 356–359
  cellular (cell) age, 355, 356
  embryo cleavage (splitting), by, 326, 351, 353, 357. *See also* Embryo, research
  germline cells, of, 347
  and nuclear transplantation, 351–354
  and somatic cell nuclear transfer, 321, 347, 356–357
  See also Clones; Legislation, of cloning; Wilmut, Ian
Coitus interruptus. *See* Contraception, coitus interruptus
Condoms, 95–96, 102, 154, 172. *See also* Contraception, barrier methods of
Congenital abnormalities (anomalies), 184–185, 195, 290. *See also* Birth defect; Screening, genetic; Sex linked disease
Consent, 37, 40, 102, 155, 157–158, 210, 245, 258, 301, 307, 311-312, 318, 333, 365. *See also* Informed consent
Contraception (contraceptives), 19, 43, 61, 81, 92–98, 99–103, 181, 207, 303
  availability of, 92, 94–96, 98, 99,102–103
  barrier methods of, 95–97, 102,
  coitus interruptus, 98
  and family planning, 19, 24, 25, 81, 138
  intrauterine devices (IUDs), 97, 99–103, 129
  male antifertility agents, 98
  oral contraceptives, 60–61, 93–95, 99–101. *See also* The minipill; The morning-after pill; The Pill
  as punishment, 99, 103
  rhythm method, 97, 181
  side effects and risks of, 94–95, 101–102
  See also Dalkon shield, Depo Provera; Norplant; Reproductive hormones
Contract pregnancy, 272. *See also* Surrogacy
Corea, Gena, 24. *See also* Feminists

Counseling, 106, 118, 138, 210, 249, 261–263, 266, 284–285, 293, 296, 307, 311–312, 322
  genetic, 157, 331, 367–369, 375–378
  See also Counselors; Informed consent
Counselors, 262–263, 311, 367–369. See also Counseling
Creutzfeldt-Jakob disease, 208, 229–235. See also Hyperovulation; Reproductive hormones
Cryopreservation (freezing)
  of embryo, 2, 207, 215–216, 220, 243, 244, 270, 275, 308, 311, 324, 342, 357–358, 362
  germline cells, of, 324,
  of ovum (eggs), 208, 220, 242–246, 295
  of sperm, 150, 160, 207, 220
  See also Donation, and The French Federation of Centers for Cryopreservation of Eggs and Sperm; Legislation, of cryopreservation; Polge, Chris
Culture media (medium), 207, 213, 219, 236–240, 242–243, 353. See also Embryo; In vitro fertilization; Ovum
Culturing (culture), 215, 221, 242, 314, 333, 353–355. See also Culture media

D and C. See Dilation and Curettage
D and E. See Dilation and Evacuation
Dalkon shield, 97, 103. See also Contraception, intrauterine devices
Dehumanization, 48, 55
Depo Provera, 94, 111. See also Contraception, oral contraceptives
DES. See Diethylstilbestrol
DI. See Donor insemination
Diaphragm, 49, 96–97. See also Contraception, barrier methods of

Diethylstilbestrol (DES), 60, 105–107, 147, 180, 184–185, 275. See also Women's health groups
Dilation and Curettage (D and C), 118–119. See also Abortion, techniques
Dilation and Evacuation (D and E), 119. See also Abortion, techniques
The disabled (disabilities), 201, 257, 327, 331, 373–379. See also Discrimination; Handicapped people; Preimplantation (genetic) diagnosis; Prenatal diagnosis; Screening
Discrimination (nondiscrimination), 3, 29, 34, 136, 169, 287, 327, 331, 364–365, 378. See also Eugenics; Feminist critiques; Sex selection
Dolly, 353–356, 356, 358. See also Clones; Cloning
Donation, 234
  of embryos, 2, 158, 207–208, 304, 308. See also Embryo
  of fetal tissue, 245, 327, 335
  and The French Federation of Centers for Cryopreservation of Eggs and Sperm (CECOS), 157–158
  of gametes, 253, 308, 310–311
  of ovum (ova, egg), 2, 207–208, 245, 253, 269–270, 273, 275–276, 286, 288, 304, 311. See also Donors, ovum; Hyperovulation; In vitro fertilization; Ovum; Surrogacy
  of sperm, 155, 157, 163, 209, 253, 304, 311, 324, 327. See also Donor insemination; Lesbians; Single women; Sperm
  See also Donors; Legislation
Donor insemination (DI), 38, 40, 43, 47, 145–147, 149–152, 154–158, 160–164, 166–169, 220
  and children, 46, 152, 155, 158, 167–169
  and secrecy, 38–41, 146, 149, 151, 157–158, 161, 166

self (alternative) insemination, 146, 149, 152, 161, 166–169
See also Artificial insemination; Donors; Legislation; Lesbians; Single women
Donors, 37–40
gamete, 315
milk, 88
ovum (ova, egg), 270, 325. *See also* Donation, ovum; Maternity; Surrogacy
registry (registration) of, 146, 318. *See also* Legislation
sperm, 47, 146, 150–151, 154, 157, 163–164, 318, 324, 325. *See also* Paternity; Screening, of donors
See also Donation
Down syndrome, 185, 196, 198, 199, 326, 362. *See also* Prenatal diagnosis; Screening, genetic; Sex linked disease
Dysmenorrhea, 51, 109–112. *See also* GnRH agonists; Menstruation

Ectogenesis, 55, 208, 317–318, 330, 370–372. *See also* Embryo research; Feminist critiques
Ectopic pregnancy. *See* Pregnancy, ectopic
Edwards, Robert, 219–220, 221, 242. *See also* Brown, Louise; In vitro fertilization; Steptoe, Patrick
Egg. *See* Ovum
Egg donation. *See* Donation, ovum
Embryo (embryos)
biopsy of, 313, 361–362
definition of, 312–313, 315, 325, 341–344, 350. *See also* Pre-embryo; Primitive streak
donation of. *See* Donation, of embryo
for experimentation, 313, 321, 331, 343. *See also* Embryo research
flushing, 43, 273, 314,
freezing. *See* Cryopreservation, of embryo

genetic screening of. *See* Screening, genetic
spare (supernumerary, surplus), 216, 243, 311–313, 324–326, 329, 345
See also Culture medium; Embryo research; Embryo transfer; In vitro fertilization; Legislation; Micromanipulation; Personhood; Preimplantation (genetic) diagnosis
Embryo research (experimentation), 47, 208, 211, 236, 245, 329–331, 337–339. *See also* Legislation, of embryo research
Embryo splitting. *See* Cloning, embryo cleavage (splitting)
Embryo (fetus, gamete) transfer, 2, 43, 151, 182–184, 212, 214, 219–221, 245, 251–254, 257, 273–274, 286, 296, 299, 301, 304, 307–308, 311, 313, 324, 326, 352–353, 357–358, 361–363, 371. *See also* Donation, of embryo; In vitro fertilization; Surrogacy
Endometriosis, 61, 100, 109–112, 181, 211–212, 223, 225–228, 304. *See also* GnRH agonists; Infertility, female; Menstruation
Environment (environmental agents or factors), 32, 34, 62, 84, 89, 131, 186, 200, 209–210, 247, 284, 289–292
Episiotomy, 69, 77, 139. *See also* Labor; Midwifery
Ergot, 60, 65, 76. *See also* Labor
Erythroblastosis fetalis, 193
ESHRE. *See* European Society of Reproduction and Embryology
Ether, 76, 290. *See also* Labor, and analgesia
Eugenics (eugenic selection or measures), 3, 24, 53–55, 57, 148, 154, 160, 200–201, 210, 299, 324, 326–327, 329, 331, 368, 373–379. *See also* Discrimination; Feminist critiques; Genetics; Preimplantation (genetic)

diagnosis; Prenatal Diagnosis; Screening; Sex selection
European Society of Reproduction and Embryology, 285, 286
Euthanasia, 374–375
Excision, 115. *See also* Female genital mutilation
Experimentation, on women, 60–61, 191, 208, 249. *See also* Feminist critiques; Hyperovulation; In vitro fertilization
Exploitation, 28–29, 126, 270, 275, 278, 324, 327. *See also* Feminist critiques

Family (kinship), 2–3, 36–41, 73, 142, 161, 167, 200, 204, 275–276, 302, 315, 357. *See also* Artificial insemination; Baby M; Donation; Legislation; Lesbians; Maternity; Parenthood; Paternity; Rights; Selection; Single women; Surrogacy
Father (fatherhood). *See* Paternity; Rights, paternal
Female determining sperm, 23. *See also* Sex selection, of sperm
Female genital mutilation, 61, 114–117
Female mortality, 23–26, 119–120. *See also* Abortion; Maternal mortality; Perinatal mortality; Sex selection
Female (women's) procreativity, 2–3, 49, 147, 209. *See also* Aristotle; Breastfeeding; Galen; Hippocrates; Labor; Maternity; Menopause; Menstruation; Pregnancy
Female seed, 8–9
Female testicle, 9, 11
Feminist critiques (concerns, issues, responses, theories, views), 29, 124, 130–131, 201, 248, 250, 277–278, 305, 333. *See also* Feminists; Reproductive autonomy
Feminists (feminist scholars, theorists) 20, 25, 44, 51, 61, 122, 277, 310, 329, 338, 341, 345, 362, 372. *See also* Corea, Gena; Feminist critiques; O'Brien, Mary, Shiva, Vandana
Fertility drugs. *See* Hyperovulation; Reproductive hormones
Fertilization. *See* Embryo; Infertility; In vitro fertilization; Pregnancy; Sperm
Fertilization rate, 24, 146, 151–152, 213–214, 221, 237, 249. *See also* In vitro fertilization, success of; Pregnancy rate
Fetal cells, 193–197, 198, 203–204, 333, 376. *See also* Amniocentesis; Chorionic villus sampling
Fetal distress, 67, 73. *See also* Fetal monitoring
Fetal (endocrinological, uterine) environment, 48, 62, 92–93, 97, 325. *See also* Contraception; Feminist critiques
Fetal life, 43. *See also* Catholic church; Personhood; Prenatal harm; Right to life
Fetal monitoring, 67–69, 132. *See also* Birth technologies; Labor
Fetal tissue transplant (or research), 245, 329, 333–335
Fetal transplant, 370–371. *See also* Ectogenesis; Embryo transfer
Feto-maternal transfusion, 195
Fibroids. *See* Myomas
The Final solution, 374, 376. *See also* Germany; Racial hygiene
Follicle-stimulating hormone (FSH). *See* Reproductive hormones, Follicle-stimulating hormone
Forceps, 60, 64–67, 73, 75–77, 119. *See also* Chamberlen family; Medicalization; Midwifery; Midwives
France, 105, 120, 155–158, 229–230, 266, 307–309
  Loi de bioethique, 307–309
  See also Donation, and The French Federation of Centers for

Index

Cryopreservation of Eggs and Sperm; Legislation
FSH. *See* Reproductive hormones, Follicle-stimulating hormone

Galen, 6–9. *See also* Ovum, theories of; Sperm, theories of
Gamete (zygote) intrafallopian transfer (GIFT, ZIFT), 208, 247, 251-254, 274. *See also* In vitro fertilization; Legislation
Gametes. *See* Embryo; Ovum; Sperm
Genetic (chromosomal or congenital) abnormality (defect, disease, disability or disorder), 25, 32, 42–43, 194–195, 220, 247, 298-299, 304, 313–314, 330, 334, 338–339, 362, 365, 367. *See also* Discrimination; Down syndrome; Neural tube defect; Preimplantation (genetic) diagnosis; Prenatal diagnosis; Screening, genetic; Sex-linked disease
Genetic diagnosis. *See* Preimplantation (genetic) diagnosis; Prenatal diagnosis
Genetic engineering, 1–3, 27–29, 55, 59, 148, 245, 329–331, 337, 339
 definition of, 27
 See also Legislation, of genetic engineering
Genetic hygiene, 368. *See also* Germany; Racial hygiene
Gene (genetic) probe, 31–32, 338
Gene therapy, 324, 339. *See also* Genetic engineering
Geneticization, 201
Germany, 210, 269, 324–328, 331, 341, 365, 373–379
 Committee of Enquiry on Prospects and Risks of Genetic Engineering, 28
 German Embryonic Protection Act (EPA), 324–327, 362
 Hitler, 375
 Law for the Prevention of Hereditarily Ill Future Generations, 374
 national socialism (national socialists), 54, 373
 Nazis, 331, 342, 373
 See also Eugenics; The final solution; Racial hygiene
Gestational mother, 48–49. *See also* Feminist critiques; Maternity; Surrogacy
GIFT. *See* Gamete intrafallopian transfer
GnRH agonists (analogs), 98, 111–112, 147, 208–209, 212–214, 222-228
 risks (safety) of, 227–228
 See also Endometriosis; Hyperovulation; In vitro fertilization; Ovulation; Reproductive hormones
Guillemin, Roger, 224. *See also* GnRH agonists; Schally, Andrew

Haldane, J.B.S., 53–56, 370
Handicapped (people or persons), 371–372, 374–375, 377. *See also* The disabled; Discrimination
The Handmaid's Tale. *See* Atwood, Margaret
hCG. *See* Reproductive hormones, human chorionic gonadotropin
Health care cost, 18, 62, 254, 286, 330. *See also* Insurance; In vitro fertilization, cost of; Public Financing; Reimbursement
Heterosexuals (heterosexual couples, families, relationships or women), 37, 57, 145–146, 156, 163, 166–169, 209–210, 257, 265–266, 273, 301, 305, 315. *See also* Feminist critiques; In vitro fertilization, access to; Legislation; Lesbians; Selection; Single women
Hippocrates, 6. *See also* Ovum, theories of; Sperm, theories of
HIV (HIV antibodies, positive, testing or virus), 95, 151–152, 156, 168-

169, 258, 273, 308, 334. *See also* AIDS; Donor insemination; Screening, of sperm
HMG. *See* Reproductive hormones, human menopausal gonadotropin
Home birth (home birthing or deliveries) 62, 63–64, 140–142. *See also* Hospital birth; Labor; Midwifery
Homosexual couples (homosexuality), 37, 163, 167, 307–308, 359, 364. *See also* Family; Lesbians; Selection
Homunculus, 1. *See also* Sperm, theories of
Hormone (or endocrine or hormone replacement) therapy, 61, 178, 191. *See also* GnRH agonists; Hyperovulation; Menopause; Reproductive hormones
Hormonal methods of contraception. *See* Contraception, oral contraceptives
Hospital, 33, 47–48, 59, 64–65, 67, 70–71, 76–77, 303–305, 309, 311-312. *See also* Lying-in wards; Medicalization; Midwifery; Sepsis
Hospital birth, 60, 62, 69, 132, 140. *See also* Home birth; Hospital; Midwifery
Human chorionic gonadotropin (hCG). *See* Reproductive hormones, human chorionic gonadotropin
Human Fertilization and Embryology Act. *See* United Kingdom, Human Fertilization and Embryology Act
Human Genome Organization, 365. *See also* United States
Human Genome Project, 194. *See also* Genetic engineering
Human Genome Research, National Center for, 365. *See also* United Kingdom, Human Advisory Commission
Human menopausal gonadotropin (hMG). *See* Reproductive

hormones, Human menopausal gonadotropin (hMG)
Human pituitary growth hormone, 229–230, 233–235. *See also* Creutzfeldt Jakob disease
Human rights. *See* Rights, human
Hydatidiform mole, 152, 186–187. *See also* Hyperovulation
Hyperovulation (hyperovulate, hyperstimulation, ovarian stimulation or ovulation induction), 146–147, 178, 180–187, 207, 209, 211–214, 220–221, 222, 225, 244, 269, 286, 294–295, 305, 308, 352, 354. *See also* In vitro fertilization; Ovulation
Hyperovulatory drugs (hormones), 155, 208, 243. *See also* Clomiphene citrate; GnRH agonists; Reproductive hormones
Hyperstimulation. *See* Hyperovulation
Hypersusceptible person, 33–34
Hysterectomy, 70, 119–120, 226, 243. *See also* Oophorectomy
Hysteroscopy, 226. *See also* Laporoscopy
Hysterotomy, 120

ICSI. *See* Intracytoplasmic sperm injection
Implantation (of eggs, embryo, ova) 92–94, 97, 99–100, 208, 211, 212 215–216, 222, 237, 251, 253, 274, 290, 301, 308, 312, 314, 354, 361, 362. *See also* Embryo transfer; In vitro fertilization
Impotence, 150
Independent living (independent-living movement), 375, 377. *See also* Handicapped people
Industrial revolution, 28, 64, 373
Infanticide, 23–24, 125. *See also* Sex selection
Infant mortality, 16–17, 77, 84, 86, 88. *See also* Perinatal mortality
Infection, 32, 60, 64, 70, 72, 75, 77, 80, 95, 97, 101, 115–116, 118, 152,

Index

172–173, 231, 247, 251, 255, 334. *See also* Antisepsis; In vitro fertilization, risks of; Sepsis
Infertility, 40, 46, 51, 101, 111, 116, 127, 145, 157, 162–163, 209-210, 211–212, 218–219, 226, 229, 240, 245, 257–258, 304, 342, 359, 370
  definition of, 284, 371
  and depression, 256–257
  female, 147, 150, 184–186, 251, 290–291. *See also* Blocked fallopian tubes; Endometriosis; Infertility; Pelvic inflammatory disease
  and global policy, 283–288
  idiopathic (unexplained or unknown), 147, 150, 208, 211, 257, 295, 304
  male, 145–147, 151, 162, 166, 171–179, 208, 221, 248–249, 290–291, 304. *See also* In vitro fertilization, and male-factor infertility; Sperm
  prevention of (preventing), 283–284, 286, 289–291, 317–318
  See also Childlessness; Counseling; Environment; In vitro fertilization; Legislation; Sterility
Infertility treatment (techniques), 145–148, 151, 180–181, 183–184, 207–210, 218, 232–234, 257, 330–331. *See also* Infertility; Selection
Infibulation, 115. *See also* Female genital mutilation
Informed consent, 62, 99, 102–103, 132–134, 249, 254, 259, 288, 293-297, 311–312, 330–331, 371. *See also* Consent; Counseling
In situ hybridization, 361. *See also* Sex selection
Insurance (insurance coverage), 71, 155, 205, 305, 310, 322, 326–327, 353–354, 365–366, 376. *See also* In vitro fertilization, cost of; Reimbursement
Interceptives, 100. *See also* Contraception; Contraceptives

Intermarriage, 152, 157. *See also* Donor insemination; Donors, registry of
Intracytoplasmic sperm injection (ICSI), 151, 154, 174, 177, 179, 208, 215, 221, 248–249, 304, 307. *See also* Infertility, male; In vitro fertilization; Sperm; Zona
Intrauterine adoption, 272. *See also* Surrogacy
In vitro fertilization (IVF), 154, 163, 178, 182, 203, 205, 207–210, 225, 244, 245, 251, 275, 283, 290, 294–295, 320, 329, 337-338, 351, 361, 370
  access to, 209, 265–267, 301, 308, 311. *See also* Lesbians; Selection and assessment; Single women
  cost of, 152, 209, 257, 285–287, 305. *See also* Health care cost; Insurance; Public financing; Reimbursement
  development of, 218–221
  and male-factor infertility, 151, 162, 211, 213, 215, 247–250, 255, 291, 325. *See also* Feminist critiques; Intracytoplasmic sperm injection
  research of, 285–286, 288, 295, 299–300, 343, 345. *See also* Embryo research
  risks of, 29, 208, 255–259, 285
  success (or failure) of, 38, 169, 208–210, 212, 214, 219, 221, 242–243, 258, 269, 274, 285, 296, 304, 321, 327, 345, 357. *See also* Birth rate; Fertilization rate; Pregnancy rate
  techniques of, 211–216
  See also Culture media; Donation; Gamete intrafallopian transfer; Hyperovulation; Legislation; Micromanipulation; Ovum; Sperm; Surrogacy
IUDs. *See* Contraception, intrauterine devices
IVF. *See* In vitro fertilization

Jewish commentators, 8. *See also* Ovum, theories of; Sperm, theories of

Kane, Elizabeth, 274
Keane, Noel, 272

Labor, 62, 65–67, 71, 132–134, 138
  and analgesia, 76. *See also* Anesthesia
  induction (to start labor), 132. *See also* Ergot
  premature (preterm) labor, 67–68, 106, 111, 305. *See also* Premature birth
  tocolytic therapy (to stop labor), 67–69
  See also Birth technologies; Fetal monitoring; Forceps; Midwifery
Lactation. *See* Breastfeeding
Lacto-engineering, 88
Laparoscopy (laparoscopic surgery), 109–110, 207, 213, 219–220, 226, 244, 252–253, 257, 269, 274, 295. *See also* Ovum, retrieval of
Laparotomy, 69, 110, 213, 220
Legislation (law, policy, provisions for, regulation of)
  of artificial (and donor) insemination, 43, 146, 154–158, 266, 310, 312, 315, 318, 324–325
  of cloning (clones), 299, 311, 313, 317–318, 321, 324, 326
  of cryopreservation, 43, 308, 311, 326, 342
  of embryo research (experimentation), 210, 299, 305, 308, 310–315, 318, 320–21, 341–345, 362–363
  of gamete (zygote) intrafallopian transfer (GIFT or ZIFT), 322, 326–327
  of genetic engineering, 318, 320–321, 324
  of in vitro fertilization (assisted conception or new reproductive technologies), 210, 245, 284–288, 298–301, 303-305, 307–308, 310–313, 315, 317–318, 320–322, 326–327
  moratorium (ban or prohibition), 106, 277, 280, 298, 314, 317, 321, 326–327, 339, 342, 378
  self-regulation, 299
  See also Australia and New Zealand; Canada; Catholic Church; France; Germany; Licensing; The Netherlands; United Kingdom; United States; Spain; Surrogacy, contracts; Sweden
Lesbians (lesbian couples, mothers, partnerships, relationships or women), 37, 151, 161, 166–169, 210, 265, 305, 324. *See also* Family; Parenthood; Selection
LH. *See* Reproductive hormones, luteinizing hormone
Licensing (licensing authority or measures), 140, 303, 307, 314–315, 318, 322, 362. *See also* Legislation
LTOT. *See* Ovum, tubal ovum transfer
Luteinizing hormone (LH). *See* Reproductive hormones, luteinizing hormone
Lying-in wards, 64. *See also* Hospitals; Medicalization

McLaren, Ann, 338–339
Male contraception. *See* Contraception
Male determining sperm, 23. *See also* Sex selection, of sperm
Male-factor infertility. *See* In vitro fertilization, and male-factor infertility
Male principle of creation, 6
Male seed, 8–9
Marital status (married couples), 155, 169, 209, 265, 314. *See also* Family; Heterosexual; Homosexual; Lesbians; Single women; Selection
Maternal mortality (death or morbidity), 64–65, 70–73, 77, 141

Index 399

Maternal serum alpha-fetoprotein analysis, 196, 198. *See also* Prenatal diagnosis
Maternity (motherhood), 1, 21, 36, 47–48, 86, 141, 166, 199–201, 208-209, 296, 358. *See also* Baby M; Family; Parenthood; Paternity; Surrogacy; Rights, maternal
Medicalization (or medical development or model)
of breastfeeding, 18. *See also* Artificial infant feeding; Infant feeding technologies
of childbirth, 2, 51, 60, 139–141, 147
of pregnancy, 51, 147
of reproduction (reproductivity), 62, 99–101
See also Feminist critiques; Hospitals; Midwifery; Midwives
Menopause, 106, 191–192, 209, 227, 245–246
pseudomenopause (early menopause), 112, 186, 190, 269. *See also* GnRH agonists; Hyperovulation
Menstruation, 8, 61, 81, 94, 100, 109–112, 150, 225–226
Micromanipulation, 27, 207, 214–216, 221, 248, 250
microimplantation or microinjection (of sperm), 146, 178, 207, 312, 325. *See also* Intracytoplasmic sperm injection; Sperm
of ovum (or zona), 214–215, 249. *See also* Zona
See also Infertility, male; In vitro fertilization, and male-factor infertility
Midwifery, 63–64, 138–143. *See also* Medicalization; Midwives
Midwives, 59–60, 62, 63, 69, 71, 75–76, 138–143, 374. *See also* Medicalization; Midwifery
Milk banking, 87–88. *See also* Artificial infant feeding; Breastfeeding; Infant-feeding technologies

The minipill, 94, 101. *See also,* Contraception, oral contraceptives
Miscarriage, 60, 105–106, 111, 120, 136, 147, 214, 290–291, 305, 313, 367. *See also* Abortion, spontaneous; Fetal tissue transplant; Ru–486
Moratorium. *See* Legislation, moratorium
The morning-after pill, 95. *See also* Contraception, oral contraceptives
Mother (motherhood). *See* Maternity
Multiple birth, 38, 183, 256, 305, 350–351. *See also* Hyperovulation; Pregnancy, multiple
Myomas (fibroids), 223, 226, 228

Nazi. *See* Germany
Nestlé, 86, 89–90. *See also* Artificial infant feeding, and baby formula
The Netherlands, 40, 105, 107, 155–156, 303–305. *See also* Legislation
Neural tube defect, 185, 187, 198, 305. *See also* Genetic abnormality; Sex linked disease
Norplant, 19, 95, 103. *See also* Contraception
Nursing. *See* Breastfeeding; Infant-feeding technologies

O'Brien, Mary, 21, 57. *See also* Feminist critiques; Feminists
Oophorectomies, 243. *See also* Hysterectomy; Sterilization
Osteoporosis, 51, 81, 190–191, 228. *See also* GnRH agonists; Menopause
Ova. *See* Ovum
Ovarian hyperstimulation syndrome, 183, 187. *See also* GnRH agonists; Hyperovulation
Ovarian suppression. *See* GnRH agonists
Ovulation, 81, 92–94, 97, 99, 149–150, 152, 155, 185, 204, 212, 219-220, 222, 242–243, 252, 273, 350
anovulation, 223, 232

See also GnRH agonists;
  Hyperovulation; Reproductive
  hormones
Ovulation induction. *See*
  Hyperovulation
Ovum (ova, egg), 13, 184, 248, 251
  banking of, 245
  donation of. *See* Donation, of ovum
    (egg)
  freezing of. *See* Cryopreservation, of
    ovum (egg)
  maturation of, 208, 242–246
  retrieval (collection, harvest) of, 213,
    220, 245, 250, 255, 269, 295, 308,
    325
  theories of, 5–13
  tubal ovum transfer (TOT), 252. *See
    also* Gamete intrafallopian
    transfer
  See also Hyperovulation;
    Micromanipulation; Ovulation

Parenthood, 36–38, 41, 138, 257, 262,
  265, 301. *See also* Family;
  Maternity; Paternity; Rights,
  parental
Partial zona dissection. *See* Zona
Paternity (fatherhood), 21, 36, 46–47,
  146, 155, 158, 161, 208–209, 358.
  See also Baby M; Family;
  Maternity; Rights, paternal
Perinatal mortality, 65, 68, 71–73, 141,
  183, 187. *See also* Infant mortality
Pelvic inflammatory disease, 101, 152.
  See also Infertility, female
Personhood
  and embryos, 300–301, 330, 342–343,
    345
  fetal (or prenatal) 47, 62, 122,
    128–129, 298.
  See also Feminist critiques; Fetal life;
    Prenatal harm
PGD. *See* Preimplantation (genetic)
  diagnosis
PID. *See* Preimplantation (genetic)
  diagnosis

The Pill, 93–94, 101, 273. *See also*
  Contraception, oral
  contraceptives
PMS. *See* Premenstrual syndrome
Polar body, 213, 350, 361
Polge, Chris, 220. *See also*
  Cryopreservation; In vitro
  fertilization
Policy. *See* Legislation
Polycystic ovarian disease (syndrome),
  223, 226, 228. *See also* GnRH
  agonists; Hyperovulation
Polyspermic fertilization (polyspermic
  ova or polyspermia), 213–214,
  249. *See also* In vitro fertilization;
  Micromanipulation; Sperm
Posthumous parenting, 38. *See also*
  Donation; Embryo
Precocious puberty, 225
Preconception arrangements, 272, 317.
  See also Contract pregnancy;
  Legislation; Surrogacy
Pre-embryo, 47, 344. *See also* Embryo,
  definition of; Primitive streak
Progenitor, 358. *See also* Clones;
  Cloning
Pregnancy (gestation)
  clinical (biochemical), 214, 296. *See
    also* In vitro fertilization, success
    of; Pregnancy rate
  coercive, 126–127
  ectopic (extrauterine), 106, 152, 184,
    214, 220, 253, 305, 334
  high risk, 68, 286
  multiple, 72, 152, 182–183, 187, 214,
    253, 255. *See also* Multiple birth
  selective reduction (abortion) of,
    255–256, 308. *See also* Abortion
  and substance abuse, 62, 130
  See also Hyperovulation; In vitro
    fertilization; Medicalization;
    Midwifery; Screening, of
    pregnancy
Pregnancy rate, 46, 179, 212–216, 220,
  225, 237, 239, 248–249, 296, 307,
  321. *See also* Fertilization; In vitro
  fertilization, success of

Index

Preimplantation (genetic) diagnosis (PID, PGD), 197, 203, 295, 308, 324, 326, 338, 361–363. *See also* Genetic diagnosis; Prenatal diagnosis; Screening, genetic
Premature (preterm) birth (babies), 88, 183, 370
Premature (preterm) labor (delivery), 67–68, 106, 111, 256, 305
Premenstrual syndrome (PMS), 109, 111–112, 228. *See also* GnRH agonists; Menstruation
Prenatal (intrauterine) adoption, 48, 272. *See also* Contract pregnancy; Preconception arrangements; Surrogacy
Prenatal diagnosis (testing), 23, 31, 42, 77, 193–197, 198–202, 363, 367–368. *See also* Screening, prenatal
Prenatal harm, 62, 128–131. *See also* Fetal life; Personhood; Reproductive harm
Primitive streak, 314, 344. *See also,* Embryo; Pre-embryo
Pro-choice, 320. *See also* Abortion; Feminist critiques; Reproductive autonomy
Progesterone. *See* Contraceptives; Reproductive hormones, progesterone
Pronatalists (pronatalist views), 246, 362. *See also* Antiabortionists; Feminist critiques; Fetal life; Personhood; Right to life
Public financing, 326. *See also* Cost; Funding; Reimbursement
PZD. *See* Zona (partial zona dissection)

Racial hygiene, 373, 375–376. *See also* The final solution; Germany
Registry. *See* Donors, registry
Reimbursement (payment), 71, 155, 163, 277, 282, 309, 311, 322. *See also* Health care cost; Insurance; In vitro fertilization, cost of; Public funding

Reproductive autonomy, 61–62, 122, 124, 208, 300, 315, 329. *See also* Feminist critiques; Reproductive choice; Rights
Reproductive choice, 127, 145, 168. *See also* Feminist critiques; Reproductive autonomy
Reproductive harm, 136–137. *See also* Prenatal harm
Reproductive hormones
  estrogen, 60, 92–95, 98, 101, 105, 112, 180, 186, 222, 227-228, 243
  Follicle-stimulating hormone (FSH), 92–93, 176, 180–182, 212–213, 222–224
  Human chorionic gonadotropin (hCG), 178, 182, 213–214, 225
  Human menopausal gonadotropin (hMG), 180–186, 225, 274
  Luteinizing hormone (LH), 92–93, 176, 180–182, 212–213, 222-226, 247, 253
  male, 146–147, 176, 226. *See also* Testosterone
  progesterone, 93–95, 97–98, 100–101, 105, 111–112, 152, 214, 222, 225, 243. *See also* Contraception
  See also GnRH agonists; Hyperovulation; In vitro fertilization; Ovulation
Reproductive rights. *See* Rights, reproductive
Rhythm method, 97. *See also* Contraception
Right to life (right-to-life activists or advocates), 122–123, 310, 341-342, 370, 377. *See also* Church; Fetal life; Personhood
Rights
  of children, 266–267
  of clones, 358–359
  of donors, 154–155
  fetal (of the embryo or fetus), 48, 122–123, 128–129, 287, 338, 342–343. *See also* Fetal life; Personhood; Prenatal harm
  human, 40, 114, 130, 284

maternal (of mothers or women's), 25, 48, 116–117, 123, 130, 278, 280, 282, 287, 299–302, 325, 327, 330. *See also* Feminist critiques; Surrogacy
parental (of parents), 102, 130, 145, 277, 282, 298, 311
paternal (of fathers or men's), 38, 145, 209, 282, 287, 301-302. *See also* Donor insemination
reproductive (to reproduce), 101, 301, 330
See also Reproductive autonomy; Reproductive choice
Risk. *See* Artificial insemination, risks; Contraception, side effects and risks of; GnRH agonists, risks of; In vitro fertilization, risks of
Roe v. Wade, 342. *See also* Abortion, access to
Roslin Institute, 353. *See also* Cloning
RU-486, 100–101, 120, 333. *See also* Abortion, as contraceptive; Contraception

Schally, Andrew, 224. *See also* GnRH agonists; Guillemin, Roger
Scientific revolution, 1, 59
Screening (testing), 37, 129, 190
of donors, 146, 154, 156–158, 322
genetic, 2–3, 31, 108, 156, 245, 299, 329, 330, 338, 357, 365, 373–379. *See also* Preimplantation (genetic) diagnosis
for in vitro fertilization (new reproductive technologies), 261, 263, 287. *See also* Selection
mass health (or population) screening, 34, 188–192
of pregnancy, 145,147
prenatal (of the embryo or fetus), 129, 147, 193, 196–197, 199–201, 209, 329, 337–338, 376. *See also* Maternal serum alpha-fetoprotein analysis; Preimplantation (genetic) diagnosis; Prenatal

diagnosis of sperm. *See* Sperm, analysis
Selected reduction (abortion). *See* Pregnancy, selective reduction of
Selection (for advanced infertility techniques), 209, 211–212, 263, 265–267, 275–276. *See also* Lesbians; Screening, for in vitro fertilization; Single women
Self insemination. *See* Artificial insemination
Self regulation. *See* Legislation, self regulation
Semen. *See* Sperm
Semen analysis. *See* Sperm, analysis
Sepsis, 64–65, 72. *See also* Antisepsis; Infection
SET. *See* Surrogate embryo transfer
Sex-linked disease (disorder or illness), 23, 326, 338, 361. *See also* Down syndrome; Genetic abnormality; Neural tube defect; Sex selection
Sex selection, 2, 23–26, 147–148, 203–205, 317–318
commercialization, of, 204–205
sex-determining gene, 203
sexing embryos, 362
sexing fetal cells in maternal blood, 203
of sperm, 23, 203, 324
See also Abortion; Feminist critiques; Infanticide; Prenatal diagnosis; Screening; Sex selective abortion
Sex selective abortion (selection for abortion), 23, 25, 203, 204. *See also* Abortion; Prenatal diagnosis; Sex selection
Sexual orientation, 33, 52, 169, 209. *See also* Family; Heterosexuals; Homosexual couples; Lesbians; Selection
Shiva, Vandana, 29. *See also* Environment; Feminists
Singer, Peter, 370
Single women (mothers), 37, 151, 166, 210, 265, 305, 307, 324. *See also*

Index   403

Family; Legislation; Lesbians; Maternity; Paternity; Selection
Somatic cell nuclear transfer. *See* Cloning, and somatic cell nuclear transfer
Sorkow, Harvey, 47, 281–282. *See also* Baby M; Stern, William; Surrogacy; Whitehead, Mary Beth
Spain, 105, 155–156, 269
Sperm (Semen)
  abnormalities of, 151, 215, 362
  analysis (separation), 24, 146, 151, 171–174, 203, 205, 213, 247, 318
  and azoopermia, 247, 249. *See also* Infertility, male
  collection of, 295
  and epididymal sperm aspiration, 177, 304
  freezing. *See* Cryopreservation
  microimplantation. *See* Intracytoplasmic sperm injection; Micromanipulation
  and oligozoospermia, 150, 247. *See also* Infertility, male
  theories of, 5–13, 21, 47. *See also* Homunculus
  See also Artificial insemination; Donation; Donors; In vitro fertilization, and male-factor infertility
Sperm antibodies, 98, 173–175, 238
Sperm banks, 151, 156, 168–169, 318, 324
Sperm donation. *See* Donation, of sperm
Spermicide, 95–97, 101. *See also* Contraception, barrier methods of
Spontaneous abortion. *See* Abortion, spontaneous
Steptoe, Patrick, 219–221, 242. *See also* Brown, Louise; Edwards, Robert; In vitro fertilization
Sterility, 247, 284, 291. *See also* Environment; Infertility
Sterilization, 99, 101
  forced (involuntary or without consent), 54–55, 102–103, 373–374
  and inducements (or incentives) 270, 288
  and vasectomy, 151, 162, 177
  See also Contraceptives; Infertility; Rights
Stern, William, 47, 280–282. *See also* Baby M; Sorkow, Harvey; Surrogacy; Whitehead, Mary Beth
Sudden infant death syndrome (SIDS), 80
Surrogacy, 36–38, 56–57, 208–209, 272–278, 308, 318
  commercial (paid) surrogacy, 305, 311, 317, 318
  Surrogate motherhood (mothers), 36, 38, 41, 43, 46, 48, 53, 208, 219, 272, 274–275, 282, 304, 324–325, 351, 353, 371
  Surrogate Mothers Limited, 49
  See also Baby M; Donation; Family; Legislation; Maternity; Paternity
Surrogate embryo transfer (SET), 273
Sweden, 39–40, 156, 158, 161, 266, 269
Syngamy, 312–313, 344

Technological fix, 25–26, 246, 254, 278
Testicular dysfunction, 247
Testosterone, 176. *See also* Reproductive hormones, male
Third World (Third World countries), 28–29, 139, 141
Thompson, Judith Jarvis, 123
TOT. *See* Ovum, tubal ovum transfer
Toxic chemicals (toxins), 290–291. *See also* Environment; Infertility; Sterility
Traditional birth attendants. *See* Midwives
Trounson, Alan, 220. *See also* In vitro fertilization
Twilight sleep, 76. *See also* Anesthesia; Labor, and analgesia

Ultrasound (sonography), 48, 77, 98, 177, 194, 196, 198–199, 204–205, 213–214, 273–274, 353

Ultrasound-guided retrieval, 207, 213, 220. *See also* Ovum, retrieval of
United Kingdom, 39–40, 47, 105, 149, 155, 158, 163, 167–168, 229, 234, 245, 269–270, 341, 367
   Human Advisory Commission, 365
   Human Fertilization and Embryology Act, 37, 156, 210, 266, 298–302, 344, 362
   The Warnock Report, 167, 265, 344
   See also Legislation
United States, 29, 39, 47, 51, 71, 103, 107, 112, 129, 133, 148, 168, 210, 229, 245, 266, 269, 275, 276, 320–322, 341, 342
Uterine bleeding, 95, 109, 112, 223, 225–226, 228

Vaginal sponge, 97. *See also* Contraception, barrier methods of
Varicocele, 173, 176–177, 247. *See also* Infertility, male
Vasectomy, 151, 175, 177. *See also* Infertility, male; Sterilization
Vasogram, 177. *See also* Infertility, male
Viral research, 329, 334. *See also* Fetal tissue transplant

The Warnock Report. *See* The United Kingdom
Warren, Mary Anne, 125
Whitehead, Mary Beth, 47, 274, 280–282. *See also* Baby M; Sorkow, Harvey; Stern, William; Surrogacy
WHO. *See* World Health Organization
Wilmut, Ian, 352. *See also* Cloning; Dolly
World Health Organization (WHO), 88, 106, 116, 138, 141, 109, 284–288
Women's Health Groups
   DES Action International, 106
   DES Cancer network, 107
   Inter-African Committee on Traditional Practices Affecting the Health of Women and Children, 116
   FORWARD, 116
   Groupe Femmes pour l'Abolition des Mutilations Sexuelles, 116
   London Black Women Health Action Project (UK), 116
   PMS Action, 111
   Women's Health Initiative (US), 51
   World Alliance for Breast-feeding Action, 90
Wrongful birth, 342

ZIFT. *See* Gamete (zygote) intrafallopian transfer
Zona (slitting, drilling, partial zona dissection (PZD) or subzonal insertion), 214–215, 221, 248–249. *See also* Intracytoplasmic sperm injection; In vitro fertilization; Micromanipulation; Ovum